"In *The Message of the Twelve* Fuhr and ~~Yates invite students of the Bible~~ into the world of the Old Testament prophets. Conversant with the best of scholarship, they orient readers to the historical and literary intricacies of the shorter prophetic books, without losing sight of their theological riches. This is essential reading for those who want to understand the message of the prophets and relay it to a new generation."

—**Mark J. Boda,** professor of Old Testament, McMaster Divinity College and professor, faculty of theology, McMaster University

"The twelve relatively short books known as the Minor Prophets give us a vision of God that pierces the darkness of our world and should evoke both healthy fear of, and humble submission to, this sovereign King of the world. Yet because these books were written in a much different time and place, they prove to be challenging to modern readers. Professors Fuhr and Yates are to be commended for producing a reliable guide to these books that will enable modern readers to grasp their profound message and to gain a greater appreciation for the God who is the central character therein. They explain with clarity and insight the message of these prophets in their ancient setting and then show us how that message is relevant in our modern context. This book will serve as an ideal introductory textbook for courses on the Minor Prophets."

—**Robert B. Chisholm Jr.,** department chair and senior professor of Old Testament studies, Dallas Theological Seminary

"Some parts of the Old Testament desperately need helpful resources to assist students of the Word to grow in their understanding of God and his expectations for his people. The prophetic books, and the Minor Prophets in particular, offer the interpreter of Scripture unique challenges, but also tremendous blessings. Fuhr and Yates have provided a *superb resource* that explains the text of each book, includes clear visuals that facilitate a reader's understanding of key features, and connects expositional details with the theological message of those books. I look forward to having this book in my personal library and making it available to my students."

—**Michael A. Grisanti,** professor of Old Testament, director of Th.M. studies, and director of TMS Israel Study Trip, The Master's Seminary

"Al Fuhr and Gary Yates have written a clear, succinct, and engaging book on the Book of the Twelve (Minor Prophets) that provides a delightful introduction to the ancient world of these fascinating, yet often neglected, prophets. The authors bring to light the irony, metaphors, and Hebrew wordplays that were employed in calling for a return to the Lord and to covenantal obedience in order to avoid judgment and foster restoration. As master teachers, Fuhr and Yates powerfully communicate the message and modern relevance of these prophets whose words and literary expressions were often like 'a bucket of ice water poured upon a bleary-eyed people.'"

—**Ted Hildebrandt,** professor of biblical studies, Gordon College

"*The Message of the Twelve* is an excellent treatment of the meaning of the Minor Prophets and their messages. The book thoroughly surveys the historical background of each Minor Prophet and correlates the teaching of each book to other sections of Scripture, including the New Testament. Each book is carefully outlined, with each section of the book given titles that are as appropriate for application in our present age as in the time the prophets presented their messages. This book is destined to be an excellent resource for serious students of God's Word as well as for modern preachers and teachers. I highly recommend this work and look forward to using it in the classroom."

—**Mark F. Rooker,** senior professor of Old Testament and Hebrew, Southeastern Baptist Theological Seminary

"The church owes Fuhr and Yates a debt of gratitude for *The Message of the Twelve.* Focusing exclusively on these neglected texts, they have given students and pastors an extended introduction that covers so much more than the usual survey. With excellent summaries of the historical background, literary features, and the role of the prophet, in addition to the exploration of each book, Fuhr and Yates provide a complete guide to their riches. *The Message of the Twelve* is thoroughly conversant with the latest scholarship, solidly conservative, and rich in literary and theological insight. I highly recommend this text for anyone interested in getting better acquainted with the wonderful, yet oft-neglected treasures that are the Minor Prophets."

—**J. Michael Thigpen,** executive director of The Evangelical Theological Society, associate professor of Old Testament, Talbot School of Theology, Biola University

THE

MESSAGE

OF THE

TWELVE

Hearing the Voice of the Minor Prophets

THE
MESSAGE
OF THE
TWELVE

RICHARD ALAN FUHR, JR.
& GARY E. YATES

ACADEMIC
NASHVILLE, TENNESSEE

The Message of The Twelve: Hearing the Voice of the Minor Prophets
Copyright © 2016 by Richard Alan Fuhr, Jr. and Gary E. Yates

Published by B&H Publishing Group
Nashville, Tennessee

ISBN: 978-1-4336-8376-3

Dewey Decimal Classification: 224.9
Subject Heading: PROPHETS / BIBLE. O.T. MINOR PROPHETS / BIBLE.
O.T.--BIOGRAPHY

Printed in the United States of America

5 6 7 8 9 10 • 25 24 23 22 21

❧❧❧

For Marilyn, Erin, Kallie and Brett ~ Gary Yates
For Alex and Max ~ Al Fuhr

❧❧❧

CONTENTS

Acknowledgments

A project such as *The Message of the Twelve* is the result of the cumulative efforts and influence of many individuals, and we want to offer our thanks to all who have helped make this work possible. We are grateful for our faithful teachers who instilled within us a love for the Old Testament prophets that has profoundly influenced our spiritual journeys and academic pursuits. We are thankful for the encouragement and support of our colleagues in the School of Divinity at Liberty University and for the students we have had the privilege of teaching over the years that have sharpened our understanding of the prophets with their questions and insights. This work on the Minor Prophets reflects decades of godly counsel and instruction from peers and professors alike.

Others were involved in a more tangible way in the production of this book. Heather Bradley carefully assisted with editorial work under significant time constraints, and Chris Thompson and the team at B&H provided invaluable assistance for each step of this project. Graduate assistants helped us as we juggled the demands of teaching and writing, and our students graciously allowed us to express in class what we were developing on paper. Most of all, we are grateful to our families for their patience as we worked on this project and for how they remind us every day of the greatness of God's love and blessing on our lives.

PREFACE

We offer this work on the Book of the Twelve (or the Minor Prophets as they are known in the English Old Testament) with the conviction that the message of these prophets is especially relevant for the church in the turbulent times in which we live. The Minor Prophets offer a compelling portrayal of God through vivid and dramatic metaphors. In judgment, the God of Israel is like a fierce warrior, a roaring lion, a raging whirlwind, and a consuming fire. And yet, the same prophets who employ these frightening images also assure us that in his work of salvation, the Lord is a faithful husband, a loving Father, a healer who restores, and a compassionate shepherd. David Wells wrote some time ago,

> It is one of the defining marks of Our Time that God is now weightless. I do not mean by this that he is ethereal but rather that he has become unimportant. He rests upon the world so inconsequentially as not to be noticeable. He has lost his saliency for human life. Those who assure the pollsters of their belief in God's existence may nonetheless consider him less interesting than television, his commands less authoritative than their appetites for affluence and influence, his judgments no more awe-inspiring than the evening

news, and his truth less compelling than the advertiser's sweet fog of flattery and lies.[1]

The prophets remind us that God cannot be pushed to the margins of our lives or trivialized and manipulated into fulfilling our personal agendas. The prophets restore a vision of God's immensity and challenge us to worship and revere him above all else.

Popular approaches often treat the prophets primarily as prognosticators and search their messages for connections to current events or for predictions about the end times. The prophets often spoke of the last days and enlarge our vision of the future kingdom of God, but they concentrated their preaching on confronting the sins of their culture and instructing the people about how to live in faithfulness and obedience to the Lord. In speaking to the crises and moral dilemmas of their day, the prophets addressed ethical issues that remain crucially important in the contemporary world, including the proper use of wealth, treatment of the poor, legal justice, war, violence, and the responsibilities of leadership. Just like Israel and Judah, the church must take to heart the prophets' call to reject religious formalism and spiritual apathy and to return to a vibrant relationship with the living God.

The prophets also help to inform a faith-filled perspective on world events in our troubled times. The God of the prophets is not a nationalistic deity merely presiding over his own people and territory but is One who judges both Israel and the nations. If the Lord exercised his sovereignty over the nations as the Assyrians and Babylonians led his people into exile, then he is equally able to accomplish his purposes in the midst of current global unrest and the threat of international terrorism. The prophets advocate trust in the Lord instead of military power and political alliances as the ultimate source of peace and security. The prophets' vision of the nations beating their swords into plows and streaming to Zion to worship the Lord offers real hope in place of empty political rhetoric that offers no real solutions for the world's problems.

We have written this overview of the Book of the Twelve for students, pastors, and all who seek to understand this neglected segment of God's Word. This part of Scripture remains obscure and unfamiliar for many

---

[1] David F. Wells, *God in the Wasteland: The Reality of Truth in a World of Fading Dreams* (Grand Rapid, MI: Eerdmans, 1995), 88.

Christians, and in teaching the prophets over the years, we have learned that many of our students would agree with Luther's assessment that the prophets "have a queer way of talking, like people who, instead of proceeding in an orderly manner, ramble off from one thing to the next, so that you cannot make head or tail of them or see what they are getting at."[2] Yet the message of the Twelve is extremely relevant, and its material, while challenging, is quite approachable with a little direction. Sermons and lessons from the Old Testament Minor Prophets are not common in our churches today, and we find this to be shortsighted, keeping the people of God ignorant about a significant portion of the Word of God. This is a tragedy. The Minor Prophets present unique interpretive challenges, but the blessings that come from careful and diligent study of this part of Scripture are worth the time and effort.

This book is divided into two major sections. The opening four chapters provide background material for the study of the Book of the Twelve as a whole. The first chapter explains the historical setting of the Book of the Twelve and the individual prophets who stand behind this corpus. The prophets deliver specific and concrete messages concerning the Assyrian and Babylonian crises facing Israel and Judah and the hopes and challenges facing the people of God in their return from exile after the Persian period. Locating the prophets within their proper historical context is foundational to proper interpretation of their message.

The second chapter explains the prophets' role as messengers of God's covenants and offers a theological context for understanding the prophetic books. Throughout the Old Testament, God exercises kingship through a series of covenants, and these covenants are central to the message of the prophets. The prophets announce judgment against the nations for their violations of the Noahic covenant and against Israel and Judah for their failure to live by the covenant commands given in the Mosaic law. The prophets were not innovators in condemning Israel's idolatry or in highlighting the need for social justice, but rather were calling the people to put into practice the original directives of the Mosaic law regarding how to love God and their neighbors. The prophetic vision of Israel's future restoration in the eschatological era of salvation is shaped by the Lord's promises of seed, land,

---

[2] Cited by Leslie C. Allen, *The Books of Joel, Obadiah, Jonah and Micah*, NICOT (Grand Rapids, MI: Eerdmans, 1976), 257.

and blessing to Abraham and his abiding commitments to the house of David. The prophets also anticipate a new covenant that would bring about the spiritual renewal and transformation of Israel when the Lord pours out his Spirit on his people. The Lord would then enable his people to obey his commands so that they might fully enjoy the blessings that were associated with the Mosaic covenant.

The third chapter focuses on the literary features of prophetic literature. The oracles of the prophets are quite different from the sermons we hear from pastors today, and the prophetic books are not like the kinds of books we are used to reading. What enables the reader to see artistry in the place of disarray is an awareness of the literary genres or forms of prophetic literature, as well as the literary and rhetorical tools used by the prophets to make their messages memorable and convincing to their often hostile or indifferent audiences. These techniques include poetic parallelism, extensive use of figurative language, wordplay, irony, and sarcasm.

This book not only seeks to offer informed literary interpretations of prophetic texts but also to help readers do the same in their own study of the Prophets. Recognition of the patterning of prophetic predictions in which they refer to near and far events together will enable readers to better grasp how the prophets inform our understanding of the future kingdom of God and how their oracles of judgment against the foreign nations of their day might apply to current nations. Awareness of how the prophets use stereotypical and figurative language to speak of the coming Day of the Lord or the future age of salvation helps the reader to avoid using the Prophets to construct a detailed road map of future events. Pastors and teachers aware of the literary and rhetorical features of the prophetic books will be better prepared to help this part of Scripture come alive for their audiences and to make applications that are faithful to the message of the text.

The fourth chapter examines the themes, motifs, and patterns that emerge from reading the Book of the Twelve as a literary unity. Scholarly study over the past thirty years has particularly focused on the Twelve as a single work rather than merely a collection of twelve separate compositions. Some of these studies have attempted to reconstruct the compositional history of the Twelve, which is beyond the scope of this book. The purpose of this chapter is to examine how the recognition of unifying themes like the Day of the Lord or the call to return to the Lord contribute to a deeper reading of the Book of the Twelve. The limited examples of repentance in the Twelve document Israel's unbelieving response to the Lord and his messengers. One of the few instances of repentance comes from the hated Ninevites, who respond to the rather reluctant preaching of the prophet Jonah, and intertextual links between Joel and Jonah particularly stress the idea that the Lord is willing to treat the nations with the same compassion and mercy that he exhibits toward his people Israel.

The second major section and the bulk of the book consist of individual chapters examining the message of the individual books of the Minor Prophets. Collectively, the prophets preach of judgment and salvation, but each has his own unique features and distinctive emphases. Hosea's family is a metaphor of Israel's infidelity. Amos warns a complacent Israel that the Lord is about to break out against them like a roaring lion and a raging storm. Joel and Zephaniah warn of an imminent Day of the Lord in times of national crisis and also look forward to the future Day of the Lord that will bring the ultimate judgment of the nations and restoration of God's people. Obadiah and Nahum preach messages of judgment against specific foreign nations. The message of Jonah is uniquely conveyed in the form of a story that recounts the surprising repentance of the Ninevites and a prophet's anger over a positive response to his preaching. In Habakkuk, dialogue between the prophet and the Lord serves as the medium for the announcement of the Lord's intention to use Babylon to judge Judah and then to subsequently judge Babylon and save his people. Haggai and Zechariah call on the postexilic community to resume rebuilding the temple in Jerusalem and to fully return to the Lord so that they might enjoy all of the blessings he has promised for his people. Malachi concludes the Twelve with a dispute between the Lord and his people that reflects the postexilic community's ongoing alienation from God, yet continues to look forward to the future restoration and the final Day of the Lord when all will be made right.

Each of these chapters examines the historical background and structure of the individual books and then provides a detailed exposition of the message of the book. The final section of each chapter analyzes the theological themes of the book and issues related to the contemporary application of the book in light of the whole canon of Scripture. Christian reading of the Twelve requires attention to connections between the Prophets and the New Testament but only after first attempting to understand the message of the prophets on their own terms and in their own historical settings. The exposition of each book provided in these chapters seeks to go beyond the standard Bible survey by presenting key interpretive issues in each book and including literary insights from the Hebrew text (with informal English transliterations for those without training in the biblical languages). The reader will need to consult exegetical commentaries and technical studies on the Twelve for more detailed discussions of interpretive issues, but in hearing the voice of the Minor Prophets, we have been careful not to sidestep interpretive points of interest. Insets, maps, photos, and charts are provided to further assist the reader in navigating the individual chapters.

ABBREVIATIONS

AB	Anchor Bible
BAR	Biblical Archaeology Review
BBR	Bulletin for Biblical Research
BLS	Bible and Literature Series
BZAW	*Beihefte zur Zeitschrift für die alttestamentliche Wissenschaft*
CTQ	Concordia Theological Quarterly
HBM	Hebrew Bible Monographs
JBL	Journal of Biblical Literature
JETS	Journal of the Evangelical Theological Society
JSOTSup	Journal for the Study of the Old Testament Supplement
NAC	New American Commentary
NIBC	New International Biblical Commentary
NICOT	New International Commentary on the Old Testament
NIVAC	New International Version Application Commentary
NSBT	New Studies in Biblical Theology
OTL	Old Testament Library Commentary
SBLSymS	Society of Biblical Literature Symposium Series
TB	Tyndale Bulletin
TOTC	Tyndale Old Testament Commentary
WBC	Word Biblical Commentary

1

The World of the Twelve:
The Historical Background and
Setting of the Book of the Twelve

Introduction

The lives of the prophets in the Book of the Twelve span a period of more than three centuries (c. 770–430 BC), and they ministered in some of Israel's most tumultuous days. The Lord had promised through Moses that he would send prophets to communicate his word to his people (Deut 18:15–22), and he kept his promise even as he prepared to bring judgment against Israel and Judah for their unfaithfulness, which had persisted for hundreds of years. The specific mission of the Twelve was threefold: to call the people to repentance so that they might avert divine judgment, to warn them of the judgment of exile when there was no repentance, and then to offer hope for the future as the people returned to the land following the exile. The Lord sent prophets to Israel and Judah during the Assyrian crisis before the fall of Samaria in 722 BC and then sent more prophets to

Judah in the Babylonian crisis before the fall of Jerusalem in 586 BC. The postexilic prophets challenged the people to rebuild the temple and to fully return to the Lord so they might experience all the blessings of restoration and renewal that he had planned for them. The Book of the Twelve reflects disappointment that full restoration had yet to occur, but holds forth the hope that the Lord would never abandon his people or his commitment to fully bless them and to extend the blessings of salvation to the nations.

The purpose of this chapter is to provide an historical survey of the times in which the Twelve lived and ministered.[1] It is important to understand the historical setting of the prophets because they preached more about their own times than they did the last days. The prophets reminded the people of God's sovereign control over the chaotic events of their day. When the Lord roars like a lion, his judgments extend beyond Israel to all the nations (Joel 3:16; Amos 1:2). The Lord controls the forces of nature, whether to direct a disobedient prophet like Jonah or to send drought and locusts to get the attention of his rebellious people. The Lord also directs the kings and armies of the nations to accomplish his purposes and to execute his judgments. Assyria was the "rod" of Yahweh's anger (Isa 10:5), Nebuchadnezzar of Babylon his "servant" (Jer 25:9; 27:6), and Cyrus of Persia his "shepherd" and "anointed one" (Isa 44:28–45:1). The destruction of Israel, Judah, Edom, and Nineveh were "days of the Lord" and not simply geopolitical events. The prophets also sought to turn the people away from military and political solutions to the crises they were facing and to help them recognize the only way they would survive was to return to the Lord before it was too late.

This chapter attempts to place the prophets in their historical context and setting, while recognizing that there was likely a lapse in time between

---

[1] For more detailed overviews and discussion of the three centuries in which the prophets of the Twelve ministered and issues of historiography related to ancient Israel, see Bill T. Arnold and Richard S. Hess, eds., *Ancient Israel's History: An Introduction to Issues and Sources* (Grand Rapids, MI: Baker, 2014), 319–425; Daniel I. Block, *Israel: Ancient Kingdom or Late Invention?* (Nashville, TN: B&H Academic, 2008); Iain Provan, V. Philips Long, and Tremper Longman, III, *A Biblical History of Israel* (Louisville, KY: Westminster John Knox, 2003), 269–303; Walter C. Kaiser Jr., *A History of Israel From the Bronze Age Through the Jewish Wars* (Nashville, TN: B&H, 1998), 351–446; and Eugene H. Merrill, *Kingdom of Priests: A History of Old Testament Israel* (Grand Rapids, MI: Baker, 1987), 373–515.

the actual ministries of the prophets and the composition of the books bearing their names. The prophets were primarily preachers who delivered their oracles orally rather than literary authors. Aaron Chalmers notes that the process by which each prophet's words became a book is unclear but likely involved three distinct movements: (1) from oral words to written words, (2) from written words to collected words, and (3) from collected words to prophetic book.[2]

The Prophets and the Assyrian Crisis

When Israel separated from Judah just after the time of Solomon in 930 BC, Jeroboam I, as Israel's first king, plunged the nation into apostasy by setting up sanctuaries that centered on the worship of golden calves (1 Kgs 12:25–33). Jeroboam sought to keep his people from going down to Jerusalem so they would not give their loyalties to the house of David, but

Israel's Classical Prophets

	Prophets to Israel	Prophets to Judah
ASSYRIAN PERIOD	Jonah* (785–775) Amos (760–750) Hosea (750–715)	Isaiah (740–681) Micah (735–690)
BABYLONIAN PERIOD		Zephaniah (630–620) Nahum (630) Habakkuk (620) Jeremiah (627–580) Obadiah (600?) Ezekiel (593–570)
PERSIAN (POSTEXILIC) PERIOD		Haggai (520) Zechariah (520–518) Joel (500?) Malachi (450–430)

*Minor prophets' names are in bold.

---

[2] Aaron Chalmers, *Interpreting the Prophets: Reading, Understanding and Preaching from the Worlds of the Prophets* (Downers Grove, IL: IVP Academic, 2015), 23.

in the process, he also led Israel away from worship at the place where the Lord had chosen to dwell among his people. Israel would walk this path of apostasy for its entire history, and 1–2 Kings notes that every Israelite king followed in the sins of Jeroboam, his father. Ahab was remembered as Israel's worst king because he and his wife Jezebel promoted Baal worship in Israel (1 Kgs 16:30–33). Even though Elijah and Elisha as prophets and Jehu as military commander and king helped to purge Baal worship from Israel, the northern kingdom never fully abandoned its idolatry, syncretism, and pagan worship practices.[3]

In many ways, Judah to the south was no better. The people worshipped at the temple in Jerusalem, but syncretism and idolatry plagued the southern kingdom as well. A handful of godly rulers reigned among the kings, but the majority of them neglected to walk in the ways of their father David or do what was right in the eyes of the Lord. Social injustice and disregard for the Lord's commands were problems in both Israel and Judah. Through the prophets, the Lord would provide one final opportunity for both Israel and Judah to return to him, but 2 Kings 17:13–18 reminds us that Israel "would not listen" and "became obstinate like their ancestors who did not believe the Lord their God." Judah likewise would fall under judgment because its people "did not keep the commands of the Lord their God but lived according to the customs Israel introduced" (2 Kgs 17:19–20).

Assyria began to look westward and to put military pressure on Israel in the ninth century BC. Ahab and a coalition of kings halted the advance of Shalmaneser III at the Battle of Qarqar in southern Syria in 853 BC, but the Assyrians exacted tribute from Jehu of Israel in their western campaign in 841. The military actions of Assyria also greatly reduced the kingdom of Aram-Damascus. This freed Israel from the domination of the Arameans, a people with whom Israel constantly fought. Just after the turn of the century, Assyria began to decline as well, forcing its rulers to deal with internal threats at home rather than focus on military expansion. The weakening of both Aram and Assyria allowed the northern kingdom to enjoy a time of

---

[3] For an overview of religious practices during the time of the divided monarchy, including the struggles with idolatry and religious syncretism in Israel and Judah, see Richard S. Hess, *Israelite Religions: An Archaeological and Biblical Survey* (Grand Rapids, MI: Baker, 2007), 247–335. Hess has separate chapters on written sources and archaeological evidence.

unprecedented prosperity under the long and effective reign of Jeroboam II (793–753 BC).[4] Jeroboam II recovered the territories that Israel had lost to the Arameans and brought most of southern Syria under Israelite control. Walter C. Kaiser comments, "In less than twenty-five years, Jeroboam II was able to take a nation that was just about to die and turn it into one of the great powers of his day."[5]

Territorial expansion was prophesied by **Jonah** (2 Kgs 14:25–28), but Jonah resisted when he was sent to preach to Nineveh, fearing that God might extend the same mercy to the hated Assyrians that he had shown to Israel (see Jonah 4:2). Many have viewed the Ninevites' favorable response to Jonah's preaching as highly implausible. However, Assyria's troubles—including military threats, revolts by vassal states, political division, and particularly intense food shortages during the years 772–755 BC—likely made the Ninevites receptive to a message of divine judgment.[6]

While Israel thrived under Jeroboam II, Judah experienced similar prosperity under the long and stable rule of Uzziah (also called Azariah) (792–740 BC). Uzziah was also able to enlarge Judah's army and to carry out successful military operations against the Philistines, Ammonites, and Edomites (2 Chr 26:6–15). This time of unparalleled blessing should have led the people of Israel and Judah to gratefully seek and serve the Lord, but their prosperity instead led to spiritual complacency and an even greater disregard of the Lord's commands. The wealthy in the land exploited the poor and needy while pretending to worship God. Despite the Lord's blessing on his kingdom, Jeroboam II did "evil in the eyes of the Lord" and carried on the apostate practices of his predecessors (2 Kgs 14:23–24, NIV). Uzziah sought the Lord until pride led to his downfall at the end of his reign (2 Chr 26:16), but Judah as a nation also drifted from the Lord because of its wealth and military strength.

Near the end of the reign of Jeroboam II, the Lord sent **Amos**, a wealthy landowner from Judah, to warn Israel that its apostasy and social injustices

---

[4] The dates for the reigns of the kings of Israel and Judah used in this chapter follow the system established by Thiele. See Edwin R. Thiele, *The Mysterious Numbers of the Hebrew Kings*, new rev. ed. (Grand Rapids, MI: Kregel, 1994).

[5] Kaiser, *A History of Israel*, 351.

[6] For a brief summary of these tumultuous times for Assyria, see John H. Walton, "Jonah," in *Zondervan Illustrated Bible Backgrounds Commentary*, vol. 5 (Grand Rapids, MI: Zondervan, 2009), 101–3.

would lead to military defeat and exile. The use of an outsider to announce Israel's judgment reflected both the seriousness of the message and the corruption of Israel's spiritual leaders. Amaziah, a priest at the sanctuary in Bethel, ordered Amos to stop preaching against "the king's sanctuary" and to return home to Judah (Amos 7:10–17). **Hosea** also began to prophesy in the last days of Jeroboam II, and his ministry continued through the turbulent years that led to the fall of Samaria in 722 BC. Hosea then migrated to Judah and continued to prophesy into the reign of King Hezekiah. Hosea's symbolic marriage and messages sought to convince the people of Israel that they needed to repent for their spiritual adultery against the Lord through their worship of false gods, disobedience to God's commands, and entangling alliances with foreign nations.

National disaster seemed like a remote possibility as Israel reveled in a golden age of prosperity, but circumstances quickly changed. An earthquake remembered in later generations occurred two years after Amos's preaching as a further warning of divine displeasure (see Amos 1:1; Zech 14:5). Jeroboam's II lengthy reign was followed by a series of bloody assassinations and violent regime changes. The major problem facing both Israel and Judah in the second half of the eighth century BC was the resurgence of the Assyrians under the energetic leadership of Tiglath-pileser III (745–727). In Judah, the Lord called **Isaiah** to prophesy in 740 BC, which was also the year that King Uzziah died. Isaiah's vision reminded him that Yahweh was Judah's true King (Isaiah 6), and he warned the people that getting right with the Lord and trusting in him as their protector was the only way they would survive the coming crisis.

Seeking to throw off Assyrian rule because of the heavy tribute they were forced to pay, Pekah of Israel and Rezin of Damascus formed an alliance. When Ahaz of Judah refused to join the coalition, the armies of Israel and Aram attacked Ahaz in an attempt to replace him with a ruler supportive of the alliance. The resulting Syro-Ephraimite War in 734–732 BC had disastrous consequences for both Israel and Judah.[7] When the more powerful armies of Israel and Aram attacked Judah, Isaiah counseled Ahaz to trust in the Lord to deliver him from his enemies. Instead, the king appealed to Tiglath-pileser III of Assyria for assistance by sending him treasures from the temple (2 Kgs 16:7–8). The Assyrian army defeated the Syro-Ephraimite

---

[7] Kaiser, *A History of Israel*, 372–74.

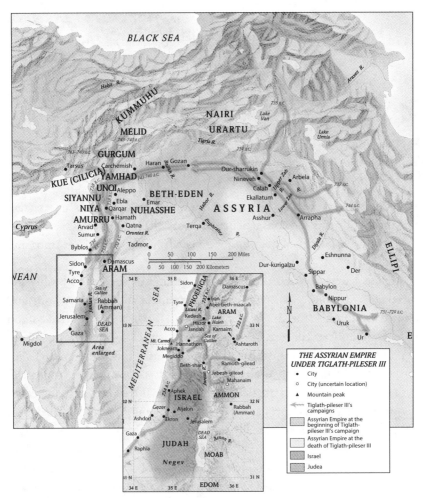

At the zenith of its power in the seventh century BC, the Neo-Assyrian Empire controlled all of the Fertile Crescent.

coalition, destroying Damascus, killing Rezin, and greatly reducing the territory of Israel (2 Kgs 16:9). After suffering the loss of many troops in the conflict, Ahaz was delivered from the immediate threat, but Judah was now also a vassal of Assyria. Ahaz was one of Judah's most wicked kings, and during his reign Judah's apostasy rivaled that of Israel to the north.

Israel survived for another decade as a vassal of Assyria, but Hoshea, in conspiracy with Egypt, rebelled against Assyria and refused to pay tribute. Assyrian King Shalmaneser V took Hoshea prisoner and then marched on Samaria in 725 BC, capturing the city three years later (2 Kgs 17:3–6). The

The Capture of Samaria (722 BC)

The annals of Assyrian King Sargon II record the capture of Samaria and the subsequent capture of the people of Israel:

> *The ruler of Samaria . . . defaulted on his taxes and declared Samaria's independence from Assyria. With the strength given me by the divine assembly, I conquered Samaria and its covenant partner, and took 27,290 prisoners of war along with their chariots.*

Israelites were taken away into captivity, and Samaria became an Assyrian province. Exile was the consequence of Israel's flagrant apostasy and disregard for the warnings of coming judgment from prophets like Amos and Hosea (2 Kgs 17:7–18).

Judah barely avoided the same fate. Ahaz was succeeded by his son Hezekiah (716–686 BC), who, unlike his father, followed the Lord and refused to submit to the king of Assyria (2 Kgs 18:1–7). The death of Sargon II motivated Hezekiah to rebel against the Assyrians early in his reign. In these early years, Hezekiah wavered between trust in the Lord and reliance on political alliances and military strategies. Isaiah warned that alliances with Egypt would fail (Isa 30:1–3; 31:1–3) and rebuked Hezekiah for showing off the temple treasures as a way of convincing Merodach-Baladan of Babylon that he was a worthy ally against Assyria (Isaiah 39). The Assyrian response to Hezekiah's revolt was severe. Sennacherib captured forty-six cities in Judah, most notably the military stronghold of Lachish some twenty-five miles southwest of Jerusalem.[8] Hezekiah paid a heavy fine to the Assyrians to spare the city of Jerusalem, but Sennacherib still sent his army to Jerusalem, demanding the surrender of the city in 701 BC (2 Kgs 18:14–35). With Jerusalem surrounded, Hezekiah turned to God and prayed that God would deliver the city (2 Kgs 19:14–19; Isa 37:14–20). Through Isaiah, the Lord assured the king that he would defend it (2 Kgs 19:20–34; Isa 37:21–35).

---

[8] Sennacherib would later decorate his palace with twelve marble friezes depicting the siege of Lachish. These reliefs provide some of the best extant pictorial depictions of warfare in the ancient Near East. For more on the capture of Lachish, see Boyd Seevers, *Warfare in the Old Testament: The Organization, Weapons, and Tactics of Ancient Near Eastern Armies* (Grand Rapids, MI: Kregel Academic, 2013), 194–201.

The angel of the Lord destroyed the Assyrian army, and Sennacherib withdrew from the city (2 Kgs 19:35–37; Isa 37:36–38). Critical scholars have viewed the account of the miraculous deliverance as legendary, but for whatever reason, it is clear that the Assyrians did not capture Jerusalem.[9]

The prophet **Micah**, from the small village of Moresheth-gath, was a younger contemporary of Isaiah who also ministered in Judah during the days of the Assyrian crisis. Micah warned that because of Judah's apostasy, Jerusalem and the temple would be reduced to rubble (Mic 3:12) and announced that the only way to avoid judgment was for the nation "to act justly, to love faithfulness, and to walk humbly" before the Lord (Mic 6:8). In the following century, the elders of the land recalled that Micah's preaching influenced Hezekiah's repentance that had led the Lord to relent from destroying Jerusalem (Jer 26:17–19).

Hezekiah's courageous faith helped to save Jerusalem, but Judah remained firmly under Assyrian control throughout the seventh century BC. After Sennacherib's assassination, the Neo-Assyrian Empire remained strong under the rule of Esarhaddon (681–669 BC) and Ashurbanipal (669–627 BC). Esarhaddon carried out a number of military campaigns against Egypt and was able to capture Thebes in 671 BC. He died and was succeeded by his son Ashurbanipal while on his way to attack Egypt two years later. In 664 BC, Ashurbanipal recaptured Memphis and destroyed Thebes. In Judah, Manasseh (687–642 BC) succeeded Hezekiah and set about to overturn his father's religious reforms. Ironically, Manasseh reigned the longest of any king in the Davidic line (fifty-five years) but is also remembered as the worst of Judah's rulers and the leader who caused Judah to do more evil than even the people who had lived in the land before Israel did (2 Kgs 21:9–11). Manasseh promoted idolatry, filled Jerusalem with violence and bloodshed, and even offered his own son as a sacrifice to the false gods (2 Kgs 21:1–9). Jewish legend states that Manasseh killed the prophet Isaiah at the beginning of his reign, and the years of his rule were characterized by an absence of prophetic voices.

Manasseh became a vassal of Assyria as early as 667 BC. He appears to have remained a loyal vassal to that nation throughout his reign, except

---

[9] For issues concerning the historicity of this event and the question of the number of military campaigns that Sennacherib led against Hezekiah, see Richard S. Hess, "Hezekiah and Sennacherib in 2 Kings 18–20," in *Zion City of Our God*, ed. Richard S. Hess and Gordon J. Wenham (Grand Rapids, MI: Eerdmans, 2004), 23–41.

for the incident recorded in 2 Chronicles 33:11–13. There, Manasseh was arrested by the Assyrians, taken to Babylon, and then released after affirming loyalty to his Assyrian overlord.[10] The Chronicler also states that the Lord allowed Manasseh to return to Jerusalem in response to the king's repentance and prayers for mercy. The writer of Kings makes no mention of Manasseh's repentance, perhaps in order to highlight the wickedness of the king's character and conduct. The apocryphal *Prayer of Manasseh* gives expression to what Manasseh's words of repentance might have been included. The Lord announced that because of Manasseh's evil he would "wipe Jerusalem clean as one wipes a bowl" (2 Kgs 21:13; see Jer 15:4).

The Prophets and the Babylonian Crisis

Amon assumed the throne after Manasseh and reigned for two years before he was assassinated; his death left the throne to his eight-year-old son Josiah (640–609 BC). In contrast to Manasseh, who was Judah's worst king, Josiah was remembered as the Davidic king who most fully obeyed the Lord (2 Kgs 23:25). Josiah purged the land of idols, pagan sanctuaries, and apostate priests. His reforms were even more extensive than those carried out by Hezekiah in the previous century. Second Chronicles 34:3 states that Josiah began to "seek" God in his eighth year (632) and to "cleanse" the land in his twelfth (628). Josiah's reforms reached their zenith with the discovery of the "book of the law" in connection with repairs to the temple in 622 BC (2 Kings 23). Josiah led the nation in a time of covenant renewal and even extended his reforms into the territories of the former northern kingdom.

One of the other significant influences behind Josiah's reforms was the preaching of the prophet **Zephaniah**. Zephaniah began to prophesy early in the reign of Josiah (Zeph 1:1), and J. J. M. Roberts suggests that the absence of direct references to the king in the prophet's oracles reflects that "Josiah was still just a boy, king in name, but under the control of royal officials."[11] Zephaniah condemned Judah's worship of false gods and warned that "the Day of the Lord" was near (Zeph 1:4–7). By taking these warnings to heart and acting on them, Josiah spared Judah from destruction. Even though the

---

[10] Kaiser, *A History of Israel*, 382.

[11] J. J. M. Roberts, *Nahum, Habakkuk, and Zephaniah*, OTL (Minneapolis, MN: Westminster John Knox, 1991), 163.

Lord had announced his intention to judge Jerusalem during the reign of Manasseh, there was still the opportunity for judgment to be averted if the people repented and sought Yahweh.

Assyria's decline enabled Josiah to expand his religious and political influence as well as allowing Egypt to reassert its claims on Syria-Palestine. The death of Ashurbanipal in 627 BC caused civil war and internal strife within Assyria that also enabled Nabopolassar to assert the independence of Babylon in 626 BC and to drive the Assyrians out of his realm completely a few short years later. Within a decade, the Babylonians and Medes were allied in a series of military attacks against the crumbling Assyrian Empire. The Medes destroyed the city of Ashur in 614 BC, and the Medo-Babylonian armies destroyed the Assyrian capital of Nineveh in 612 BC, fulfilling **Nahum's** prophecies against the city. The Egyptian army, under Pharaoh Neco II, marched north in 609 BC to support what was left of the Assyrian army. Viewing the rise of Babylon as an opportunity to bring an end to Assyrian domination, Josiah sought to impede the northern advance of the Egyptian army and was killed at Megiddo at the age of thirty-nine. Despite his righteous reign and godly reforms, Josiah acted contrary to God's will in opposing the Egyptians (see 2 Chr 35:22). The Babylonians and Medes subsequently defeated the Assyrians and Egyptians at Haran. In 605 BC, Nebuchadnezzar destroyed the last Assyrian fortress at Carchemish and drove the Egyptians out of Syria. Nebuchadnezzar marched southward, asserting Babylonian control over all of Syria-Palestine and taking away the first group of exiles from Judah, including Daniel and members of other prominent Judean families. Nebuchadnezzar returned to Babylon in September of 605 BC to assume the throne, following the death of his father Nabopolassar. Judah became a vassal of the Neo-Babylonian Empire.

The rise of the Neo-Babylonian Empire coincided with a flurry of prophetic activity within Judah. As judgment drew closer, the Lord provided every possible opportunity for the people of Judah to hear of his plans to use Babylon as his instrument of judgment so that Judah might repent. **Jeremiah** began his ministry in 626 BC and warned of the coming enemy from the north as he called on Judah to "return" to the Lord. Jeremiah ministered beyond the fall of Jerusalem in 586 BC, and he suffered great opposition and persecution as he warned that Judah's exile in Babylon would last for seventy years. As Babylon rose to power, **Habakkuk** struggled with the

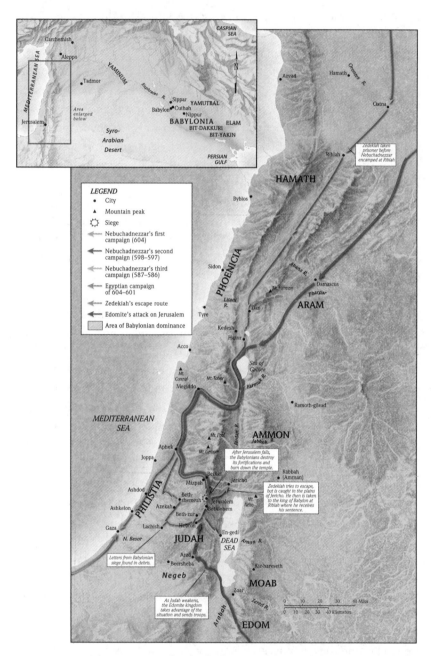

*The campaigns of Nebuchadnezzar against Judah culminated with
the fall of Jerusalem and the destruction of the temple in 586 BC.*

Lord's justice in using the violent and wicked Babylonians to punish Judah (Hab 1:12–2:1), but the Lord announced to the prophet that he would also judge Babylon after using that nation as his instrument of judgment against Judah (Hab 2:6–20). No matter how dire the circumstances, Habakkuk would trust in the Lord and wait for him to bring the promised deliverance of his people (Habakkuk 3).

Josiah's reforms delayed, but could not permanently reverse, the Lord's decree of judgment against Judah. After Josiah's death, Judah quickly returned to its sinful ways. Returning from his defeat at Haran in 609 BC, Neco II of Egypt removed Jehoahaz from the throne and took him away as a prisoner, placing his brother Jehoiakim on the throne in his place (2 Kgs 23:33–34). Jehoiakim remained loyal to the Egyptians until 605 BC, when he switched his allegiances to Babylon after Nebuchadnezzar's victory at Carchemish. Jehoiakim vacillated between Egypt and Babylon for his entire reign. In 602/601 BC, Nebuchadnezzar took Jehoiakim as prisoner to Babylon, seizing treasures from the temple as a fine, but then allowed him to return to Jerusalem (2 Chr 36:6–7). Jehoiakim's final rebellion against Babylon led to Nebuchadnezzar's capture of Jerusalem in 597 BC, but Jehoiakim died before the Babylonians reached the city. The book of Jeremiah documents Jehoiakim's evil behavior and his hostility toward the Lord's prophets. When concerned officials had the scroll of Jeremiah's prophecies of judgment read to the king in 605 BC, the king destroyed the scroll and sought to have Jeremiah arrested (Jeremiah 36). Jehoiakim's rebellious posture toward the word of the Lord meant the judgment that could have been avoided was now inevitable.

When Nebuchadnezzar overpowered the city of Jerusalem in 597 BC, he took away as prisoner Jehoiachin, the eighteen-year-old king who had only been on the throne for three months (2 Kgs 24:10–17). Nebuchadnezzar also deported more than 10,000 exiles from Judah at this time, including Ezekiel, who would become a prophetic voice for the exiles in Babylon.[12]

---

[12] There appears to be a discrepancy between the figure 10,000 in 2 Kings 24:14 and the smaller numbers given for the deportations to Babylon in Jeremiah 52:28–30. The figure of 10,000 may refer to the total number of captives taken to Babylon in all the deportations. See Peter van der Veen, "Sixth-Century Issues: The Fall of Jerusalem, the Exile, and the Return," in *Ancient Israel's History*, 383–84. Van der Veen (pp. 387–96), while acknowledging that a large portion of Judahites remained in the land after the fall of Jerusalem, discusses the archaeological evidence countering the theory that the biblical texts related to this era provide a propagandistic and historically unreliable account of the Babylonian exile.

Nebuchadnezzar replaced Jehoiachin with his uncle Mattaniah and gave him the throne name Zedekiah. Zedekiah was a weak and indecisive leader who lacked the courage to follow Jeremiah's prophetic counsel to submit to Babylon so that Judah might be spared further destruction (Jeremiah 37–38). Following instead the advice of his royal officials and military leaders, Zedekiah rebelled against Babylon with disastrous results.

The Capture of Jerusalem, 597 BC

The Babylonian Chronicle gives the following record of Nebuchadnezzar's Capture of Jerusalem in 597 BC:

Year 7 [of Nebuchadnezzar]. In the month of Kislev [December 598], the king of Babylonia mobilized his troops and marched to the west. He encamped against the city of Judah [Jerusalem], and on the second of Adar [March 16, 597], he captured the city and seized [its] king. A king of his choice he appointed there; he to[ok] its heavy tribute and carried it off to Babylon.

Nebuchadnezzar's armies carried out an eighteen-month siege on Jerusalem in 588–586 BC and this time burned the city, its walls, and the temple. Many were killed and others were taken away as captives in this third wave of exile. Zedekiah was captured at Riblah while attempting to flee from the Babylonians (2 Kgs 25:5–7; Jer 39:4–6). The Babylonians forced him to watch the execution of his two sons before blinding him and taking him away to Babylon as a prisoner. Jehoiachin and Zedekiah would remain in Babylon for the remainder of their lives. The nation of Judah had come to an end, and there was no longer a Davidic king on the throne. To many, it appeared as if the Lord had terminated his special relationship with the people of Israel and had voided his covenant promises to Abraham and David.

The kingdom of Edom bordered Judah on the south, and the Edomites were the descendants of Esau, brother of Israel's patriarch. Hostilities between the Edomites and Israelites had existed from before the time Israel had entered the land, and tensions between Edom and Judah flared once again in the Babylonian crisis. By 600 BC, Edom had seized territory and attacked Judah's military fortifications in the south. Edomite troops participated with Babylon in the siege and destruction of Jerusalem, and the Edomites also attacked Judean refugees as they fled from the Babylonians. Shortly after these events, **Obadiah** condemned the Edomites for their violence against Judah. He announced that Edom would "be covered with shame and destroyed forever" (Obadiah 10) for rejoicing over Judah's fall and using it for their own gain. Nabonidus and the Babylonians conquered Edom in 553 BC, and the Nabateans later defeated the Edomites, driving them out of their land by the end of the fourth century BC.

Along with calling the people to repentance and announcing the coming judgment when repentance did not occur, it was the mission of the prophets to proclaim coming restoration and to offer hope. The prophets had preached judgment on the basis of the Mosaic covenant; they would offer hope on the basis of the Abrahamic and the Davidic covenants. Isaiah, Jeremiah, and Ezekiel even promised the Lord would make a new covenant with Israel that would erase the failures of the past and provide enablement for future obedience. This hope of return, renewal, and restoration is also an important component of the message of the Book of the Twelve.

Following the fall of Jerusalem in 586 BC, there were Jews living in exile in Babylon, those who had remained in the land, and Jewish refugees who had fled to Egypt. Jeremiah remained in the land to minister to the people there and was later kidnapped and taken to Egypt. Another deportation of Jews from the land would occur in 582 BC in connection with the assassination of Gedaliah, the Babylonian-appointed governor of Judah (see 2 Kgs 25:25; Jer 41:1–3). **Ezekiel** was called to be a prophetic voice to the exiles in Babylon in 593 BC. **Daniel**, who rose to prominent positions in both the Babylonian and Persian governments, also became an important prophetic voice in revealing the Lord's future plans for Israel. Jeremiah had prophesied that the exile would last for seventy years (Jer 25:11–12; 29:10). Near the end of those seventy years, Daniel prayed for the Lord to keep his promises and to restore his people (Daniel 9). As an expansion on Jeremiah's original prophecy, Daniel received a vision clarifying that the full restoration of Israel would not occur for "seventy weeks" (Dan 9:24–27). The people would return from exile in Babylon in fulfillment of Jeremiah's prophecy, but the complete and final restoration of Israel would not occur for a long and undefined period of time.

The Prophets in the Postexilic (Persian) Period

Cyrus II of Persia rose to power in 559 BC and, after uniting the Persians and the Medes, marched on the Babylonians in 539. He won a major victory over the Babylonian army at Opis and then took the city of Babylon without resistance, bringing to an end the short-lived Neo-Babylonian Empire. Cyrus issued a decree in 538 BC, allowing the Jews to return to their homeland (2 Chr 36:23–24; Ezra 1:2–4; 6:3–5). The Cyrus Cylinder, discovered in

The Cyrus Cylinder: In this inscription, Cyrus claims to have allowed captive peoples to return to their homeland, and to have restored temples, and to have returned images of the gods to those temples throughout Mesopotamia. These policies allowed Jewish exiles to return to their homeland beginning in 538 BC.

1879, reveals the general Persian policy of allowing conquered peoples to return to their homelands and rebuild their temples. Cyrus hoped to gain from the revenue of thriving provinces, to receive favor from foreign gods, and to establish buffers against his enemies at the extreme boundaries of his empire. Eugene H. Merrill writes that this aspect of Persian policy "was nothing short of brilliant."[13] The majority of Jews living in exile had acclimated to their surroundings and remained in foreign lands, but a group of nearly 50,000 returned to Judah (Ezra 2:64–65).

The circumstances faced by the returnees to Judah hardly matched the idyllic conditions envisioned by the prophets before and during the time of the exile as they spoke of Israel's restoration and renewal. The impoverished postexilic community remained under Persian control and was surrounded by enemies who opposed their resettlement. The people faced the enormous task of rebuilding their towns, restoring their fields and vineyards

---

[13] Merrill, *Kingdom of Priests*, 491. The policy of the Assyrians and Babylonians was to displace conquered peoples and to resettle them in various parts of their empires as a way of discouraging revolts and rebellion (see 2 Kings 17:23–24; 25:11–21).

to productivity, and renewing some sense of community. The walls of Jerusalem and the temple were in ruins. Most importantly, the people had come home, but they had not fully returned to the Lord. As during the Assyrian and Babylonian crises, the Lord would raise up prophets to confront, direct, and encourage his people in the midst of the challenges they faced in returning to the land.

The first group of Jewish returnees laid the foundation for the temple and rebuilt the altar for sacrifices in 536 BC under the leadership of Zerubbabel the governor and Joshua the high priest. Zerubbabel was the grandson of the deposed Jehoiachin, and his leadership role reflected in a small way the Lord's continued commitment to the house of David. The laying of the foundation for the temple was a time of both great joy and sorrow as the elders remembered the glory of Solomon's temple that had been destroyed (Ezra 3:10–13). Opposition led by the Samaritans would ultimately lead to the shutting down of the rebuilding project for sixteen years. In 520 BC, the Lord commissioned the prophets **Haggai** and **Zechariah** to encourage the people to finish the task of rebuilding the temple (Ezra 5:1–2). Within three weeks of Haggai's first oracle, the people were back at work, and the Lord promised—through Haggai and Zechariah—to bless and prosper the people because of their obedience.

More opposition ensued when Tattenai, the provincial governor of Trans-Euphrates, wrote a letter to Darius seeking to again stop the rebuilding of the temple (Ezra 5). Darius ordered a careful search of the Persian archives and found a copy of the decree of Cyrus that had allowed the Jews to return to their homeland and to rebuild their sanctuary (Ezra 6:8). The king ordered Tattenai to cease from interfering with the rebuilding and to provide financial resources for the construction project (Ezra 6:6–12). The Jerusalem temple was completed and rededicated in 515 BC.

The revitalization of Judah that accompanied the rebuilding of the temple eventually waned as the people returned to their spiritual lethargy and disregard for the Word of God. They had failed to learn—even from the exile—the necessity of covenant faithfulness to the Lord and continued the sinful practices of previous generations that had led to the exile in the first place. Dating the book of **Joel** is extremely difficult, but the view taken in this work is that Joel belongs to the postexilic period. Perhaps around 500 BC, Judah suffered a devastating locust plague that wiped out much of the land's agricultural produce; Joel warned that an even greater judgment, in the form of an invading army, was on its way. Joel called for a sacred assembly in which the people would repent, confess their sins, and pray for the Lord's mercy (Joel 2:13–17). A positive response from the people to Joel's counsel appears to have led the Lord to relent from executing the judgment he had threatened (Joel 2:18–27).

As the final voice in the Book of the Twelve, **Malachi** reflects that Israel remained rebellious and alienated from God. When Malachi affirms Yahweh's love for Israel, the people challenge his claim, and they question if there is any justice with God or any value in serving him. The issues of corrupt priesthood and worship (Mal 1:6–2:9; Neh 13:4–9), intermarriage with foreigners and divorce (Ezra 9–10; Neh 13:23–37), social injustice (Mal 3:5; Neh 5:1–12), abuse of the Sabbath (Mal 2:8–9; Neh 13:5–22), and failure to pay tithes (Mal 3:8–10; Neh 13:32–39; 13:10–14) in the preaching of Malachi are similar to concerns addressed by Ezra and Nehemiah. This suggests that Malachi prophesied either just before or during the time of the reforms carried out by Ezra and Nehemiah following their returns to the land in 458 and 445 BC.[14]

Conclusion

The historical period to which the Book of the Twelve belonged concluded without Israel ever experiencing the full restoration the Lord promised through his prophets. Malachi announced that the Lord would send "Elijah the prophet before the great and awesome Day of the LORD" (Mal 4:5), signifying that another time of great judgment would precede Israel's ultimate restoration. The New Testament era opens with John the Baptist announcing the impending arrival of God's kingdom and of Jesus the Messiah who would fulfill the promises of the prophets. Despite the disappointing history of the prophets, their promises of salvation and restoration for Israel and the nations would not fail. The Lord would overcome even the unbelief of his own people to bring those promises to pass.

---

[14] David W. Baker, *Joel, Obadiah, Malachi*, NIVAC (Grand Rapids, MI: Zondervan, 2006), 208.

2

The Role of the Twelve: Messengers of God's Covenants

Introduction

When many people think of a prophet, they picture a bearded prognosticator with a crystal ball, a Nostradamus-like figure foretelling the future. In reference to biblical prophecy, the idea usually involves the cosmic display of God's final judgment on humanity, a counting down to the last days before God's wrath is meted out on the world. Prophecy conferences tend to support such thinking, and the most popular books on biblical prophecy usually center on the fulfillment of prophetic texts on a global scale within *our* immediate future. However, as much as sensationalism appeals to the senses, many readers of biblical prophecy—when they actually turn to the text itself—are disappointed to find that the prophets were not as interested in our future as they were in the futures of a distant, foreign people, foretelling events that were indeed prophetic for them, but that for us fall into the realm of ancient history. Furthermore, the role of foretelling the future was often secondary to the role of forth-telling; that is, preaching the heart of God to his people. When the reader understands this distinction, a whole new world opens up as the words of the prophets take on a relevance much more in line with their role in proclaiming the word of God to a stiff-necked, obstinate people.

The Prophets as Forth-Tellers

The primary role of the prophets was to proclaim the word of God as "covenant reinforcement mediators," preaching to the people a message of blessing for obedience and cursing for disobedience, reinforced through fresh and sometimes shocking rhetoric.[1] Although the prophets refined and extended the details of covenant fulfillment, the basis of their message was nothing new, rooted as it was in the promises of the Mosaic covenant. Nevertheless, the way they framed the message was both new and innovative; their role was to get the attention of the people and to remind them of covenant obligations before the proverbial hammer dropped. In fulfilling this primary role, the prophets did fill a secondary role as foretellers of future things—but their prognostications were always set within the context of covenant obligation and fulfillment. They foretold the historical details of what would later take place as a result of Yahweh's covenant faithfulness and Israel's covenant unfaithfulness.

Most of the content within prophetic oracles was prompted by the covenants God made with his people. Of first concern to the prophets was the bilateral Mosaic covenant—established on Sinai (Exod 19:5; Leviticus 26), renewed in Moab (Deuteronomy 28–30), and enforced through the words of the prophets. Within the framework of the Mosaic covenant, the law functioned as the stipulations of Israel's covenant obligations.[2] In return for corporate obedience to the law, Yahweh obligated himself to bless Israel. In the case of disobedience, however, Israel was promised the scourge of curse and exile—a fate described in Deuteronomy 28:15–68 and prophetically

---

[1] Gordon D. Fee and Douglas Stuart, *How to Read the Bible for All Its Worth*, 4th ed. (Grand Rapids, MI: Zondervan, 2014), 190.

[2] Ibid., 169–75.

forecast in Deuteronomy 29 and 30. What Moses promised, the prophets reinforced, actively proclaiming a message that preceded them by hundreds of years—the choice of life or death, blessing or cursing (Deut 30:11–20).

The Mosaic covenant was not the only covenant to anchor prophetic messages. The oracles of salvation were anchored in the promises of the unilateral covenants; the unconditional blessings of the Abrahamic, Davidic, and new covenants are acknowledged by the prophets as the basis for eschatological hope. As much as the oracles of judgment were tied to violations of the bilateral Mosaic covenant, so the blessings promised by the oracles of salvation were based in the Abrahamic, Davidic, and new covenants. Every eschatological promise within the Prophets links back to some aspect of God's promises in the unilateral covenants (see Gen 12:1–3; 15:18–20; 2 Sam 7:12–16; Deut 30:4–6). Certainly the prophets expand and refine aspects of these covenants, but they do not replace them, nor do they prophesy apart from them.

Although the prophets announced horrific judgment based on the curses of the bilateral Mosaic covenant (Deut 28:15–68), there was always a sense of conditionality in their role as preachers, a divine "perhaps" seen in their frequent calls to repentance. As "covenant enforcement mediators," the prophets were preachers, not simply proclaimers. They sought to call Israel back into covenant conformity, back to the knowledge of Yahweh. In proclaiming judgment, they did everything to steer Israel in the right direction, knowing that Yahweh was longsuffering. Perhaps there was still time; perhaps Yahweh would relent; perhaps Israel would obey and receive covenant blessing rather than cursing. Yet as history unfolded, Israel remained on the path of destruction, and eventually the full force of the covenant curses came to fruition (2 Kgs 17:7–23; 25:1–17). Nevertheless, as central as the conditional curses were to the preaching of the prophets, they were not the end of their message. The prophets also proclaimed a glorious, unconditional restoration anchored in the unilateral promises of God. In this, the prophets were also preachers of hope.

As God's prosecuting attorneys,[3] the prophets brought an indictment against Israel (or the nations) that revolved around five primary areas of

---

[3] The role of bringing indictment against the people was often framed according to the form of a courtroom motif. In this sense, J. Daniel Hays makes a clever analogy in stating that the prophets "serve as Yahweh's prosecuting attorneys." See C. Marvin Pate, J. Scott Duvall, J. Daniel Hays, E. Randolph Richards, Preben Vang, and W. Dennis Tucker Jr., *The Story of Israel: A Biblical Theology* (Grand Rapids, MI: InterVarsity, 2004), 93.

violation: (1) idolatry, (2) social injustice, (3) violence, (4) hypocritical ritualism, and (5) spiritual apathy.[4] As forth-tellers, the prophets called the
people (and their leadership) out for their sins, proclaiming an impending
judgment unless they would repent. Categorically, the content of indictment within the Minor Prophets overwhelmingly fits into the five areas of
covenant violation listed above, although there are certainly variables within
each category.

Idolatry: Often framing it with the image of "spiritual adultery," the
prophets spoke out against Israel's constant engagement with the idols of
foreign lands. These idols included Baal, his consort Asherah, and a host
of related agricultural deities. This sin, among Israel's many others, was the
primary catalyst that brought the wrath of God's judgment to bear.[5] God's
concern over this most basic reflection of covenant faithfulness permeates
the Twelve, but Hosea is the book that most richly encapsulates the heart of
God on the matter of idolatry.

Social Injustice: God's concern was for the poor, not in reference to social
equality, but in terms of social justice—the prophets made it abundantly
clear that God hates corruption and ill-gotten gain made at the expense of
the powerless. Aspects of social justice included care for the poor, the widows, and the orphans, honesty in trade and transaction, and truth in litiga-
tion (justice "at the gates"). The prophets who spoke out most often against
social injustice were Amos and Micah, although virtually all of the Twelve
reference some aspect of God's concern for justice in the land.

Violence: Although the ancient world was often harsh—a warrior culture where bloodletting was regular and sometimes justified—the prophets
made it clear that excessive, unjustified violence would not go unpunished.
God's indictment against violence was often set in conjunction with aspects
of social injustice (Mic 2:2; 6:12), but it sometimes focused independently
on the revelry of the act itself (Obadiah 10–14). The prophets therefore

---

[4] This list is an adaptation stemming from work produced by J. Daniel Hays, although
"violence" and "spiritual apathy" have been added. See J. Daniel Hays, *The Message of
the Prophets* (Grand Rapids, MI: Zondervan, 2011), 63–69 and J. Daniel Hays in Pate,
Duvall, Hays, Richards, Vang, and Tucker, *The Story of Israel: A Biblical Theology*, 93.

[5] This is implied throughout the Prophets and explained by the narrator of 2 Kings
17:7–23.

spoke out against the violent, both in Israel and Judah (Hab 1:2–4) as well as among the nations (Amos 1:3–2:3; Nah 3:1, 19; 2:8–13).[6]

Hypocritical Ritualism: Ironically, the Israel that blatantly disregarded the law in matters of social justice and unilateral devotion to Yahweh readily sought the ritual aspects of the law as a means to justify themselves. The prophets do not charge Israel with wrongdoing in keeping the ritual components of the law; rather, they charge Israel in light of her misguided, hypocritical attitude in assuming ritual devotion could somehow absolve the sins of idolatry and social injustice. Amos and Micah especially highlight Israel's hypocrisy associated with ritual devotion in the face of social injustice (Amos 5:21–24; Mic 6:6–8).

Spiritual Apathy: The postexilic prophets Haggai and Malachi highlight the apathetic excuses of the people, calling them to consider their misplaced priorities. The people were suffering physical consequences for their lack of spiritual commitment. The prophetic message therefore sought to redirect them to a proper devotion to Yahweh, lest a greater scourge fall on them. Although spiritual apathy was a condition permeating all of society, it began with the spiritual leaders of Israel. Therefore, the prophets would often direct their indictment over spiritual apathy to the priests on whom that responsibility rested (see Mal 1:6–2:9).

The Prophets as Foretellers

As argued above, the prophets spoke words of indictment, calling the people out for their sins. Accompanying their prosecution, the prophets announced near-term, impending judgment. As divine spokesmen, however, the prophets also announced distant prognostications revealing God's program for the restoration of his people. Ultimately, God's program of restoration would bring a blessing to all the families of the earth through the Messiah (Gen 12:3). Therefore, as foretellers, the prophets announced the future in reference to both judgment and blessing, contemporary and eschatological. Accounting for the positive and negative, along with various audiences and

---

[6] The Old Testament prophets frequently proclaimed God's vengeance against the nations, answering excessive violence with God's violent wrath. See Jerome F. D. Creach, *Violence in Scripture* (Louisville, KY: Westminster John Knox, 2013), 163–72.

referents, foretelling prophecy can be generally categorized by three broad periods of fulfillment: (1) near-term, (2) middle-term, and (3) far-term.[7]

Near-Term Fulfillment: Prophecies fulfilled in the near term are those that came to pass within, or shortly after, the lifetime of the prophet and his original audience. Near-term prophecies usually involve announcements of judgment reflecting various aspects of impending exile, including the destruction of Samaria in 722 BC and Jerusalem in 586. However, they often relate to the destruction of enemy nations, presumably providing hope for the oppressed people of God (see Obadiah and Nahum). Although near-term prophecies were hardly hollow warnings, they were couched in an aura of conditionality. Depending on whether or not the audience repented upon hearing the prophetic call, near-term announcements of judgment could be either deferred (see Jonah 3:4) or delayed (see Mic 3:12).

Middle-Term Fulfillment: These are prophecies that were fulfilled centuries after being spoken by the prophet. Although they were fulfilled long after their original audience had passed, from the perspective of the modern reader, they entail matters of ancient history.[8] The most common prophecies involving the middle term are those fulfilled in the first coming of Christ. Notable examples from the Twelve include Micah 5:2 and Zechariah 9:9.

Far-Term Fulfillment: These entail prophecies yet to find fulfillment, even from the perspective of the modern reader. They are eschatological—yet to be fulfilled, but not necessarily directed at our future. Far-term prophecies involve God's final judgment on the nations (Joel 3:9–16; Zeph 3:8), along with the blessings of a future Davidic kingdom (Amos 9:11–14). They describe the restoration and gathering of Israel replanted into the land, under one Davidic King, living in peace and prosperity forever (Hos 2:21–23; 3:5; and Mic 4:1–5).

---

[7] Between and through these periods, one frequently discovers patterns and tiers (or levels) of fulfillment. Progressive patterns of prophecy in and between prophetic books are a striking reflection of divine origin.

[8] This point highlights one of the more important hermeneutical precepts in studying the Old Testament Prophets: to fully understand biblical prophecy, one must first have a working knowledge of biblical history.

The Prophets as Authors

It is clear from the written text of the Twelve that the prophets were God's spokesmen who lived in real space and time, preaching the prophetic word to an ancient audience through the spoken oracle. What is less clear is the role of the prophet as an author, one who carefully *wrote* the prophetic word, compiling, arranging, and authoring the books that we now consider the Word of God. Nahum is the only book among the Twelve that is introduced as a "book," providing some glimpse into the original intent of its composition.[9] Outside of the Twelve, there is clear indication of scribal activity with Baruch's service to Jeremiah (Jer 32:12; 36:4, 32; 45:1), but the other writing prophets are largely silent in reference to their scribal activities or relationships.

What we do know is that there is some level of departure between the spoken words of the prophets and the written words of the prophets. This is not to suggest any less authority in the written oracle, nor does it suggest inaccuracies or corruption between the spoken word and the written word. What it does suggest is that the written word was necessarily composed sometime after the spoken word. This is apparent by the extended periods traversed by the historical superscriptions introducing certain prophetic books, such as Hosea and Micah.

Consider the book of Hosea as an example. In reference to composition, it is possible that the Hosea book could have been written during the lifetime of Hosea or sometime near the conclusion of his prophetic ministry (during the reign of Hezekiah). If written during Hosea's lifetime, the prophet himself may have composed the book that bears his name. However, it is more likely that Hosea would have had a scribal companion, over whose writing Hosea would have had direct oversight and authority. What is certain is that many of the oracles in Hosea occurred during the earlier period of his ministry, before the fall of Samaria in 722 BC. And yet the superscription indicates that Hosea prophesied into the reign of Hezekiah, which began in 716. So clearly there was some degree of departure from the spoken oracle to the written word, even *if* the book was composed during Hosea's lifetime.

---

[9] In other words, Nahum may have begun as a written text, never proclaimed by the prophet in the traditional, oral sense. A similar situation is implied with the book of Jonah, a well-crafted narrative *about* the life and ministry of the prophet.

Alternatively, the Hosea book *could* have been composed after the prophet had passed from the scene while his authority still carried influence in the community. If the final compilation and composition of the prophet's oracles were authored by someone standing under the authority of the prophet, the book would have carried authority even if not penned directly by the prophet himself.[10] Prophetic penmanship would not have been necessary to sustain prophetic authority or inspiration in the Book of the Twelve.

The nature of prophetic books as anthologies suggests the possibility of inspired editorial activity within the scope of the prophet's time . . . or even shortly afterwards. Editorial activity may have been responsible for the literary craftsmanship of the written text, including the aesthetic features of parallelism, chiasm, inclusio, and literary wordplay. The written text would have been selectively arranged and configured for maximum impact, again reflecting diverse oracles spoken over a period of years to a potentially diverse audience. In all this, the "authored" book would have carried all of the authority of the prophet and the inspiration of the Holy Spirit; it is the written text that is inspired within the canon, not the spoken word lost through the passage of time. In this, it is true that the prophets may have had a role as authors—yet in some cases perhaps their authority carried over so that the role of authorship was fulfilled by others, all the while superintended by God the Holy Spirit.[11]

---

[10] Although the actual events and means pertaining to the composition of prophetic books is somewhat shrouded in mystery, the authority and inspiration of the text is not in jeopardy as the authority of an ancient text did not necessarily rest in its authorship. See John H. Walton and D. Brent Sandy, *The Lost World of Scripture: Ancient Literary Culture and Biblical Authority* (Grand Rapids, MI: InterVarsity, 2013), 60–68.

[11] A parallel may be drawn from the Gospels. While frequently representing the words of Jesus, there is distance in time, language, and authorship between the authoritative words that Jesus spoke and the inspired text authored by the Gospel writers.

3

The Words of the Twelve: Literary Genres and Rhetorical Devices within the Minor Prophets

Introduction

One of the primary roles of the prophets was communicating God's message through vivid and often shocking rhetoric, getting the people's attention first through the spoken word, and subsequently, through the written word. The prophets' messages were communicated not only by what they said, but—more importantly—by how they said it. The language of the prophets is at once imagery rich and aesthetically powerful, adding shock value and new flavor to an old, sometimes stale message of covenant enforcement. The prophets were charged with waking God's people out of their spiritual stupor; their words were like a bucket of ice water poured over a bleary-eyed people. For all their eccentricity, the prophets were artistic geniuses, crafting their words to maximize the effectiveness of their message. Just as the prophets Jeremiah and Ezekiel performed strange acts to get their messages across, the words of the writing prophets, and the Twelve in particular, took on the role of literary performance, designed to shock the reader into response. Unless one learns to read the Prophets with an eye toward rhetorical strategy, there is the risk of missing the function of their rhetoric and the performance of their language.[1] There is the risk of missing the point altogether.

If prophetic literature is meant to speak to the heart more than the mind, then it is no surprise that most of the writing prophets addressed audiences in the form of poetry rather than prose. For all its challenges, poetry simply facilitates the performing function of prophecy better than prose. This is certainly true within the Book of the Twelve, where most of the prophets exhibit a higher propensity to poetry than prose.[2] This, of course, does not eliminate prose literature from the prophetic books. Indeed, the postexilic prophets contain at least as much prose as poetry. What it means is that the reader of the Twelve must have an eye to read poetry as poetry, seeing the characteristics of poetic form as essential "performers" of the prophetic script. Otherwise, the reader runs the risk of missing what the prophetic text is *really* saying.

The primary genre of most individual prophetic books is anthology. There are exceptions among the Twelve, but it is the general trait of Old Testament prophetic books. As anthologies, prophetic books are collections of oracles and associated subgenres—a literary collage representing, in some cases, decades of prophetic ministry.[3] As such, most prophetic books are difficult to outline, as they belie logical, linear progression. Yet prophetic anthologies are not without structure. The collections of individual units

---

[1] In the Prophets, it is true that "the function of language may prevail over form." However, one must learn to read, understand, and appreciate the form of prophetic language in order to discern the function of that language. Furthermore, the function of prophetic language is not simply to inform the reader, or even to shock the reader, but to illicit a response. See D. Brent Sandy, *Plowshares and Pruning Hooks: Rethinking the Language of Biblical Prophecy and Apocalyptic* (Downers Grove, IL: InterVaristy, 2002), 80–82.

[2] The notable exception to this is Jonah, but even the second chapter of Jonah is comprised almost entirely of a psalm.

[3] On identifying literary units within prophetic literature, see Aaron Chalmers, *Interpreting the Prophets: Reading, Understanding and Preaching from the Worlds of the Prophets* (Downers Grove, IL: InterVarsity, 2015), 94–98.

that comprise most prophetic books do reflect thematic and literary cohesion, often facilitated through repeated catchwords and thematic content. Many prophetic books reflect repeated literary cycles or alternating panels of judgment and salvation. Prophetic books, including all of the Twelve, demonstrate a high degree of structural artistry through individual segments within the broader texts. Primary among these features is *chiasm*, where the second half of a unit repeats the first half in reverse order. Although chiasm can be over exaggerated,[4] there are many obvious examples within the Twelve. Also, *inclusio* features prominently within the Twelve, creating thematic or literary "bookends" to demonstrate cohesion by structurally wrapping a segment of text.

Each of the Minor Prophets exhibits unique literary characteristics, reflecting a variety of prophetic subgenres. They are collections packed with individual, discernible literary units. Although a linear structural arrangement is often absent between literary units, each unit itself is likely to be highly structured. This does not eliminate structural components between literary units, and there are certainly thematic and literary connections tying units together within prophectic books. Individual literary units reflecting a variety of prophetic subgenres are the building blocks of prophetic books. In this, both the content and the structure of an individual unit are determined by its literary subgenre.[5]

Following the role of the prophet, the words of the Twelve can be broadly separated into three categories: (1) announcements of judgment, (2) oracles of salvation, and (3) calls to repentance. Supporting these categories is a broad cast of literary subgenres adding color and flavor to the standard prophetic pronouncements. Not all among the Twelve exhibit each of these categories of pronouncement, much less all of their attendant subgenres. And there are a few books that are unique to themselves (i.e., Jonah).

---

[4] Chiasm is often clear, but in many cases, especially when "discovered" through repetition of thematic content, it is highly interpretive. Perhaps the most exhaustive commentary recognizing extensive chiasm in the Old Testament belongs to David A. Dorsey, *The Literary Structure of the Old Testament: A Commentary on Genesis—Malachi* (Grand Rapids, MI: Baker, 1999). See pages 265–324 for many helpful, albeit interpretive, suggestions of chiasm in the Minor Prophets.

[5] Structure and content determine genre, but genre also determines structure and content. See Peter Cotterell and Max Turner, *Linguistics and Biblical Interpretation* (Downers Grove, IL: InterVarsity, 1989), 99–100.

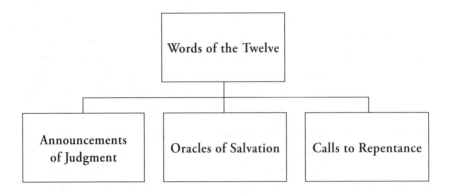

However, the majority of prophetic script either reflects each of the categories of pronouncement or supports the broader function of the three, and all prophetic books utilize a variety of subgenres to fulfill their mission of communicating the Word of God.

Announcements of judgment are typically communicated in prophetic literature through the spoken oracle. The pronouncement is either stated to be from the Lord ("the Lord says"), or it is assumed through the Lord's spokesman, the prophet. The two primary elements of the prophetic judgment speech are *accusation* and *announcement*.[6] Accusation features the Lord's charge against the guilty party, while the announcement of judgment reveals the description of judgment called for by the guilty verdict. To facilitate these basic elements, a variety of literary subgenres is used to perform the task.

Woe Oracles: A woe oracle announces judgment through the vehicle of pronouncing "woe" upon the accused. These speeches had the effect of proclaiming death for the accused. Examples in the Twelve include Amos 5:18–24; 6:1–7; Micah 2:1–5; Nahum 3:1–4; Habakkuk 2:6–20; and Zephaniah 3:1–5.

Laments: A lament is a funeral dirge, a song of mourning for the fallen. In prophetic literature, the lament takes on the ominous role of mourning the fallen before the fact, essentially singing a dirge as a pronouncement of certain doom. Examples in the Twelve include Amos 5:1–7; Micah 1:8–16; and Zephaniah 1:10–13.

---

[6] Andreas J. Köstenberger and Richard D. Patterson, *Invitation to Biblical Interpretation: Exploring the Hermeneutical Triad of History, Literature, and Theology* (Grand Rapids, MI: Kregel, 2011), 321–22.

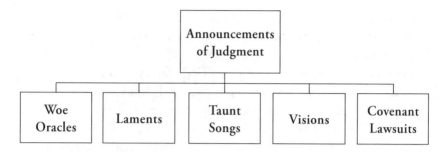

Taunt Songs: The taunt song was a formalized mockery of one's opponent, a common practice in ancient warrior societies.[7] In prophetic literature, the taunt is employed as a colorful and vivid means of proclaiming the defeat of Yahweh's enemies. Examples in the Twelve include Nahum 2:11–13; 3:5–13; and Habakkuk 2:6–20 (a taunt song consisting of a woe speech).

Visions: Although prophetic visions are not the exclusive domain of judgment speeches, prophets would often receive visions of future judgment and communicate that through their speeches and their writing. Examples in the Twelve include Amos 7:1–9; 8:1–3; and Nahum 2:3–10; 3:14–17.

Covenant Lawsuits: Although most announcements of judgment carry overtones of legal indictment (the guilty are in violation of covenant law), the prophets would often craft their speeches with the language of a formalized lawsuit. Features of covenant lawsuit include the summoning of witnesses, a list of charges against the accused, and the sentencing of the guilty party.[8] Examples in the Twelve include Hosea 4:1–14 and Micah 6:1–16.

In prophetic literature it is common for judgment and salvation to be proclaimed as opposing realities, with judgment the result of covenant disobedience and deliverance the result of covenant faithfulness. However, the ultimate restoration of God's blessings on his covenant people is proclaimed as eschatological realities, with the expectation of fulfillment based in *his* faithfulness to the unilateral covenants *he* made with Israel. Therefore, the prophets typically proclaim God's salvation as eschatological blessing with oracles that foretell a blessed future to come *after* the ashes of judgment have cleared. Nevertheless, an expectation of future blessing functioned to bring hope in the present; thus, the prophets proclaimed impending judgment

---

[7] Leland Ryken, *A Complete Handbook of Literary Forms in the Bible* (Wheaton, IL: Crossway, 2014), 193–94.

[8] Köstenberger and Patterson, *Invitation to Biblical Interpretation*, 325–26.

and a distant blessing "in that day" for motivation in their present day. In the literature of the prophets, oracles of judgment and salvation are rarely distanced on the page as much as they are in time.

As a means to reassure the people of God's faithfulness to his covenant promises, especially after proclamations of overwhelming judgment, salvation oracles often function as concluding, capstone endings to prophetic anthologies. These oracles typically include two facets: (1) the messenger formula, and (2) the word of salvation.[9] The messenger formula was the "thus saith the Lord" introduction, the authentication that such a grand promise was guaranteed to come to pass and that its basis was in the very authority of God himself. The word of salvation was simply the content of prophetic expectation, the blessings of that future day. The content of the word of salvation was typically facilitated through the subgenres of kingdom oracle and apocalyptic vision.

Kingdom Oracles: These oracles proclaim the establishment of Israel's final kingdom. This eschatological kingdom is characterized by a return to the land by a dispersed remnant that will be ruled by a future Davidic king. One facet of the king's rule is that it extends beyond the borders of Israel, including the subjugation and incorporation of all nations. In concert with the establishment of this future kingdom, these oracles often blend elements of judgment with the restoration that leads to the establishment of the final era of blessing.[10] Examples in the Twelve include Joel 3:9–21; Amos 9:11–15; Obadiah 15–21; Micah 4:1–5; and Zephaniah 3:11–13, 18–20.

Apocalyptic Vision: Some oracles of salvation feature elements of apocalyptic literature, including visions characterized by symbolic language that describes cosmic catastrophe and renewal. Apocalyptic language in the Prophets often blends judgment with salvation, merging the two in the course of bringing about eschatological fulfillment. Examples in the Twelve include Joel 2:28–32 and the night visions of Zechariah 1–6.

The prophets were not simply messengers of judgment and salvation. They were preachers calling God's people to repentance, holding out hope that perhaps with a change of course, God might relent from bringing

---

[9] Willem A. VanGemeren, "Oracles of Salvation," in *Cracking Old Testament Codes: A Guide to Interpreting the Literary Genres of the Old Testament*, ed. D. Brent Sandy and Ronald L. Giese Jr. (Nashville, TN: B&H, 1995), 142.

[10] Köstenberger and Patterson, *Invitation to Biblical Interpretation*, 327–28.

certain judgment. In the written text, the call to repentance comes as a direct address to the people, a plea on the part of the prophet and an offer on the part of God. The prophetic call to repentance is a hortatory subgenre, urging a course of action rather than simply instructing the people. The call to repentance typically follows an announcement of impending judgment and provides a facet of hope based in the character of a longsuffering God. Examples in the Twelve include Hosea 6:1–3; Joel 2:12–17; and Zephaniah 2:1–3.

Complementing the primary genres of direct prophetic oracle, the words of the Twelve are supported by a cast of additional subgenres, including narrative, prophetic dialogue, disputation speeches, and the lyrical praise of psalms and hymns.[11]

Narrative: Simple narrative is not as common in the Twelve as in the Major Prophets. A few books among the Twelve are nevertheless complemented with short narrative reports, including Amos 7:10–17 and Haggai 1:12–15. Zechariah 7 and 8 present God's words to the prophet within a narrative framework. Additionally, the greater portion of Jonah is written as a narrative, albeit with highly structured, satirical overtones.[12]

Prophetic Dialogue: The book of Habakkuk is largely structured around a question and response dialogue set between the prophet and Yahweh. The prophets not only report the word of the Lord, but they also interact with their God. Besides Habakkuk 1 and 2, such dialogue is found in Amos 7 and 8.

Disputation Speeches: Disputation involves a hypothetical dialogue cast in literary form. For the prophets, the strategic function of disputation was to use the people's own words against them in demonstration of their guilt.[13] Prophetic disputation typically features assertion, quotation, and refutation, all staged in the context of hypothetical dialogue. The premier example of

---

[11] This is not an exhaustive list of prophetic subgenres, and it does not reflect the variables associated with rhetorical strategies and devices (such as rhetorical question). Additional subgenres found among the Twelve include prophetic drama (Hosea 1:1–9; 3:1–5), proverbial riddle (Hosea 14:9), numerical formula (Amos 1–2), and example story (Amos 5:3; 6:9).

[12] Leland Ryken, *Words of Delight: A Literary Introduction to the Bible* (Grand Rapids, MI: Baker, 1987), 337–40.

[13] Grant R. Osborne, *The Hermeneutical Spiral: A Comprehensive Introduction to Biblical Interpretation* (Downers Grove, IL: InterVarsity, 1991), 216.

this in the Twelve, if not the whole Bible, is the disputation speeches of Malachi.

Psalms and Hymns: The prophets often used the language of the Psalter to express praise and thanksgiving, exalting the name of Yahweh through a genre familiar to the temple courts of Israel. Among the Twelve there are hymnic elements incorporated into the oracles and announcements of the prophets (Amos 4:13; 5:8; 9:5–6; and Nah 1:2–8) as well as full psalms incorporated into the books (Jonah 2:2–9 and Hab 3:1–19).

Although the books within the Twelve are largely built around collected literary units—subgenres that form the brick and mortar of prophetic literature—it is insufficient to simply describe them as books built around collections of prophetic subgenres. The performing function of prophetic literature is carried by its aesthetic characteristics, by the color and flavor created through the use of imagery, figurative language, and the capacity of Hebrew poetry to communicate the heart of God to his people. Simply stated, there is more to a literary reading of the Twelve than the recognition of subgenres and literary units.

As noted earlier, poetry communicates emotion better than prose, and through the pens of the prophets, it also facilitates a response on the part of the reader. If the whole Word of God is "living and effective and sharper than any double-edged sword" (Heb 4:12), the Prophets are the tip of the blade, penetrating deep into the heart of the reader. In modern vernacular, the words of the prophets are like laser-guided missiles—precision instruments that penetrate the deepest underground bunkers, even the hardest of hearts. But what is the fuel behind these laser-guided missiles? What provides the extra edge to penetrate the heart, even to speak beyond the mind? Simply put, it is the language the prophets use, the way they speak—it is the way they write.

Although the literary features of the Twelve warrant a long list of characteristics and elements, most of what makes the words of the Twelve so powerful and compelling can be summarized by four primary features: (1) rich imagery and figures of speech, (2) terse language with focused repetition, (3) irony and sarcasm, and (4) Hebrew wordplay.

Rich Imagery and Figures of Speech

To suggest that the words of the Twelve are imagery rich is itself an under-statement. Figurative language provides the color and texture essential to biblical prophecy; without it, "prophecy would be little more than tedious diatribe—recitations of failures and dashed hopes, with an occasional offer of hope for the repentant."[14] While the prophets employ a full range of figu-rative language in their rhetoric, there are a few particular figures of speech that are especially useful in facilitating the role of the prophet; that is, in bringing shock value to the page. These are metaphor and hyperbole.

Metaphor: Metaphor refers to any number of figures of speech where one thing symbolically represents another. Technically, this may include figures of comparison such as simile and hypocatastasis, or figures of substitution, such as metonymy and synecdoche.[15] While there is merit in making tech-nical distinctions between figures of speech, for our purposes "metaphor" simply describes any figure of speech where one thing represents another in an expressive, analogical relationship.

Metaphors add visual imagery to the prophetic text unlike any other lit-erary device. They bring color and vividness while simultaneously compress-ing ideas into a memorable picture. They add a degree of ambiguity that facilitates reflection, while also conveying the abstract in concrete terms. Metaphors are so integral to the language of prophecy that they may even appear to reflect the reality itself.[16] Thus, the reader of biblical prophecy must discern between image and substance, all the while recognizing that the fullness of reality is being conveyed through the imagery of metaphor.

There are hundreds, if not thousands, of examples of metaphor in the Old Testament Prophets. Among the Twelve, perhaps Hosea is the prophet best known for his rich use of metaphor. In the pages of Hosea, God is pictured

---

[14] Sandy, *Plowshares and Pruning Hooks*, 72.

[15] Simile can be technically defined as a comparison in which one thing resembles another through the use of "like" or "as," while metaphor is a comparison in which one thing is, acts like, or represents another mediated through a form of the verb "to be." Hypocatastasis is a comparison facilitated through direct naming, while metonymy sim-ply substitutes one word for another. Synecdoche is "the substituting of a part of some-thing for the whole or the whole for the part." See Roy B. Zuck, *Basic Bible Interpretation* (Colorado Springs, CO: Chariot Victor, 1991), 148–51; and Leland Ryken, *A Complete Handbook of Literary Forms in the Bible*.

[16] Sandy, *Plowshares and Pruning Hooks*, 72.

as a jealous husband (2:2–13), a frustrated shepherd (4:16), destructive rot (5:12), and a ferocious lion (5:14; 13:7–8). He is also pictured as a healing physician (6:1–2), a doting parent (11:3–4), regenerating dew (14:5), and a flourishing tree (14:8). Meanwhile, Israel is described as the unfaithful wife (1:2–9), a flittering dove (7:11), a faulty bow (7:16), a wayward donkey, and an unproductive tree (9:16). Often, the metaphors in Hosea demonstrate the contrast between God and Israel in stark detail—not through technical, analytical description, but through the imagery of metaphor.

Hyperbole: Hyperbole is a deliberate exaggeration used to heighten or convey a point. It is used in poetry and prose, and it can be found throughout the Bible. Yet for the prophets, hyperbole is a tool specially crafted for their trade; it turns up the volume of their rhetoric and provides the shock value so needed by their message. Hyperbole is applied to the language of judgment and salvation—in a sense, the prophets speak of judgment in the most exaggerated, intensified terms possible, and then they draw the pendulum equally high in describing the blessings of restoration.[17]

Recognition of the role of hyperbole in the Twelve does not negate the reality of the severity of God's wrath or the extent of God's blessings in Scripture, especially when understood within the eschatological context foreseen by the prophets. But their language was meant to motivate with the wringing of the neck, not the gentle turning of the head. Hyperbole facilitated this function well, describing to the fullest extent Israel's guilt (Amos 5:10–13; Mic 7:1–7) and the displeasure this brought to God (Amos 5:18–23). Hyperbole was instrumental in warning the people of the depth and extent of God's wrath (Zeph 1:2–3, 17–18), while also assuring God's elect of an equally impressive restoration (Joel 3:18–20; Amos 9:13).

Terse Language with Focused Repetition

Like all Hebrew poetry, the language of the prophets is terse—short on words yet long in power. But while terse in syntax, the prophets are anything but concise in verbiage. Repetition is an iconic feature of Hebrew poetry, and the prophets use this feature to throw combination punches at their audience again and again. The routine feature of parallelism provides

---

[17] For more on prophetic hyperbole, see Sandy, *Plowshares and Pruning Hooks*, 87–102.

a kind of one-two punch, wearing down their opponents, and the repetition often escalates throughout a unit until the climatic knock-out punch is delivered. Through parallelism and various related forms of repetition, the prophets pound the pulpit with their words—short, parallel lines that convey an intensity of thought, even if lacking in logical, progressive structural development.

Parallelism: Parallelism is the foremost common characteristic of Hebrew poetry; therefore, it should come as no surprise that parallelism features prominently within the rhetoric of the prophets. Essentially, parallelism is the practice of balancing lines of poetry through a correspondence of words or ideas. These parallel lines then function in concert to communicate unified, intensified concepts.

Although there are numerous kinds of parallelism in Hebrew poetry, the two most common forms in the Prophets are "synonymous" parallelism and "climatic" parallelism. "Antithetical," "synthetic," and "emblematic" parallelism are common in Wisdom literature and the Psalter, but less frequently employed by the prophets.

Synonymous parallelism: The thoughts in each line correspond synonymously, saying similar things with matching words. Consider Micah 5:10b–12:

> I will remove your horses from you
> and wreck your chariots.
> [11] I will remove the cities of your land
> and tear down all your fortresses.
> [12] I will remove sorceries from your hands,
> and you will not have any more fortune-tellers.

In Micah 5:10b, "remove your horses" corresponds synonymously with "wreck your chariots." In verse 11, "remove the cities of your land" corresponds with "tear down all your fortresses," and in verse 12, "I will remove sorceries" corresponds with "you will not have any more fortune-tellers." In each case, the second line is essentially saying the same thing as the first line. The repetition in the second line enhances the intensity of the idea introduced by the first line. But the second line is not saying anything significantly different from the first line. With synonymous parallelism, the second line intensifies the concept introduced in the first line, but it does not develop it.

Climactic parallelism: Through corresponding, successive lines thoughts build in detail and descriptive force, conveying the impression of escalation. This technique is often found in three-and four-line stanzas. In formal examples, a portion of the opening line may be repeated in successive lines throughout the stanza. Consider Amos 3:15:

> I will demolish the winter house
> and the summer house;
> the houses inlaid with ivory will be destroyed,
> and the great houses will come to an end.

In this example, the idea of God destroying the houses of the wealthy carries throughout all four lines. The repetition provides an expanding sense of just how much excess the rich possessed in Amos's day. Each line is essentially saying the same thing, but the collection of parallel lines provides a fully developed, intensified description of God's judgment against the houses of Israel's elite.

As demonstrated in the prior two examples, parallelism in the Prophets is more than simply a matter of conformity to literary style and structure. The prophets used parallelism as an effective tool to heighten the intensity of their rhetoric, so the reader must see that as the critical function. Parallel lines always work in concert with one another and should be interpreted thus. Looking for distinctions in meaning between parallel lines will rarely produce fruit, and will often result in counterproductive analysis. The point is conveyed through the correspondence between lines.

Repetition: The repetition of words and phrases are used in a variety of ways in the Twelve, usually with the effect of heightening and intensifying the rhetoric of prophetic oracles. For instance, the repetition of the statement "yet you did not return to Me," in the stanzas of Amos 4:6–11 brings cohesion and intensification to Amos's indictment. As each stanza concludes with this statement, the sense of Israel's guilt builds, preparing the reader for the climatic pronouncement of judgment in 4:12: "Israel, prepare to meet your God!" Repetition links each stanza of verses 6–11 together, while heightening the sense of Israel's guilt in the process.

Zephaniah's repetition of synonyms in his description of the Day of the Lord provides an example of repetition in close proximity—conveying the effect of an overwhelming barrage (Zeph 1:14–16). In other examples, repetition of words and phrases spans across whole books, tying individual units together through catchwords and common motifs. Zephaniah includes numerous examples of catchwords, some apparent from the Hebrew (such as *paqad*: 1:8-9 [punish]; 2:7 [return]; 2:9 [plunder]), and others in English translation ("shame"; see 3:5, 11; "gather"; 3:8, 18–20). Additionally, Zephaniah includes repeated phrases, such as "I will sweep away" (1:2–3), "face of the earth" (1:2–3), "fire of His jealousy" (1:18; 3:8), and the many references to the Day of the Lord. Every one of the Twelve contains repeated words and phrases that give each book a distinctive flavor.

Irony and Sarcasm

Irony permeates the language of the prophets. This should not shock the reader, as there is a certain theological irony that courses throughout the book of the Twelve, highlighted by Nineveh's repentance upon hearing a five-word sermon (Jonah 3:4). God's people were dull headed, so perhaps where the shock of metaphor or the pounding of repetition failed, the sting of irony might succeed. It could be said that God is a God of poetic justice, and the Twelve certainly made this message apparent. For instance, the ironic twist of poetic justice is clear in Amos 6:1–7. In Amos's indictment of the "notable people" of the "first of the nations," who "anoint themselves with the finest of oils," he proclaims that they will continue to go first in line—as "the first of the captives" led into exile!

Supporting their message of poetic justice, the words of the Twelve were often sarcastic. Again, perhaps Amos is best known among the Twelve for his biting sarcasm. Consider, for example, the "cows of Bashan" (Amos 4:1), the wealthy women of Samaria who oppressed the poor and crushed the needy, who even commanded their "lords" (*'adonim*) to serve them. Notice that Amos prods these fat cows, these wealthy women who rely on religious ritual—the same ones who oppress the poor—to bring the tithe for the poor every three days (4:4) instead of every three years! Such is the love that these women have for their freewill offerings (4:5).

Hebrew Wordplay

A variation to the more common repetition and irony used by the prophets is wordplay. In wordplay, the prophet would capitalize on the semantic range of words to convey a twist in meaning or draw associations between words to highlight a bit of irony. The prophets also repeated words that sound alike (or look alike) as a means to draw attention to their message.

A great example of semantic wordplay involves the repetition of the Hebrew word *ra`ah* in Jonah 3:10–4:1. "Then God saw their actions—that they had turned from their evil [*ra`ah*] ways—so God relented from the disaster [*ra`ah*] He had threatened to do to them. And He did not do it. But Jonah was greatly displeased [*ra`ah* times two; the intensification is communicated through the repetition of the word in Hebrew] and became furious."

The semantic flexibility of the Hebrew term *ra`ah* provides Jonah the opportunity for wordplay, but it is the creativity of the text that capitalizes on the ironic twist supported by the selective use of *ra`a*. That creativity supports the message of the book and should not be missed.

As with semantic wordplay, sound-alike wordplay ("assonance") is easily missed due to the necessity of translation. Significant examples are highlighted throughout this handbook, and technical commentaries on the Twelve rarely bypass notable cases of assonance. A few of the better examples highlighted in this work include Amos 8:2; Obadiah 10–14; Micah 1:10–17; and Zephaniah 2:4.

4

THE BOOK OF THE TWELVE: APPROACHING THE MINOR PROPHETS AS A CANONICAL UNITY

Introduction

Augustine is believed to be the first to have referred to the twelve smaller books among the Latter Prophets in the Hebrew canon as the "Minor Prophets." The Jews referred to this collection as the "Book of the Twelve" because they recognized them as a single literary work from ancient times. Scholarly study of the Book of the Twelve since the 1990s has particularly focused on the literary unity of the Twelve as a single collection rather than twelve separate writings.[1] James Nogalski explains that study of the Twelve as a unified composition examines the use of catchwords that link together the individual books and the shared themes and motifs found in these books.[2] The approach taken in this work places primary emphasis on the distinctive message of each individual book but also pays attention to the theological message of the Twelve that emerges when these books are read as a collective whole.[3] The focus here is more on presenting the thematic unity of the Twelve than attempting to reconstruct how the Book of the Twelve might have been composed or edited as a single literary work.[4]

By as early as 200 BC, it appears that the Book of the Twelve was written on a single scroll and recognized as a single book.[5] The book of Sirach (c. 180 BC) found in the Apocrypha mentions the twelve prophets alongside Isaiah, Jeremiah, and Ezekiel: "May the bones of the Twelve Prophets send forth new life from where they lie, for they comforted the people of Jacob and delivered them with confident hope" (49:10 NRSV). The fact

---

[1] For an example of an evangelical scholar providing a unified reading of the Book of the Twelve, see Paul R. House, *The Unity of the Twelve*, BLS 27; JSOTSup 97 (Sheffield: Almond, 1990). House views the Twelve to be arranged around three major themes: (1) the sin of Israel (Hosea–Micah); (2) the punishment of sin (Nehemiah–Zephaniah); and (3) the restoration (Haggai–Malachi). While this structure is perhaps somewhat oversimplified, it provides a good starting point for examining the Twelve as a literary unity. See also Rolf Rendtorff, "How To Read the Book of the Twelve as a Theological Unity," in *Reading and Hearing the Book of the Twelve*, SBLSymS 15 (Atlanta, GA: SBL, 2000), 139–51.

[2] James Nogalski, *Literary Precursors to the Book of the Twelve*, BZAW 217 (New York, NY: Walter deGruyter, 1993), 13.

[3] For critique of the trend to read the Book of the Twelve as a unity, see Ehud ben Zvi, "Twelve Prophetic Books or 'The Twelve': A Few Preliminary Considerations," in *Forming Prophetic Literature: Essays on Isaiah and the Twelve in Honor of John D. W. Watts*, JSOTSup 235 (Sheffield, UK: Sheffield Academic Press, 1996), 125–56. Ben Zvi notes the fluidity of the order of the books and argues that evidence for viewing the Twelve as a unity is too late to clearly demonstrate a purposeful composition and redaction of the Twelve as a single work. Ben Zvi provides helpful cautions, while acknowledging that the books in the Twelve likely reflect shared vocabulary, concepts, and forms of discourse, as well as specific intertextual connections.

[4] David L. Peterson has described the Book of the Twelve as a "thematicized anthology." See David L. Peterson, "A Book of the Twelve?," in *Reading and Hearing the Book of the Twelve*, 3–10.

[5] The various ancient evidences for the recognition of the unity of the Book of the Twelve provided in this paragraph summarize Nogalski. Ibid., 2–3.

that Josephus (*Ag. Ap.* 1.40) and 4 Ezra 14 in the first century AD refer to the number of books in the Hebrew canon as twenty-two and twenty-four respectively also reflects that they viewed the Twelve as a single work. The oldest Hebrew manuscripts of the Twelve from Qumran (Dead Sea Scrolls) reflect that they were written on a single scroll. Of the eight partial manuscripts that have been found, several have more than one book and confirm the order of the present Hebrew Bible.[6] The Septuagint, the Greek translation of the Old Testament, reflects a different ordering, but the Twelve always appear together, with other prophetic writings either preceding or following the Twelve as a group. The Babylonian Talmud (*Baba Batra 13b–15a*) references the Twelve as a single composition, and the Masoretic scribes responsible for preservation of the received text of the Hebrew Bible also treated the Twelve as one book.

Chronology and Catchwords as Evidences of Unity in the Twelve

One of the primary organizing principles for the Book of the Twelve is chronology. Six of the twelve books have historical superscriptions in their introductions:

1. Hosea
2. Amos
3. Micah
4. Zephaniah
5. Haggai
6. Zechariah

These six books with superscriptions provide an overall chronological sequence for the Book of the Twelve. Hosea, Amos, and Micah prophesy during the Assyrian crisis in the eighth century BC. Zephaniah is a prophet during the Babylonian crisis that culminates with the fall of Judah and Jerusalem in 586 BC. Haggai and Zechariah are postexilic prophets

---

[6] One possible exception would be 4Q76 Malachi, where a few letters that appear after the book of Malachi may belong to the book of Jonah.

who begin their ministry in 520 BC as they encourage the people to finish rebuilding the temple, following the return from exile.[7]

Chronology was also a key factor in the placement of four of the six books that do not have historical superscriptions. Jonah was a prophet to Israel in the eighth century BC during the reign of Jeroboam II, and the book of Jonah appears in the section of the predominantly Assyrian prophets that extends from Hosea to Micah. Nahum and Habakkuk with Zephaniah form a section of books that focus on the Babylonian crisis. Nahum prophesied the fall of Nineveh in 612 BC, and Habakkuk announced the Lord's intentions to use Babylon to judge sinful Judah and then to also punish Babylon for its crimes. Malachi appropriately appears at the end of the Twelve because his ministry follows Haggai and Zechariah at the end of the prophetic era.

Chronology, however, is not the only factor in determining the order and arrangement of the Book of the Twelve. The date of Joel is disputed, but the current scholarly consensus is that Joel prophesied during the postexilic period or just prior to the Babylonian exile. Obadiah also appears in the Assyrian section, but this prophet's ministry likely belongs to the time of the Babylonian crisis in the following century.

Along with chronology, it also appears that common themes and connecting catchwords between books were determining factors in the arrangement of the Twelve. Nogalski observes, "Throughout the Book of the Twelve,

---

[7] The Hebrew Masoretic Text (MT) and the Greek Septuagint (LXX) reflect a slightly different arrangement of the Book of the Twelve. The order of the six books with superscriptions (Hosea, Amos, Micah, Zephaniah, Haggai, and Zechariah) is the same in both the MT and LXX relative to each other. The last six books in the Twelve are also in the same order in the MT and LXX, and Nahum–Malachi reflect a chronological arrangement. The differences between the MT and LXX order have to do with how the books of Joel, Obadiah, and Jonah are interspersed among the eighth-century prophets in the first half. The MT reflects an order of Hosea, Joel, Amos, Obadiah, Jonah, and Micah. The LXX order is Hosea, Amos, Micah, Joel, Obadiah, and Jonah. The scholarly consensus is that the Masoretic order is likely the original and that the LXX simply placed Amos and Micah after Hosea because their superscriptions located them in the same basic time period and then retained the order found in the MT for the other books. See Nogalski, Ibid., 2. Other possible orders of arrangement are suggested by some Greek manuscripts, canon lists from the church fathers, and extra-biblical literature from the Second Temple or early Christian era (e.g. *The Ascension of Isaiah* and *The Lives of the Prophets*). See Ben Zvi, "Twelve Prophetic Books," 134, n. 25.

the end of one writing contains significant words that reappear in the opening sections of the next writing."[8] The use of catchwords in the Twelve indicates that the individual books in this collection are to be read together and
in light of each other. The book of Hosea concludes with a promise that the
Lord will restore Israel to the land after the exile and that he will bless his
people with agricultural fertility (Hos 14:4–9). The Lord will provide for
Israel an abundance with regard to "grain," "vine," and "wine" (14:7). In
the opening message of the book of Joel that follows, the prophet portrays a
devastating locust plague that has descended on the land as judgment from
the Lord, and the locusts have devoured the "grain," the "new wine," the
"grapevine," and various other agricultural products (Joel 1:10–12). These
linking references to grain, wine, and vine in Hosea and Joel contrast the
future blessing of Israel with the present realities of judgment.[9]

At the end of Joel, the prophet announces, "The LORD will roar from
Zion and raise His voice from Jerusalem" as he comes in judgment to judge
the nations and to deliver Israel (Joel 3:16). This same expression depicting
the Lord as a roaring lion and a devastating storm opens the book of Amos
(Amos 1:2). References to the judgment of Tyre and Philistia in Joel 3:4 also
line up with oracles of judgment against these same peoples in Amos 1:6
and 9. The vision of Israel's glorious future in which "the mountains will
drip with sweet wine, and the hills will flow with milk" in Joel 3:18 matches
almost identical words in the concluding vision of the future kingdom in
Amos 9:13. Joel and Amos are linked thematically by these corresponding
words of judgment and hope. Even though Joel may have chronologically
appeared as one of the last of the Minor Prophets, the book of Joel is positioned in its present location because of its thematic connections to Amos.
It also seems likely that Joel is located near the beginning of the Book of
the Twelve because it introduces themes that are prominent throughout this
collection.

---

[8] Nogalski, 20.

[9] The specific examples of catchwords developed in this paragraph and in the sections below (along with others) are more fully developed and explained by Nogalski,
Ibid., 20–57. Nogalski and a number of other scholars attempt to use these catchwords
to reconstruct the growth and development of the twelve over time. The focus in this
study is more simply on how these verbal parallels reflect literary unity and serve to
highlight key theological themes within the Twelve.

The concluding vision of the eschatological kingdom in Amos 9:11–15 includes the promise that the people of Israel will "possess the remnant of Edom" (9:12). The book of Obadiah that immediately follows consists of an oracle of judgment against Edom, the descendants of Esau and long-time enemies of Israel. Obadiah is chronologically displaced, but it thematically connects to the books that precede and follow. The book of Jonah also focuses on God's warnings of judgment against a foreign people, the Ninevites of Assyria. Obadiah opens with the declaration, "We have heard a message from the LORD; a messenger has been sent among the nations." In Jonah 1:2, the Lord commands Jonah to go and preach against the city of Nineveh.

In the final chapter of Jonah, the prophet finally reveals that his reason for not going to Nineveh was his knowledge that the Lord was "a merciful and compassionate God, slow to become angry, rich in faithful love, and One who relents from sending disaster" (Jonah 4:2). Jonah did not want to go and preach judgment against Nineveh because he knew there was the possibility that their repentance might lead God to relent from sending judgment. Jonah here recites the Lord's words about himself from Exodus 34:6–7, a passage that forms one of the central theological confessions in the Old Testament (see Num 14:18; 2 Chr 30:9; Neh 9:17; Pss 86:15; 103:8; 111:4; 145:8). The wording of this confession is also echoed in the closing message of Micah as the basis for the promise that the Lord would ultimately forgive Israel's sins (Mic 7:18–20). The confession of Exodus 34:6–7 first appears in the Book of the Twelve in Joel 2 as the motivation for Joel's call for the people of Judah to repent so that the Lord might turn away from his judgment (Joel 2:12–14). Following Micah, Nahum immediately opens with a reference to the confession of Exodus 34:6–7 that focuses on God's judgment of sinners as the basis for the message of judgment against Nineveh (Nah 1:3).

References to the confession of Exodus 34:6–7 link together several books in the front half of the Book of the Twelve.[10] As the people of Israel endured the crises surrounding the ministries of the Minor Prophets, it was important for them to understand that the Lord not only would judge, but would also forgive based on his compassion and covenant faithfulness

---

[10] See further, Raymond C. Van Leeuwen, "Scribal Wisdom and Theodicy in the Book of the Twelve," in *In Search of Wisdom: Essays in Memory of John G. Gammie*, ed. L. G. Perdue and Scott Wiseman (Louisville, KY: Westminster John Knox, 1993), 31–49.

revealed in the confession of Exodus 34:6–7. The Lord had shown this compassion by not destroying Israel when they sinned by worshipping the golden calf at the beginning of the covenant relationship (see Exodus 32), and he would not destroy his people or annul his covenant with Israel even when he sent them into exile. The books of Jonah and Nahum also reflect that the Lord would act even toward the nations with a compassionate and gracious justice. These qualities were not just part of the Lord's covenant with Israel; they were central to his very nature and to his dealings with all peoples.

Thematic connections and catchwords between the individual books of the Book of the Twelve carry through to the end of the collection. Haggai and Zechariah were postexilic prophets who both called for the return-ees to rebuild the Jerusalem temple, and the books of their prophecies are linked together as well. Haggai's promise that the Lord would restore Israel's dominion by overturning the Gentile kingdoms in Haggai 2:20–23, with its references to "the earth" and "horses" and "riders," closely parallels Zechariah's opening vision of four angelic horsemen who patrol the earth and prepare for the coming judgment of the nations that have afflicted Israel (Zechariah 1:8–17). References to Zerubbabel as "My servant" in Haggai 2:23 and to "My servants the prophets" in Zechariah 1:6 also link the books together. The introductory formula "an oracle, word of the LORD" (*massaʾ devar-yhwh*) repeated in Zechariah 9:1; 12:1; and Malachi 1:1 serves to link the last two books in the collection.[11]

Unifying Themes in the Book of the Twelve

Israel's Failure to Repent in Response to the Prophetic Word

The Book of the Twelve documents the unbelieving responses of Israel and Judah to the prophetic word for more than three centuries. The prophets repeatedly call the people to repentance. Hosea exhorts the people, "Come, let us return to the LORD" (Hos 6:1). Joel tells the people that they must turn to the Lord with all their heart (Joel 2:13). Amos offers positive motivations for repentance: "Seek the Yahweh and live" and "Seek good and not evil so

---

[11] This exact heading appears in only these three specific places in all of the Hebrew Bible.

that you may live" (Amos 5:6, 14). Through the preaching of Zechariah and Malachi, the Lord calls out to his people: "Return to Me, and I will return to you" (Zech 1:3; Mal 3:7). The Hebrew verb "repent/return" (*shuv*) literally means "to turn around," and some form of this word appears eighty-three (or eighty-four) times in the Book of the Twelve. As an introduction to the Twelve, the book of Hosea uses the verb *shuv* twenty-two times.[12] Jason T. LeCureux suggests that the central message of the Book of the Twelve is, "As the people struggle to turn [*shuv*] from covenant failure toward YHWH in repentance and receive his blessing, YHWH struggles to turn [*shuv*] from judgment toward his people in grace."[13]

When repentance is not forthcoming in response to the preaching of the prophets, it becomes necessary for the Lord to bring judgment. One of the striking features of the Book of the Twelve is that there are only four specific examples of positive response to the preaching of the prophets:

1. Joel 2:12–17: This text implies (but does not explicitly state) that the people responded to Joel's call for a sacred assembly to confess their sins and pray for God's mercy. The Lord's promise that he would turn judgment into blessing in 2:18–27 indicates the people's obedience to the prophetic word.

2. Jonah 3:1–10: In response to Jonah's warnings of impending judgment and with no offer or promise of divine favor, the king and people of Nineveh turned from their evil ways and sought God's mercy through prayer and fasting. Because of this positive response, the Lord relented from sending the threatened judgment.

3. Haggai 1:12–14 and Zechariah 1:3–6: The postexilic community responded almost immediately to the calls from Haggai and Zechariah to begin rebuilding the temple. The work resumed in 520 BC, and the temple was completed in 515 BC.

4. Malachi 3:16: After rebuilding the temple, the postexilic community once again slipped into spiritual apathy and rebellion, but a

---

[12] See Craig Bowman, "Reading the Twelve as One: Hosea 1–3 as an Introduction to the Book of the Twelve (Minor Prophets)," *Stone-Campbell Journal* 9 (2006): 41–59. Bowman argues that Hosea 1–3 orients all of the Twelve toward this theme of "Return to the Lord."

[13] Jason T. LeCureux, *The Thematic Unity of the Book of the Twelve*, HBM 41 (Sheffield, UK: Sheffield Phoenix, 2012), 39.

small segment of the population "feared" the Lord and heeded Malachi's preaching. The Lord's command to record the names of these individuals in a "book of remembrance" reflected that he would reward them for their obedience.

It is telling that in over three centuries of preaching in the Book of the Twelve, there are few examples of positive response to the prophetic word—and the most prominent response comes from the hated Assyrians!

In fact, a literary pattern of repentance and relapse emerges from a reading of the Twelve as a whole that highlights the people's unbelieving response to the prophets. In this pattern, each group that repents in the Twelve subsequently relapses into disobedience and becomes the object of God's judgment. This literary pattern helps to highlight the seriousness of persistent unbelief and unresponsiveness to the prophetic word.

As the opening book of the Twelve, Hosea stresses Israel's unwillingness, and even inability, to return to the Lord (Hos 5:4; 7:10, 14–16). The prophet Amos charges that the people of Israel have not "returned" (*shuv*)

The Pattern of Repentance and Relapse in the Book of the Twelve		
ISRAEL	NINEVEH	POSTEXILIC COMMUNITY
Narrative of Repentance: Joel 2:12 Israel repents and God spares from judgment.	Narrative of Repentance: Jonah 3—the people and king of Nineveh repent and God spares from judgment.	Narrative of Repentance: Post-exilic Israel obeys calls to rebuild temple and "returns to the LORD" (Haggai 1; Zechariah 1).
Relapse and warning of judgment of exile for Israel (Amos) and Judah (Micah, Habakkuk, Zephaniah).	Relapse and warning of judgment and destruction for Nineveh (Nahum).	Relapse and warning of further judgment for post-exilic community (Malachi). **Narrative of partial repentance in Malachi 3:16–18** with a warning of final judgment for the wicked.

to the Lord (Amos 4:6, 8–11). The leaders of the northern kingdom order Amos to stop preaching against the king's sanctuary (Amos 7:10–17), and the leaders of Judah command Micah to stop preaching about the coming destruction of Jerusalem (Mic 2:6). Unbelief and disobedience ultimately lead to exile for both Israel and Judah.

Surprisingly, it is the foreign Ninevites/Assyrians in the book of Jonah who provide the most thorough example of repentance in the Twelve, but Nahum announces judgment on Nineveh when they also return to their sinful ways. The verbal parallels between Joel 2:12–17 and Jonah 3:4–10 serve to highlight the idea that the pagan Assyrians embodied what the Lord desired from his own people. If the Lord extended his mercy to the Ninevites when they repented, one can only imagine how much more he would have extended his grace to his own people.

The postexilic community returned to the land and rebuilt the temple, but their complete restoration would not occur until the people fully returned to the Lord by obeying his precepts (Zech 8:16–23). At the end of the Twelve, the Lord continues to call out to his people: "Return to Me, and I will return to you." As LeCureux explains, "Even those who had returned

NINEVEH AS THE SURPRISE EXAMPLE OF REPENTANCE: A COMPARISON OF JOEL 2:12–17 AND JONAH 3:4–10	
JOEL 2:12–17	*JONAH 3:4–10*
Call for fasting (2:12)	Nineveh's extreme fasting includes even their animals (3:5, 7)
Call for mourning (2:12–13)	Ninevites wear sackcloth and sit in ashes (3:5–6, 8)
Call for people to "turn/return" (*shuv*) to the Lord (2:12–13)	Ninevites "turn" (*shuv*) from their sinful ways (3:8, 10)
Possibility of divine mercy: "Who knows? He may 'turn' (*shuv*) and 'relent' (*nacham*)" (2:14)	"Who knows? God may 'turn' (*shuv*) and 'relent' (*nacham*)" (3:9)
Exodus 34:6–7 as basis for why God "relents" (*nacham*) from sending "disaster" (*ra'*) against Israel (Joel 2:13)	Exodus 34:6–7 as basis for why God "relents" (*nacham*) from sending "disaster" (*ra'*) against Israel (Jonah 4:2)

from exile and were in the process of rebuilding the temple, must still return to YHWH."[14] As a result, the Book of the Twelve highlights the theological message that the need for repentance and return is "an ongoing dynamic for all time; one that has occurred throughout Israel's past and will continue into the present."[15]

The postexilic prophets spoke of the necessity of divine judgment beyond the exile to fully purge Israel of its evil ways. The only hope for Israel's future lay in the Lord's promise that he would act decisively to transform his people by healing their apostasy (Hos 14:1–3), pouring out his Spirit upon them (Joel 2:28–32), and giving them "a spirit of grace and prayer" (Zech 12:10), ultimately enabling them to become a faithful people.

The Day of the Lord

The Lord repeatedly sent his prophets to announce the coming Day of the Lord, and this theme is especially prominent in the Book of the Twelve. The expression "Day of the Lord" (*yôm yhwh*) appears in Joel 1:15; 2:1, 11, 31; 3:14; Amos 5:18, 20; Obadiah 15; and Zephaniah 1:7, 14. There are also references to the "Day of the Lord's wrath/anger" (Zeph 2:2–3) and numerous references to "the day" or "that day" (see Hos 1:5; 2:16, 18; 5:9; Amos 2:16; 3:14; Obad 1:12–14; Mic 7:12; Zeph 1:9–10; Zech 9:16; 14:13, 20–21). Rolf Rendtorff understands a key message of the Twelve to be that "the day of the Lord is both darkness and light."[16] The prominence of this theme in the book of Joel likely explains its placement at the beginning of the Twelve, and the ominous warning that "the Day of the LORD is near" is a recurring theme (see Joel 1:15; 2:1; 3:14; Obadiah 15; Zeph 1:7, 14).

Christian readers often associate the Day of the Lord exclusively with the eschaton and the events surrounding the second coming of Jesus, but the Old Testament prophets used this term to refer to events that occurred in their day as well as in the distant future. The Day of the Lord is both near and far and refers to any time Yahweh dramatically intervenes in human history. As Jeffrey J. Niehaus explains, "Every Day of the Lord is a foreshadowing of that final and dreadful—and glorious—Day of the Lord when the

---

[14] Ibid., 109.
[15] Ibid., 231.
[16] Rendtorff, "How To Read the Book of the Twelve as a Theological Unity," 75–87.

sun will turn dark, the moon will turn to blood, the heavenly bodies will be shaken, and the Son of Man will return on the clouds with great power and glory."[17] The judgments of the present anticipate the great and final judgment of Israel and the nations in the last days that will usher in the kingdom of God on earth.

The concept of the Day of the Lord originated in Israel's worship and holy war traditions that celebrated the Lord as the Divine Warrior who fought on Israel's behalf throughout its history.[18] The people and leaders of Israel had developed a presumptuous confidence that the Lord would always deliver them—even apart from their obedience to him—and unscrupulous prophets fed this presumption with empty promises of peace and unconditional blessing. It was the task of the true prophets to correct this defective theology and to warn the people of the grim reality of coming judgment, military defeat, and exile. The prophet Amos warned the people of longing for the arrival of the Day of the Lord and announced that it would be a day of judgment rather than a Day of deliverance (Amos 5:18–20).

The Broken and Restored Covenant

The Book of the Twelve as a literary unit tells the story of the broken and restored covenant between the Lord and Israel. The prophets were the Lord's prosecuting attorneys, indicting Israel and Judah for their unfaithfulness. Their indictments center on charges of idolatry, false worship, failure to practice social justice, and general disregard for the Lord's commands. The prophets announced that if the people did not turn from their sinful ways, the Lord would judge them by bringing against them the covenant curses that Moses had warned them about prior to their entrance into the land (see Leviticus 26; Deuteronomy 28).

Despite these severe judgments, the Lord would remain enduringly committed to his covenant people and his covenant promises. In Hosea 11:8–9, the LORD painfully asks, "How can I give you up?" as he executes judgment on his people and then assures that he would "not vent the full

---

[17] Jeffrey J. Niehaus, *Biblical Theology, Vol. 1: The Common Grace Covenants* (Wooster, OH: Weaver Book, 2014), 217–18.

[18] Robin Routledge, *Old Testament Theology: A Thematic Approach* (Downers Grove, IL: InterVarsity, 2008), 274–75.

fury" of his wrath or "turn back to destroy Ephraim." Amos 9:8 warns that the Lord would "destroy" Israel "from the face of the earth" but also promises that he would not "totally destroy the house of Jacob." The Lord's love and mercy would ultimately trump his anger and wrath. After the exile, the Lord brought the people back to the land and promised to bless them as they rebuilt the temple and renewed their covenantal commitments to him. The return from exile anticipated the even greater return of the future when the Lord will fully restore his people, and the nations will be included in the blessings of Israel's salvation.

The beginning and end of the Book of the Twelve highlight the marriage metaphor as a picture of the Lord's abiding love for Israel. At the beginning of the Twelve, Hosea's failed marriage with Gomer is representative of the broken marriage between the Lord and Israel (Hosea 1–3). The people have broken covenant with the Lord and have loved and served other gods. Malachi ends the Book of the Twelve where Hosea begins by highlighting Israel's apostasy. John D. W. Watts has noted that Hosea and Malachi provide bookends for the Twelve in the way that these books uniquely focus on the love of God.[19] The word "love" ('ahav) in all its forms appears only twenty-eight times in the Twelve, and then it only refers to God's love for Israel in Hosea 3:1; 9:15; 11:1; 14:3–4; and Malachi 1:2–3.[20] Yahweh loved his people Israel, but the Lord himself is never the object of Israel's "love" (Hos 2:5, 7, 10, 12; 3:1; 9:1, 10; 12:7).[21] Rather than following the Lord, Israel pursued the other gods she had turned to as her "lovers." Just as Hosea restored his unfaithful wife (Hos 3:1–5), the Lord would ultimately "speak kindly" to Israel so that she would finally love him as she should (Hos 2:14–23).

Israel continues to respond in the wrong ways to the Lord's love. When the Lord affirms his love for Israel, the people reply, "How have you loved us?" (Mal 1:2). Centuries of judgment, military defeat, exile, and deprivation had led the people to question the Lord's love, but it was actually his love that protected them from total destruction. Despite the experience of

---

[19] John D. W. Watts, "A Frame for the Book of the Twelve: Hosea 1–3 and Malachi," in *Reading and Hearing the Book of the Twelve*, 209–17.

[20] Ibid., 212.

[21] Mark J. Boda, *A Severe Mercy: Sin and Its Remedy in the Old Testament*, Siphrut 1 (Winona Lake, IN: Eisenbrauns, 2009), 295.

divine discipline, the people's disposition toward the Lord had not changed, and Israel remained both an unfaithful wife and a rebellious son (Mal 1:6). The future judgments of the final Day of the Lord would be necessary for Israel to return fully to the Lord and to embrace him as her husband. At the end of the Twelve, the Lord promises to turn the hearts of fathers and children in Israel to each other (Mal 4:6), and the restoration of family relations at the human level would be the evidence of the renewed relationship between the Lord and Israel. Israel's persistent apostasy would test the Lord's patience but could never extinguish his passionate love for her.

The Book of the Twelve focuses on the reversal of the curses the Lord brought against his people, and it promises a return to the land following the exile. These prophets first warned that judgment was coming in the form of military invasion and defeat. Hosea announced that the Lord was coming against his people like a lion and a bear (Hos 13:7–8) and that he would use the armies of enemy nations to carry out his attack. Nations would be gathered against Israel, fortresses would be destroyed, and the people would live as exiles in a foreign land (Hos 9:3, 6; 10:14–15; 13:16). Israel would be "swallowed up" and cast aside "like discarded pottery" (Hos 8:8). Joel warned the army of locusts that had invaded the land would precede a human army, bringing even greater devastation (Joel 2:1–11).

Amos portrays the coming military defeat of Israel with frightening detail. As in Hosea, the Lord would roar against his people like a lion by using enemy armies (Amos 1:2; 6:14). He had already sent enemy armies against an unresponsive Israel (Amos 4:10–11), and the armies to come would wipe out nearly all of Israel's fighting force (Amos 2:15–16; 5:1–3). Israel's citadels and fortifications would not provide protection (Amos 6:8–9), and the survivors of the war would be carried away into exile (Amos 5:5, 27; 6:7; 7:11, 17). Micah prophesied that enemy armies would turn both Samaria and Jerusalem into a heap of ruins (Mic 1:6; 3:12). Habakkuk and Zephaniah announce that the Lord planned to use Babylon to punish Judah (Hab 1:6–11; Zeph 1:14–18; 3:8).

The Lord's judgment would bring his people to the brink of destruction, but he would also save them and restore them to their land. The Lord promises through Hosea to destroy the weapons of war used against Israel so they might dwell securely in the land (Hos 2:18) and through Amos that he would restore Israel's fortunes—they would "never again be uprooted from the land" (Amos 9:14–15). Obadiah's oracle against Edom and Nahum's message of doom against Nineveh reflect how the Lord would turn the tables on the nations that had assaulted Israel and Judah. Habakkuk's prophecies reveal that the Lord would destroy Babylon after he had used Babylon to inflict judgment on Judah (Hab 2:2–20). The Lord would wage war in final judgment against all the nations that had fought against his people (Joel 3:1–16; Zeph 3:6–8; Hab 3:1–15). In preparation for this final battle, the Lord calls on the nations to beat "your plows into swords and your pruning knives into spears" (Joel 3:10); in contrast, he promises that the nations would one day turn their "swords into plows, and their spears into pruning knives" (Mic 4:3). A recurring promise in the Twelve is that the Lord would "restore the fortunes" (*shuv shevut*) of his downtrodden people (Hos 6:12; Joel 3:1; Amos 9:14; Zeph 2:7; 3:20).

The return from Babylonian exile represented an initial and partial fulfillment of the Lord's promises to restore his people, but it hardly lived up to all that the prophets had anticipated for Israel's renewal as a nation. The postexilic prophets looked forward to a return beyond the return when the Lord would "shake the heavens and earth" and permanently deliver his people from all enemies (Haggai 2:20–23; Zech 9:14–16). Zechariah envisioned that the cycle of judgment, exile, and return would occur on an even grander scale in the last days (Zech 12:1–9; 14:1–5, 12–15). Ultimately, the Book of the Twelve looks forward to the time when the nations that attacked Zion would instead make pilgrimage to Jerusalem to worship Yahweh and share in the blessings of Israel's salvation (Mic 4:1–5; Zech 14:16–19). Zephaniah prophesies that the Lord would reverse the curse of Babel against the nations (see Genesis 11) and "restore pure speech to the peoples so that all of them may call on the name of Yahweh and serve Him with a single purpose" (Zeph 3:9).

The Book of the Twelve also highlights the reversal from agricultural ruin to abundant prosperity. In the restoration, each person would "sit under his vine and fig tree," (Zech 3:10; Mic 4:4). Hosea announced that Israel's trust in the Baals and Asherahs for blessing would bring futility instead of fertility. The Lord would take away Israel's grain and wine because they had honored Baal as the source of their provision, and the land would not produce enough crops to sustain the people (Hos 2:8–12; 9:1–2). Despite the practice of pagan fertility rites, Israel's women would not be able to conceive and bear children; the children that were born to them would be lost in war (Hos 9:11–14, 16–17). However, the Lord would become "like the rain" and "the spring showers that water the land" when he restored his people (Hos 6:3), and Israel would flourish like the lily, the olive tree, and the pine while enjoying the bounty of the land (Hos 14:5–8).

Joel and Amos prophesy at times when Israel experienced the covenant curse of locust invasions that ruined the land and its crops (Joel 1:5–12; Amos 4:9; see Deut 28:38). When the people responded positively to Joel's call for repentance and prayer, the Lord promised to prosper them by sending grain, wine, and oil and to "repay" Israel for what the locusts had destroyed so they would have plenty to eat (Joel 2:18–27). But Amos warned of further judgment because even the covenant curses on the land had not caused the people to "return" to the Lord (Amos 4:6–13; 7:1–3). Both prophets anticipated a future time of blessing when the mountains would drip with wine and milk as Israel planted vineyards and gardens (Joel 3:18; Amos 9:13–15).

The postexilic community remained impoverished because the people had not fully returned to the Lord. Haggai rebuked the people for failing to rebuild the temple and reminded them that they had "planted much but harvested little" and had put their wages "into a bag with a hole in it" because of their disobedience and misplaced priorities (Hag 1:6–11). When the people resumed rebuilding the temple, Haggai encouraged them that the Lord would bless them with abundance from that point forward (Hag 2:15–19). In line with the Mosaic covenant, Malachi connected Judah's poverty and lack of food to the failure of the people to honor the Lord with their tithes (Mal 3:7–10). Malachi promised that when Israel obeyed and honored the Lord, he would prosper them to the extent that all the nations would consider them a blessed people (Mal 3:11–12). Zechariah also looked forward to the time when "the vine will yield its fruit, the land will yield its produce, and the skies will yield their dew" (Zech 8:12). The Book of the Twelve opens with the Lord taking away the vine, wine, and grain from Israel but concludes with promises that the Lord would restore the fruit of the land.

The Promise of a New David

The restoration of Israel would also include the fulfillment of the Lord's covenant promise to establish the throne of David forever, and some of the most important Messianic prophecies in the Hebrew Bible are found in the

Book of the Twelve.[22] After the collapse of the Davidic throne, the Lord would restore the Davidic dynasty and raise up a new David over his people (Hos 3:5; Amos 9:11–12). This future king would come from Bethlehem, like David, and would bring peace to Israel by extending his rule over the nations (Mic 5:2–6).

Messianic hopes especially flourished in the postexilic era. Jeremiah had prophesied that the Lord was removing Jehoiachin as his "signet ring" (Jer 22:24) with that ruler's exile to Babylon in 597 BC. The subsequent end of the Davidic dynasty in 586 BC meant that David's sons would no longer serve as the Lord's vice-regents. However, Haggai announced after the return from exile that the appointment of Zerubbabel as governor of Judah was proof that the Lord was restoring David's family to its honored position as "signet ring" (Hag 2:20–23). The limited authority of Zerubbabel anticipated the future rule of the house of David over the nations. Jeremiah had also promised that the Lord would raise up a "Righteous Branch" from the line of David to rule over Israel (Jer 23:5–6; 33:15–16), and Zechariah reiterated this promise, pointing to the leadership provided by Zerubbabel and Joshua (the high priest) as anticipation of the rule of this future Davidic "Branch" (Zech 3:8–10; 6:10–15).

Zechariah also prophesied that the future Davidic king would present himself to the people as a man of peace, riding on a donkey, and that his rule would extend "from sea to sea" (Zech 9:9–10). The Lord would extend his mercy to both the nation of Israel and the house of David and would make the Davidic king to be "like God" as he led the people (Zech 12:8–14). Ironically, this restoration would occur only after the Lord had caused both Israel and the house of David to mourn at the realization that they had rejected the Lord by "piercing" (crucifying) their Messiah (see Zech 12:10; John 19:37). The New Testament presents Jesus as the One who fulfills these messianic prophecies, both as a son of David and as the eternal Son of God whose reign would never end.

---

[22] For a more extended treatment of the messianic passages in the Book of the Twelve, see Herbert W. Bateman, Darrell L. Bock, and Gordon H. Johnston, *Jesus the Messiah: Tracing the Promises, Expectations, and Coming of Israel's King* (Grand Rapids, MI: Kregel Academic, 2012), 107–32, 191–209.

KEY MESSIANIC TEXTS IN THE BOOK OF THE TWELVE
HOSEA 3:5
AMOS 9:11–15
MICAH 5:2–6
HAGGAI 2:20–23
ZECHARIAH 3:8–10; 6:10–15; 9:9–10; 12:8–14

Conclusion

The Book of the Twelve transforms the words of twelve distinct prophets into a cohesive account of the Lord's dealings with his people over the last three centuries of Old Testament history. The Lord warns Israel and Judah through his prophets that various "Day of the Lord" judgments are imminent because of their disobedience, and these judgments fall in rapid succession because the people are largely unresponsive to the prophets' warnings. These judgments, however, are not the end of the story. The Lord remains committed to his covenant people and his covenant promises. The history of failure, disobedience, and judgment would give way to a future day when the Lord would judge the nations and restore Israel. The return from exile was merely a preview of an even greater time of blessing when Israel would enjoy the abundance of their land and live under the peaceful and righteous rule of the Lord and the future ideal Davidic ruler. The Book of the Twelve provides a unique and cohesive perspective on how the Lord accomplishes his purposes through both judgment and salvation.

5

THE BOOK OF HOSEA

Introduction

Hosea has all the intrigue of a love story gone wrong; it is the kind of sordid tale too often replicated as entertainment. The dramatic introduction to Hosea, however, is not meant to titillate, but to shock the senses.[1] Hosea draws the reader into the very heart of God, torn between the righteous indignation of a jealous husband and the unfathomable love of a father for his wayward son.[2] Through prophetic drama, intense language, and historical reflection, Hosea brings a case against Israel, indicting her for her sins of idolatry and political treason or—in the imagery of Hosea—the sin of

---

[1] Hosea is not the earliest among the twelve Minor Prophets, with Amos's ministry predating Hosea's by a few decades. However, its message provides a fitting thematic introduction to the Book of the Twelve.

[2] Although the husband/wife analogy is primary, Hosea 11 clearly draws on a second analogy, the father/son relationship.

spiritual adultery. The book of Hosea sets the tone for Israel's guilt and God's just recompense, while establishing the ever-present reality of God's *hesed* love.

Hosea is perhaps best known not for the intense poetic imagery within its oracles, but for the prophet's marriage to the adulterous woman Gomer. While the story of Hosea's life is intriguing, to focus here is to miss the point of the book. Rather than simply narrating Hosea's life, the book draws the reader into the analogous story of God's relationship with Israel. The story of Hosea's dysfunctional marriage to Gomer sets the stage for the prophetic message that permeates all fourteen chapters of the book—the message that Israel has been unfaithful and, like Gomer, has committed grave offense against the husband of her youth, Yahweh.

To understand the theological message of the Hosea book, one must first understand the historical context in which Hosea prophesied to Israel. Hosea's ministry began during the reign of Uzziah in Judah (792–740 BC) and Jeroboam II in Israel (793–753 BC), extending at least thirty years into the reign of Hezekiah (716–686 BC). Hosea's prophetic calling occurred during a period of relative peace and prosperity for the divided kingdom, with the threat of foreign domination suppressed by internal corrosion within the Assyrian Empire. In the years following Jeroboam II's death, the northern kingdom of Israel quickly declined as the Assyrian Empire expanded its reach into neighboring territories. By 738 BC, Israel was paying tribute to the Assyrian king Tiglath-Pileser III, and by 725 BC, trusting in alliances made with Egypt. Israel's last king, Hoshea, rebelled against Shalmaneser V, king of Assyria. In retaliation, the Assyrian armies besieged Samaria, and by 722 BC, Israel had fallen, its cities destroyed and its people taken into exile.

Hosea's prophecies are almost entirely directed at the northern kingdom of Israel, and Hosea's familiarity with Israel's geography indicates that he was likely a citizen of the north.[3] Nevertheless, within the text there are various references to Judah that convey both judgment as well as restorative expectation (1:7; 4:15; 5:5, 10, 13, 14; 6:4, 11; 8:14; 11:12; 12:2). Additionally, it is peculiar that the introduction to the book dates Hosea's ministry as extending into the reign of Hezekiah, king of Judah. Perhaps the mention

---

[3] Additionally, scholars have long noted the many difficulties in the Hebrew text of Hosea, perhaps due to the Hebrew reflecting a "Northern dialect." See Duane A. Garrett, *Hosea, Joel*, NAC (Nashville, TN: B&H, 1997), 26.

of four Judean kings, along with the occasional mention of Judah in oracles, indicates that Hosea escaped the destruction of Samaria by fleeing to Judah, thereby finishing his prophetic ministry while residing there.

In terms of content, the text of Hosea indicates significant familiarity with Israel's history and its Scriptures. Indeed, historical reflection and inter-textual allusions are a hallmark of Hosea's prophecies. Hosea also exhibits frequent use of Hebrew wordplay, including repetition, alliteration, and assonance. But the book of Hosea is perhaps best characterized by its rich use of shocking metaphors to describe particular characteristics of the God/Israel relationship (as if the analogy of an adulterous wife was not shocking enough). In judgment, God is a ferocious lion about to tear apart its prey (5:14; 13:7–8), while in mercy he is depicted as a lioness whose roar calls her cubs home (11:10–11). God's faithfulness is as sure as seasonal rains (6:3) and as nourishing as dew to the fields (14:5). In contrast, Israel's lack of faithfulness is as disappointing as a morning mist during drought and as fleeting as morning dew under a searing sun (6:4). Israel is described as sowing the wind, and reaping the whirlwind (8:7). The imagery in Hosea startles the senses, inviting the reader to *feel* God's suffering over his beloved people.

Structure

Finding clean structural lines in Hosea is a fool's game at best, as generations of scholars have struggled to find an overarching framework for the book.[4] The reader does, however, find a clear break between the prophetic drama of chapters 1–3 and the series of covenant lawsuits, historical reflections, and heart-strung musings that carry through the rest of the book (chapters 4–14). Perhaps the most distinctive structural components within Hosea are the alternating panels describing either judgment or salvation. Although there are distinct literary units within these panels, and short transitional segments between them, the tug-of-war between God's desire for grace and his inclination to justice comprise the structural backbone of the book.

---

[4] For a survey of structural approaches, see Garrett, *Hosea, Joel*, 30–39; and Mark F. Rooker, "Hosea," in *The World and the Word: An Introduction to the Old Testament* (Nashville, TN: B&H, 2011), 416–17.

Impending Doom	Intermediary Discipline	Call to Repentance	Eternal Hope
1:2–6; 8–9			1:7, 10–2:1
2:2–13			2:14–23
	3:1–4		3:5
4:1–5:14	5:15a	6:1–3	5:15b
6:4–11:7		10:12	11:8–11
11:12–13:16		14:1–3	14:4–8

Through these panels lie multiple subgenres, including prophetic drama, historical reflection, woe speeches, trial speeches, calls to repentance, and salvation oracles. Additionally, Hosea closes with a proverb, a prophetic word to the wise that challenges the reader to seek the knowledge of the Lord. Although Israel lacked the "knowledge of God," and paid dearly for it, Hosea implores future generations to carefully consider the price of judgment and of abandoning the Lord who once drew them with "gentle cords" (11:4 NKJV). This is a fitting and unique conclusion to a book that requires deep, introspective thought in both heart and mind.

Exposition

1:1 (Introduction)

Hosea opens with an introduction affirming the divine origin of the prophet's message, along with a list of reigning kings that provide a historical framework behind the prophetic content of the book. Four Judean kings are referenced, beginning with Uzziah (792–740 BC) and ending with Hezekiah (716–686 BC). Additionally, Jeroboam II (793–753 BC) is referenced as the sole representative from the northern kingdom of Israel. While six additional kings ruled Israel after Jeroboam II, these are not mentioned in the introduction, perhaps due to their short reigns, illegitimate claims to the throne, and the fact that they presided over the eventual fall of the northern kingdom in 722 BC. Additionally, the fact that Hosea's introduction includes an emphasis on Judean monarchs suggests that he may have ended his ministry in Judah after the fall of the northern kingdom, even though his message is primarily directed to the north.[5] What is clear from the introduction is that Hosea's ministry spanned a period of at least forty years, thus suggesting that the words collected within the book reflect multiple prophetic episodes from Hosea's life.

Panel 1 (1:2–2:1)

1:2–6; 8–9 "And I will not be your God" (Prophetic Drama and Symbolic Names: Describing God's Rejection of Israel)

With the exception of Jonah, biographical narrative is rare in the Book of the Twelve; the words of the prophets take center stage over the stories of their lives. Yet Hosea begins with a shocking revelation from his own life—God's command for him to "marry a promiscuous wife and have children of promiscuity" (1:2a). Obedient to that command, Hosea marries Gomer, daughter of Dibliam, who, in time, conceives three children: Jezreel, Lo-ruhammah, and Lo-ammi (1:2–9).[6] Aside from the ambiguous information provided in chapter three, the reader is left with very little biographical detail concerning Hosea's marriage. Was Gomer a promiscuous woman prior to the marriage, or did she become one after it? What kind of day-to-day relationship did Hosea have with Gomer and the children? Speculate we might, but in truth we will never know. Although the events of Hosea's marriage are historical, the text itself is not a biography. Rather, as prophetic drama, the focus of the text is the correspondence between Hosea's marriage and God's relationship to adulterous Israel (1:2). To be clear, this does not deny the historicity of the account. Indeed, God would often shock his people not only through the words of the prophets, but through their actions as well. Jeremiah was commanded not to marry in Judah (Jer 16:1–4); Ezekiel was commanded not to weep for his deceased

---

[5] While speculative, this approach may better explain the numerous references to Judah throughout the text without needing to concede to critical assumptions that all Judean references come from the hand of a later Judean redactor. If Hosea's ministry extended into Hezekiah's reign, then one should expect references to Judah within the Hosea book.

[6] Although laden with symbolic value and analogical function, there is no inherent reason to question the historicity of Hosea's marriage. The fact that the name of Gomer's father, Dibliam, is mentioned at all provides striking support for the historicity of the story.

wife (Ezek 24:15–27). Isaiah was commanded to walk around naked for three years (Isaiah 20), while Jeremiah was commanded to walk around wearing chains and yokes of wood (Jeremiah 27). Ezekiel was commanded to cook his food over human waste; and while the Lord conceded to allow him to use cow dung (Ezek 4:12–15), distasteful directives are not unique to the life of Hosea. Affirming God's command to Hosea as historical, it nevertheless is the analogical function that is important. The Hosea book is more a story about God's relationship with his promiscuous wife Israel than it is a story about Hosea's relationship with his promiscuous wife Gomer.

Throughout the first two chapters of Hosea, the names of the three children take on special significance as they illustrate God's rejection and restoration of Israel through striking wordplay. As Gomer conceives and bears a son, the Lord commands Hosea to name him "Jezreel," a name that literally means "God will scatter" (1:4). The term has many layers of prophetic and historical significance, and these layers must be understood to fully appreciate the theological depth housed within this name. Peeling back the first layer, historical reference is made to the city of Jezreel, where Jehu slaughtered the house of Ahab, establishing his own dynasty, of which Jeroboam II was a descendant (2 Kgs 9:7–10:28). Although God sanctioned this judgment over the house of Omri, Jehu did not walk in the ways of the Lord, but followed after the Baals in the same manner as those who preceded him (2 Kgs 10:30–31). For this reason, in an act of poetic justice, God would visit the house of Jehu in the same place (Jezreel), and with the same bloody judgment.[7] The prophecy was fulfilled when Shallum assassinated Zechariah, the forth (and last) of Jehu's descendants to reign over Israel (2 Kgs 15:10). Furthermore, it was in the Valley of Jezreel that God would bring an end to the northern kingdom (Hosea 1:5). This came to pass through a succession of military engagements between Israel and Assyria (743–722 BC). In the fertile valley meaning "God will scatter," the

---

[7] Although many translations imply that this judgment would come as an act of vengeance *for* the bloodshed brought by the hand of Jehu, this causes a dilemma in that God commanded Jehu to carry out this act of bloodshed (2 Kings 9:7). The Hebrew word used here, *paqad*, literally means "to visit." Contextually, it is preferable to understand this as an act of poetic justice. That God would "visit" the *same kind* of bloodshed upon the house of Jehu (due to his unfaithfulness in not walking in the ways of the Lord; 2 Kings 10:31) eliminates the ethical (and logical) dilemma of God avenging an act that he commanded. See Garrett, *Hosea, Joel*, 55–57.

Image of the Jezreel Valley

Assyrian armies waged the campaigns that ultimately led to Israel's exile, when God scattered them to the outskirts of the Assyrian Empire (1:5).

The second child born to Gomer is given the name "Lo-ruhammah," variously translated "No Compassion," "not pitied," or "not loved" (1:6).[8] If the name "Jezreel" did not get the attention of Hosea's contemporaries, then certainly the name "No Compassion" would! Whether the little girl was Hosea's child is unclear, and the reader is left with uncertainty about whether or not she was rejected or accepted by Hosea. What is clear is that her name symbolized God's rejection of Israel. No longer would God spare Israel from judgment, no longer would he "forgive their guilt" (1:6c NET).

---

[8] The HCSB translates the name "No Compassion," and the ESV translates the name as "No Mercy." The NIV transliterates but includes a footnote stating the meaning as "Not loved." The NET Bible translates it, "No Pity," placing the transliteration in the main text within parentheses.

After weaning Lo-ruhammah, Gomer gives birth to a third child, given the symbolic name "Lo-ammi" (1:8–9). This third child carries the most haunting name, as it literally means "Not My People," suggesting a stark rejection of God's covenant people. The concise description does not specify whether Gomer or the child was literally rejected by Hosea at this juncture in their relationship. Nevertheless, the analogical language of rejection is quite clear, harkening Exodus 6:7 and reversing God's claim of the people of Israel as his own. What is less clear theologically is whether this rejection constitutes a covenant divorce of Israel. Notwithstanding the language of restitution in the following oracles (1:10–2:1; 2:23), it is difficult to escape the imagery of rejection that this name symbolizes, whether it constitutes a divorce or simply a separation of some kind.

1:7, 10–2:1 "They will be called: Sons of the living God" (Reversal: Symbolic Names Describing God's Restoration of His People)

Hosea is saturated with the language of reversal. There is perhaps no clearer example of divine reversal in Scripture than between Hosea 1:8–9 and 1:10–2:1. Following stark statements of rejection associated with the names of the children, reversal comes in the form of an abrupt, hyperbolic shift in fortunes: "Yet the number of Israelites will be like the sand of the sea" (1:10a), and "in the place where they were told: 'You are not My people, they will be called: Sons of the living God'" (1:10b). Interestingly, sandwiched between the oracles concerning Lo-ruhammah and Lo-ammi, Hosea prophesies a historical precursor of God's great eschatological deliverance—the historical deliverance of Judah from the threat of Sennacherib, king of Assyria (1:7). In 701 BC, God revealed himself as Deliverer when in one night, 185,000 Assyrian soldiers were slaughtered by the Angel of the Lord. They were killed as they were encamped around Jerusalem. God thus spared Judah the same fate as had befallen Israel (Isa 37:36–37).[9]

The salvation oracle that comprises Hosea 1:10–2:1 is set in stark contrast to the ominous judgments symbolized by the names of Gomer's

---

[9] Some argue that 1:7 is unoriginal to Hosea. However, the introduction to the book indicates that Hosea prophesied into the reign of Hezekiah, and the impending threat of the Assyrians was the prophetic and political focus in Hezekiah's Judah. Furthermore it stands to reason that Hosea, as a prophet, could indeed predict the future, both far and near.

children. Playing off of the symbolic names, the reversal of fortunes prophesied in 1:10–2:1 points to a day of covenant blessing and restoration as positive as the preceding message of rejection was negative. Those who were told they were "not My people" will be called "Sons of the living God" (1:10). The imagery portrayed in the male child "Lo-ammi" comes to full reversal; the son rejected as illegitimate has been received fully as a rightful heir, and the people deemed "not My people" have become "sons of the living God!"[10]

Referencing both Israel and Judah, and evoking the same theology of re-gathering and reunification later envisioned by Ezekiel, Hosea 1:11 parallels Ezekiel 36:9–11 and 37:18–25 in reference to the people, land, and king.[11] Where God had "scattered" in judgment, he would now "gather" in restoration. Where God had dispersed his people, bringing an end to Israel, he would now sow the seed of his people back into the land. There, in the Valley of "God's scattering," this seed would take root, and "come up out of the land," (NKJV); "for great shall be the day of Jezreel" (ESV)!

Finally, the salvation reversal closes in 2:1 with allusion back to Lo-ruhammah, "No Compassion." In escalating, parallel fashion, all three children are mentioned in terms of positive reversal: "Jezreel"

Jezreel

יזרעאל

Jezreel's name means "God will sow." The Valley of Jezreel is located in Israel. It is the place where Barak defeated Sisera in Judges 4 and where Jezebel was thrown out of a window and eaten by dogs (2 Kgs 9:30–35). In Hosea 1:5, God promises to "break the bow of Israel in the Valley of Jezreel." In conjunction with the name, Hosea plays on the theme of reaping and sowing when describing the coming exile of Israel and their future restoration.

---

[10] The reference to "the place" in 1:10, while ambiguous, is not incidental. The implication of this spatial reference is that this prophecy finds its ultimate fulfillment in the land, in line with the prophetic expectation of Ezekiel in the new covenant (Ezekiel 37:21–28).

[11] Ezekiel 36:9–11 uses sowing imagery to depict Israel's being replanted into the land, while Ezekiel 37:15–28 describes the rejoining of the divided kingdoms into one kingdom (Ezekiel 37:21–22), ruled in their own land (Ezekiel 37:21, 25), by one head (Ezekiel 37:22), the Davidic king (Ezekiel 37:24–25).

Lo-ruhammah	**Lo-ammi**
לא-רחמה	לא-עמי
Lo-ruhammah was Gomer's second child. The girl's name means "No Compassion" and alludes first to coming judgment. However, in reversal, God promises a future day of restoration where he will show his people compassion and love (2:1, 23).	The name Lo-ammi means "Not my people," symbolizing God's rejection of his people. As with the other names, Hosea reverses the symbolic language of judgment to proclaim restoration, once again calling Israel "My people" (2:23).

(1:11), "Ammi" (2:1a), and "Ruhammah" (2:1b). Those sown back into the land ("Jezreel"), who are once again called "My People" ("Ammi")—these have received the mercy ("Ruhammah") of God!

Panel 2 (2:2–23)

2:2–13 "She is not My wife and I am not her husband." (Accusation against the Adulterous Mother)

Although not technically that of a courtroom setting, the imagery of accusation and rebuke brings to mind the drama of a legal dispute in Hosea 2:2–13.[12] Yet this is no standard trial. In a very odd manner, the children of an adulterous woman are called upon to rebuke their own mother. Here the analogy between Hosea's family and the nation of Israel remains intact. The focus is on Israel, and the children have come to represent the citizenry of a

---

[12] There may be some debate surrounding whether or not the statement in Hosea 2:2, "For she is not my wife and I am not her husband," is a legal decree of divorce (whether for Hosea and Gomer or for God and Israel). The text itself is not clear on either end, and, in any case, the language of reversal throughout Hosea suggests that the condition was not permanent. Rather than a declaration of divorce, it may be that the statement is simply affirming the condition of this broken relationship. Israel has played the harlot with the Baals, and now Yahweh, her husband, will give her over to her lovers. The language of abandonment saturates the oracle through verse thirteen.

corrupt nation. In an ironic twist, it is not the prophet who rebukes, nor is it God, but the citizens themselves are called upon to rebuke their adulterous mother Israel (2:2). The children of Israel had become "Lo-ammi," and were now expected to bring accusation against their mother for these disastrous results. Because of their mother, the children would receive no compassion (2:4), and as they followed the lead of their mother, so they would also experience judgment with her. The citizens of Israel are the offspring of an adulterous nation, and her sins have indeed become theirs. The remedy of repentance and restoration is as paradoxical as the charges introduced in 2:2. In effect, the "Israelites can become God's people only by renouncing Israel!"[13]

In addition to the language of abandonment, there is an emphasis in chapter two on agricultural provision. Through conscious repetition, Hosea lists the agricultural provisions that Israel had attributed to Baal (2:5), even though it was Yahweh who had provided them. To further heighten the imagery of unfaithfulness, Israel is described as taking those provisions given by God and then, quite ironically, preparing them for the ritual worship of Baal (2:8). Therefore, in abandoning Israel to her "lovers," God gives the people over to Baal, a suitor who cannot provide—who will leave her utterly forsaken (2:9–13).

2:14–23 "I WILL TAKE YOU TO BE MY WIFE FOREVER" (REVERSAL: A SALVATION ORACLE HIGHLIGHTING GOD'S RESTORED RELATIONSHIP WITH ISRAEL)

Although many recognize Hosea 2:14–23 as a distinct salvation oracle (often viewed as beginning in 2:16), the many points of allusion and repetition between chapters one and two indicate that they function together as a unit. However, this does not equate uniform tone and flavor. The language of abandonment in 2:2–13 reverses abruptly, beginning with 2:14, and continues to escalate toward a salvation climax in 2:23. In language reminiscent of Isaiah 40, Yahweh is depicted as a lover courting his beloved once again, speaking tenderly to her—speaking words of comfort and restoration (v. 14).

Typical of Hosea, the picture of God's comfort and restoration is enhanced by historical allusion. The Valley of Achor ("trouble"), deemed as

---

[13] Garrett, *Hosea, Joel*, 76.

such for the archetypical sin of Achan (Josh 7:26), has become a "gateway of hope,"—an avenue of return for the re-gathering of Israel. Furthering the sense of reversal, "in that day,"[14] Israel will call Yahweh "My husband" (*'ishi*) rather than "My Baal" (*ba`ali*), a transliterated term meaning "lord" or "master" (v. 16). It was certainly possible to describe a husband as a *ba`al*, or even to describe Yahweh as a *ba`al*. However, Baalism (in the proper sense of the term, referring to the worship of the Canaanite deity) would be removed so far from Israel that such confusion in language would no longer be possible (v. 17). The wordplay is obvious—God becomes more than a *ba`al* when the "Baals" are removed from Israel. Furthermore, the contrast between *'ishi* and *ba`ali*, both of which can refer to a husband, highlights reversal in the relationship between Yahweh and Israel. "In that day," the worship of Israel will be characterized by love and devotion rather than duty and fear.[15]

Continuing the marriage analogy, Yahweh will take Israel to be his "wife forever," his spouse in "righteousness, justice, love, and compassion" (v. 19). He will take his "wife in faithfulness," that she may "know" the Lord (v. 20). This is a future, new covenant expectation, not the present reality of unfaithful, eighth-century Israel.[16] As the oracle progresses with heightened expectation, Hosea looks forward to a day in which reversal will be complete, implemented by Yahweh alone (note the "I will" statements in this oracle). On "that day" God will respond (v. 21), and he will again refresh the land with provisions that Baal could not provide (note the repetition "grain, new wine, and oil" listed in 2:5–9).

Mirroring the imagery symbolized in the names of the three children, the oracle circles back to again reference "Jezreel" (v. 22). Conjuring a beautiful, two-sided picture of blessing, God first sows his people back into the land (v. 23) and then subsequently provides the produce from the land to sustain them (v. 21–22). Through the use of wordplay, the reversal of fortunes is fulfilled: the "Jezreel" of God's judgment has in fact become the

---

[14] "In that day" is a common eschatological marker that often introduces or escalates a salvation oracle. It is an abbreviated reference to the "Day of the Lord."

[15] Elizabeth Achtemeier, *Minor Prophets I*, Understanding the Bible Commentary Series (Grand Rapids, MI: Baker, 1996), 26–27.

[16] Tying this oracle to the rest of Hosea, it is significant that these same terms are used to indict Israel in the introduction to chapter four ("There is no truth, no faithful love, no knowledge of God in the land!").

"Jezreel" of God's blessing, and God has compassion on those once called "No Compassion" (v. 23). In climactic dialogue, God says to "Lo-ammi," "You are My People," and Lo-ammi responds, "You are my God!" (v. 23).

Panel 3 (3:1–5)

3:1–4 "You must live with me many days" (Prophetic Drama and a Prophet's Glimpse into the Future)

Moving from oracle back to prophetic drama, the circumstances of Hosea's life are again put in focus. With frustrating brevity, the reader is given a first person account of Hosea's reconciliation to Gomer. Although not mentioned by name, there is little doubt that the adulterous woman in 3:1 is Gomer. Also, while vague, the description of events in chapter three appear subsequent to the birth of the three children in chapter one. With those interpretive assumptions in mind, what is the point of God's command to "Go again; show love to a woman who is loved by another man and is an adulterer." (3:1)? The initial point of the analogy seems clear: to demonstrate the love that God has for adulterous Israel (3:1). In this the drama unfolds to reveal that Gomer was in need of redemption. The text does not explain what transpired to bring her to that point, or exactly what conditions led to her enslavement. It only reveals that she was purchased for a specific price, roughly the cost of a slave.[17] Furthermore, Hosea recounts the stark probation under which this relationship resumes (3:3). Gomer will live with Hosea for "many days." During this unspecified but lengthy period, Gomer is to remain chaste, and Hosea will abstain from any sexual relations with her.

Although the account of Hosea's life concludes there (without mention of the resumption of normal marital relations), the analogy is taken further and comprises one of the most significant prophetic snapshots of Israel's future in Scripture. Before the glory of the "last days" (v. 5), Israel will live for "many days" (v. 4) "without king or prince, without sacrifice or sacred

---

[17] The combined price of shekels and barley would have equaled to roughly thirty shekels, the price of a slave according to Exodus 21:32. See Hans Walter Wolff, *Hosea*, Hermeneia (Philadelphia, PA: Fortress Press, 1974), 61. Alternatively, Douglas Stuart argues that the amount equates to a "bride price" for eschatological Israel, Yahweh's new bride. See Douglas Stuart, *Hosea-Jonah*, WBC (Waco, TX: Word, 1987), 66.

pillar, and without ephod or household idols." Indeed, since her exile, to varying degrees, Israel has lived without the full implements of her national and religious systems. She has also been chaste; idolatry was cleansed from the land following the Babylonian exile, and Israel has largely remained zealous in her rejection of paganism since then.[18] From the exile forward, she has not had a king or prince, but has lived under the political domination of foreign kings. Although the temple was rebuilt under Zerubbabel, and the law was reinstituted under Ezra, Israel has remained in a religious and political state of limbo, still waiting for her kingdom to come.[19]

3:5 "In the last days" (God's Eschatological Restoration of Israel)

The language of Hosea 3:5 is terse yet profound, providing prophetic confirmation of Davidic headship "in the last days." While some question the inclusion of "David their king" as a later addition, this is unnecessary. Hosea, as a true prophet, affirms the same Davidic theology as Isaiah, Jeremiah, and Ezekiel, a theology based in the covenant God made with David (2 Sam 7:12–16).[20] Furthermore, the language of Israel's blessing "in the last days" is a thread that runs throughout the Old Testament. Isaiah and Micah saw the conditions of kingdom blessing "in the last days" (Isa 2:2–4; Mic 4:1–3), and Jacob framed his blessings (including messianic strains pertaining to Judah) as occurring "in the latter days" (Gen 49:1, 9–12 NKJV). Balaam prophesied of Israel's dominion "in the latter days" (Num 24:14–19 NKJV), and Moses warned of evil that would befall Israel "in the latter days" (Deut 31:29 NKJV). The prophets indeed were prophets and, as such, could predict the future. Even if the primary function of the prophets was to proclaim the word of God to their contemporaries (as forth-tellers), this does not diminish their role to proclaim the future as foretellers. In this most powerful statement of Israel's future hope, Hosea does exactly that.

---

[18] This is quite startling given the influence of the Persians, Greeks, and Romans upon her society.

[19] With the destruction of the temple in AD 70, the hope of normal religious activity was further diminished.

[20] See as examples Isaiah 11:1; Jeremiah 23:5; 33:15; and Ezekiel 37:24–25.

Panel 4 (4:1–6:1–3)

4:1–5:14 "no truth, no faithful love, and no knowledge of God in the land" (The Legal Case against Israel)

Chapter four marks a clear break in Hosea. Although there are allusions back to the prophetic drama of chapters 1–3, especially in reference to the motif of spiritual adultery, Hosea 4–14 never again references Hosea's biographical situation. Rather, the text demonstrates the depth of Israel's guilt, the consequential abandonment of Israel, and the Lord's restoration of his bride. Throughout chapters 4–14, repetition, wordplay, and threaded motifs provide continuity between alternating panels of judgment and salvation.

Chapter four is introduced with a "charge" (*riv*) brought against the "inhabitants of the land" (4:1a, NKJV), laying out three distinct statements of indictment: "There is no truth, no faithful love, and no knowledge of God in the land!" (4:1b). Chapters four and five evoke courtroom imagery as evidence for these charges is set forth. That there is no "truth" (*'emet*) is evidenced by Israel's lack of spiritual integrity; not only do her citizens curse and lie to one another (4:2a), their leaders are "like those who move boundary markers" (5:10), who are "determined to follow what is worthless" (5:11).[21] That there is no "faithful love" (*hesed*) between individuals is clear, given the killing, stealing, and bloodshed typical in the land (4:2). That there is no *hesed* toward God is equally clear, given Israel's wanton betrayal of the Lord (5:7a). Finally, it is charged that there is no knowledge (*da`at*) of God in the land. This fact is enhanced through repeated emphasis in the indictments that follow. The people are destroyed for a lack of knowledge because the priests of Israel neglected to impart the knowledge of the Lord (4:6). The "spirit of promiscuity is among them," for "they do not know the Lord" (5:4). With prophetic fervor, Hosea delineates the consequences of spiritual ignorance: "A people that lacks understanding will come to ruin!" (4:14b NET).

---

[21] Note that the "princes of Judah" (5:10a) are structurally parallel to "Ephraim" (5:11a), suggesting that the Judah reference is original to the Hosea book.

"No truth, no faithful love, no knowledge of God"		
אמת	emet	"firmness, faithfulness, truth"
חסד	hesed	"goodness, kindness"
דעת	da`at	"knowledge"

Throughout chapters four and five, Hosea merges the literal and meta-phorical senses of what it meant to commit adultery. The people went after the idols of Baal, committing spiritual adultery against their God (4:12). But in the worship of Baal, the people themselves committed literal prosti-tution, engaging in sexual promiscuity associated with Canaanite fertility rites and worship practices.[22] And thus Hosea describes the rites of cultic, physical promiscuity in conjunction with the act of spiritual adultery. The daughters of Israel engaged in cultic prostitution on the high places where Baal was worshipped (4:13), and the men of Israel joined themselves to cultic prostitutes as a sacrifice to Baal (4:14). All the while, the Lord brought judgment against Israel. In an ironic twist, their worship of Baal, the god of agricultural fertility, brought hunger and drought, and though they made a ritual act of sex-ual intercourse, they could not pro-duce offspring to replenish their own population (4:10).

The priests in Israel were charged with the responsibility of bringing

Baalism and Cultic Prostitution

In Semitic languages, the term *baal* means "owner," "master," or "lord." It was also the name of a god in ancient Near Eastern cultures who rose to prominence in the Canaanite pantheon. He was the god of fertility for the land and its occupants. Sexual rites characterized Baal worship and the temples of Baal employed cultic prostitutes.

---

[22] For further discussion of the issue of the concept of "sacred prostitution" in ancient Near Eastern religions, see Richard S. Hess, *Israelite Religions: An Archaeological and Biblical Survey* (Grand Rapids, MI: Baker, 2007), 332–35. Texts like Hosea 4:14; Genesis 38:15, 21–22, Deuteronomy 23:17–18 reflect that prostitutes served at cultic sites, but the nature of their activity is debated. Prostitution may have simply been a means of providing income for the cult rather than serving as a means of securing fertility from the gods.

the knowledge of God to the people. However, chapter five brings a charge of guilt against the priests for not knowing the Lord. Guilty charges are also brought against the king, suggesting the noble's role in shepherding the flock of Israel (v. 4). Even the guilt of Judah does not go unnoticed (v. 5b). On five occasions Judah is referenced in the chapter (5:5, 10, 12, 13, 14), and in each case the references to Judah are intertwined through the structure of the text, suggesting that these are original to the book. The indictment of both sides of the divided kingdom provides a precursor to the eventual reunification of the kingdoms (1:11). As such, the references to Judah in chapter five should not be viewed as secondary additions, but as integral to the theological message of Hosea.

5:15 "I will depart" (Prophetic Glimpse of Intermediary Distance)

Using the imagery of a lion that has carried off its prey (v. 14), and later returns to its lair (v. 15a), the analogy shifts from judgment to probation. This is reminiscent of the description of Hosea's redemption of Gomer in the prophetic drama (3:4). The lion has returned to its lair, and now Israel must await its day of restoration.

5:15 "they will search" (Prophetic Glimpse of Restoration)

As God departs, Israel searches in vain to find him. Only when the nation repents will the Lord be found. Mirroring the picture of redemption in 3:5, Israel finds the Lord only when she seeks the true knowledge of the Lord.

6:1–3 "Come, let us return" (Call to Repentance [Now]: A Glimpse Ahead to Eschatological Restoration [Later])

While chapter five concludes with the expectation of future repentance, chapter six opens with a present tense call to repentance. Although Israel would not, in Hosea's day, return to the Lord (7:10), the prophet nevertheless pleaded the case. If Israel would return, Yahweh would heal (6:1a) rather than wound (6:1b; see 5:12–13); he would bind rather than tear (note the reversal of the imagery of the lion tearing its prey; see 5:14).

Hosea envisions the results of repentance, enhanced with escalating numerical parallelism: "He will revive us after two days, and on the third day He will raise us up" (6:2). Although Israel is ultimately redeemed through the work of Christ, there is nothing in the context or the language of Hosea 6:2 to suggest that this is a prophecy regarding the resurrection of Christ.[23] Rather, Hosea is building an expectation of promise and blessing. If Israel were to pursue the knowledge of God (6:3a), returning to the Lord (6:1a), she could expect that God would be faithful to respond. He would come with the certainty of the dawn (6:3). Furthering the metaphor, God's faithfulness is described as the seasonal rains, a regular, expected climatological phenomenon in the land of Israel.[24]

Panel 5 (6:4–11:11)

6:4–11:7 "THEY SOW THE WIND AND REAP THE WHIRLWIND" (MUSINGS OF JUDGMENT: HISTORICAL REFLECTION AND ORACLES OF JUDGMENT)

Following a brief call to repentance, Hosea reverts to judgment speeches, reflecting on past and present events to sustain the case for judgment. In addition to historical reflection, the collection of speeches within these chapters includes a rich and vast array of metaphors to describe Israel's guilt and God's wrath. The metaphors often carry throughout the book, using contrast and comparison to heighten the effect. Transitioning from the call to repentance (6:1–3) back to a judgment speech (6:4–6), God's faithfulness is contrasted with the unfaithfulness of Ephraim (a synecdoche for Israel used often in Hosea) and Judah (parallel to Ephraim). While Yahweh's *hesed* is as certain as the dawn and should be expected like the seasonal rains (6:3), Israel's *hesed* ("loyalty" HCSB) is as unreliable as the morning dew, vanishing away with the parting of the dawn (6:4). Israel's *hesed* is as disappointing as a morning cloud that comes prior to the rainy season. Although it evokes an anticipation of life-giving rains, it departs only to leave the land parched under the searing sun.

---

[23] This is not to suggest that interpreters have never understood Hosea 6:2 as a reference to resurrection. For an excursus of historical approaches to Hosea 6:2 and the question of resurrection, especially in view of 1 Corinthians 15:4, see Wolff, *Hosea*, 117–18.

[24] In an agrarian world prone to drought and dependent on seasonal rain, the ancient Israelites were very much aware of seasonal patterns. During the rainy season (Oct–April), it was important that the early rains came to allow seeds to germinate, while the later rains were important to bring the crops to maturity prior to harvest. See "Rain," in the *Dictionary of Biblical Imagery* (Downers Grove, IL: InterVarsity, 1998), 694.

While Hosea 6:1–3 is distinguished from 6:4–6 by tone and person (note the third person shift back to first person), the metaphors retain continuity. Additionally, the words of the text continue to play off of one another. Although Israel lacked *hesed*, it was *hesed* that God desired (6:6a). In Hosea 6:3, Israel is called to pursue the knowledge (*da`at*) of Yahweh. It is not sacrifice, but rather the knowledge of God that brings the only hope of averting impending doom (6:5–6).

Hosea 7:3–7 pictures the corruption of Israel as an oven heated by a baker, consuming the rulers of Israel. The interpretive details of the allegory are difficult to discern, but the allusion to the political intrigue of the final years of the northern kingdom of Israel is clear. Four of Israel's last six kings were assassinated by conspirators (2 Kgs 15:10, 14, 25, 30), and Israel's final decades were characterized by political opportunism and corruption.[25] Although they rose up to commit murder among themselves and called on foreign powers to save them (7:11), they never once called upon the one King who could save them (7:7).

Following the imagery of the baker, and even the political and religious syncretism of Ephraim is compared to a half-baked cake, one that the baker failed to turn (7:8, NKJV). Furthermore, the corruption of Ephraim is compared to gray hairs on an aging head (7:9). Much like the aging process, which is not seen day to day but is apparent over time (as a picture album will attest), so the religious corruption of Israel permeates in gradual, unnoticed sequence.[26] The ignorance of Israel is central to the point of these metaphors;[27] like a cake burning on one side (though not apparent on the other), or like gray hairs on an aging man, so the decay of Israel consumes, even though "he did not notice."

Moreover, Ephraim is compared to a "senseless dove" (7:11), while God is compared to the bird catcher (7:12) and an eagle descending from above (8:1). The "senseless dove," flittering between alliances with Egypt and Assyria, should have been confident in the Lord's protection. Ironically, as

---

[25] For a brief summary of potential historical referents, see David Allen Hubbard, *Hosea*, TOTC 24 (Downers Grove, IL: InterVarsity), 142–46.

[26] For an alternate interpretation understanding "gray hairs" as "hairs of mold" on stale bread (thus continuing the baker's cake metaphor), see Garrett, *Hosea, Joel*, 170.

[27] Achtemeier, *Minor Prophets I*, 59.

a result of her alliances *with* these powers for protection *from* these powers, Israel "will return to Egypt" and eat "unclean food" in Assyria (9:3).

Israel is furthermore described as a "faulty bow," ever aiming, but never hitting the target (7:16). She is described as a donkey in heat, going after her foreign "lovers" (8:9), and her promiscuity is enacted "on every grain-threshing floor" (9:1). Therefore, in an ironic twist, the threshing floor will not sustain, it will not feed them (9:2). Metaphors such as these, and many others, permeate the text of Hosea 6:4–10:15, providing rhetorical continuity throughout these judgment speeches. In summary, because Israel has "sown the wind" of folly, she will "reap the whirlwind" of judgment (8:7).

Although the Hosea book is characterized by the metaphor that follows the story of Hosea's marriage, Hosea 11:1–7 introduces a new metaphor, portraying God as the Father of a rebellious son. This segment of Hosea is notorious for interpretive difficulties, and the "fulfillment" of 11:1 presents its own set of challenges (see Matt 2:15).[28] Yet the central point of the metaphor is clear: while God loved Israel as a father loves his son, the child was ungrateful, rebelling against the father who cared for him. This father/son relationship began with the historical exodus out of Egypt, but due to rebellion, will culminate in exile. Although God "lifted the yoke from their neck" (11:4 NET),[29] and "bent down to give them food" (v. 4), Israel was "bent on turning" from God (v. 7a). Therefore they would be placed under the yoke of the king of Assyria (v. 5).

---

[28] Matthew's use of Hosea 11:1 is not a matter of standard exegesis, for it is clear that Hosea was referring to a past event in the history of Israel, not predicting a future event in the life of Messiah. However, Hosea develops a pattern moving from past exodus (11:1) to future exodus (11:10–11), and Matthew furthers the pattern as he applies it to Jesus. In this sense, Matthew's recognition of a theological pattern fulfilled in Christ infers more than simple analogy; Jesus is the fulfillment of a typological pattern understood by the prophet himself. See Garrett, *Hosea, Joel*, 220–22; and Craig L. Blomberg, "Matthew," in *Commentary on the New Testament Use of the Old Testament* (Grand Rapids, MI: Baker, 2007), 7–8.

[29] While most translations see in verse four a shift to animal imagery, others emend the Masoretic Text to retain the imagery of a child ("I was to them like those who lift infants to their cheeks"; NRSV). For the exegetical argument favoring this translation, see Wolff, *Hosea*, 199–200.

10:12 "Sow righteousness for yourselves and reap faithful love"" (A Call to Repentance)

With the same agricultural imagery used to announce judgment, Hosea shifts the metaphor to call Israel to repentance. Israel is a "trained heifer," equipped to plow righteousness (10:11), but she has instead plowed wickedness and reaped injustice (10:13). Bringing the imagery home to his audience, Hosea now calls Israel to sow righteousness and reap *hesed*, or "faithful love" (v. 12a). Although this call to repentance does not conclude one segment or begin another, it nevertheless functions as a reminder of God's inclination to forgive.

11:8–11 "How can I give you up, Ephraim?" (Musings of Salvation)

The extended judgment speeches that began with Hosea 6:4 now reach a conclusion as the panel shifts from judgment to salvation, a precursor to the final oracle of salvation that concludes the book (14:1–8). The rhetorical questions of 11:8 set the tonal shift from judgment to salvation, and as the heart of God muses, his compassion is stirred. Although Israel will experience judgment, she will also experience future restoration. As surely as God is God (v. 9), he will call his people from captivity, reestablishing them in their homes (implied dwelling in the land; v. 11). In a masterful use of metaphor, Hosea reverses negative images of judgment and presents them as positive points in anticipation of future deliverance. The God who in wrath is described as a roaring lion tearing apart his prey (5:14–15; 13:7–8) is now described as a lioness "roaring" to call her cubs home (11:10). Israel, who was once described as a "senseless dove" flittering between Egypt and Assyria (7:11), is now described as a dove flying home from foreign lands to again dwell in the land of God's possession (11:11).

Panel 6 (11:12–14:8)

11:12–13:16 "Therefore they forgot Me" (Musings of Judgment: Historical Reflection and Oracles of Judgment)

In a manner typical of Hosea, reflections on future blessing are abruptly shifted by the reminder of present sin. Returning to the language of indictment, Hosea describes Ephraim as encircling God with lies (11:12a; allusion back to "no truth" in 4:1), and feeding on the wind (12:1a; allusion back to reaping "the whirlwind" in 8:7). While the preceding salvation oracle envisioned a day when Israel would return from Egypt and Assyria (11:11), the reader is again reminded that in Hosea's day Israel was engaged in making "covenant" alliances with these same foreign powers (12:1b).[30] And while Israel remains the focal point of Hosea's warning, Judah is not exempt (11:12b).[31]

As in earlier judgment speeches, Hosea continues to be characterized by historical reflection and metaphor. Historical reflections include Jacob's struggle with Esau (12:3; see Gen 25:26), supporting the charge that Israel has from its inception been full of deceit (11:12). In his struggle with God (12:3; see Gen 32:24–29), Jacob was a precursor to a struggle that would continue to Hosea's day, and as God spoke to Jacob at Bethel (12:4; see Gen 28:10–19), so God was continuing to call his people to repentance (12:5–6).[32] The God who brought Israel out of Egypt would again have her dwell in tents, perhaps reflecting the judgment of the wilderness wanderings (12:9). Although Israel has sojourned before (12:12), through the ministry of a prophet (Moses) she found deliverance (12:13). God was now attempting to lead Israel through the mouth of another prophet, Hosea (12:10).

Metaphors throughout this section of Hosea include the description of Israel (and its idols) as morning mist, early dew, chaff, and smoke (13:3), all evoking the image of transience. God is described as a lion, a leopard, and a bear—wild beasts who will tear Israel up in fury (13:7–8). In an odd and somewhat obscure metaphor, Israel is described as an unwise son who is unwilling to come forth from the womb when the time for delivery has

---

[30] Note the irony in God's "covenant" people making "covenants" with foreign powers. The covenant under which Israel was governed ensured their destruction for such covenant unfaithfulness (Deuteronomy 4:25–29).

[31] Some English translations render the second half of 11:12 as a positive affirmation of Judah, suggesting that Judah, unlike Ephraim, still "walks" with Yahweh (NKJV, ESV, NRSV, NLT, and NET). Others render this as a statement against Judah, suggesting that Judah "wanders" from Yahweh and is drawn toward false gods (NIV, NASB). The HCSB is ambiguous, translating the verse, "Judah still wanders with God and is faithful to the holy ones."

[32] Embedded within chapter twelve is a brief call to repentance following the historical reflection of Jacob's struggle with God at Bethel. This is similar to other calls to repentance, but here it is directly linked to the historical illustration at hand.

come (13:13). Although Israel should be drawn to life, in its obstinacy, it chooses to die in the womb.

Two especially difficult verses are found in this panel that may or may not reflect abrupt transition between judgment and mercy, depending on the interpretive conclusions reflected across English translations. The first among these is Hosea 13:9. The first line in this verse is straightforward, but the second line is variously translated as representing God as either destroyer or redeemer. The HCSB renders the verse, "I will destroy you, Israel; you have no help but Me," retaining a certain degree of neutrality in the second line. The NKJV implies a reversal of judgment in its translation: "O Israel, you are destroyed, But your help *is* from Me" implying that God will move from judgment to salvation based upon his own covenant love for Israel. The NASB takes another track, translating 13:9, "*It is* your destruction, O Israel, That *you are* against Me, against your help," implying that responsibility for Israel's judgment rests on the shoulders of her obstinacy. The NET Bible translates the verse, "I will destroy you, O Israel! Who is there to help you?" This translation suggests that Israel will not find help from its king or any other alliances it may make with foreign kings. The Hebrew text of Hosea is notoriously laden with difficult grammatical constructions and textual oddities that create exegetical challenges in translation.[33]

The second and perhaps more complex example is Hosea 13:14. There are generally two interpretive options, the first viewing this as an outburst of hope and expectation of deliverance, and the second viewing verse fourteen as a continuation of the judgment speech that precedes and follows. The first option is reflected by the HCSB, KJV, NKJV, and NIV. The HCSB reads:

I will ransom them from the power of Sheol.
I will redeem them from death.
Death, where are your barbs?
Sheol, where is your sting?
Compassion is hidden from My eyes.

---

[33] Although the focus of our exposition is on literary technique, it is worth noting the importance of comparing translations for English Bible readers. Differences in translation tend to act as "red flags," indicating exegetical or text-based issues that may be significant. Perhaps no book of the Bible is more laden with issues in translation than the book of Hosea. For a survey of verses that defy uniform agreement among translations, see Hosea 4:4; 6:11; 7:14, 16; 8:10–11; 11:2, 5, 7, 12; 12:7; 13:9, 14.

The obvious difficulty with this translation is that the last line clearly states the Lord will not show compassion to Israel. The NIV remedies this by placing the last line with verse fifteen, making it the introduction to the resumed judgment speech.

Some translations avoid an overtly positive or negative translation by rendering the first four lines as rhetorical questions. This approach is reflected by the NASB, NRSV, and ESV. Through the use of rhetorical question, the interpretive thrust of these statements is left rather ambiguous. Other translations frame the first two lines as rhetorical questions but add negative answers and then frame the third and fourth lines as a call for personified death to bring its plagues, thus taking a negative stance (NLT, NET, and CEV). In this view, the final line flows seamlessly with the preceding lines of the verse. This is perhaps best seen in the NET:

> Will I deliver them from the power of Sheol? No, I will not!
> Will I redeem them from death? No, I will not!
> O Death, bring on your plagues!
> O Sheol, bring on your destruction!
> My eyes will not show any compassion!

As seen above, translations are quite varied, reflecting the interpretive difficulties within the Hebrew text and the uncertain flow of Hosea's speech. Nevertheless, either interpretive approach, whether positive or negative, fits well with the general thrust of Hosea's message.[34]

14:1–3 "Israel, return to Yahweh your God" (A Call to Repentance)

In a final call to repentance, as a precursor to the envisioned salvation of "Orphan Israel" (14:3 NET), Hosea puts the very words of repentance into the mouth of God's wayward nation. In so doing, Yahweh ensures that he—not Assyria, not horses, nor idols—he himself will save.

---

[34] Furthermore, Paul's use of a portion of Hosea 13:14 in 1 Corinthians 15:55 is clear. Whatever the approach taken to the translation of Hosea 13:14, there is nothing lost to the theology of either Hosea or Paul.

14:4–8 "I will freely love them" (Musings of Salvation)

In a closing oracle of salvation, Hosea describes God's restorative and nurturing relationship to Israel. Based in the "return" (*shuv*) of Israel to Yahweh (14:1a), God will heal Israel, love them freely, and "turn" (*shuv*) his anger away (14:4). The wordplay in 14:1–4 is significant; not only does Hosea capitalize on the varied application of the verb *shuv*, he also highlights Israel's healing from their "apostate" (*meshuvatah*) condition (v. 4a). This is reflected in the use of a noun (*meshuvatah*) based in the same root as the surrounding verbs (*shuv*).

Earlier in the book, the metaphor of "dew" was used negatively to describe Israel's vanishing faithfulness (6:4) and impending destruction (13:3). Now, instead of transience, the metaphor evokes the nourishing characteristics of morning dew; God will nourish Israel as the dew nourishes the land, resulting in the growth and produce of God's goodness and provision (14:4–7).

Shifting from first person (14:4–5a) to third person (14:5b–7), the oracle reverts again in conclusion with God addressing Israel in a direct and forthright manner (14:8). Through rhetorical question, God affirms their abandonment of idols (v. 8a), and confirms that he alone is the One from whom they derive their sustenance (v. 8d) and the shade of protection (v. 8b–c). Earlier, Hosea describes the worship of Baal under the trees adorning the high places, for their "shade is pleasant" (4:13). Now God is the "luxuriant cypress" under which shelter is found (NET).

14:9 (A Word to the Wise—A Wisdom Postscript)

Hosea ends with a wisdom postscript exhorting his readers toward understanding. It is not simply a matter of Hosea encouraging his readers to think hard about his message. While it is true that the Hebrew text of Hosea is "subtle, allusive, elliptical, and at times obscure," this is not the reason for Hosea's final word of exhortation.[35] Rather, Hosea uses a proverbial postscript to direct his readers toward the "knowledge of the Lord," the very thing that was missing in the spiritual and political leadership of Israel. In his conclusion, Hosea effectively captures the heart of Hebrew wisdom found in Proverbs 1:7, "The fear of the Lord is the beginning of knowledge;

---

[35] Garrett, *Hosea, Joel*, 281–82.

fools despise wisdom and discipline." The inference to the message of Hosea is clear: the wise will find the knowledge of God by his word, but fools will despise the prophetic word.[36]

Theological Message and Application of Hosea

The theological message of Hosea is wrapped in the clothes of metaphor, and the central metaphor of Hosea involves the image and repercussions of adultery. Idolatry is the focal point of Israel's guilt, and the theology of Hosea strains to communicate the depth to which Israel's unfaithfulness affects God. The metaphor and the message of the book are not simply about wayward Israel—it is, in fact, a book about the suffering of God and the extent to which the sins of his people affect him. The prophetic drama of Hosea's marriage reflects this clearly, as "the pain in the heart of the prophet became a parable of the anguish in the heart of God."[37]

The guilt of idolatry is not merely supported by Hosea's dramatic circumstances; as a prophet, Hosea proclaims Israel's guilt and announces the consequences of her unfaithfulness. Various forms of the Hebrew word for prostitution can be found throughout the book of Hosea, with twelve of those occurrences found in chapters four and five.[38] The wayward leadership of mother Israel, represented by her political and religious institutions, along with her children, the common folk of the land, have together joined themselves to idols (4:17) and dealt "treacherously with the Lord" (5:7; 6:7 NKJV).[39]

Due to Israel's unfaithfulness, Yahweh, the jilted husband, will bring judgment against his wayward spouse. Consequently, the book of Hosea is stacked with judgment speeches picturing the consequences of Israel's sin.

---

[36] On the postscript of Hosea functioning as a motto for the book of the Twelve, and as a bridge between Hosea and Joel, see Christopher R. Seitz, *Prophecy and Hermeneutics: Toward a New Introduction to the Prophets* (Grand Rapids, MI: Baker, 2007), 126, 215.

[37] James Limburg, *Hosea-Micah*, Interpretation (Louisville, KY: Westminster John Knox, 2011), 10.

[38] J. Daniel Hays, *The Message of the Prophets* (Grand Rapids, MI: Zondervan, 2010), 270.

[39] A distinction should be made in the central metaphor of the book between the mother (political/religious Israel) and her children (the people of Israel). Both are guilty of idolatry, but it is the mother who has led her children astray. See Garrett, *Hosea, Joel*, 39–40.

Hebrew Words for Adultery Found in Hosea	
Naaph	3:1; 4:2, 13–14; 7:4
Naaphuph	2:2, 4
Zanah	1:2; 2:5, 7; 3:3; 4:10, 12–15, 18; 5:3; 9:1
Zenunim	1:2; 2:2, 4, 12; 5:4
Zenuth	4:11; 6:10
Zuwr	5:7; 7:9; 8:7, 12

Indictment turns to sentencing, and the wrath of God is displayed in full measure by the language of the prophet. God suffers as a jilted husband precisely because he loves his wayward spouse and her children. Although they had no *hesed* love for God, nevertheless he cannot deny his *hesed* love for them. And thus the tension between God's sense of justice and his desire for mercy is put on full display throughout the book of Hosea. Perhaps the reader learns more about the heart of God through Hosea than anywhere else in the Old Testament. Yahweh is pulled between judgment and mercy, and indeed, his people do receive judgment; the institutions of the promiscuous mother, Israel, are for a time eliminated from the land (3:4). Yet in the end, his *hesed* love wins, and Israel is ultimately (and eschatologically) restored back into her land. Her children will come home (1:11; 2:23; 3:5), and her governance will submit faithfully to one ruler (1:11), one God (2:23), and one Lord (3:5). Indeed, she will be reunited with her one Husband, and she will remember the names of the Baals no more (2:17).

The book of Hosea strikes the reader as theologically intimate, providing deep insight into the heart of God. Therefore, one might forego the practical, focusing only on the theological message of the book. Yet with a little reflection, one can draw broad principles for application from the message of Hosea. And with further inspection, many of the particulars within the book will strike right to the heart of the reader.

The sin of idolatry must be considered in any application of the book. Hosea is not the only Old Testament prophet to speak out against idolatry, but no prophet describes the impact of this sin in quite the same manner as Hosea. Idolatry is not simply a breach of contractual agreement. Idolatry is spiritual adultery—a breach of the most intimate kind. It is this image that

God uses to describe the practice of idol worship. How often do we consider spiritual unfaithfulness as an intimate breach of relationship, as an affront to the God we adore?

The ancient Israelites were pulled toward idols that would promise fertility of land and womb. For the hope of crops and offspring, the people traded the God who was Lord over everything for a god who was as transient as the seasons. Although modern western man may balk at the notion of worshipping idols of wood, silver, and gold, the New Testament clearly equates the worship of money, possessions, and any other thing that comes before God as idolatry (Eph 5:5; Col 3:5).[40] This ought to be a sober warning for modern believers, where temptation to follow the "idols" of our day is as pervasive as the temptation to follow Baal was in Hosea's time.[41] In Hosea's day, the prevailing culture lied by ensuring prosperity through the worship of Baal. In our day, culture lies in worshipping prosperity itself.

Second, we would be remiss if we failed to recognize the grace of God as a primary teaching point in the book of Hosea. Although the people failed to demonstrate *hesed* to God and fellow man, God was steadfast in his "faithful love" toward Israel. Hosea's presentation of God is not one that ignores, lessens, or trivializes sin. The anger of God over sin is on full display in Hosea, and the consequences of sin are clearly stated the many judgment speeches within the book. Yet one cannot help but see the tension between God's sense of justice and his desire for mercy based on his *hesed* love for wayward Israel. Although Israel has of her own accord "reap[ed] the whirlwind" (8:7), God still has a hope and a future for Israel, and her children will one day be called "Sons of the living God" (1:10). By extension, the same *hesed* that will bring reversal to the fortunes of Israel now brings salvation to those whom God calls (Rom 9:24–26), even those who call upon the name of the Lord (Rom 10:13).

---

[40] Paul lived in a world where idols of silver, stone, and gold were still worshipped in a pervasive manner. And yet for the New Testament church, his warning was not oriented around the temptations of the Greco-Roman pantheon, but rather, the temptations of possessions.

[41] Although Western culture rejects idolatry in the traditional sense, this is not universally true in the modern world. Considering the idols of Hinduism and various Eastern sects, the worship of idols attracts a higher number of devotees today than at any other time in history.

Finally, it is worth noting that the conclusion of the book itself prompts the reader to action. The wise will find in the words of Hosea the knowledge of the Lord. This knowledge is not simply intellectual, but it is relational. The book of Hosea is calling the reader into renewed relationship with Yahweh. The wise will understand this as the message of Hosea.

6

The Book of Joel

Introduction

In the aftermath of the terrorist attacks on September 11, 2001, media outlets reported that church attendance in America increased by as much as 25 percent. This upsurge in religious interest unfortunately had little lasting impact and, after finding initial comfort during a time of crisis, people quickly settled back into their old patterns of religious devotion. The book of Joel reveals a turning to God following a time of national calamity in ancient Israel—a severe locust plague. The people's apparent repentance led the Lord to bring blessing in the place of judgment (Joel 2:18–27). Israel's history could have looked much different had the kind of response to the prophetic word that is modeled in Joel 2 been more frequent.

The prophet Joel, whose name means "Yahweh is God," is not mentioned elsewhere in the Old Testament, and the book provides few clues as to its precise date and setting. Dates for Joel range from the ninth century

BC through the postexilic period, as late as the fourth century BC. The view taken here is that Joel's ministry most likely took place in the postexilic period, though any conclusions on date and setting are tentative at best.

Joel prophesies in the aftermath of a terrible locust plague that has ruined the land and its crops. He proclaims the locust plague is just the beginning of judgment and that another "Day of the LORD is near" (1:15). Joel calls for sacred assembly and fasting so the people might repent of their sinful ways and return to the Lord. When the people respond positively to these calls for repentance, the threats of judgment turn into promises of blessing. The Lord promises to reverse the agricultural ruin of the land and even to "repay" his people for the years that the locusts have eaten (2:25). These immediate blessings associated with restoring the land's fertility are merely the prelude to Israel's ultimate restoration, when the Lord will pour out his Spirit on his people, deliver them from the nations that seek to destroy them, and bless them with permanent peace and prosperity.

Locust plagues are a common occurrence in the Middle East, so this detail offers no help in dating the book. The location of Joel near the beginning of the Twelve is more likely for thematic reasons than chronological ones. The end of Joel (3:16, 18) closely parallels the beginning and end of Amos (Amos 1:2; 9:13). Joel was also likely placed at the front of this collection because of its focus on the Day of the Lord and the fact that Joel 2:12–17 provides the paradigmatic response of repentance that the Lord desired from his people. The earlier dates assigned to Joel are problematic in light of the reference to the captivity of the people in 3:2–3.

The fact that the temple is standing and operational (see 1:9, 13–14, 16; 2:17) also precludes a date from 586–516 BC, between its destruction and rebuilding. Joel speaks in 3:2–3 of the Dispersion of Jews into foreign lands as having already occurred, which seems to require a date for the book no earlier than after the fall of Samaria and the northern kingdom in 722 BC. Many date the book just prior to the Babylonian invasion of Judah in 605 BC or the final fall of Jerusalem in 586 BC. They understand Joel's warnings of the coming "Day of the LORD" (see 1:15; 2:1) as referring to the coming of the Babylonian army. Zephaniah also warns that "the Day of the LORD is near" in connection with the Babylonian crisis (see Zeph 1:14–18).

Other evidence more specifically suggests, even if not conclusively proving, a postexilic setting for the book. Joel lacks a reference to the king or monarchy and offers no polemic against idol worship. There are more than a dozen intertextual references to other prophetic texts in Joel, but use of this evidence for dating purposes is problematic because of the difficulty in determining the direction of influence. Baker notes, however, that the quotation of Obadiah 17 in Joel 2:32, with the additional "as the Lord promised," would seem to indicate that Joel followed Obadiah, who likely writes in the aftermath of the fall of Jerusalem (see Introduction to Obadiah).[1]

The enemies of Judah mentioned in the book—Tyre, Sidon, and Philistia (3:4) as well as Egypt and Edom (3:19)—are not of great help in dating the book because all of these nations had long histories of conflict with Israel and Judah. The lack of any reference to Assyria and Babylon is more difficult to explain in a preexilic context. The fact that Tyre, Sidon, and Philistia had sold Jewish captives as slaves to the Greeks (3:6) could have occurred before or after the fall of Jerusalem. The Greeks had a greater presence in the Near East during the Persian period but would also have had contact with the region in the seventh and eighth centuries.[2] The prime example of Edom's violence to Judah was its participation with Babylon in the assault on Jerusalem (see Ps 137:7–9; Obadiah 10–16; Ezek 25:12–14; Lam 4:21–22).

A date for Joel's ministry of about 500 BC or shortly thereafter seems the most plausible option. The temple is in operation, but enough time has passed since its dedication that the leaders and people have once again slipped in their commitment to the Lord. Other postexilic prophets reflect that disobedience and spiritual lethargy remained a problem even after the people returned to the land. The reference to armies (or locusts) scaling the wall of the city in 2:7 is figurative and does not require the book, if postexilic, to have been written after Nehemiah's rebuilding of the walls of Jerusalem in 445 BC, as some have argued.[3] There are no clear connections between Joel and Malachi or Ezra-Nehemiah that would make a strong argument for dating Joel at the same time as these figures. The destruction

---

[1] David W. Baker, *Joel, Obadiah, Malachi*, NIVAC (Grand Rapids, MI: Zondervan, 2006), 26.

[2] Duane A. Garrett, *Hosea, Joel: An Exegetical and Theological Exposition of Scripture*, NAC (Nashville, TN: B&H, 1997), 292.

[3] Leslie C. Allen, *The Books of Joel, Obadiah, Jonah and Micah*, NICOT (Grand Rapids, MI: Eerdmans, 1976), 23.

of Sidon (see 3:4) by the Persians in 345 BC indicates that the book was composed before this time.[4]

Fortunately, the message of Joel concerning how the Lord responds to the penitent prayers of the people or the Lord's promises for Israel's future are in no way impacted by the exact date and setting of the book. If the book was composed in part as a liturgical text in connection with Judah's sacred assembly, the lack of historical precision would allow for its repeated usage in other crises facing the people of God.

Locusts or Armies or Both?

The relationship between chapters one and two in Joel is perhaps the most difficult interpretive issue in the book. As already noted, Joel carried out his ministry in the aftermath of a devastating locust plague. Interpreters are divided as to whether the locusts described in 1:3–6 and 2:2–11 refer to actual insects, to human armies, or to both. One view sees human armies in both chapters, another sees locusts in both chapters, and a third view sees the description of a past locust plague in chapter one and the warning of an imminent invasion by an enemy army (either human forces or an apocalyptic army) in chapter two. This debate is created in part by the fact that human armies are metaphorically compared to locusts in other biblical texts (see Judg 6:5; 7:12; Jer 46:23; 51:14).[5] The focus on the destruction of crops and subsequent food shortages in Joel 1 strongly suggests that an actual locust invasion is in view in that chapter. The Lord had warned through Moses that he would send the covenant curses of famine, crop failure, and locust plague if the people failed to keep his commands (Deut 28:38–42; see Lev 26:20, 26; 1 Kgs 8:37; 2 Chr 6:28; 7:13). Amos, in the book immediately following Joel, also speaks of locusts invading the land as punishment for Israel's sins (Amos 4:9; 7:1–3). The locusts are portrayed as an army in Joel 1 to emphasize their power and strength (see Prov 30:27).

The locust-like features of the army in chapter two make it possible that this chapter also portrays a locust invasion. Chapter one refers to an event that has already taken place, while chapter two depicts something that is still future, and so this invasion would be subsequent to the events

---

[4] Ibid., 20.

[5] Douglas Stuart, *Hosea-Jonah*, WBC 31 (Waco, TX: Word, 1987), 232.

in chapter one rather than a description of the same event. The view taken here is that chapter two portrays the invasion of an actual army.[6] Duane Garrett argues that the military language in chapter two "is too strong to be taken as accidental or metaphorical."[7] Joel 1 focuses on the destruction of crops and the loss of grain, wine, and oil, but Joel 2 mentions nothing about crop destruction and focuses instead on the capture of a city. The progression from curses in nature to curses in battle is also what is portrayed in Deutonomy 28:38–65.[8] The recurring use of "like" or "as" in 2:4–7 would seem to suggest that the army is being compared to something else, but the Hebrew preposition for "like" (*ke-*) can also be used as an expression to describe exactly or precisely what something is like. In 1:15, the Day of the Lord comes "as (*ke-*) devastation from the Almighty, because divine destruction is what this 'day' is in every way."[9] This army invades Judah from the north (2:20), the direction from which enemies invading the land normally come (see Jer 1:14–15; 4:6; 6:1), while locust invasions normally come from the south.[10] The depiction of locusts like an army in chapter one and of an army like locusts in chapter two masterfully demonstrates how these two judgments are connected to one another and how the Lord's judgment intensifies when the people fail to respond with repentance.

Scriptural Echoes in Joel

One of the distinctive features of the book of Joel is the striking number of parallels with other texts in the Hebrew Bible. Determining the direction of influence for these allusions and echoes is difficult, but the addition of "as the LORD promised" to the quote of Obadiah 17 in Joel 2:32 likely indicates

---

[6] For a summary of the arguments in favor of the view that chapter two also describes a locust swarm, see Michael A. Grisanti, "Joel," in *The World and the Word: An Introduction to the Old Testament* (Nashville, TN: B&H, 2011), 425–26.

[7] Garrett, *Hosea, Joel*, 339.

[8] Ibid.

[9] Ibid., 298–99. See also Robert B. Chisholm Jr., *Handbook on the Prophets* (Grand Rapids, MI: Baker, 370–71). For discussion of this use of the preposition *ke-* (*kaph veritalis*) and other examples, see Bruce K. Waltke and Michael O'Connor, *An Introduction to Biblical Hebrew Syntax* (Winona Lake, IN: Eisenbrauns, 1990), 203. Ezekiel 26:10 also depicts invading enemy forces "as (*ke-*) an army entering a breached city."

[10] Chisholm, ibid., 371.

The Destructive Power of Locust Invasions

The following from *National Geographic* reflects the devastating effects of a locust invasion and explains how these insects continue to provide an ongoing problem for agricultural production in the Middle East today:

The desert locust is notorious. Found in Africa, the Middle East, and Asia, they inhabit some 60 countries and can cover one-fifth of Earth's land surface. Desert locust plagues may threaten the economic livelihood of one-tenth of the world's humans.

A desert locust swarm can be 460 square miles (1,200 square kilometers) in size and pack between 40 and 80 million locusts into less than half a square mile (one square kilometer).

Each locust can eat its weight in plants each day, so a swarm of such size would eat 423 million pounds (192 million kilograms) of plants every day.

Like the individual animals within them, locust swarms are typically in motion and can cover vast distances. In 1954, a swarm flew from northwest Africa to Great Britain. In 1988, another made the lengthy trek from West Africa to the Caribbean. *

---

* http://animals.nationalgeographic.com/animals/bugs/locust/

that Joel is quoting Obadiah.[11] The late date of Joel would fit well with the numerous references to earlier biblical materials, and Joel may have employed the words of other prophets as a means of enhancing the authority of his message and showing that his message belongs within the larger prophetic tradition.

In his study of Joel's use of Scripture, John Strazicich has developed the manner in which the first half of the book of Joel (1:1–2:17) appropriates and reapplies earlier texts in primarily negative ways as a means of encouraging repentance.[12] The locust plague against Egypt in Exodus 10 is now directed

---

[11] Baker, *Joel, Obadiah, Malachi*, 26.

[12] John Strazicich, *Joel's Use of Scripture and Scripture's Use of Joel: Appropriation and Resignification in Second Temple Judaism and Early Christianity*, Biblical Interpretation Series, 82 (Leiden, Netherlands: Brill, 2007), 59–162.

against Judah. Judah is now facing another Day of the Lord (see Isa 13:6; Ezek 30:2–3), and the people must now repent and pray at the temple in the manner advocated by Solomon in 1 Kings 8. In the second half of the book (2:18–3:21), Joel's vision of Israel's glorious future is informed by earlier prophetic promises and biblical imagery.[13] The promised defeat of the northern army and the pouring out of the Spirit in Joel 2:20, 28–29 echoes the vision of the defeat of Gog and the renewal of Israel in Ezekiel 38–39. Jerusalem will become like a new Eden (Joel 3:18; see Gen 2:10; Ezek 47:1–2). The promise of agricultural bounty in Joel 2:19 recalls the promises concerning the fertility of the land given when Israel first entered the land (see Deut 11:12–15). Before the nations turn their "swords into plows" (Isa 2:4), they must first beat their "plows into swords" (Joel 3:10).

Joel contains a number of these parallels to other books in the Twelve, including these:

1.	1:15	Obadiah 15; Zeph 1:7
2.	2:2	Zeph 1:14–15
3.	2:6	Nah 2:10
4.	2:13	Jonah 3:9; Mic 7:16–18; Nah 1:3 (see Exod 34:6)
5.	2:31	Mic 4:5
6.	2:32	Obadiah 17
7.	3:5	Obadiah 15
8.	3:10	Mic 4:3 (see Isa 2:4)
9.	3:16	Amos 1:2
10.	3:18	Amos 9:13*

* For a fuller listing of other biblical parallels in Joel, see Baker, *Joel, Obadiah, Malachi,* 26; and James L. Crenshaw, *Joel: A New Translation with Introduction and Commentary,* AB 24 (New York, NY: Doubleday, 1995), 26–28.

Regardless of the direction of influence, these textual connections with other books in the Twelve enhance the unity of this corpus. James Nogalski suggests that the book of Joel serves as a "literary anchor" for the Twelve in the way that Joel's "Day of the Lord" sayings anticipate recurring references to the Day of the Lord in the Twelve as a whole and provide a "transcendent

---

[13] Ibid., 163–252.

historical paradigm" of God's work of judgment and salvation that unfolds in the books that follow.[14] The final editors responsible for the shaping of the Twelve could have added these quotes and allusions as a means of reflecting explicit connections between the messages of the individual prophets, but it is just as plausible that Joel incorporated the words of other prophets into his own preaching, or that prophets later than Joel did the same with his oracles. In other instances, the parallels may be due to common expressions or shared traditions between the prophets.

Structure

Joel reflects a two-part structure. The first section (1:1–2:17) contains the prophet's call for lament and repentance. This section further divides into the call for lament in response to the recent locust invasion in chapter one and the second appeal for a sacred assembly in light of the imminent threat of further judgment in 2:1–17. The introduction of a positive word of hope in 2:18 clearly divides the two halves of the book, and this second section provides the Lord's response to the people and the promise of restoration. The possibility of the Lord showing mercy in 2:12–17 becomes a reality as he promises to turn their punishment into blessing. The expression "after this" ('achare ken) in 2:28 also divides the second half of the book into two parts, with 2:18–27 describing the more immediate reversal of the locust plague, and 2:28–3:21 portraying the eschatological restoration of Israel and judgment of the nations.

The two halves of the book share a number of similar or common expressions, including "the Day of the LORD is coming" (2:1; 3:4); the Day of the Lord as "terrible/great" (gadol) and "dreadful/awe-inspiring" (yara') (2:11,28); the Lord "raising his voice" (2:11; 3:16); and the quaking of heaven and earth (2:10; 3:16).[15] These shared expressions demonstrate the unity of the book and the pervasiveness of the day of the Lord motif.

---

[14] James D. Nogalski, "Joel as 'Literary Anchor' for the Book of the Twelve," in *Reading and Hearing the Book of the Twelve*, SBLSymS 15 (Atlanta, GA: Society of Biblical Literature, 2000), 91–109.

[15] Joel Barker, *From the Depths of Despair to the Promise of Presence: A Rhetorical Reading of the Book of Joel*, Siphrut 11 (Winona Lake, IN: Eisenbrauns, 2014), 168.

JOEL 1:1–2:17: THE CALL FOR REPENTANCE IN LIGHT OF THE DAY OF THE LORD		JOEL 2:18–3:21: THE RESTORATION OF ISRAEL AND THE FINAL DAY OF THE LORD	
Call for Sacred Assembly to Lament (1:1–14)	Call for Sacred Assembly to Repent (2:1–17)	Promise for the Near Future (2:18–27)	Promise for the Distant Future (2:18–3:21)
Focus on past judgment of locust plague	Focus on a coming judgment	Reversal of the Locust Plague	Restoration of Israel and Judgment of the Nations
"the Day of the LORD is near" (1:15) "the Day of the LORD is coming" (2:1) "the Day of the LORD is terrible and dreadful" (2:11)		"the great and awe-inspiring Day of the LORD" (2:31) "the Day of the LORD is near" (3:14) "In that day . . ." (3:18)	

Exposition

1:1–14 "ANNOUNCE A SACRED FAST; PROCLAIM AN ASSEMBLY" (CALL FOR LAMENT IN RESPONSE TO THE LOCUST INVASION)

This opening section calls for the community to gather at the temple in order to lament and pray for the Lord to show mercy in the aftermath of a devastating locust plague. Sacred assemblies for the purpose of prayer, repentance, and spiritual renewal were a normal response in times of national crisis (see 2 Kgs 23:1–3; Ezra 9; Psalms 44; 60; Jer 6:26; 36:9). The prophet employs eighteen imperatives in calling the community to assemble, and verbs of mourning are especially prominent in this section—"weep" (*bakah*) (v. 5), "wail" (*halal*) (vv. 5, 11, 13), "grieve" (*'alah*) (v. 8), "mourn/grieve" (*'aval*) (vv. 9–10), and "be ashamed" (*bosh*) (v. 11). Mention of the wearing of sackcloth in verses 8 and 13 reflects the somber mood of the passage. While calling for repentance, the prophet never identifies the specific sins or crimes that the people committed. References to the "elders" (*zaqen*) and "inhabitant/residents of the land" (*yoshve ha'arets*) in 1:2 and 14 provide a frame around this section. This crisis affects the entire nation, but Joel also addresses specific groups within the community.

Joel first entreats the elders and inhabitants of the land to reflect on how the severity of the locust plague indicates that this disaster is judgment from God (vv. 2–4). Locust plagues were a fairly common occurrence, but no previous generation had seen an invasion like this one. Whereas Moses commanded the Israelites to recount for subsequent generations the salvation story of the exodus and Passover (Exod 12:24–27), the prophet here instructs the people to recount for future generations the terrible judgment they have just experienced.[16] The Lord had brought a devastating locust plague on the Egyptians as well (Exod 10:2–4), but now the same punishment was falling on Israel.[17] Commentators are divided as to whether the three names for locusts in verse 4 and 2:25 refer to different species or to different stages of development, but the use of these three terms, as well as the repetition of the verbs "has left" and "has eaten," conveys the totality of the destruction caused by the locusts swarming through the land.

The first segment of the population that Joel addresses is the "drunkards" who would be deprived of the wine that they loved (vv. 5–7). The prophet strategically mentions this group first because the people as a whole need to awaken from spiritual stupor and return to the Lord. Wine was a common drink regularly used at meals, but drinking to excess was a symptom of selfish indulgence and disregard for the Lord (see Isa 5:11–12, 21). The locusts would devour the vines with the ferocity of a lion, and they would even strip bare the bark on the fig trees. The "vine" and "fig tree" are often mentioned together as symbols of prosperity (1 Kgs 4:25; Mic 4:4; Hag 2:19; Zech 3:10), so their loss here reflects the poverty the Lord is inflicting on the people as punishment for their sins.

The prophet again addresses the people as a whole and calls for them to mourn like a grieving widow, focusing specifically on how the present crisis has impacted the priests and Israel's worship practices (vv. 8–10). The image of a grieving bride dressed in the mourning garb of sackcloth (a black material made out of goat's hair) evokes powerful emotion. The term for "young woman" (*bethulah*) may suggest a woman who was betrothed to her husband in a marriage that was not yet consummated, adding to

---

[16] Garrett, *Hosea, Joel*, 314.
[17] Ibid., 315.

the intensity of the grief.[18] Garrett comments: "The sorrow and loss of an unconsummated marriage illustrates the sorrow of a lost harvest."[19] This passage is similar to Isaiah's "song of the vineyard" (Isa 5:1–7), in which a wedding song employing the imagery of harvesting a vineyard turns images associated with celebration into a warning of judgment. There is a funeral in place of a wedding.

The priests would mourn over the devastation of the land because they would be unable to present the grain and drink offerings to the Lord as commanded. Coming to the temple to present sacrifices and offerings or to participate in the national feasts was not just an obligation. These services were times of great joy and celebration in the presence of God (see Lev 23:40). Without the foodstuffs needed to present offerings, the people would be unable to fully enjoy the blessings of fellowship with the Lord. The priests and Levites who had no land would also be deprived of the food they normally received from the tithes of the grain, wine, and oil (see Lev 2:10; 27:30–33; Deut 14:22–29; 26:1–15).[20]

The farmers and vintners are called to mourn because their crops are ruined (Joel 1:11–12). The mention of eight different crops to indicate completeness when a sevenfold list would have sufficed demonstrates the totality of the destruction.[21] The order of the crops may also reflect the various harvests of the agricultural year for Israel, with the wheat and barley in the spring and the grape, figs, and fruit trees in the summer, leading into the Festival of Booths in the fall.[22]

Various wordplays and repetitions add to the dramatic effect of the prophet's appeal in this chapter. The "cutting off" (*karat*) of the wine (v. 5) precedes the "cutting off" (*karat*) of the grain and drink offerings (v. 9). The verbs "mourn" (*'aval*) and "destroyed" (*shadad*) are alternated in verses 9–10, and the fact that both the people and land are in mourning reflects the intensity of the crisis. The "drying up" (*yavash*) of the new wine (v. 10), the vine (v. 12), and the fruit trees (v. 12) causes the farmers to "be

---

[18] Ibid., 319. For the use of *bethulah* to refer to a betrothed woman, see Deuteronomy 22:23, 28.

[19] Ibid.

[20] Marvin A. Sweeney, *The Twelve Prophets*, Vol. 1, Berit Olam (Collegeville, MN: Liturgical Press, 2000), 158.

[21] Chisholm, *Handbook on the Prophets*, 369.

[22] Barker, *From the Depths of Despair*, 86.

ashamed" (*hovishu*) (v. 11) and the joy of the people to "dry up" (*yavash*) (v. 12). The destruction of the crops means no communal celebration of an abundant harvest.

The sacred assembly for which the prophet called for was to begin with the priests putting on sackcloth and spending the night in prayer. The leaders and the people were to join in a "sacred fast" (see Judg 20:26; 1 Sam 14:24; Jer 36:6–9). Allen Ross explains that "prophetic instructions to proclaim a fast were almost synonymous with a call to repentance," and fasting was an important element of such gatherings because "it is difficult to concentrate on spiritual matters while indulging in physical pleasures."[23] The connection between fasting and repentance is reflected in the fact that fasting was required on the Day of Atonement (Lev 16:29–31).

1:15–20 "The Day of the LORD is near" (The Warning of More Judgment to Come)

The prophet joins with the people in their lament because he shares in their loss and foresees that more judgment is on the way. This section introduces the phrase "Day of the LORD," an expression that becomes a central theme in the Twelve (see 2:1, 11, 31; 3:14). The Day of the Lord is the time when Yahweh will come to judge his enemies, and the prophets warn of various judgments the Lord plans to bring against his people in the near future, culminating with the final Day of the Lord in the eschatological future. In the first half of Joel, the prophet preaches concerning the Day of the Lord that is coming soon, while his focus shifts to the distant future in the second half. When Joel warns that the "Day of the LORD is near," he is not suggesting that the locust invasion was not a Day of the Lord, but rather that an even more intense judgment is on its way. These Day of the Lord judgments reoccur in the Twelve because the people refuse to turn from their sinful ways.

The judgment of Judah would come as "destruction" (*shod*) from the "Almighty" (*shadday*). Joel highlights the impact of the people's sin on nature and the environment, as do other prophets (see Hos 2:12; Jer 9:10; 12:4). Sin and rebellion against God introduce chaos and disharmony into God's

---

[23] Allen P. Ross, *Recalling the Hope of Glory: Biblical Worship From the Garden to the New Creation* (Grand Rapids, MI: Kregel, 2006), 239.

creation. In the Noahic flood, the judgment of human violence resulted in the undoing of creation. Jeremiah figuratively presents the Babylonian invasion of Judah as returning the creation to its condition of "void and without form" (Jer 4:23; see Gen 1:2). The Lord promises through Hosea that in the eschatological restoration he will make a covenant with the animals by putting an end to the human war and violence that have brought such suffering into the creation (Hos 2:18).

2:1–11 "They storm the city" (The Warning of an Approaching Army)

Judah now faces a new crisis, the impending attack of an enemy army. This new threat suggests the people have not yet fully responded to the prophetic call for repentance and prayer. The prophet portrays an invading army storming the land, with Zion (Jerusalem) in its sights as its ultimate target. The role of watchmen stationed on the city walls was to warn of approaching armies (see 2 Sam 18:24–27; 2 Kgs 9:17–20), and here Joel serves as a prophetic watchman (see Jer 6:17; Ezek 3:17; 33:2–7; Hos 9:8). The Lord issues a command to sound the ram's horn (which functioned like a modern air raid siren)[24] to warn the people of the impending attack (see Judg 3:27; 6:34; Jer 4:19–21; 6:1). The opening and closing verses of this section identify this assault as "the Day of the LORD" for Judah because Yahweh himself leads and directs the invading army against his disobedient people.

The prophet vividly describes the approaching army rushing toward Jerusalem in Joel 2:2–11. This massive and powerful army is unlike any ever seen. Prophetic hyperbole enlarges the threat as a means of motivating the people to repentance. This army covers the land with darkness and ominous clouds like the arrival of a devastating thunderstorm (v. 2). The army also devours the land like a consuming fire (v. 3). The land in front of them is green and verdant like Eden; the land behind them is a scorched desert. This image reverses other prophetic promises that Israel in her restoration would become like the garden of Eden (Isa 51:3; Ezek 36:35).[25] This army is like a swarm of locusts in its size, strength, and swiftness of movement (Joel 2:4–9). The noise of its approach terrifies the troops. Their

---

[24] Allen, *The Books of Joel. Obadiah, Jonah, and Micah*, 67.

[25] Baker, *Joel, Obadiah, Malachi*, 71–72.

relentlessness and fearlessness renders useless any attempt to withstand them, and fortresses offer no protection because of their ability to scale walls and climb through windows with ease. The attacking army is so ferocious that it causes the earth to shake and the lights in the sky to cease shining (v. 10).

The cosmic nature of this imagery conveys that the Lord marches at the head of this army as its leader. Darkness is often associated with the Day of the Lord, in contrast to the people's expectation that this day would be a time of light and salvation (see 2:31; Amos 4:13; 5:18–20; Zeph 1:15). Darkness, clouds, fire, heavenly chariots, deafening noise, and cosmic upheaval are common features in theophany passages that portray the Lord's appearance, when he wages war against his enemies (see Judg 5:4–5; Ps 18:7–15; Mic 1:3; Nah 1:2–6; Hab 3:3–12).[26] The "cloud" of the Lord's presence had protected Israel at the Red Sea and led them in the wilderness (see Exod 13:21–22; 14:19–21; 40:35–38), but now his presence brings judgment. He afflicts his people with the same darkness he brought upon Egypt (Exod 10:21–22). The Lord had promised to defeat the enemy nations that assaulted Zion (see Psalms 48; 76) and had miraculously delivered Jerusalem from the Assyrians in 701 BC (see 2 Kings 18–19; Isaiah 36–37), but now he leads the attack on Jerusalem.

The actual identity of this army, if Joel belongs to the postexilic period, is unknown. If Joel is placed just prior to the exile, the invading army would be identified with Babylon. The prophet employs these apocalyptic images to emphasize the severity of the crisis and the fact that this army does the Lord's bidding (see Jer 4:5–8, 13, 23–26; 5:5–17; 6:21–23), though some have seen here a reference to a supernatural or heavenly army.

2:12–17 "Tear your hearts, not just your clothes, and return to the LORD your God" (Another Call for Repentance and Sacred Assembly)

As in the previous chapter, the prophet calls for the people to assemble and cry out to the Lord. The first explicit call for the people to "turn/return"

---

[26] For more on theophany texts and imagery in the Old Testament, see Jeffrey J. Niehaus, *God at Sinai: Covenant and Theophany in the Bible and Ancient Near East*, Studies in OT Biblical Theology (Grand Rapids, MI: Zondervan, 1995).

(*shuv*) to the Lord in the book is issued here (vv. 12–13). The ritual of tearing one's garments is not enough; the people are to approach the Lord with a broken heart. The motivation for repentance is the possibility that the Lord would graciously extend a blessing in the place of sending judgment. Joel reminds the people of the theological confession first expressed after Israel worshipped the golden calf (see Exod 34:6–7): Yahweh is "gracious and compassionate, slow to anger, rich in faithful in love." He also adds that the Lord "relents from sending disaster." As the "Who knows?" in verse 14 reflects, repentance does not guarantee divine favor and blessing, but the possibility that God would "relent" (*naham*) and send blessing in the place of judgment, as he did at Sinai and at other times in Israel's history (see Exod 32:12–14; Numbers 14; Jer 18:7–10; Mic 3:9–12 with Jer 26:17–19; Amos 7:1–3; Jer 26:3–7; 36:3–7), always exists.

"Blow the horn in Zion" in Joel 2:15 echoes verse 1, and the sounding of the horn here calls the people to assemble at the temple for a "sacred fast" (see Lev 25:9; 2 Chr 15:14; Ps 150:3). The urgency of this assembly is such that it must include all segments of the population, from the eldest down to nursing infants. The crisis is so severe that even the newly married, who were exempt from military duty (see Deut 20:7), must present themselves before the Lord.[27] The priests intercede for the Lord to show mercy to the people, basing their appeal—as Moses had at Sinai—on the Lord's reputation among the nations. Those people would say, "Where is God?" if he allowed Israel to be destroyed (see Exod 32:12–14).

2:18–27 "I will repay you for the years that the swarming locust ate" (The Lord's Gracious Response and the Reversal of Judgment)

The text does not explicitly state how the people responded to Joel's call for repentance, but what follows in 2:18–20 indicates that they obeyed through on what the prophet had commanded. Leslie Allen comments: "Evidently the people did gather to a national service of fasting and lamentation, and the priests duly offered prayers on behalf of a genuinely repentant

---

[27] Ronald L. Troxel, "The Problem of Time in Joel," *Journal of Biblical Literature* 132 (2013): 94.

community."[28] Though some translations view verses 18–19 as promises of what the Lord would do for Israel in the future, the verb forms used are typical of narratives that describe past events. Here they describe how the Lord responded to the prayers and repentance of the people at the time of the sacred assembly ("became jealous," "spared," and "answered").[29] Their repentance brought immediate blessing.

The Lord informs the people that in the near future, he will restore their harvests and drive away the northern army he had threatened to send against them (vv. 19–20). The "grain, wine, and oil" that was taken away would be restored. The fruit trees would produce their "riches." The commands to wear sackcloth, to weep, and to wail are now replaced with calls for the people to "rejoice and be glad" (vv. 21, 23). The wild animals and pastures that had suffered because of human sin (1:18–20) would now rejoice together with the people (v. 22). The autumn and spring rains would lead to plentiful grain and wine. Through such productivity, the Lord would compensate the people for the harvests the locust invasions had destroyed, and they would have plenty to eat. Yet, even greater than any agricultural blessing was the promise of the Lord's presence (v. 27).

2:28–32 "I will pour out My Spirt on all humanity" (Israel's Restoration and the Promise of the Spirit)

What the Lord does for the people in the present anticipates the even greater blessings he has in store for them in the more distant future. "After this" clearly indicates a time subsequent to the more immediate blessings of

---

[28] Allen, *The Books of Joel, Obadiah, Jonah, and Micah*, 86.

[29] These types of verbs are referred to in the grammars as preterites or imperfects with a *waw* consecutive. They are translated this way in the HCSB, ESV, NRSV, TNK, and NET. They are viewed as functioning like prophetic futures and read as future promises in the NIV, NASB, NKJV, and KJV. For the view that these verbs should be taken as prophetic perfects, see, for example, James D. Nogalski, *The Book of the Twelve: Hosea-Jonah*, Smith & Helwys Bible Commentary (Macon, GA: Smith & Helwys, 2011), 234–37; Stuart, *Hosea-Jonah*, 257–59; and Sweeney, *The Twelve Prophets*, 1:69. For the view that these verbs should be taken as preterites narrating past events, see Allen, *The Books of Joel, Obadiah, Jonah, and Micah*, 86–88; Chisholm, *Handbook on the Prophets*, 373; Troxel, "The Problem of Time in Joel," 78–83; and Hans Walter Wolff, *Joel and Amos: A Commentary on the Books of the Prophets Joel and Amos*, Hermeneia (Minneapolis, MN: Fortress, 1977), 57–60.

The Working of the Holy Spirit in the Old Testament

Prophetic promises concerning the future outpouring of the Spirit should not be read to imply that the Spirit's transforming work was absent under the old covenant. The Lord's commands for Israel to "love the Lord with all their heart" (Deut 6:4) and to "circumcise" their hearts (Deut 10:16) imply internal spiritual enablement to carry out these directives. David prayed for the Lord to "create a clean heart" (Ps 51:10) within him. There can be no creation of a clean heart apart from the Spirit's working. When OT saints reflect the actions and qualities that the NT attributes to the working of the Spirit (in praise, holiness, love for God's law; see Eph 5:18–20), one should assume that the Spirit is producing those characteristics even if this is not explicitly stated. The sanctifying work of the Spirit in the lives of individuals is not the primary focus of Old Testament revelation concerning the Spirit.

The difference between the working of the Spirit in the old and new covenants is one of degree rather than one of complete discontinuity. When speaking of the Spirit's future work, the prophets were not envisioning something completely new that had never happened. The indwelling Spirit controls the heart of the New Testament believer to a far greater degree because the love of God that compels obedience has been revealed in a fuller way in the person and work of Jesus (see Rom 5:5). The new covenant envisions that all members of the covenant community will be truly regenerate, in contrast to the old covenant that included both believers and unbelievers within a national covenant. Spirit baptism that places the believing individual into the body of Christ (1 Cor 12:13) also appears to be a unique aspect of the Spirit's working in the new covenant.[1]

---

[1] For further discussion of the Spirit's working in the OT, see David G. Firth and Paul D. Wegner (ed.), *Presence, Power, and Promise: The Role of the Spirit of God in the Old Testament* (Downers Grove, IL: InterVarsity, 2011); and Leon J. Wood, *The Holy Spirit in the Old Testament* (Eugene, OR: Wipf and Stock, 1998).

reversing the locust invasion. Verses 28–29 promise the outpouring of God's Spirit. Throughout the Old Testament, the Lord primarily bestows his Spirit on kings (1 Sam 16:13–14; Isa 11:2), prophets (1 Sam 10:6; 19:20–24;

Isa 61:1; Mic 3:8), and other leaders (Exod 31:3; 35:31; Judg 3:10; 6:34; 14:6) to equip and empower them for service. The Lord promises that the Sprit will be poured out on "all humanity" (lit. "on all flesh"), which here refers to the Spirit being given to all the people of Israel without regard to age, gender, or social status. The prophets portray the eschatological era as an age of the Spirit (see Isa 32:15–16; 59:20–21; Ezek 36:26–28; 39:29; Zech 12:10).

The Spirit will be the channel of God's revelation and will enable all of the people to prophesy. At Sinai, the people had requested that the Lord speak to them through Moses as a prophetic intermediary (Exod 20:18–19), but the future outpouring of the Spirit will remove the need for intermediaries. In this way the giving of the Spirit would fulfill Moses's desire for all of the people to be prophets (Num 11:29). In Isaiah 59:21, the Lord promises to put his words in the people's mouths as he had done with the prophets. Even more expansive is the promise of Jerermiah 31:34 that every individual would know the Lord to the extent that no one would need to be taught by others. The Lord also promises to place his Spirit within the people of Israel in the eschatological age so that they will have the desire and ability to fully obey his commands. The giving of a new heart and imparting of the indwelling Spirit (Ezek 36:26–28) would be the transforming means by which the Lord would write his law on the people's hearts (Jer 31:33; 32:38–39).

In Joel 2:30–32, the prophet announces that the pouring out of the Spirit would come at a time of worldwide judgment in the form of cosmic signs and catastrophic events. The signs in the heavens announce the arrival of the bloodshed and warfare belonging to the final Day of the Lord. The darkening of the sun and the turning of the moon to blood likely refers to an eclipse, often viewed in the ancient world as an omen of coming disaster. A lunar eclipse causes the moon to become blood-red in appearance.[30] The promise in the midst of this announcement of coming doom is that the Lord will save those who call upon his name, and the remnant saved from this judgment will become his people.

---

[30] Mark W. Chavalas, "Joel," in *The Zondervan Illustrated Bible Backgrounds Commentary*, Vol 5 (Grand Rapids, MI: Zondervan, 2009), 48.

3:1–21 "Multitudes, multitudes in the valley of decision!" (The Judgment of the Nations and Israel's Final Deliverance)

Israel's future restoration will include the judgment of the nations for their crimes against the Lord's people (vv. 1–8). The nations would again assault Israel, but the Lord would then "enter into judgment" (*shaphat*) against them at the Valley of Jeho*shaphat* ("the Lord judges"). In the days of Jehoshaphat, the Lord defeated a coalition of enemy nations without Judah's armies even having to fight in the valley of Beracah (2 Chr 20:1–20). The Lord would once again directly intervene for his people. His judgment would begin in the near future against Tyre, Sidon, and Philistia. Because they had robbed Judah's treasures and sold Judah's people as slaves, the Lord would cause their own children to be sold into slavery as just recompense for their wicked behavior.

The judgments the Lord was about to execute against the nations responsible for Judah's exile anticipates his final judgment against all wicked nations in the last days (Joel 3:9–16). Micah and Isaiah anticipate a future day of peace when the nations "will beat their swords into plows" (Mic 4:3; Isa 2:4), but this must be preceded by a time when they "beat their plows into swords" and assemble against the Lord and his people in one final act of rebellion. God calls on his heavenly hosts to strike his enemies like reapers, swinging sickles into grain and trampling them like grapes in the winepress. The "Day of the LORD is near" warning earlier directed toward God's people (1:15) is now turned against the nations. The Lord, roaring as a lion and marching out as a warrior from Zion, will cause the lights in the heavens to go dark and the earth to quake. Still, in the midst of this cosmic disturbance, he will provide refuge for Israel.

When the Lord establishes his rule over the earth, the city of Jerusalem will never again be overrun by foreigners (vv. 17–21). Dwelling in the security of the Lord's protection, the people of Israel will enjoy the abundant fertility of their land. The promise that the mountains and hills will flow with wine and milk marks a complete reversal of the conditions of drought and famine brought on by the locust invasion in the first half of the book. Egypt and Edom, representative of all the enemy nations, would become barren wastelands because of their violence against Israel. In contrast, Israel would be inhabited forever, and the Lord would graciously pardon his people's sins.

Theological Message and Application of Joel

The message of Joel serves as a reminder of the seriousness of obedience for those who live in a covenant relationship with the Lord. Before Israel entered the land, Moses instructed people that their decision to obey the Lord's commands was a matter of life and death (Deut 30:15); the Lord would bless them if they obeyed and curse them if they disobeyed (Leviticus 26; Deuteronomy 28). The people's unfaithfulness to the Lord had brought the covenant curses of famine and deprivation, just as Moses warned. The covenantal history of Israel provides a powerful illustration of the general spiritual principle of sowing and reaping (see Gal 6:7–9). Israel had literally reaped the harvest of its disobedience.

While the Lord requires obedience, he is also merciful and compassionate to forgive sin and relent from judgment when his sinful people turn to him in repentance. Joel particularly stresses that God is responsive to the genuinely penitent cries of his people. As the confession of Exodus 34:6–7, quoted in Joel 2:13, stresses, one way the Lord demonstrates his covenantal faithfulness to his people is by his willingness to forgive them when they are unfaithful to him. Even at the time of eschatological judgment, all who call on the name of the Lord will be saved (Joel 2:32). The New Testament gives that promise a Christological focus—it is all who call on the name of Jesus as Lord who will be saved from God's wrath and judgment (Rom 10:13).

The Lord's compassion in turning judgment to blessing in Joel's day anticipates the full and final restoration of Israel in the last days. Israel would face more judgment because of its refusal to return to the Lord, but these future judgments would also lead to the Lord pouring out his Spirit on Israel so they would know and serve him. The New Testament reveals that the fulfillment of the promises of Joel 2:28–32 would occur in stages. The initial fulfillment of the eschatological pouring out of the Holy Spirit began on the Day of Pentecost (see Acts 2:16–21) and continues into the present as the Spirit indwells each individual believer as well as the church collectively (see Rom 8:9; 1 Cor 3:16; 6:19). The Spirit will also be poured out on the people of Israel at the time of their eschatological renewal when they turn to the Lord and believe in Jesus as their Messiah (see Isa 59:20–21; Zech 12:10; Rom 11:26–28). Joel's ominous warnings of catastrophe and warfare (2:30) also seem to be fulfilled in stages. Following Pentecost, the Romans destroyed Jerusalem in AD 70, providing a preview of the cosmic and political upheaval that would occur in the final Day of the Lord (see Rev 6:12–13; 8:7–13).

Joel 3 is one of several prophetic texts that portray the judgment of the last days as including an eschatological battle in which the Lord destroys the nations that assault Israel or that assemble in armed rebellion against him (see Isa 66:18; Ezekiel 38–39; Mic 5:5–9; Zephaniah 3; Zechariah 12, 14). The purpose of this judgment will be to establish the Lord's sovereignty over the nations that have rebelled against him and to execute justice on behalf of God's oppressed people. Beyond that, this judgment would also purge Israel of its sin and pride (Zeph 3:11; Zech 13:8–9) and purify the nations so they might also become worshippers of the true God (see Zeph 3:8–9; Zech 14:6). In the New Testament, the book of Revelation portrays the demonically influenced kings of the nations gathering for war at Armageddon (Rev 16:12–16). It promises the ultimate victory of Jesus over his enemies as he destroys them with the power of his word at his Second Coming (Rev 19:11–16). Revelation 20:7–9 portrays yet another assault of the nations on Jerusalem when Satan is released from the abyss, following the millennial reign of Christ. The nations will "beat [their] plows into swords" (Joel 3:10) so that ultimately they can "beat [their] swords into plows" (Isa 2:4; Mic 4:3). God's eternal kingdom will finally bring a lasting peace, and war will be no more.

7

THE BOOK OF AMOS

Introduction

Wealth is a relative thing. The average middle class American enjoys comforts that only kings and emperors enjoyed in the ancient world. Most twenty-first century American Christians live in peace and prosperity, enjoying the fruits of their labor as the blessing of God. Certainly such achievements should not be belittled or envied—through personal responsibility in an innovative, free market society, the path to prosperity is a relatively open road. Yet in many parts of the world, the path to wealth is still paved by corruption. When considering the global population, Jesus's words concerning the poor still ring true.[1] The poor are always with us, often on a massive and overwhelming scale. Poverty may come as a result of laziness and foolish

---

[1] Matthew 26:11; Mark 14:7

111

behavior, but it to often as a result of violence, corruption, social injustice, and crimes against humanity.

Amos preached in an environment of unparalleled prosperity for the upper class of Israel, though the vast majority of people still lived in poverty and oppression. The political expansion of Jeroboam II ensured a false sense of geopolitical security (see 2 Kgs 14:23–29); the Assyrian Empire was temporarily subdued by its own internal strife, and Israel had little to fear from other external threats. The ruling class had come to see their blessings as a sign of God's favor, yet they were blind to the suffering of the population they suppressed. Moreover, they were blind to the coming wrath of God. What seemed nearly impossible during the reign of Jeroboam II—the destruction of the northern kingdom of Israel—was actually only decades away.

Structure

The structure of Amos is clear, albeit complex. Following an introduction (1:1) and summary oracle (1:2), the main body of Amos consists of three sets of judgment oracles (1:3–2:16; 3:1–4:12; 5:1–6:14), five visions (7:1–3; 7:4–6; 7:7–9; 8:1–3; 9:1–4), and a concluding salvation oracle (9:11–15). Within these primary units lie a rich variety of literary devices.

The first set of oracles utilizes numerical formulas to proclaim judgment against the nations, ultimately functioning as an indictment against Israel. The second set of judgment speeches contain rhetorical disputation, courtroom imagery, and biting sarcasm, and the third set of oracles uses a combination of lament and woe speeches to proclaim the impending death of Israel.

The five visions can be grouped into two structurally similar pairs, with the fifth vision independent of the prior four. In the first pair (7:1–6), Amos intercedes for the nation after receiving a vision of their coming destruction. In the second pair (7:7–9; 8:1–3) judgment is inevitable, and there is no prophetic intercession given. Between the third and fourth vision, a biographical interlude provides a narrative context for Amos's message of judgment. An announcement of judgment (8:4–14) provides a link between the fourth and fifth vision (9:1–4). Finally, the salvation oracle concluding the book can be viewed as two kingdom oracles (9:11–12; 13–15).

Of significant interest to the structure and theology of Amos are the hymns that exalt the power of Yahweh and bring attention to the reverence due to his name (4:13; 5:8–9; 9:5–6). Each hymn celebrates his role as a divine warrior, fully capable of bringing judgment to Israel in the most cataclysmic way.

Exposition

1:1 (Introduction)

The introduction to the book of Amos contains helpful clues in determining an approximate date for Amos's prophetic ministry. Reference to Uzziah, king of Judah, and Jeroboam II, king of Israel, narrows the range for Amos's ministry to 767–753 BC. Interestingly, Amos's ministry is stated to have occurred "two years before the earthquake." Although the memory of this earthquake would have remained in popular recollection for many generations, the text leaves the date unspecified, and archeological evidence is inconclusive in determining an exact date for such an ancient event.[2]

Beyond establishing a historical marker for Amos's ministry, the mention of this earthquake has the function of validating the prophetic authority behind Amos's warnings of judgment. Amos's message resounded with a depiction of God as one who "strides on the heights of the earth" (4:13), who "touches the earth" and "it melts" (9:5), and who has laid the "foundation of His vault on the earth" (9:6). Furthermore, he smashes the large house "to pieces, and the small house to rubble" (6:11). If Amos proclaimed the words of this book two years prior to the great earthquake, then history has, in a sense, validated the content of its message even prior to its composition as a book.

In addition to establishing a historical context, the introduction to the book provides a glimpse into the personal background of the prophet. Amos was a citizen of Judah called to prophesy to the upper class rulers of Israel. He was an outcast, a foreigner living among people who were not his own. Nor was he a prophet by profession. Amos was a "sheep breeder" and tender

---

[2] An often-cited date for the earthquake is 760 BC, in part supported by archeological excavations in Hazor and Samaria. See Yigal Yadin, *Hazor II: An Account of the Second Season of Excavations, 1956* (Jerusalem, Israel: Magnes Press, 1960); and R. Reed Lessing, "Amos's Earthquake in the Book of the Twelve," *Concordia Theological Quarterly* 74 (2010): 243–59.

of "sycamore figs," called by God out of his rural homeland to prophesy to the hostile leadership of Israel.

1:2–2:16 (The Trap is set for Israel)

1:2 "The Lord roars from Zion" (An Introductory Oracle of Judgment)

The summary oracle that sets the tone for the rest of the book presents Yahweh as a roaring lion whose voice brings destruction to the most treasured lands of Israel (the rich pasturelands and forested heights of Mount Carmel). The imagery of a roaring lion was meant to engender fear in the minds of the ancients who were, defenseless against the raw power of the "King of Beasts." The lion metaphor is used throughout the prophets with great fluidity. Joel 3:16, using almost identical language to Amos 1:2, directs the roar of Yahweh against the nations, thus providing reassurance to God's people, Israel. Hosea, while using the lion metaphor in describing God's wrath, also presents Yahweh as a lioness whose roar calls her cubs home (Hos 11:10). But for Amos, the intent of the metaphor is clear: Yahweh has roared, and the people ought to tremble in fear and anticipation of judgment.

1:3–2:16 "For three crimes, even four" (An Oracle of Entrapment: Numerical Formula Announcing Judgment upon the Nations, Judah, and Israel)

The prophets frequently proclaim judgment against the nations as a means to encourage the people of Israel. Amos's prophetic ministry was addressed to the northern kingdom of Israel (7:10–17), so his pronouncements of judgment against six surrounding foreign nations, along with the southern kingdom of Judah, must have been met with hopeful expectation (see 5:14, 18). However, the prophet used their sense of assurance to trap them in their own deception. Utilizing a kind of "rhetoric of entrapment," Amos masterfully drew Israel into thinking that God was pronouncing judgment upon their enemies for their own benefit, only to turn the tables on them and pronounce his most damning judgments in an unexpected eighth oracle against his own people, Israel.

The eight-part series of escalating oracles (1:3–2:16) employs a numerical pattern, suggesting a heightened degree of guilt; in essence, with three sins God's cup of wrath is filled, with the fourth it has overflowed. The numerical formula introduces each successive nation with the pattern, "For three crimes of [name of city or nation], and for four, I will not bring it back," followed by an accusation of specific guilt and a pronouncement of judgment (for the first seven nations, this judgment is stated to come by fire).[3] Interestingly, each installment of the numerical formula is followed not by a list of four crimes, but just one. Each indictment against the nations comprised a sin so egregious that any sane person would agree that such a crime must be avenged; but nevertheless, only one crime is highlighted.[4] Perhaps it is significant that only the eighth oracle against Israel lists the expected four crimes for which God's full wrath is justified.

The series begins with an oracle pronounced against Damascus, the capital city of the Arameans (1:3–5). Aram (Syria) was located to the northeast of Israel, and it was a constant threat to the security of the northern territories of Israel. The reason for its judgment is "because they threshed Gilead with iron sledges" (1:3), evoking the agricultural imagery of the threshing floor. Yet the threshing of grain is not in view, but rather, the people of Gilead who have been torn and crushed by repeated incursions into their land.

For such cruel treatment of civilian populations, Damascus would suffer the fire of divine wrath. Through the heightening effect of parallelism, God's wrath moves from the house of royalty (Hazael and Ben-Hadad) to the defenses of the capital city (Damascus) to the inhabitants of the furthest reaches of Aramean territory.[5] Finally, the people of Aram are judged to "go captive to Kir," the very place from which they came (9:7). The irony in this statement should not be missed; in effect, God had brought the Arameans

---

[3] The formulaic statement of judgment literally reads, "I will not bring it back," although most translations, including the HCSB, clarify this as a promise not to withhold judgment.

[4] These single crimes are often expanded in verse through parallelism. This has the effect of heightening the intensity of guilt, even though each oracle only lists one distinct crime.

[5] Although the exact locations and identities of the "Valley of Aven" (Valley of Wickedness) and "Beth Eden" (House of Pleasure) are uncertain, these may correspond with the northern and southernmost boundaries of the Aramean kingdom.

Amos's Escalating Repetition		
Nation	Numerical Introduction	Crime
Damascus (1:3–5)	I will not relent from punishing Damascus for three crimes, even four (1:3)	because they threshed Gilead with iron sledges
Gaza (1:6–8)	I will not relent from punishing Gaza for three crimes, even four (1:6)	because they exiled a whole community
Tyre (1:9–10)	I will not relent from punishing Tyre, for three crimes, even four (1:9)	because they handed over a whole community of exiles to Edom and broke a treaty of brotherhood
Edom (1:11–12)	I will not relent from punishing Edom for three crimes, even four (1:11)	because he pursued his brother with the sword
Ammon (1:13–15)	I will not relent from punishing the Ammonites for three crimes, even four (1:13)	because they ripped open the pregnant women of Gilead in order to enlarge their territory
Moab (2:1–3)	I will not relent from punishing Moab for three crimes, even four (2:1)	because he burned the bones of the king of Edom to lime
Judah (2:4–5)	I will not relent from punishing Judah for three crimes, even four (2:4)	because they have rejected the instruction of the Lord and have not kept His statutes.
Israel (2:6–16)	I will not relent from punishing Israel for three crimes, even four (2:6)	because they sell a righteous person for silver and a needy person for a pair of sandals.

in the Oracles of Chapters 1–2		
Judgment	**Results**	**Final Declaration**
Therefore, I will send fire against Hazael's palace	consume Ben-Hadad's citadels	The Lord has spoken.
Therefore, I will send fire against the walls of Gaza	it will consume its citadels	The Lord God has spoken.
Therefore, I will send fire against the walls of Tyre	it will consume its citadels	
Therefore, I will send fire against Teman	it will consume the citadels of Bozrah	
Therefore, I will set fire to the walls of Rabbah	it will consume its citadels	The Lord has spoken.
Therefore, I will send fire against Moab	it will consume the citadels of Kerioth	The Lord has spoken.
Therefore, I will send fire against Judah	it will consume the citadels of Jerusalem	
Look, I am about to crush you in your place as a wagon full of sheaves crushes grain.		This is the Lord's declaration. x2

out of Kir, and in judgment he would send them back. This was fulfilled in 732 BC when the Assyrians conquered Damascus and deported its inhabitants to Kir (2 Kgs 16:9).

The second oracle moves from the northeast of Israel to the southwest, targeting the Philistines, historical enemies of Israel from before the period of Saul and David (1:6–8). The chief cities of Philistia are listed as guilty and judged: Gaza, Ashdod, Ashkelon, and Ekron, with a final blow directed at the "remainder of the Philistines" (v. 8). As with the first oracle, parallelism escalates the effect of totality in judgment, yet in essence, Philistia is indicted for only one crime—having taken "captive the whole captivity, to deliver *them* up to Edom" (v. 6 NKJV). The details of this event are uncertain, although the Philistine incursion into Judah during the reign of Jehoram is a possible referent (2 Chr 21:16–17). The fulfillment of the destruction of the Philistine cities may have occurred shortly after the proclamation of this oracle by the hand of Uzziah (2 Chr 26:6), or later, by Hezekiah (2 Kgs 18:8).[6]

The third oracle is directed against Tyre, the chief Phoenician city to the northeast of Israel (1:9–10). Similar to the crime of the Philistines, Tyre is indicted for "hand[ing] over a whole community of exiles to Edom" (v. 9b). But Tyre is even more fully culpable because she has transgressed against a "treaty of brotherhood" (v. 9c). The event to which this crime refers is uncertain, and the fulfillment of judgment against Tyre is not realized until 332 BC when the city was conquered by Alexander the Great.

The fourth oracle is leveled against Edom, a nation to which the prophets often directed God's message of wrath. Edom was southeast of Israel, but perhaps more important than geographical movement is the escalation of guilt between oracles. The Philistines had sold captives into slavery to the Edomites, as had the Phoenicians. Now, the slave traders themselves would be judged. Furthermore, the Phoenicians were guilty of breaking a treaty of brotherhood with Israel, but now Edom has broken actual bloodlines with Israel, having "pursued his brother with the sword" (v. 11). Again, parallelism is employed to heighten the effect of Edom's guilt and judgment. Although the exact timing and nature of this judgment is uncertain, it appears to have taken effect by the time of Malachi (Mal 1:3–5).

---

[6] In the late eighth century BC, the Philistine cities and territories were conquered by the Assyrians, perhaps bringing this prophecy to its final stage of fulfillment.

The shocking indictments continue into the fifth oracle as the cup of wrath overflows against Ammon, a nation inhabiting the land to the east of the Jordan River. God's wrath would not be "revoked" against Ammon because she had "ripped open Gilead's pregnant women" for the sole purpose of enlarging her own territory (v. 13 NET). Such shocking behavior was common in ancient Near Eastern warfare and has continued down through the centuries. When one looks at the atrocities of Nazi Germany or Imperial Japan during World War II, for the purpose of "enlarging their territories," the devastation of these nations at the end of the war seems a just recompense for their crimes. In a similar manner, the judgments of God against Ammon would have been viewed by Israel as just and right. Like Aram before her (v. 3), Ammon had committed terrible crimes against Israel (Gilead, in particular); thus, Amos's message of judgment against Ammon would have been welcomed by an Israelite audience.

As Amos wraps up his oracles against the nations, attention is drawn to Moab, located south of Ammon and north of Edom. Ironically, the crime committed by Moab is not against Israel, but against Edom. Again emphasizing the depth of pagan depravity, Moab is indicted for "burn[ing] the bones of the king of Edom to lime" (2:1b). As with the prior oracles within this set, the oracle against Moab intensifies the description of judgment through climactic parallelism.

The seventh oracle is directed against Judah. Presumably, when the message was spoken, Amos's original audience would have expected this seventh oracle to be the capstone of the series. After the division of Israel, the northern kingdom and the southern kingdom regularly waged war against one another. There was little love lost between Israel and Judah during the time of Amos's ministry, and the Israelites would have certainly rejoiced to hear that Judah was not exempt from the Lord's wrath. The repetition of certain key features from past oracles indicate the same pattern of divine indictment and judgment against Judah: (1) the numerical formula is intact, (2) the introductory formula is followed by one crime (subsequent indictment is only a literary heightening through parallelism), (3) divine "fire" is sent against the nation, and, (4) its "citadels" are consumed. Yet the crime for which Judah is guilty is unlike that of the foreign nations. It is not a crime against humanity, but rather, a crime against God—a breach of the covenant made between God and his people. At the very least, it is clear that

God takes obedience to his law seriously and is certain to judge his people who reject it.[7]

The logical concluding point to this set of oracles would have been the seventh oracle. Every nation surrounding Israel had been named, and the number seven typically signified completion. To conclude with Judah would have been especially striking coming from a Judahite prophet, perhaps signaling why Amos was not prophesying to his own people in Jerusalem. (His message would not have been welcomed there!) But something was missing. The numerical formula was never fulfilled; in none of the seven oracles is any nation indicted for the expected four transgressions. Clearly the cup had overflowed, but ultimately, against whom? The answer comes in an unexpected eighth oracle, far more extensive than the others, and directed against Israel.

Although the oracle is introduced with the same numerical formula as the others, the listed crimes expand beyond a single distinct transgression.[8] Israel's judgment is warranted because she has waged war against her own people, and each of the listed crimes indicts Israel for various aspects of social injustice. Israel has (1) aggressively pursued the debtor (2:6b–7a); (2) oppressed the slave, even sexually (2:7b); (3) broken the law that protected the debtor (2:8); and, (4) encouraged sin among the consecrated, while suppressing the word of God through the prophets (2:12). Amos's rhetoric of entrapment has come to serve its purpose; even when compared to the ghastly crimes committed by the nations, even when compared to Judah's rebellion against the Law and the Prophets, Israel's guilt rises above the rest.

A recurring motif throughout the book of Amos is social justice. In a time of relative prosperity under Jeroboam II, Israel's first-class citizens were

---

[7] Critical scholarship has long held that this seventh oracle is a redaction added to the text during or after the Babylonian exile. Such an approach begins with the assumption that prophets cannot or do not foretell the future, an assumption that is void if the prophets really do, in fact, prophesy by the Spirit of God. Furthermore, the fulfillment of the destruction of certain cities and nations in the prior six oracles did not take place within the eighth century. In fact, the destruction of Tyre took place over two centuries after the destruction of Jerusalem. Edom, Ammon, and Moab all fell to the Babylonians in the sixth century BC.

[8] See Robert B. Chisholm Jr. "'For Three Sins . . . Even for Four': The Numerical Sayings in Amos," in *Vital Old Testament Issues: Examining Textual and Topical Questions*, ed. Roy Zuck (Grand Rapids, MI: Kregel, 1996), 191–92.

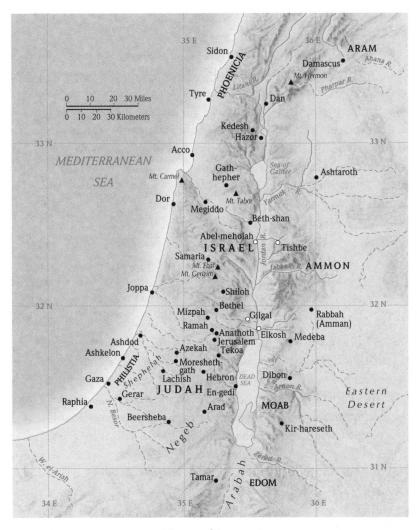

Nations of Amos 1–2

guilty not simply of neglecting the poor, but of committing aggressive crimes against them. They were quick to sell the debtor into slavery ("they sell a righteous person for silver and a needy person for a pair of sandals"), and they trampled the "heads of the poor on the dust of the ground" (2:6b–7a). In the context of social oppression, it is likely that 2:7b refers to a slave girl being abused sexually, and 2:8 is a clear violation of Exodus 22:26–27, where a poor man's garment taken in pledge was to be returned to him every evening. But not only did they lie down on garments taken in pledge, they did so by "every altar," even celebrating the demise of the debtor in their own house of worship!

Separating the third and fourth crimes of the eighth oracle recounts the history of God's gracious relationship to Israel, enhancing her culpability and guilt (2:9–11). God was a deliverer and a warrior who fought on behalf of Israel, giving her the land that she now possessed. Established in the land, Nazirites and prophets were called out from among them, yet Israel silenced the prophets and profaned the consecrated (2:11–12). For this reason, God would turn against them, crushing them as a weighted cart crushes grain (v. 13).[9] Continuing the chiastic structure, as God was once a warrior who fought on behalf of Israel (2:9–10), he would now fight against her. She would "flee naked on that day" (2:14–16; see Deut 28:25).

3:1–4:13 (The Guilt of Israel)

3:1–2 "I HAVE KNOWN ONLY YOU" (AN ORACLE CASING ISRAEL'S GUILT)

Amos 3:1 begins the second major segment of Amos, which concludes with 6:14. Within this broader segment, various sub-genres aid in communicating the prophetic message, many of which provide boundary features pointing to contextual shifts in the text. The clearest markers come in the form of three commands to "listen" (shema') to the word of the Lord (3:1; 4:1; 5:1), thereby reinforcing the voice of the One who "roars from Zion" (1:2).[10]

Yahweh has spoken his word "against" (repeated twice for emphasis) Israel, a people established under a unique relationship with God. The practical expectation of this relationship was obedience, and based on that obedience, Israel could expect protection and blessing. Yet instead of obedience God received rebellion, and, to their great dismay, Israel would now receive judgment. Contrary to the expectation of the people, their elect position would not bring unequivocal blessing. Their unique position as God's

---

[9] The imagery of verse 13 can be understood in the passive sense of God being "weighed down" by the sins of the people (NASB, NKJV, "I am weighed down by you . . ."), or actively as God crushing Israel in judgment (ESV, HCSB, NIV, "I will crush you . . .").

[10] See Mark F. Rooker, "Amos," in *The World and the Word: An Introduction to the Old Testament* (Nashville, TN: B&H, 2011), 434.

chosen obligated them to obedience, and now that same position obligated God to judgment. Again, the message of Amos ran counter to the expectations of the people (5:18–20).

3:3–8 "WHO WILL NOT PROPHESY?" (PROPHETIC DISPUTATION SPEECH: A SERIES OF RHETORICAL QUESTIONS AIMING TO VALIDATE THE MESSAGE AND THE MESSENGER)

Amos 3:3–8 provides an independent argument validating the prophet and his message. Through a series of rhetorical questions, Amos continues his rhetoric of entrapment by engaging his hearers in self-evident logic. The purpose is two-fold: first, the prophet provides a defense of his prophetic calling, a point that was especially relevant given that Amos was a non-professional prophet hailing from a small village in Judah. Second, Amos 3:3–8 validates the veracity of the prophetic message. The logic borne out by this rhetorical unit suggests that God is the One responsible for calamity, and indeed, the signs are already in place (3:6b; 4:6–11). As Jeremiah argues nearly two centuries later, God is the potter behind the destruction of the clay, and has every right—even an obligation—to bring judgment on his people.

The pattern throughout this rhetorical disputation is self-evident cause-and-effect relationship. The questions in verses three through five are each answerable with a resounding "of course not!" Indeed, two cannot share the same path unless they are agreed as to their destination (v. 3); lions do not roar unless they have caught prey (v. 4; utilizing parallel succession); birds do not fall from the sky unless snared, and traps do not snap unless triggered (v. 5; again, using parallel succession). Verse 6a reverses the cause-and-effect relationship, yet the logic is still intact: if a trumpet is blown in the city, then yes, the people will certainly be afraid. Moving to his point, again using parallelism to tighten the logical correspondence, Amos brings the initial sequence to conclusion: if there is a calamity in the city (the effect of judgment), then yes, the Lord must certainly be the responsible agent (v. 6b).

Tying his two purposes together, Amos concludes the broader unit by pressing the logical relationship between prophecy and judgment (3:7–8). If calamity is coming (and yes, it is), then surely a prophet will proclaim it (v. 7). If a prophet is prophesying, then it is the Lord who has spoken (v. 8b); if the Lord has indeed spoken, then the people ought to be afraid (v. 8a). Falling back on the metaphor of 1:2, the lion has roared; the response of the people ought to be fear. The Lord has spoken, and thus Amos must prophecy.

3:9–15 "Proclaim on the citadels . . ." (An Ironic Lawsuit within an Announcement of Judgment)

Taking 3:9–15 as a single unit bound by the theme of "plundered citadels,"[11] this announcement of judgment contains "judicial overtones" laced with rich irony.[12] From the citadels of Ashdod and Egypt, witnesses are called to Samaria to witness the oppression within her midst, for God's "people are incapable of doing right" (v. 10). Although God's people Israel were meant to be a beacon of light and a testimony to the nations, now the nations are called to testify against her, for she, who had received the law of God and knew what was right, seemed incapable of putting it into practice. The irony of the indictment should not be missed, yet the judgment is equally striking. Those who stored up the plunder of violent oppression in their citadels (v. 10b) would have those same citadels plundered by a violent foreign enemy (v. 11; see also 3:12; 4:2–3).[13]

Amos 3:12–15 continues the same line of argument introduced in 3:9–11. The violent overthrow of Israel's oppressing class is described in terms that only a breeder of sheep would fully appreciate (1:1; 7:14). Just as a shepherd retrieves "two legs or a piece of an ear" from a lamb mauled by a lion, so the remnant of Israel would be taken out in bits and pieces (v. 12). Continuing the line of irony, Amos shifts attention to one of Israel's centers of religious ritual, Bethel. The "horns of the altar" in Bethel were viewed as a place of refuge (1 Kgs 1:50; 2:28), but they would provide no such safety

---

[11] One of the binding themes in the oracles against the nations is that judgment would come against their citadels. However, the eighth oracle against Israel does not use this language; rather, it is picked up and expanded in Amos 3:9–15.

[12] While not an organized covenant lawsuit, 3:9–11 contains imagery that evokes judicial concepts such as jury, testimony, and evidence in the courtroom of justice. See Elizabeth Achtemeier, *Minor Prophets I*, Understanding the Bible Commentary Series (Grand Rapids, MI: Baker Academic, 1996), 193–94.

[13] The theme of plundered citadels continues into verse 15 by reference to the houses of the wealthy.

or refuge in the day of the Lord's visitation (v. 14).[14] In the course of destruction the very horns of the altar would be cut off, so that when reached, there would be nothing to grab!

4:1–5 "Cows of Bashan" (Sarcasm within an Announcement of Judgment)

Among the prophets, Amos has no equal in the use of biting sarcasm. This literary feature is on full display in Amos 4:1–5. Amos begins by addressing the wealthy women of Samaria as "cows of Bashan" (v. 1). These were the wives of the rich who fattened themselves off the backs of the poor. Bashan was a fertile grazing region in the northeast of Israel, and Amos's audience knew that he was essentially calling these women "fat cows." While such shock value was fully in-line with the prophet's rhetoric, there may have been a secondary function behind these words. With the certainty of judgment on the horizon, Amos may have been suggesting that these wealthy women were being fattened for the slaughter.[15]

There is additional irony in Amos's words as the "cows of Bashan" command their husbands, or literally, their "masters" or "lords" ('adonim), to bring wine that they may drink. Elsewhere, Amos describes these women as "drink[ing] wine by the bowlful" (6:6), so excess is certainly in view, but the irony of fattened cattle commanding their masters is a powerful picture.

Moving from accusation to announcement, Amos proclaims the coming judgment in exile imagery, although the exegetical details of Amos 4:2–3 are notoriously difficult. The HCSB, along with the NKJV and NIV, support the following translation of Amos 4:2b: "Look, the days are coming, when you will be taken away with hooks, every last one of you with fishhooks." On the other hand, the NET Bible understands the verse as describing the deportees taken away in baskets and fisherman's pots. In either case, the description is equally ominous. If taken in fishhooks, Amos may be describing the Assyrian practice of deporting populations by lines of individuals

---

[14] Bethel, the "house of God," was desecrated by Jeroboam I (1 Kings 12:25–33), continuing as a center for idol worship until its destruction in 722 BC. The altar at Bethel is referenced frequently by the prophets Amos and Hosea. Its "horns" were projections that rose from each of the four corners of the altar.

[15] This viewpoint is better supported if verse 2b is a description of exiles being packed as fish for the market. See Robert B. Chisholm Jr., *Handbook on the Prophets* (Grand Rapids, MI: Baker Academic, 2002), 388.

lashed together by hooks protruding through the lower lip.[16] If taken in fish baskets, then the deportees are described as dead fish packed and transported to the fish-market.[17] In either case, the imagery of exile is haunting. It was fulfilled a generation later when the citizens of Samaria were taken away by the brutal Assyrians.[18]

One must continue to appreciate the sarcasm introduced in 4:1 to properly grasp the intention of Amos in 4:4–5. Amos instructs the people to go to their revered centers of worship (Bethel and Gilgal) and offer sacrifices, tithes, and freewill offerings. Through imperative and climactic parallelism, Amos appears to be encouraging "rebellious" offerings. But again, the sarcasm should not be missed. The people had a misplaced trust in their cultic rituals of sacrifice, tithing, and freewill offerings (4:5b; 5:21–22). Although the people loved to display their outward affections, the Lord was disgusted by them (5:21). The invitation to rebel through sacrifice drips with sarcasm; but to intensify the effect, Amos also instructs them to bring their "sacrifices every morning, [their] tenths every three days" (v. 4b). What is especially striking here is that Amos instructs the people to bring "tenths" (tithes) every three days (*yomim*).[19] Among the tithes required of ancient Israel, each was offered annually, not daily, and only one was offered every three years, the tithe for the Levite and for the poor (the irony behind this should be obvious). Because the first class of Israel had come to place so much confidence in their religious rituals and offerings, instead of tithing for the poor every three years, according to their logic, why not do it every three days? After all, this "is what you Israelites love to do" (v. 5b)!

---

[16] Gary V. Smith, *Hosea, Amos, Micah*, NIVAC (Grand Rapids, MI: Zondervan, 2001), 288.

[17] For a detailed exegetical survey of the passage, along with an argument supporting the "fisherman's pots" translation, see Shalom Paul, *Amos*, Hermeneia (Minneapolis, MN: Fortress Press, 1991), 130–36.

[18] Although Assyria is never mentioned by name in the book of Amos, there are clear inferences to the impending Assyrian conquest. This was fulfilled in 722 BC, roughly forty years after Amos prophesied (762 BC).

[19] Some translations, perhaps missing the sarcasm and rather thinking to align *yomim* with the tithe given to the Levite and the poor (Deuteronomy 14:28; 26:12), have translated Amos 4:4b "every three years" rather than "every three days." See the KJV and NIV as examples.

4:6–12 "Yet you did not return to Me" (Escalating Repetition to Highlight Covenant Ignorance)

Amos 4:6–12 has clear distinguishing marks that set it apart within the book. Beginning in verse 6, the refrain, "Yet you did not return to Me," is repeated five times (vs. 6, 8, 9, 10, 11), followed in each case with a rehearsal of the name of Yahweh. Thematically, this section correlates back to the covenant curses detailed in Deuteronomy 28. Israel had been warned of suffering that would come as a result of national disobedience to the law; the curses were now warning Israel of the coming exile that would manifest the capstone of divine judgment.

Although Israel had plenty of opportunity for reflection and repentance, given her past and present sufferings, she refused to return to God. Therefore, because Israel did not come to God in repentance, God would come to her in judgment (v. 12). Instead of meeting God in the expectation of blessing (5:14; 18–20), Israel would meet God in the full measure of his wrath (v. 12b).

4:13 "Yahweh, the God of Hosts is His name" (A Hymn to Exalt the Name of Yahweh)

Amos 4:13 is the first of three hymns found within the book (4:13; 5:8–9; 9:5–6). Thematically, all three exalt the power of Yahweh and celebrate his role over creation. A common thread in each is the emphasis on the name of Yahweh. Awe over that name is a prominent motif throughout Amos, perhaps reaching a highpoint in these hymns.[20]

As interpreters of the Amos book, it is critical to understand how these hymns function. While a hymn of praise may encourage heartfelt worship, in Amos 4:13 the hymn prompts awe and fear. The God who Israel will meet in judgment (v. 12) is the same God who "forms the mountains," makes the "dawn out of darkness" (in modern terms, rotates the earth), and "strides on the heights of the earth." In the context of judgment, this was an awesome and terrible reminder of what *this* God was capable of bringing against Israel.

---

[20] It is uncertain whether these hymns originate with Amos or if they were adapted from preexistent material.

Similarities between Amos 4 and Deuteronomy 28–29	
Amos	Deuteronomy
4:6 "I gave you **absolutely nothing to eat** in all your cities, a **shortage of food** in all your communities . . ."	28:48 "you will serve your enemies . . . **in famine**, thirst, nakedness, and a **lack of everything**."
4:7–8 "**I also withheld the rain** from you while there were still three months until harvest. I sent rain on one city but no rain on another . . .Two or three cities staggered to another city to drink water but were not satisfied . . ."	28:23–24 "The sky above you will be bronze, and the earth beneath you iron. **The LORD will turn the rain of your land into falling dust;** it will descend on you from the sky until you are destroyed."
4:9 "I struck you with blight and mildew; the **locust** devoured your many gardens and **vineyards**, your fig trees and **olive trees** . . ."	28:38–40 "You will sow much seed in the field but harvest little, because **locusts** will devour it. You will plant and cultivate **vineyards** but not drink the wine or gather the grapes . . . You will have **olive trees** throughout your territory but not anoint yourself with oil, because your olives will drop off."
4:10 "I sent **plagues** like those of **Egypt** . . ."	28:60 "He will afflict you again with all the **diseases of Egypt** . . ."
4:11 "I overthrew some of you as **I overthrew Sodom and Gomorrah** . . ."	29:23 "All its soil will be a burning waste of sulfur and salt, unsown, producing nothing, with no plant growing on it, **just like the fall of Sodom and Gomorrah** . . ."

5:1–6:14 (The Death of Israel)

5:1, 16–17 (A LAMENTATION FOR ISRAEL – *INCLUSIO* OF LAMENT FRAMING A CALL TO REPENTANCE)

Amos 5:1–17 comprises an oracle of judgment in the form of a lament. The lament is introduced in 5:1 and proclaimed in 5:2, yet carries through until bookended by the announcement of wailing in 5:16–17. Thematically, the lament continues through the woe oracles introduced in 5:18 and 6:1. Hearing one's own funeral announcement from the mouth of a prophet should have brought great fear and dread. Yet even in the midst of such dire prediction, the opportunity for repentance was still intact. The lament brackets the only true call to repentance within the book (5:4–7, 14–15).

5:2 "Virgin Israel will never rise again" (A Lament)

Picturing Israel as a "fallen virgin," perhaps to evoke the imagery of a maiden cut off before her prime (rather than lost purity), the lament opens in a succinct four-line parallel stanza. The lament is heightened through parallelism and hyperbole, with fallen Israel stated to "never rise again." In the language of the prophets, such a proclamation expressed the severity of judgment. From a human vantage point, her judgment was not a matter of temporary discipline.[21] Amos nevertheless sees a future for Israel, as the Lord "will not totally destroy the house of Jacob" (9:8) and "will restore the fallen booth of David" (9:11).[22] But in the immediate sense, there was no hope for Israel aside from national repentance (5:4–15).

5:3 "ten left in the house of Israel" (Numerical De-escalation by Example Story)

To further the effect of the lament, Amos includes an example story to illustrate the severity of judgment. Through numerical de-escalation, Amos describes a 90 percent mortality rate among Israel's troops. To assume a remnant from the remaining 10 percent is to miss the point; rather than provide hope for a remnant, this example story illustrates the severity of judgment leading to the death of Israel.

5:4–7 "Seek Me and live!" (A Call to Repentance)

The irony of finding a call to repentance (5:4–15) framed by an oracle of lament (5:1–3, 16–17) highlights the stark contrast between the opposing

---

[21] On "prophetic hyperbole," and the functional use of hyperbole in the language of the prophets, see D. Brent Sandy, *Plowshares and Pruning Hooks: Rethinking the Language of Biblical Prophecy and Apocalyptic* (Grand Rapids, MI: InterVarsity, 2002), 75–102.

[22] Even if 9:11–15 is seen as applying distinctly to Judah (the "booth of David"), other prophets, most particularly Ezekiel, see a reunification of the divided kingdoms restored to the land under one Davidic King (Ezekiel 37:15–28; 39:21–29).

future options set before Israel. Either Israel would experience the impending death forecast by her own funeral dirge, or she would seek God and live, an option repeated three times within the call to repentance (5:4, 6, 14).

Like other oracles within Amos, the call to repentance is introduced as a message from Yahweh. Yet within the call there is a shift from the first person, "Seek Me and live" (vs. 4–5) to the third person, "Seek Yahweh and live" (vs. 6–7), perhaps highlighting the authentic relationship between the prophet and God. Additionally, Amos is clear that Yahweh was not found by sacred location; Bethel (the "house of God") would be reduced to 'aven ("nothing"). Gilgal, the first encampment in Joshua's conquest of the land, would "certainly go into exile" (v. 5). For rhetorical effect, Amos employs alliteration and "sound-play" within this text. The Hebrew phrase translated "will certainly go into exile" sounds like the name "Gilgal" repeated, thus capturing the attention of the original audience through the repetition of Hebrew consonants.[23] Such an effect was generated by Egyptian Islamists on September 11, 2012, when they marched the streets of Cairo chanting, "Obama, we are all Osama." Any American hearing that chant immediately understood the chilling effect of wordplay.

5:8–9 "Yahweh is His name" (A Hymn to Exalt the Name of Yahweh)

Like the hymn that precedes it (4:13), this hymn draws attention to the role of Yahweh as Creator. Although the broader context of judgment is still in play, the hymn in 5:8–9 also praises God as capable of forgiving the repentant as well as establishing justice in the land. This is illustrated by the contrast between Israel, who turns "justice into wormwood," and Yahweh, who "turns darkness into dawn" (v. 6, 8b). The God who should be feared in judgment (4:13; see also 5:9) can also be trusted as One who is quick to forgive.

The hymn's placement at this location may have an additional function related to structure. Scholars have long recognized chiastic structure within the boundaries of lamentation (5:1–17). In this arrangement, the center lies in the hymn at this focal point: "Yahweh is His name."

---

[23] The statement "Gilgal will certainly go into exile" reads in the Hebrew as *haggilgal galoh yigleh*. The wordplay is obvious. See Chisholm, *Handbook on the Prophets*, 390.

Chiastic Structure of Amos 5:1–17

A. Lamentation over fallen Israel (5:1–3)
  B. Call to repentance: "Seek Me (Yahweh) and live!" (5:4–6)
    C. Accusation against Israel: "Throw[ing] righteousness to the ground" (5:7)
      D. Hymn: Celebration of Yahweh as Creator (5:8a–b)
        E. Epicenter: Yahweh is His name (5:8c)
      D'. Hymn: Celebration of Yahweh as Warrior (5:9)
    C'. Accusation against Israel: "Oppress[ing] the righteous" (5:10–13)
  B'. Call to repentance: "Seek good . . . that you may live" (5:14–15)
A'. Wailing over fallen Israel (5:16–17)

5:10–13 "For the Days are Evil" (An Announcement of Judgment)

Shifting from accusation (vs. 10–11a) to an announcement of judgment (v. 11b) and then back to accusation (v. 12; v. 13 functions as a summary statement for 10–12), the segment from 5:10–13 reiterates the theme of social injustice. In the city gate where the elders judged cases of civil dispute, the few who stood for justice were despised and hated (v. 10). Repeating the image of trampling on the poor (see 2:7), Amos condemns the extraction of "grain taxes" from the sustenance farmer. The law did not provide for such taxation, and the injustice of farmers starving because of the extraction of their harvests strikes to the core of abusive power.[24]

The judgment against those who "trample on the poor" mirrors the promise of curse in Deutonomy 28:30, again reinforcing Amos's role as a mediator of the covenant (v. 11b). Following this brief announcement of judgment, Amos returns to accusation, repeating for effect the crime of diverting justice at the gate, which took place through the sin of bribery (v. 12). So prevalent was this culture of corruption that the few voices of justice are described as keeping silent for their own good and safety.

---

[24] Modern parallels are unfortunately plentiful, especially when communist governments extract the harvests of farmers only to leave the farmers starving in spite of the produce of their labor. The Ukrainian famines in the 1930s or North Korean famines in the 1990s provide examples of such injustice.

5:14–15 "Hate evil and love good" (A Call to Repentance)

Repeating the call to repentance, Amos affirms that seeking Yahweh is not a matter of religious ritual and location (5:4–7), but of seeking "good and not evil." The chiastic structure of the unit pictures the image of "turning" in repentance, and with such turning came the hope of God's grace to Israel (v. 15).

5:16–17 "I will pass among you" (An Announcement of Death)

The lament announced in Amos 5:1 formally closes in verses 16–17, with the Hebrew term for "wailing" (*misped*) repeated three times for emphasis. So expansive will the death toll be that professional mourners will not be sufficient to mourn for all the dead; even farmers will be called to mourning (v. 16). The lament closes with a chilling promise from the voice of Yahweh: "For I will pass through you" (v. 17 NKJV). Although this language is repeated later in Amos's visions (7:8; 8:2), the more significant point is the allusion back to the Exodus Passover.[25] When Yahweh passed *through* the land of Egypt on that night, death fell upon the firstborn of the land (Exod 12:12). Yet for Israel, Yahweh instead passed *over* them, and thus spared their firstborn sons from death. These prophetic words must have been especially chilling; in effect, the God who had once passed *over* them would now pass *through* them in judgment.[26]

5:18–27 "Woe to you who long for the Day of the Lord!" (Woe Speech against the Hypocrite and Idolater)

Following thematically with the prior lamentation, Amos 5:18–27 takes on the form of a woe speech.[27] Although Amos has previously alluded to the misguided confidence that Israel placed in her elaborate cult, the motif of misguided expectation rises to prominence in this unit. Calling attention to this misguided conception, Amos proclaims "woe," or "death," to those

---

[25] On the prophetic technique of historical allusion and alteration, see Aaron Chalmers, *Interpreting the Prophets: Reading, Understanding and Preaching from the Worlds of the Prophets* (Downers Grove, IL: InterVarsity, 2015), 89–91.

[26] Additional allusions to the plagues of Egypt in Amos include (4:10; 7:8).

[27] Given the thematic unity, it is possible that the woe speech is simply a continuation of the lament. See Chisholm, *Handbook on the Prophets*, 392–94.

who desired the Day of the Lord. The people had come to expect that the Day of the Lord would be a day of salvation, a day when God would exalt Israel over the nations. This day would include military victory, economic blessing, and an expansion of territory; interestingly, the limited expansion of territory under Jeroboam II was seen by some as a precursor to that day of blessing. However, Amos turns this misguided expectation into an announcement of judgment. In contrast to Israel's expectation, the Day of the Lord would be a day when Yahweh would fight *against* Israel, not *for* her. Through repetition and climactic parallelism, Amos describes the day not as a day of joyful light, but of dreaded darkness (5:18b, 20). In a series of related illustrations, Amos describes the day as one in which a man flees a lion, and quite ironically, meets a bear, or when he reaches a house and places his hand against a wall (signifying refuge and rest) only to have a serpent bite him (v. 19). When God turns against Israel, there will be no place of refuge.

In no uncertain manner, God declares his feelings ("I hate, I despise") toward the rituals Israel pursued so expectantly (v. 21). God's rejection of the listed sacrifices is described using Hebrew verbs that relate directly to each ritual: God will not "savor" their burnt offerings, nor will he "look upon" their peace offerings or "listen" to their festive songs.[28] Rather than the rituals Israel practiced, God desired for the culture of corruption (5:10–13) to be replaced with a culture of justice, where righteousness would flow "like an unfailing stream" (v. 24).

Amos 5:25–27 is notoriously difficult to interpret, and translations reveal the wide range of options. The major difference is in how one understands the rhetorical question in verse 25, "House of Israel, was it sacrifices and grain offerings that you presented to Me during the 40 years in the wilderness?" If one concludes that the implied answer to the rhetorical question is "no," then history demonstrates sacrifice is not as significant as Israel might assume. Following suit, if the worship of idols takes place after devotion to Yahweh, then judgment will surely follow (this understanding may find support in Deut 32:17). But if the implied answer is "yes," then verse 26 can be understood with the transition "sure, but," essentially arguing against syncretistic worship. In the first approach, the shortsightedness of placing trust in religious ritual is exposed. In the second, the religious

---

[28] Achtemeier, *Minor Prophets I*, 211.

hypocrisy of eighth-century Israel is condemned. Either conclusion leads to the judgment of exile. Although Assyria is not mentioned by name, it is inferred by the geographical marker, "beyond Damascus" (v. 27). As a result of Israel's abuse of the poor, religious hypocrisy, and practice of idolatry, she would be sent into captivity in a foreign land.

6:1–8 "Woe to those who are at ease in Zion" (Woe Speech against the First of Israel)

Chapter six continues the judgment oracles with a woe speech leveled against the first-class citizens of Israel.[29] Utilizing wordplay to communicate a sense of poetic justice, the "first class" citizens of the "first" (*re'shit*) nation who use the "finest" (*re'shit*) oils will be the "first" (*ro'sh*, derived from the same root as *re'shit*) to go into captivity (v. 7).

Additionally, Amos 6:1–8 reminds the reader of judgments and abuses cited earlier. In the rhetorical questions of verse two, the reader is reminded of the judgments against the nations (1:3–2:3), and most notably, the fact that Judah and Israel are also subject to God's judgment (2:4–16). Verses three and four remind the reader of the excessive features of their first-class lifestyle (3:9–15), and verse five reminds of the hypocrisy of their worship (5:21–23). Verse six brings the reader back to the excesses of the wealthy women of Samaria and their disdain for the poor (4:1–2), and finally, the announcement of judgment in verse seven mirrors the conclusion of the previous woe speech (5:27).

Assuming that verse eight functions together with 6:1–7 (6:1 highlights the death of the city, 6:8 ends with the city "handed over"), the judgment of Israel's coming captivity is reiterated not as a stale matter of cause and effect, but as a matter linked to the heart of God. As Israel "despised" (*ta'ev*) the one who speaks with integrity (5:10), so Yahweh "loathed" (*ta'ev*) Jacob's pride (6:8), the sin attitude that led Israel into hypocrisy, a false sense of security, and the social corruption that would drive her into captivity.

---

[29] Both "Zion" and "Mount Samaria" are referenced in the parallelism of Amos 6:1. While Amos's message targets the northern kingdom of Israel, this is not the only reference to Judah and its capital, Jerusalem (2:4–5; 9:11).

6:9–10 "Silence!" (A Continuation of the Example Story in Amos 5:3)

The poetic series of judgment oracles that comprises Amos 3–6 is interrupted by a prose "example story" in 6:9–10. Thematically, this example story is tied to the overall message of impending judgment, and it reads as a continuation of the example story in 5:3. As ten are left to the house of Israel (5:3d), so these ten, now remaining in one house, shall also die (6:9). The purpose of the example story in 5:3 is to emphasize the severity of judgment; in 6:9–10, the story continues with an emphasis on the God who brings that judgment. Ironically, those who in their pride once dismissed any expectation of judgment (6:3a), now fearfully expect judgment at the mere whisper of his name (6:10). Those who refused to revere the name of Yahweh (4:13; 5:8; 9:6); these would now cower in fear at the mention of his name.

6:11–14 "Do horses gallop on the cliffs?" (Disputation with an Announcement of Judgment)

In a disputation authenticating the surety of God's judgment, Amos concludes the broader series of judgment speeches with a clear prophetic statement of what lies in Israel's near future. Reinforcing the oracle of 3:9–15, Amos again states that it is God who brings judgment at the command of his voice (compare 3:15 to 6:11). Then, using rhetorical disputation reminiscent of 3:3–8, Amos asks, "Do horses gallop on cliffs; does anyone plow there with oxen?" (v. 12a). The implied answer is "no, that would be absurd . . ." Yet just as absurdly, Israel has managed to "turn justice into poison, and the fruit of righteousness into wormwood" (v. 12b; compare to 5:7). Additionally, Israel had rejoiced in her own conquests, including the town of "Lo-debar," transliterated from the Hebrew words meaning "nothing" (v. 13). Quite sarcastically, Amos accuses Israel of rejoicing in the military might responsible for the conquest of "nothing."[30]

For reason of Israel's own pride, God would raise up a nation against her who would afflict her from the entrance of Hamath (in the north) to the Brook of the Arabah (in the south). For Amos's contemporaries, such a

---

[30] 2 Samuel 9:4–5; 17:27 mention Lo-Debar. It was the home of Mephiboseth, Jonathan's son. This may have been a small town conquered by the expansion of territory under Jeroboam II (2 Kings 14:23–27).

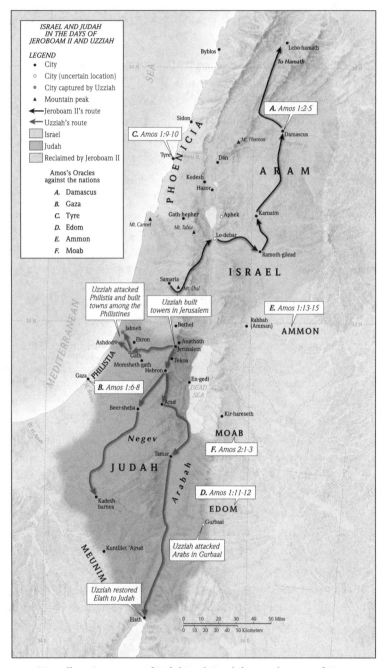

Map illustrating scope of Judah and Israel during the time of Amos

description would have been quite shocking, as Jeroboam II had just expanded the territory of Israel to these very boundaries (2 Kgs 14:25). Just one generation later, God would raise up the Assyrians to conquer the territory that had become the pride of Israel.

7:1–9:6 (Five Visions of Amos)

Chapter seven begins a shift to the prophetic subgenre of vision (with a narrative interlude). The first two visions follow a similar structural and thematic pattern (7:1–3, 4–6), as do the third and fourth visions (7:7–9; 8:1–3). The fifth vision, on the other hand, is quite unique in form and function (9:1–4).

7:1–3 "Please forgive!" (The Vision of Locusts)

Amos 7:1–2a introduces the first vision, an event that, due to prophetic intervention, never came to pass. Amos was shown a vision of locusts, a dreadful thought in a world where one locust plague could result in the near extinction of a nation. The "spring crop" implied that these were the resources that would sustain Israel through the dry summer season and, if affecting those crops taken after the "king's hay" (perhaps the extraction of grain taxes; see 5:11), this was the worst possible scenario for the populace of Israel. In poetic script, Amos pleads the case for Israel (7:2b), knowing the impending disaster soon to fall upon her. Yahweh hears the prophet's intervention, and relents (7:3).

7:4–6 "Please stop!" (The Vision of Fire)

Parallel to the vision of locusts, the vision of fire is also met with prophetic intervention. The "judgment by fire" is likely an imaginative description of a supernaturally severe drought, one that would dry up underground water sources and leave the landscape devastated. Although one might infer a movement from the prophet's plea to "forgive" in the first vision to the more desperate "stop" in the second, this is likely nothing more than a slight literary adjustment between parallel visions.

Two important points can be gleaned from the visions. First it was not enough for Amos, as a prophet, to proclaim the coming judgment of God. Rather, in the pattern of Moses (Deut 9:17–20, 25–29), Jeremiah (Jer 7:16–17; 9:1; 15:1), and Ezekiel (Ezek 13:5), Amos fulfills his prophetic calling by interceding on behalf of the people.[31] Amos's ministry of intercession is especially striking when one sees the response of Israel's leadership in the following narrative (7:10–12): if Amaziah the priest knew just how close Israel was to judgment, and how Amos had interceded on their behalf not once but twice, perhaps he would have embraced Amos as a national hero rather than rejecting him as a treasonous foe.

Second, as a theological point, it is striking that God is the one who "relented" of judgment, while the people of Israel were too hard-hearted (and hard-headed) to repent of their sins. The prophets present a God who is quick to relent of judgment; this is even stated propositionally in texts such as Joel 2:13 and Jonah 4:2. But God's mercies should not be taken for granted; there is a line that, once crossed, cannot be retraced.

7:7–9 "I am setting a plumb line among My people Israel" (The Vision of the Plumb Line)

Although there are similar features among the first four visions of Amos, there are also distinctions. In the second two visions (7:7–9; 8:1–3), instead of simply seeing an anticipated event and responding, Amos sees a symbolic picture and is prompted to dialogue with God over its interpretation. Furthermore, God's response is strikingly different. Instead of relenting from judgment, the line has been crossed; God will not relent.

In the third vision, Amos sees a "plumb line," with the Lord standing on a wall holding the line in his hand.[32] As the line drops down against the vertical wall, the wall is shown to be crooked. The implication of the vision is clear: Israel has failed to meet the standard set by the builder, and now the wall must be destroyed. In judgment, God will "no longer spare them," a possible allusion back to Amos 5:17 and the Passover event. Announcing the details of this judgment (with chiastic structure in v. 9), the religious

---

[31] Achtemeier, *Minor Prophets I*, 219.

[32] The Hebrew word behind the translation "plumb line" is found only in this passage, and there is some debate regarding its meaning. For a discussion on the exegetical options, including the translation "tin," see Paul, *Amos*, 233–36.

fortifications of Israel are laid waste as God rises with sword against the house of Jeroboam.[33]

7:10–17 "Go, prophesy to My people Israel" (Autobiographical Interlude)

The third and fourth visions are interrupted by an autobiographical interlude, positioned to provide a historical context for Amos's visions while also providing justification for the unrelenting nature of the announced judgments. Amaziah, the priest in Bethel (a frequent target of Amos's words), sends a report to Jeroboam II that essentially mirrors the announcement of judgment in Amos 7:9. The literary position linking the words of the letter (v. 11) to the prior vision (v. 9) is significant; equally significant is the link between historical event and prophetic literature that this text reveals. Amos's words were spoken and heard before they were written and read, and Amos's prophecies must be understood within the context of the sociopolitical setting of his day.

According to Amaziah, the "land" (v. 10) was unable to "endure" the words of Amos (whose name means "burden"—the wordplay is likely intentional, although the terms are not identical in the Hebrew). Because Amos announced that the people of Israel would be led away as captives from their "homeland" (v. 11), Amaziah tells Amos to flee back to his own "land," the land of Judah (v. 12). Amos responds boldly to the high priest. Beginning with a defense of his divine call and motivation (Amos was not prophesying for financial gain), Amos verbally blasts Amaziah, shifting the judgment from the house of Jeroboam II (v. 11) to the house of Amaziah (v. 17). In an ironic twist, Amos turns Amaziah's report back on his own head—Amaziah's wife would turn to harlotry (horrifying, considering that Amaziah was a priest), his sons and daughters would fall by the sword, and his "land" would be divided and given to another while he died "on pagan soil."

---

[33] Commentators are divided over the fulfillment of this announcement. While the destruction of sanctuaries points to the Assyrian invasion forty years after the ministry of Amos (an invasion and captivity implied elsewhere throughout Amos), some see a more immediate fulfillment in the assassination of Zechariah, son of Jeroboam, and the effective end to the dynasty of Jehu (2 Kings 15:12).

8:1–3 "The end has come" (The Vision of Summer Fruit)

Following the historical interlude, the text immediately proceeds to the fourth vision, where Amos is shown a basket of summer fruit. In dialogue similar to that in the third vision, the Lord explains the meaning of the vision, again alluding to Passover symbolism (7:8; 8:2). Reinforcing the finality of the decision for judgment, the summer fruit (over-ripe fruit) symbolized that an end had come upon Israel; judgment was now inevitable (8:2). Thematically, just as over-ripe fruit could not be brought back from spoil, Israel would not be brought back from destruction. Linguistically, Amos crafts a play on words in the vision; the Hebrew for "summer fruit" is *qayits*, a "sound alike" to the Hebrew word for "end," *qets*.

Like the third vision, the fourth ends in a poetic description of Israel's death; the songs of the temple that Israel rejoiced over (see 5:23; 6:5) would become wailing in that day (see 5:16–17), and the dead would be picked up in silence (see 6:10).

8:4–14 "I will never forget all their deeds" (Announcement of Judgment)

Amos 8:4–14 begins a new unit, an announcement of judgment that bridges the gap between the fourth and fifth visions. Amos again calls out those who oppress the poor and "trample on the needy" (see 2:7). Their hypocrisy is enhanced by their social corruption, seeking every "lawful" opportunity to oppress the poor by falsifying scales and selling fewer goods for a higher price (v. 5).

Their crimes in the marketplace were not limited to grain and wheat. In Amos 2:6, Israel is guilty of "*sell[ing]* the righteous for silver, and the poor for a pair of sandals" (NKJV). Now Amos completes the cycle, describing the desire of these corrupt merchants: "We can *buy* the poor with silver and the needy for a pair of sandals" (8:6). Those who were in the business of buying and selling marketplace goods were now in the business of buying and selling humans. Ironically, those who led the poor into the desperate straits of slavery would close the deal through the financial transaction of buying and selling those same people.

In response, Yahweh proclaims his judgment in no uncertain terms: "I will never forget all their deeds" (v. 7b)! To enforce the surety of this promise, Yahweh swears it as an oath (v. 7a). There is exegetical ambiguity in the oath: Some translations view the oath as a sarcastic reference to Israel's pride, "by the *pride* of Jacob" (NKJV, NASB, ESV, NET), while others view it as a reference to a proper name, presumably God himself; "by the *Pride* of Jacob" (HCSB, NIV, NLT). In favor of the former approach, Amos 6:8 states that God "loath[es] Jacob's pride," clearly a reference to the arrogance of Israel's first-class citizenry (6:1–7). In this interpretation, the oath reflects sarcasm as Yahweh seals the announcement of judgment, swearing by the very pride that led Israel to believe they were beyond the reach of God's wrath.

On the other hand, in favor of the translation that understands the "Pride of Jacob" as metonymy for God, and thereby, God swearing "by himself" (for there is no one higher), one might find correlation in Amos 4:2, "The Lord God has sworn by His holiness." Furthermore, with this approach, there is a greater sense of irony when the Israelites swear "by the guilt of Samaria" (if the "guilt of Samaria" is an idol; see 8:14). While Israel swears by an idol, Yahweh swears "by himself."

The oracle continues by describing the judgment of God in catastrophic (even apocalyptic) terms. Ironically, those who celebrated feasts (see 5:21) would mourn, and those who sang songs (see 5:23) would lament; the nation that turned justice to bitterness (see 5:7) would experience its end as a "bitter day" (v. 10). Furthermore, the Day of the Lord (8:9, 11, 13) is described as a day in which the word of the Lord cannot be found. In that day, the young men and women will "faint from thirst," demonstrating the drought of the words of God. Those who swear by idols will meet their final demise (8:13–14).[34]

9:1–4 "I will fix My eyes on them for harm and not for good" (The Vision of the Lord Standing at the Altar)

The fifth vision of Amos lacks the structural and thematic characteristics found in the first four visions, but it is nonetheless introduced as a vision: "I saw the Lord standing beside the altar" (v. 1a). Amos "sees" an oracle of judgment—the Lord commanding the destruction of the altar and its edifice. In judgment, Yahweh ominously states that he will slay "the rest of them" with the sword, evoking the image of no escape (9:1; compare 5:19 to 9:3 for a similar use of imagery). Furthermore, 9:1–4 clearly portrays

---

[34] This is ironic given Israel's earlier rejection of the prophets (2:12) and Amos's prophetic ministry (7:12).

an ironic relationship to the previous oracle. In the Day of the Lord, when there is a "famine" of "hearing the words of" Yahweh (8:11), the people will seek God, but not find him (8:12). Now, in 9:1–4, the people will flee the Lord, but they will not be able to escape him!

9:5–6 "Yahweh is His name" (A Hymn to Exalt the Name of Yahweh)

In the last of the three hymns of Amos, Yahweh is presented as the divine warrior who wages war with cosmic might, whose power is that over nature itself (compare 8:8 to 9:5). Again, the hymn functions within the text of Amos as a polemical device; first, to draw attention to the name (identity) of the God who Israel had neglected to fear, and second, to argue, in effect, that "if *this* is the God who has declared war against us, then indeed, we are utterly defeated!"

9:7–15 (The Salvation of Israel)

9:7–10 "I will not totally destroy the house of Jacob" (Precursor to Salvation)

The primary emphasis throughout the book of Amos has been the accusation of guilt and the announcement of judgment, communicated through a range of rich imagery, rhetorical devices, and prophetic sub-genres. Aside from a hint of grace in chapter five (5:15), the words of Amos have been devoid of hope. In the concluding oracles, however, Amos turns from the inevitability of judgment to the hope of salvation. Amos 9:7–10 provides a transition, first teaching that Yahweh's judgment is not indiscriminant before proclaiming the full restoration of Israel's blessings in the land (9:11–15).

Beginning with a series of rhetorical questions (v. 7), Yahweh, in effect, asks Israel, "Have no other nations had 'exodus' experiences, have no other nations been planted in lands that were not theirs?" The answer is "of course not"—Israel should know that just as God has planted her in the land, he could surely uproot her (v. 8a). Yet this was not the end of Israel, nor the end of the point being made; although Israel was not unique in her conquest of the land, she was unique in the covenant God had made with her (v. 8b). For this reason, God would be discerning in judgment, sifting Israel

(vv. 9–10) and preserving a remnant through which Israel's covenant blessings would be fully realized (9:11–15).

9:11–12 "I will restore the fallen booth of David" (Salvation Oracle #1)

Reflecting the flexible nature of "Day of the Lord" language, the day that Israel hoped for (5:14, 18), but was told to dread (5:20; 8:9, 11, 13), has now become a day of hope and restoration (9:11, 13). Although a unified Israel ruled by the Davidic dynasty seemed a distant memory for the now divided Israel, the "fallen booth" of David will one day be raised up by God to repossess the land. But this text suggests more than a repossession of territory.[35] The text alludes, at least in the Septuagint translation, to the incorporation of the Gentiles into the program of God. Interestingly, the LXX is quoted by James in Acts 15:16–17 to support just such an application. Perhaps God in his providence commandeered an extension of this prophecy, even if through an ancient translation of the Hebrew.[36]

9:13–15 "They will never again be up rooted from the land I have given them" (Salvation Oracle #2)

While the first salvation oracle promised restoration of the Davidic kingdom, the second oracle focuses on the experience of kingdom blessings in the land (9:13–15). Using hyperbolic imagery, Amos describes days of such agricultural prosperity that the harvest cannot be reaped before it is time once again to replant. The hills "flow" with the sweet produce of the harvest (v. 13). Perhaps more significantly, these are days of national replanting in the land, where the captives would be brought back from captivity and the ruined cities would be rebuilt. Most importantly, God would plant them in the "land" ('adamah), never again to be removed or destroyed from the face of the "earth" (9:8; 'adamah).

---

[35] Although, territory is an expected aspect of the Davidic covenant (Psalm 2; 72:8–11).

[36] Although the Hebrew for "Edom" and "mankind" are distinguishable, it is understandable how the Septuagint translators would have arrived at their translation. Perhaps God intended all along that the Davidic conquest of "Edom" would translate (no pun intended) to the Davidic salvation of "mankind." For exegetical notes, see Jeffrey Niehaus, "Amos," in *The Minor Prophets: An Exegetical & Expositional Commentary*, Vol. 1; ed. Thomas Edward McComiskey (Grand Rapids, MI: Baker, 1992), 491–92.

Theological Message and Application of Amos

The message of Amos centers on the accusation of sin and subsequent announcements of judgment. Although rich in tone and imagery, the message of Amos is consistent. Israel's transgressions constitute a grave inhumanity on par with that of the nations (1:3–2:3). A culture of corruption had developed in Israel, with little regard for the sanctity of human life. Adding insult to social injustice, Israel rejoiced over her elaborate yet hypocritical religious system. The spiritually obtuse leadership of Israel even expected God's favor and blessing for their religious pomp; in their view, the prosperity experienced in Jeroboam II's reign was a precursor of blessings to come. But Amos's message was a sharp slap in the face to Israel. She who expected the Day of the Lord as a day of blessing would soon discover that it would come as a day of curses and captivity (5:18–20, 27; 6:7–8).

In the context of Amos's contemporaries, the "lion's roar" (1:2; 3:8) would be felt within a generation—the Assyrians rose to prominence in the ancient Near-Eastern world and ruthlessly destroyed the Israelite kingdom, taking its people into captivity and replacing its population with other conquered people groups. Although there are no explicit references to Assyria within the book of Amos, implied references are frequent. History clearly brings Amos's warnings to fulfillment in 722 BC.

While Amos lacks integrated references to eschatological restoration, it should come as no surprise to see the prophet from Judah closing his message with an oracle of Davidic hope, a reversal from the "dark" day of God's judgment to the "bright" day that Israel expected. In his closing words, Amos brings to light a day of new covenant blessing, where Israel would be re-gathered and replanted in the land, never to be uprooted again (9:14–15; see Hos 1:11; 2:23; Ezekiel 37; 39:21–29).

Theologically, one motif stands above the rest—fear and reverence at the awesome name of Yahweh. The theology of Amos exalts the power and name of Yahweh in his judgments and salvation. This is especially prominent in the hymns dispersed throughout the book. Even so, the entire text of Amos reflects a repeated emphasis on the name of Yahweh, a necessary reminder of the reverence due to his name. Not only did the people have a false perception of themselves. They had diminished their God, demonstrating through their actions a complete lack of reverence for the name of Yahweh. Amos made clear the name that was to be exalted above all other names.

Complementing the theological teachings of the book is an array of practical teachings. First, in view of Amos's repeated indictments against social injustice, any application of the book must consider what God is saying to his people today regarding their treatment of the underprivileged, the downcast, and the helpless within society. The text of Amos makes it clear that God considers crimes of extortion, bribery, cheating, usury, and the like on par with violence and murder: all are considered crimes against humanity. On a national level, social injustice exists where pay day loan operations are established in the poorest neighborhoods, along with abortion clinics. And while social injustice in the United States is relatively benign, there are many places in the world today where businesses must budget bribes, courtrooms are a sham, and children are sold into sexual slavery every day. On a more personal level, who has not at one time or another been tempted to take advantage of the mishaps of others in order to achieve personal gain? Or perhaps, in a sin of omission, who among us has been anointed "with the finest oils," yet failed to grieve for the affliction of the poor (6:6)?

Second, Amos speaks out against the practice of vain religious ritualism, especially when practiced in a spirit of hypocrisy. Although God's people today may not be celebrating feasts and observing sacred assemblies of the same variety as those practiced in Amos's day, one wonders what God's attitude is toward our Sunday morning celebrations. Is there any reason why he might say "I hate, I despise" your Sunday services (5:21), or "take away from Me the noise of your songs" (5:23)?

Finally, in the area of religious expectation, how different are many North American church-goers today from the ancient Israelites, believing that God's eyes are set on them only for good and not for harm (9:4)? The message of Amos is clear: God's judgment is discerning on both ends, and those deserving of judgment will receive it (9:10). When polled, the majority of Americans say they believe they are going to heaven, even though they may believe in a hell. Within the churches, the vast majority believe that they are in "favor" with God. One must wonder if this kind of thinking is reflective of the same spiritual obtuseness seen in Amos's day. What would a modern-day Amos preach to the churches of America?

8

THE BOOK OF OBADIAH

Introduction

Perhaps nothing reflects the brokenness of our world as much as brothers at war or people of kinship perpetrating atrocities against one another. The first murder in the Bible was a fratricide. The conflict between Ishmael and Isaac has endured for four millennia and remains at a boiling point. Of all the American soldiers who have died in wars, nearly half of them died in the Civil War, where brother fought against brother. More than five million people were killed in the Korean War in the 1950s, and deep ideological differences remain between North and South Korea. Violent civil wars in Rwanda, Bosnia-Herzegovina, and Iraq in recent years have resulted in millions of deaths and untold suffering. Recent headlines tell the horrific stories of Islamic militants selling abducted Iraqi children as sex slaves and killing other children by crucifixion or burying them alive. Because of his perfect love, God grieves over this violence. Because he is the righteous Judge, God also holds the nations accountable for their crimes.

The book of Obadiah addresses the brotherly conflict between Israel/ Judah, the descendants of Jacob, and Edom, the descendants of Jacob's twin brother Esau. The message of Obadiah is that God would completely destroy Edom for the violence she had committed against Judah and that he would ultimately restore Israel. The book of Obadiah reminds us of God's justice as he punishes Edom in accordance with its crimes as well as remembering his special love for Israel, his elect people. In their long history of conflict, Israel was in many ways as guilty as Edom, but the Lord would use the restoration of Israel as the means by which he would extend the blessings of salvation to the nations as well.

Edom was a small kingdom to the southeast of Judah. It lay in the rugged and mountainous terrain between the Dead Sea and the Gulf of Aqaba. Edom is sometimes referred to as Seir (Gen 32:3; 36:20–21). Israel and Edom were bitter rivals throughout the Old Testament era. Though they were allies at times (see Deut 2:2–6; 2 Kgs 3:9), their relationship was more often characterized by hostility and conflict. The people of Edom refused to allow Israel to pass through their territory on the way to the Promised Land (Num 20:14–21). When Saul became king in Israel, he won military victories against Edom and the other peoples surrounding Israel (1 Sam 14:47). David also defeated Edom, built garrisons throughout Edom to protect Israel's borders, and made the Edomites his subjects (2 Sam 8:13–14). The Lord raised up Hadad the Edomite as an adversary to Solomon to punish him for his apostasy (1 Kgs 11:14), and Edom finally regained its independence from Judah around 840 BC during the reign of Jehoram (2 Kgs 8:20–22; 2 Chr 21:8–10). King Amaziah (c. 800 BC) engaged in a particularly brutal campaign against Edom, in which he is said to have killed 10,000 Edomites and then to have killed another 10,000 captives by throwing them off a cliff (2 Kgs 14:7; 2 Chr 25:12). The absence of natural boundaries between Judah and Edom contributed to this perpetual conflict.

Near the middle of the eighth century, Amos condemns the Philistines for selling captives (most likely from Judah) to the Edomites (Amos 1:6). He condemns the Edomites for their violence against Judah as a brother nation (Amos 1:11–12). During the reign of Ahaz, Edom raided Judah and took captives (2 Chr 28:17). In the Babylonian crisis, envoys from Edom journeyed to Jerusalem in 593 BC to discuss plans for a coalition against

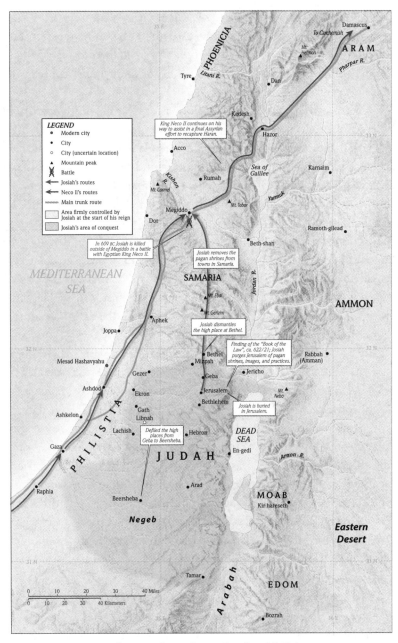

Edom in relationship to Israel and Judah.

Babylon, but the Edomites ultimately allied with Babylon in their assault on Jerusalem in 588–586 BC. Edom used the Babylonian invasion as an opportunity to seize territory from Judah, and archaeological evidence, including military dispatches from Arad, in southern Judah confirms this conflict between Judah and Edom.

Interpreters have dated Obadiah from as early as the ninth century BC to as late as the fourth century BC.[1] The lack of precise historical data in this brief work makes it difficult to assign an exact date for the book. The name Obadiah ("servant of the Lord") is common and refers to twelve different individuals in the Hebrew Bible. The Babylonian Talmud (*b. Sanh. 39*) identifies the prophet with Obadiah, the steward of Ahab (1 Kgs 18:1–15), but there is no indication that this Obadiah was a prophet, nor are there any specific connections between the two figures. Of all the conflicts between Edom and Israel, the Babylonian invasion seems to best fit the description in Obadiah 10–14, particularly the references to Edom's participation in the looting of Jerusalem. The time of Obadiah's ministry likely falls, then, between the destruction of Jerusalem in 586 BC and the defeat of Edom by Nabonidus and the Babylonians in 553.

Other biblical texts confirm Edom's participation with Babylon in the assault on Jerusalem (Ps 137:7; Isa 34:5–17; Lam 4:21–22; Ezek 25:12–14; 35:1–15), and additional prophetic oracles are directed against Edom (Isa 63:1–6; Jer 49:7–22; Amos 1:11–12; 9:12; Mal 1:2–5). Obadiah 1–5 closely parallels the oracle against Edom in Jeremiah 49:14–16. The two prophets were contemporaries and may have simply used a common source. Daniel Block states that at least half of the verses in Obadiah appear to be adaptations of other prophetic oracles against Edom.[2] Inspiration does not preclude the possibility of Obadiah hearing the Lord speak through his prophetic predecessors, and these intertextual references add "the weight of prophetic tradition" to Obadiah's own message against Edom.[3] At only 291 words, Obadiah is the shortest book in the Hebrew canon.

---

[1] For more detailed discussion of the various dates and proposals, see Daniel I. Block, *Obadiah: The Kingship Belongs to YHWH*, Hearing the Message of Scripture 27 (Grand Rapids, MI: Zondervan, 2013), 22–27.

[2] Ibid., 38.

[3] Ibid., 40.

Structure

The book of Obadiah divides into two major sections—the oracle of judgment against Edom in verses 1–14 and a more general announcement of the coming Day of the Lord against all nations in verses 15–21. The Lord would deal with Edom because of its treatment of Judah (v. 10), and his standard for judging the nations would also be, "As you have done, so it will be done to you" (v. 15).

The oracle against Edom in verses 1–14 contains the two basic elements of a judgment speech, with the announcement of judgment coming first (vv. 1–9), followed by the accusation of the crimes that forms the basis of the judgment (vv. 10–14). The announcement in verses 1–9 also reflects an A-B-A pattern in which statements of the Lord's direct involvement in Edom's destruction envelop a portrayal of the human armies that would invade this land:

A		The Lord will "bring down" Edom (vv. 1–4).
	B	The nations that have made a treaty with Edom will "deceive and conquer" (vv. 5–7).
A		The Lord will "eliminate the wise ones of Edom" and terrify its troops (vv. 8–9).*

---

* Block, *Obadiah: The Kingship Belongs to YHWH*, Hearing the Message of Scripture 27, 57

This structure reflects Yahweh's sovereign control over the nations that carry out his judgments.

The oracle concerning the "Day of the LORD" in verses 15–21 also divides into two sections. These sections contrast the judgment of the nations, particularly Edom (vv. 15–18), and the future blessing of Israel that would include its geographical expansion and subjugation of Edom (vv. 19–21). References to "mount" (*har*) Zion (vv. 16, 17, 21) and the "hill country" (*har*) of Esau (v. 19) accentuate the contrasting destinies of Edom and Israel.

Exposition

1–9 The Lord to Edom: "I will bring you down" (The Coming Judgment of Edom)

The opening announcement of judgment in verses 1–4 begins with a report of the Lord summoning an army to wage war against Edom. The Lord issues similar summons to war against the nations and even his own people elsewhere (see Jer 6:8; 51:27–28). The use of the perfect tense "We have heard" and "has been sent" in verse 1 might seem to suggest that the prophet is describing an event that has recently occurred. But the perfect tense verbs here are likely prophetic perfects, which present a future event as if it has already happened in order to stress the certainty of the prophecy's fulfillment. The Lord would humiliate Edom by reducing its status among the nations, and the word "insignificant" is moved to the front of the sentence in verse 2 for emphasis. The word for "despised" (*bazah*), giving the nations' estimation of Edom, is used by Esau in reference to Genesis 25:34 to describe his disregard for his birthright.[4]

Edom presumptuously believed itself to be invulnerable to enemy attack—its rugged terrain with deep ravines and rocky cliffs easily defended against invasion. Edom's capital Bozrah was strategically located in the highlands, and the stronghold of Sela ("rock/crag") located three miles to the north was a natural rock fortress. The prophet compared Edom to an eagle that soared into the heavens and made its nest in the clefts of the rocks. In response to Edom's boast, "Who can bring me down (*yarad*) to the ground?" (v. 3), the Lord announced that he would "bring down" (*yarad*) Edom from its lofty heights (v. 4).

Though Edom thought itself impenetrable to outside invaders, her destruction would be complete (vv. 5–6). The invading armies would pillage Edom even more thoroughly than thieves breaking into a house or gleaners harvesting a vineyard. Thieves steal as much as they want but typically leave a few things behind, and grape pickers usually leave some fruit on the vines (see Lev 19:10; 23:22; Deut 24:19–22). In contrast, Edom's plunderers would leave nothing behind; they would even search out and steal Edom's "hidden treasures." David Baker notes that Edom's wealth came from trade

---

[4] Mark F. Rooker, "The Book of Obadiah," in *The World and the Word: An Introduction to the Old Testament* (Nashville, TN: B&H Academic, 2011), 442, n. 5.

that passed through her land on the King's Highway (Num 20:17) and from her copper mines and grape production (see Isa 63:1–6).[5] The most shocking detail of the plunder is that it would be carried out by Edom's former allies. In the same way that she had betrayed Israel, Edom's treaty partners would betray her. The statement, "He will be unaware of it" at the end of verse 7 is unclear, but it likely refers to how Edom would be caught unawares by the treachery of her allies.

As the divine warrior, the Lord himself would fight against Edom to bring about her destruction (vv. 8–9). He would eliminate both Edom's military advisors and the troops who fought for them. Edom took great pride in its ancient wisdom traditions. Job's friend Eliphaz came from Teman (Gen 36:10–11), and perhaps even Job himself lived within Edom's borders (see Lam 4:21).[6] Nevertheless, Edom's counselors would be unable to construct any kind of strategy to thwart the Lord from carrying out his plans, and these advisors would themselves become a part of the great "slaughter" that the Lord planned for Edom.

10–14 "You will be covered with shame . . . because of violence done to your brother Jacob" (The Lord Avenges His People)

The specific reason for Edom's judgment was its "violence" against Judah (vv. 10–14). The Edomites had gloated over Judah's demise, looted treasures, and captured Judean refugees fleeing the land to turn them over to the Babylonians. Edom viewed Judah's misfortune as an opportunity to fill its own coffers and expand its territories. The Abrahamic covenant stipulated that the Lord would "curse" those that mistreated his people (Gen 12:1–3), and the prophet Zechariah would later declare that whoever harmed Israel was touching the apple of God's eye (Zech 2:8). The nine-fold repetition of the word "day" (*yom*) in verses 12–14 is a reminder that the disaster that befell Jerusalem was a Day of the Lord judgment for Judah. The Lord had sanctioned the Babylonians, as his instrument of judgment, to attack Jerusalem, but he had not authorized the Edomites to participate in this

---

[5] David W. Baker, *Joel, Obadiah, Malachi*, NIVAC (Grand Rapids, MI: Zondervan, 2006), 169–70.

[6] C. Hassell Bullock, *An Introduction to the Old Testament Prophetic Books*, updated ed. (Chicago, IL: Moody, 2007), 309.

judgment. They would, then, be held accountable for their crimes. The wordplay between Judah's "disaster" (*'edam*—"their disaster" and *'ed* two more times in v. 13) and the name "Edom" (*'edom*) hints at the fact that the calamity Judah had experienced would soon befall Edom.[7] The Day of the Lord was past for Judah but was soon to arrive for Edom.

Edom's crimes against Judah were particularly heinous in that they were committed against a brother nation. Nogalski comments that "the long tradition of alliance and blood kinship would make the actions of Edom in many ways more despicable than those of Babylon, which never claimed to be an ally, a friend, or a brother."[8] The use of a series of eight prohibitions to portray the crimes that Edom had committed against Judah perhaps reflects the covenant stipulations found in the Ten Commandments and specifically highlights Edom's crimes as a breach of covenant.[9]

15–21 "The Day of the Lord is near . . ." (The Coming Judgment of the Nations)

The final announcement of judgment expands outward to include all peoples. After God's "day" of judgment against Judah, he would turn his anger against all other nations. The Edomites were foolish to gloat over Judah's downfall when a similar "Day of the LORD" was waiting for them. The statement, "As you have done, so it will be done to you; what you deserve will return on your own head" summarizes the central theological premise of the book of Obadiah. The Lord's punishment of Edom would be one in which the punishment would fit the crime. Wordplays found in verses 8–14 also highlight this idea of divine justice. The Lord would "eliminate" (*'avad*) Edom's wise men (v. 8) because Edom had rejoiced in the day of Judah's "destruction" (*'avad*) (v. 12). The Edomites would be "destroyed" (*karat*) (vv. 9–10) because they had "cut off" (*karat*) Judah's refugees (v. 14). This principle of divine justice is especially prominent in the Old Testament Prophets and is also reflected in the *lex talonis* ("an eye for an eye") laws regarding

---

[7] Marvin A. Sweeney, *The Book of the Twelve*, Vol. 1, Berit Olam (Collegeville, MN: Liturgical Press, 2000), 293.

[8] James D. Nogalski, *The Book of the Twelve: Hosea-Jonah*, Smyth & Helwys Bible Commentary (Macon, GA: Smyth & Helwys, 2011), 387.

[9] Sweeney, *The Book of the Twelve*, 1:293.

retaliation in the Mosaic law (Exod 21:24; Lev 24:19–20; Deut 19:21).[10] The Lord acts with both justice and mercy toward sinful humans. His judgments, while they may be severe, are never excessive or beyond the bounds of what are appropriate.

The warning that "the Day of the LORD is near" is a recurring message in the Prophets, especially in the Book of the Twelve (see Isa 13:6; Ezek 30:3; Joel 1:15; 2:1; 3:14; Zeph 1:7, 14). The Day of the Lord refers to historical judgments that were carried out in the times of the prophets. The "Day of the LORD" can also refer to the eschatological judgments of Israel and the nations that would occur in the last days (see Isa 2:12–21; Joel 3; Zechariah 14; Mal 4:5). The prophetic technique of telescoping often brings these near and far aspects of the Day of the Lord together as one event, as Obadiah appears to do here. Judgment would soon fall on Edom and the surrounding nations, but this "Day of the LORD" occurring within history anticipated the final "day" in which God would judge the nations and fully restore his people Israel.

Some interpreters understand the addressee of the statement, "As you have drunk . . ." in verse 16 to be Edom. This reading would see a reference to Edom's drunken celebration of the fall of Jerusalem. The problem with this reading, however, is that Edom is addressed in verse 15 and in every other instance except one (forty times total) in the second person singular, and the verb in verse 16 is the second person plural form.[11] The Lord is instead likely speaking here to the people of Judah and assuring them that he would punish the nations just as he had punished his own people. The people of Judah had drunk of the wine of God's wrath, but now their judgment was ending, and the nations would reel and stagger under the Lord's intoxicating judgment (see Ps 75:8; Isa 51:17–23; Jer 25:15–29; 48:26–27; Ezek 23:31–35). Yahweh's promise to judge Israel's enemies would offer hope to the discouraged exiles who believed that the Lord had forgotten and abandoned them (see Isa 40:27; 49:14–15). New Testament believers have an even greater assurance—Jesus Christ has drunk the "cup" of God's

---

[10] Mark J. Boda, *A Severe Mercy: Sin and Its Remedy in the Old Testament*, Siphrut 1 (Winona Lake, IN: Eisenbrauns, 2009), 315.

[11] Baker, *Joel, Obadiah, Malachi*, 189–90.

wrath through his death on the cross, so they are free from the sentence of divine wrath and condemnation (Mark 14:36).[12]

The promise of restoration for Israel at Mount Zion (v. 17) contrasts with the slaughter that would take place in the mountains of Esau (vv. 8–9). Jerusalem would never again fall to its enemies. Edom had done violence to Jacob (v. 10), but Jacob would become a "blazing fire" that would completely consume Edom (v. 18). Israel's remnant would become a mighty army that would humiliate its former oppressors. The destruction of Edom and other enemy nations would enable the dispossessed Israelites to regain their lands. Some form of the root word "to possess" (yarash) appears five times in verses 17–21.[13] Obadiah's prophecy echoes the earlier oracle of Balaam that Edom would become an Israelite "possession" (yereshah) (Num 24:18).[14]

Verses 18–20 picture the people of Israel expanding in all directions and enlarging their territories to the full extent of the Promised Land (see Josh 13:2–6). The Israelites would move south from the Negev into Edom and from the Shephelah west into Philistine territory along the coast. The Benjamites would move northeast to take control of Gilead, recalling the deliverance of Jabesh Gilead by Saul the Benjamite (1 Sam 11:1–11). The exiles of Israel would occupy Zerephath on the Phoenician coast to the far north, and the exiles from Judah would conquer the Negev in the south. The mention of Zerephath brings to mind Elijah and how he had demonstrated the greatness of Yahweh in Baal's home territory (see 1 Kgs 17:8–24). Yahweh would demonstrate his power in an even greater way by giving Israel possession of the territories belonging to the Canaanites, a people the Israelites had been unable to dispossess in the past. Ancient inscriptional evidence suggests that Sepharad refers to Sardis in Asia Minor.[15] The great distances to which his people were exiled would not prevent the Lord from fulfilling his promise to restore them to their homeland.

In verse 21, the prophet promises that the Lord would raise up military deliverers in Jerusalem who would conquer Edom, providing one final contrast between "Mount Zion" (har tsiyon) and "the hill country of Esau" (har

---

[12] Leslie C. Allen, The Books of Joel, Obadiah, Jonah, and Micah, NICOT (Grand Rapids, MI: Eerdmans, 1976), 162.

[13] Block, Obadiah: The Kingship Belongs to YHWH, 95.

[14] Ibid., 93.

[15] Ibid., 100.

Does the OT Sanction Nationalistic Hatred?

Some of the most vengeful language in the OT is directed against the Edomites. We even read this curse (or imprecation) against Edom and Babylon for their violence against Jerusalem in Psalm 137:7–9: "Remember, LORD, what the Edomites said that day at Jerusalem: Destroy it! Destroy it down to its foundations!' Daughter Babylon, doomed to destruction, happy is the one who pays you back what you have done to us. Happy is he who takes your little ones and dashes them against the rocks." The presence of such violent prayers or the severity of the judgment that the prophets envision for Israel's enemies in Scripture is shocking for many reasons, but the following salient points need to be remembered when assessing these parts of the OT message:

1. God's people often cry out for justice in the midst of desperate circumstances.

2. Judgment/imprecation language asks for God to act in accordance with his covenantal commitments—"curse those who curse you" (Gen 12:3); "an eye for an eye" (Exod 21:24).

3. Edom's violence would also have constituted a violation of the Noahic covenant that prohibited the shedding of blood (Gen 9:5–6; see Isa 24:1–5; 26:21).

4. By using judgment/imprecation language, God's people are committing retribution over to God, not taking it into their own hands.

5. Judgment/imprecation language often uses highly figurative and hyperbolic language for rhetorical effect and employs curse language that was common to ancient Near Eastern culture.

6. The prophets focus more on God's punishment of Israel than on the nations for their crimes.

7. God and his prophets express grief over the terrible judgments coming on the nations (see Isa 16:9–11).

8. The judgments that have occurred in history using war and military conflict reflect an imperfect justice, but they anticipate the perfect justice that God will mete out in the final judgment.

`esau). The term "Saviors" (*moshi`im*) is used in Judges to refer to the military leaders the Lord raises up to deliver Israel from foreign oppressors (see Judg 3:9, 15; 6:36; 12:3). This promised expansion of Israel did not occur in the postexilic period and thus points forward to the final restoration of Israel in the last days. The concluding word of Obadiah is a promise that the Lord will rule over the nations as King. Yahweh's kingship is eternal, but the prophets also anticipate a future time when the nations will recognize and submit to his sovereign rule.

The judgment of Edom prophesied by Obadiah was carried out when Nabonidus, the final Neo-Babylonian king, defeated and annexed Edom in 553 BC. At the end of the Book of the Twelve, Malachi makes reference to the crushing defeat Edom experienced and announces that she would never recover or rebuild (Mal 1:1–4). By the end of the fourth century BC, the Nabateans had driven the Edomites out of the land and had established Petra as their capital. The region in the Negev around Edom came to be known as Idumea, and the Herodian dynasty was of mixed Judean/Edomite origin. The conflict between Edom and Israel carries over into the New Testament as Herod the Great, of Edomite descent, attempts to destroy Jesus at his birth and bring an end to the One who would fulfill the prophetic promises concerning Israel's future (see Matt 2:1–18).[16]

Theological Message and Application of Obadiah

Yahweh is the Lord and judge of all nations, and all people must ultimately answer to him. The many "days" of judgment the Lord has executed against his enemies in the past confirm the certainty of the final Day of the Lord, in which he will judge the entire earth and all humanity (see 2 Pet 3:10–13). The fate of historical Edom is representative of the judgment that awaits all nations and peoples who oppose God. This idea is most clearly seen in prophetic texts where the judgment of Edom precedes the coming of Israel's eschatological restoration (Isaiah 34–35; Ezekiel 35–37; Isaiah 63–66). The Lord returning as a warrior from Bozrah after treading at the winepress in Isaiah 63:1–6 becomes an image for Jesus at his Second Coming, executing vengeance on his enemies (Rev 19:11–16).

---

[16] Tremper Longman III and Raymond B. Dillard, *An Introduction to the Old Testament*, 2nd ed. (Grand Rapids, MI: Zondervan, 2006), 442.

In the Prophets, the cause of the Lord's judgment is often excessive human pride. This overweening pride and arrogance not only characterized the superpowers like Babylon (Isaiah 13–14; Dan 4:28–30) and Assyria (Isa 10:12–17; 36:15–20), but also the smaller nation states surrounding Israel (Isa 16:6; Ezek 28:1–5; Zeph 2:8–10) and even Israel herself (Isa 17:7–11). Some measure of nationalistic pride and patriotism is natural, but in fallen humans it often leads to war, violence, and the dehumanizing of other peoples standing in the way of misguided nationalistic ambitions. Most of all, human pride disregards accountability to God and seeks to elevate humans to equal status with him (see Gen 3:5; Isa 14:12–14). The Lord's final judgment will ultimately bring an end to sinful human pride (Isa 2:12–21).

The judgment of exile was not the end for Israel, and the Lord would not abandon his covenant people or the promises he had made to them. The judgment of the nations would become the salvation of Israel (Obad 17–21). The ending of Obadiah closely parallels the closing verses of Amos (9:11–12), which also promise the incorporation of Edom into the future kingdom of God through forced military subjugation. The larger canonical witness provides a more positive promise of the inclusion of the nations into the kingdom of God as worshippers of the Lord and participants in the blessings of Israel's restoration (Isa 2:1–4; 19:19–24; 49:5–6; 60:1–3; Mic 4:1–5; Zeph 3:9; Zech 14:16). In the full light of New Testament revelation, Gentiles are grafted into the olive tree of Israel as the people of God (Rom 11:12–24), and Jews and Gentiles equally share in the spiritual blessings that come through Jesus Christ (Gal 3:28–29; Eph 2:11–22).

9

THE BOOK OF JONAH

Introduction

Jonah's unique commission reflects the wideness of God's mercy.

The reference to "Jonah son of Amittai" in 2 Kings 14:25 places the ministry of Jonah in the reign of Jeroboam II, in Israel, from 793–753 BC. According to 2 Kings 14:23–25, Jonah prophesied the expansion of Israel's borders in the north to Lebo Hamath, which was carried out by Jeroboam II during his long and prosperous reign. Israel's military success was evidence of God's grace because Jeroboam II, like all of Israel's other kings, had not followed the Lord (2 Kgs 14:27).

Jonah's favorable message to Israel makes it all the more surprising that the Lord chose Jonah to proclaim a message that led to God showing mercy to the hated Assyrians. In the previous century, the Assyrians had expanded westward and had forced Israel's kings to pay tribute, but a time of internal weakness and economic instability in Assyria allowed for

*A relief from the palace of Ashurbanipal at Nineveh show-
ing Assyrian soldiers subjecting captives to a series of tortures.*

Jeroboam II's extension of Israel's territories. Nineveh was a major city in
Assyria and would, in subsequent generations, become the center of the
Assyrian Empire. The Lord sent Jonah on a unique preaching mission to
this foreign city to announce its impending destruction, but with the intent
that this warning of divine judgment would lead to repentance. Jonah's message led to the sparing of the people who would ultimately bring about the
fall of Israel in 722 BC; in Jonah 4:2, we learn that the possibility of the
Lord sparing Nineveh is why Jonah initially fled from the Lord rather than
fulfilling his mission.

The Question of Historicity

Scholars have debated the historicity and literary genre of the book of Jonah.
Most modern scholars have treated the book as a parable, allegory, or satire,
but a number of evangelical scholars have continued to defend the historicity of the book. Arguments against the historicity of Jonah have focused on

God's Mercy and Assyria's Cruelty

The depth of God's mercy to the Ninevites is more fully appreciated against the backdrop of the severe cruelty that the Assyrians practiced toward other peoples in their military conquests. Their actions are reflected in the relief of Assyrian soldiers torturing Elamite prisoners of war that is from the palace of Ashurbanipal at Nineveh and is attested in the annals of Ashurnasirpal:

"I captured many troops alive: I cut off of some their arms [and] hands; I cut off of others their noses, ears, [and] extremities. I gouged out the eyes of many troops. I made one pile of the living [and] one of heads. I hung their heads on trees around the city."

With their blood I dyed the mountain red like wool, [and] the rest of them the ravines and torrents of the mountain swallowed. I carried off captives [and] possessions from them. I cut off the heads of their fighters [and] built [therewith] a tower before their city. I burnt their adolescent boys and girls."

See Erika Bleibtreu, "Grisly Assyrian Record of Torture and Death," *BAR* 17 (1991): 1–11.

(1) the supernatural elements in the story, particularly how Jonah survives in the belly of the fish for three days; (2) the improbability of or lack of evidence for the repentance of Nineveh; (3) historical inaccuracies or exaggerations in the book; and (4) literary features of the story that suggest its fictional character. Apologists for the historicity of the book have often pointed to other historical incidents in which individuals were swallowed by large aquatic creatures, but the credibility of these stories is often in question.[1] Additionally, as Billy Page notes, such an approach "shows a posture of defensiveness that is unnecessary, counter-productive, and violates the nature of the biblical accounts."[2] The book presents what happens to Jonah as a miracle that occurs only because of God's direct intervention. The fact

---

[1] For a list of these, see Billy K. Smith and Frank S. Page, *Amos, Obadiah, Jonah*, NAC 19B (Nashville, TN: B&H Academic, 1995), 240, n. 4; and R. K. Harrison, *Introduction to the Old Testament* (Peabody, MA: Hendrickson, 2004), 908–9.

[2] Smith and Page, *Amos, Obadiah, Jonah*, 240.

that God "appoints" the fish to be at just the right place at the right time and that Jonah emerges from the fish with no ill-effects reflects the supernatural nature of the events depicted in the story. Barring presuppositions against the possibility of miraculous occurrences, supernatural elements in the stories of Moses, Elijah, and Elisha do not preclude us from reading those narratives as depicting real events. The same would seem to be true with regard to the book of Jonah.

The lack of outside confirmation for the events in Jonah is not surprising, in light of the overall paucity of Assyrian historical records from Jonah's specific time period. Additionally, it is not entirely clear to what degree the Ninevites repented of their sinful acts, how long this repentance lasted, or whether this repentance ultimately had a significant impact on the nation of Assyria at large. There is nothing in the story of Jonah to suggest a national revival, and we know that within a few decades Nineveh returned to its sinful and violent practices. This led the prophet Nahum to announce the impending destruction of the city in the century following Jonah.

While it may seem improbable that the Ninevites would respond so positively to the message of Jonah, Assyria's internal troubles and economic hardships during Jonah's lifetime may have made the people of Nineveh especially receptive to the announcement of divine judgment, even from an unknown god. A solar eclipse that occurred on June 15, 763 BC, in addition to an earthquake, several famines, and political rebellions that occurred between the years 765–756, may have served as portents of divine wrath.[3] John Walton also argues that the fact Jonah was a foreigner added greater weight to his message: "He is doing the Assyrians a favor and has gone to a great deal of trouble to do so. He has nothing to gain, so the idea that he is compelled by deity is the most plausible explanation."[4] There is also some evidence that the city of Nineveh venerated the fish deity, Nanshe, which would have enhanced the people's esteem for Jonah's message if they were aware of the circumstances that brought the prophet to their city.

The lack of historical precision with names and dates is just as true of the exodus narratives as it is of the story of Jonah. The supposed historical inaccuracies or exaggerations in the story present a more substantive issue.

---

[3] Donald J. Wiseman, "Jonah's Nineveh," *Tyndale Bulletin* 30 (1979): 44–51.

[4] John H. Walton, "Jonah," in *The Zondervan Illustrated Bible Backgrounds Commentary*, Vol. 5 (Grand Rapids, MI: Zondervan, 2009), 114.

The book describes Nineveh as "an extremely large city (lit. 'a great city to/before God'), a three-day walk" (3:3), and states that it had a population of "more than 120,000 people" (4:11). While it was not the capital city of the Assyrian Empire, as it would later become under the reign of Sennacherib (705–681 BC), Walton estimates that eighth-century Nineveh had a circumference of three miles and covered an area of 300 acres or 1.5 square miles.[5] Population estimates for Nineveh in the seventh century BC are roughly 300,000, so the number of 120,000 seems in line for the time of Jonah, particularly if the total includes the entire province of Nineveh that likely extended from Kahlu, more than twenty miles to the south, to Khorsabad, some twelve miles to the north.[6] The reference to the "three-day walk" in 3:3 would suggest a journey of forty-five–sixty miles, so this is likely not a reference to the size of the city as much as it is a reference to how long it would require Jonah to complete his preaching mission. Preaching to the entire city could have involved visits to the temple, the palace, and stops at each of the major gates of the city so that all the people would have the opportunity to hear the message. The mention of the "king of Nineveh" in 3:6 is also problematic. We have similar references to Ahab as the "king of Samaria" (1 Kgs 21:1) and to Benhadad of Syria as the "king of Damascus" (2 Chr 24:23), but Nineveh was not the capital city at the time of Jonah, and there is no evidence to suggest that it was a royal residence. The term "king" (*melek*) could also refer to the local governor who ruled over the city or province of Nineveh. In conclusion, historical issues do not present an insurmountable obstacle to reading Jonah as depicting events that actually occurred.

Literary approaches have tended to treat the book of Jonah as midrashic legend, allegory, or some type of didactic parable or short story. A midrashic approach would view the book as an embellished legend about Jonah that provides commentary on a passage like Exodus 34:6. Allegorical approaches view the character of Jonah as representative of the nation of Israel and the swallowing of Jonah by the fish as figurative for the Babylonian exile as punishment for Israel's failure to fulfill its mission of proclaiming God's Word to the Gentiles. Reading Jonah as a parable or short story emphasizes the didactic purpose of

---

[5] Ibid., 113.
[6] Ibid.

the book—the need to balance God's justice and mercy or an indictment of Israel's nationalism and lack of concern for the Gentile nations.[7]

The literary artistry of Jonah is an impressive feature of the book. The name "Jonah" means "dove," which suggests that the prophet in some way represents the people of Israel as a whole (see Ps 74:19; Hos 7:11; 11:11). The book of Jonah also contains elements of parody and satire that portray Jonah in an extremely negative light and that make him worthy of mocking and derision. Jonah's highly stylized prayer in chapter two likely does not reflect the exact prayer the prophet prayed in the belly of the fish. Hebrew narratives as a whole often contain highly literary features; without specific genre indicators marking the book as an allegory or parable, reading the book of Jonah as a prophetic narrative referring to actual events in the prophet's life seems to be the most natural reading of the text. The statements of Jesus concerning the repentance of Nineveh and Jonah's three days in the fish (Matt 12:39–41; Luke 11:29–30) add weight to the claims for the historicity of Jonah.

While an historical reading of Jonah is preferred here, it is also important to remember that belief in the historicity of Jonah is not "a litmus test of orthodoxy" and that the events in Jonah are not central to redemptive history in the same way as the exodus or the resurrection of Christ.[8] Jesus, when referencing the story of Jonah, may have simply been making an analogy or appealing to the traditional Jewish understanding of the book. What ultimately matters here is recognition of the truthfulness of the message of the book concerning the mercy of God and his redemptive concern for all peoples.

Structure

The book of Jonah has two major sections built around God's two calls for Jonah to go and preach in Nineveh. In chapters 1–2, Jonah chooses to flee from the Lord rather than carry out his commission and ends up in the belly of the fish, from which the Lord delivers him. In chapters 3–4, Jonah obeys the Lord, and the people of Nineveh repent and are spared from judgment

---

[7] For further discussion of these various literary approaches, see Smith and Page, *Amos, Obadiah, Jonah*, 209–16.

[8] Robert B. Chisholm Jr., *Handbook on the Prophets* (Grand Rapids, MI: Baker, 2009), 408.

in spite of Jonah's strenuous objections. The symmetry between the two sections reflects the literary artistry of the book and serves to highlight the contrast between Jonah's thankfulness for his own deliverance from death at sea and his anger over the sparing of Nineveh:

A	Jonah and the pagan sailors who turn to the Lord (chap. 1)
B	Jonah and the Lord: Jonah's song of thanksgiving for his salvation (chap. 2)
A'	Jonah and the pagan Ninevites who turn to the Lord (chap. 3)
B'	Jonah and the Lord: Jonah's anger over the Lord's compassion on Nineveh (chap. 4

In chapters 1 and 3, the pagans with whom Jonah interacts are more responsive to God and his ways than the prophet. The parallels between the two chapters are extensive.

These parallels highlight the pattern of God's willingness to show mercy even when he has warned of impending judgment if people turn to him in faith and repentance. God's compassion and forgiveness are for all peoples and not just for Jonah and the Israelites. The contrasting responses of Jonah to his own salvation and the sparing of Nineveh in chapters two and four are a reminder that those who have experienced God's mercy have no right to object to God's mercy to others, even the wicked Assyrians. The issue is not just Jonah's selfishness but how he responds to the working out of God's justice and mercy with regard to the Ninevites. The poetic composition in Jonah 2 is not a secondary addition, as some commentators have suggested, but is central to the overall structure and message of the book. The joining together of prose and poetic texts is a common feature of Hebrew literature (see Exodus 14–15; Judges 4–5; Isaiah 6–8, 34–39; Jeremiah 30–33).

Jonah's Disobedient Response to God's Call (Jonah 1)	Jonah's Obedient Response to God's Call (Jonah 3)
1:1–2 God's command: "Get up! Go to . . . Nineveh."	3:1–2 God's command: ""Get up! Go to . . . Nineveh."
1:3 Jonah's response: "Jonah got up to flee. . . ."	3:3 Jonah's response: "Jonah got up and went."
1:4 Report of an impending disaster: "the LORD hurled a violent wind on the sea."	3:4 Warning of impending disaster: "In 40 days Nineveh will be demolished!"
1:5 Response of the sailors: They were afraid and cried out to their gods.	3:5 Response of the people: They believed in God and showed signs of repentance.
1:6 The message of the captain to Jonah: "Get up! Call to your god. Maybe this god will consider us, and we won't perish."	3:8–9 The message of the king to the people: "Everyone must call out earnestly to God . . . Who knows? God may turn and relent; He may turn from His burning anger so that we will not perish."
1:14 The response of the sailors: They cry out to God and pray for his mercy.	3:5–9 The response of the Ninevites: They believe in Jonah's message and fast and repent of their evil ways.
1:15 The Lord's response: The storm stilled and the sailors were spared.	3:10 The Lord "relented" from sending judgment and the Ninevites were spared.

Exposition

1:1–17 Jonah's Flight from the Lord

1:1–3 "Jonah got up to flee" (Jonah's Refusal to Go to Nineveh)

The story begins with Jonah's refusal to obey his prophetic commission. Jonah is to go to Nineveh and preach against the city because its wickedness has come to the Lord's attention and will not go unpunished. Instead of "rising" and "going" as commanded by the Lord, Jonah arises to flee by going to Joppa and boarding a ship to Tarshish. Prophets like Moses

(Exodus 3–4), Isaiah (Isa 6:5), and Jeremiah (Jer 1:6) expressed objections to the Lord's calling on their lives, but Jonah's direct disobedience is unique. The reason for Jonah's refusal to heed the Lord's calling is not revealed until near the end of the story—the prophet objects to the possibility of the Lord showing mercy to the Ninevites (see 4:2). The location of Tarshish is disputed, but most scholars have identified it with either Tartessos in Spain or Tarsus in Asia Minor. The significance of Tarshish is that it lies across the Mediterranean in exactly the opposite direction of Nineveh.

Jonah's real intention is to flee "from the Lord's presence." The prophet's own confession in 1:9 that the Lord is the Creator of both the "sea and the dry land" reflects the futility of his flight, as does the assertion of Amos 9:2–3 that one cannot escape from the Lord by digging into Sheol, climbing up to the heavens, or hiding at the bottom of the sea (see also Ps 139:7–12). No matter how hard he tried, Jonah can neither evade the Lord or his calling.

1:4–16 "THE LORD HURLED A VIOLENT WIND ON THE SEA" (THE LORD SENDS A PERFECT STORM)

In verses 4–16, the Lord sends a fierce storm to get the attention of his wayward prophet. The storm demonstrates the Lord's control over Jonah's life even outside the Promised Land.[9] The narrator skillfully weaves together details of the storm with Jonah's dialogue with the sailors on the ship. Several key wordplays and repetitions are important to the unfolding of this story in Hebrew. The adjective "great" (*gadol*) describes the severity of the wind and storm three times in verses 4 and 12. The ship is personified in verse 4 as "thinking" (*hashav*) that it would break apart. Any storm that can frighten a ship is no ordinary storm. The Lord "hurls" (*tul*) this storm on the sea like a warrior hurling a javelin (v. 4), and the sailors aboard the ship respond by "hurling" (*tul*) their cargo overboard in an attempt to keep the ship from sinking (v. 5). The seas, however, continue "raging against them more and more" with increasing intensity (vs. 11, 13) until the sailors follow Jonah's advice and "hurl" (*tul*) him into the sea (vs. 12, 15).

The threefold repetition of the verb "to go down" (*yarad*) in chapter one describes Jonah's descent as he flees from the Lord. Jonah "went down" to Joppa; then he "went down" to board the ship (v. 3); and then he "goes down" into the hull of the ship (v. 5). His downward descent eventually

---

[9] Douglas Stuart, *Hosea-Jonah*, WBC 31 (Waco, TX: Word, 1987), 456.

leads to Jonah being thrown overboard into the sea and then "going down" (*yarad*) toward Sheol, the abode of the dead (2:6). Running away from God leads Jonah to the brink of death, and it is only the Lord's rescue via the fish that keeps Jonah from descending to a grave at the bottom of the sea.

The thrice-repeated verb "to fear" (*yara*) reflects a movement in the opposite direction for the pagan sailors aboard the ship with Jonah. The sailors "were afraid" (*yara*) because of the terrible storm, and each of them cried out to their different gods (v. 5). Their fear intensifies (lit. "they feared a fear") in verse 10 when they learn of Jonah's identity and that he is fleeing from the God of heaven who made "the sea" and "dry land." The sailors are coming to a gradual recognition of the identity of the one true God. When the seas calm after they throw Jonah overboard, the sailors' fear intensifies again in verse 16, and this time, "they feared the Lord even more" (lit. "they feared the Lord with a great fear"). The sailors have moved from the fear of dying, to terror over a powerful and unknown God, to genuine reverence for the Lord.[10] The "fear of the LORD is the beginning of knowledge" (Prov 1:7) and the "reverence" for God that motivates a life of worship and obedience (see Deut 10:12; Pss 22:23; 25:14). The Lord spared the sailors from death in response to their prayers, and they make the same response as Jonah (2:9) to the Lord's deliverance by offering sacrifices and making vows. These details reflect that we should see their response to the Lord as a genuine conversion. Daniel Timmer explains, "The sailors' actions clearly show a reorientation of heart and life in the context of a monotheistic relationship with Yahweh."[11]

The irony of this opening episode in the story of Jonah is that the pagan outsiders are much more spiritually attuned and sensitive than the prophetic insider. The sailors come to fear the Lord, while Jonah remains hardened in rebellion. While the sailors frantically cry out to their gods, Jonah is asleep in the bottom of the ship.[12] The verb "to sleep" (*radam*) can refer to the state in which one receives a vision from the Lord (see Gen 15:12; Job 4:13;

---

[10] James Bruckner, *Jonah, Nahum, Habakkuk, Zephaniah*, NIVAC (Grand Rapids, MI: Zondervan, 2004), 49.

[11] Daniel C. Timmer, *A Gracious and Compassionate God: Mission, Salvation, and Spirituality in the Book of Jonah*, NSBT (Downers Grove, IL: InterVarsity, 2011), 115.

[12] Contrast the image of Jonah sleeping here with that of Jesus in Matthew 8:23–27. Jesus is also asleep on a boat during a "great storm," but sleep reflects his confidence in the Father's protection. He awakens to calm the storm and save his disciples.

33:15; Dan 8:18; 10:9), but here it reflects Jonah's apathy toward his circumstances and his obliviousness to the Lord's working in the storm.[13]

In verse 6, the captain of the ship implores Jonah to "rise up and cry out" (*qum* + *qara*), employing two of the same verbs used by the Lord when sending Jonah to Nineveh in verse 2. No matter how hard Jonah tries, he cannot evade or avoid his calling. Nevertheless, Jonah has no interest in acting like a prophet, and he becomes a parody as the anti-prophet. The sailors act more like prophets than Jonah does. Jonah does not pray for the sailors in the way that prophets like Moses and Samuel interceded for others in the past (see Exodus 32; Numbers 14; 1 Samuel 12). He provides no message from the Lord that would help the sailors with the peril they are facing. Other prophets raise the possibility of divine mercy and favor if their hearers will turn to the Lord (Joel 2:12–14), but here it is the captain who must suggest this possibility to Jonah.[14] In chapter three, it will be the king of Nineveh, rather than Jonah, who again raises the possibility of divine relenting from judgment (3:9).

In the absence of prophetic counsel, the sailors must turn to the casting of lots in order to receive revelatory insight from God. Jonah only speaks of the Lord after the sailors determine by lot that he is the cause of the storm. Jonah's orthodox confession has a hollow ring to it in that he acknowledges Yahweh as the Creator of the "sea" and "dry land," but acts as if he can flee from God by heading out to sea on a ship. The role reversal of the sailors acting like prophets continues when they confront Jonah with his wrongdoing in verse 10. Godly prophets often lived through times of calamity because of God's judgment on the people to whom they ministered, but here is it is the prophet himself who has brought calamity on the sailors.

Rather than fulfilling his prophetic mission, Jonah only wants to die, and he instructs the sailors to throw him overboard so that the seas will calm. Jonah has no revelatory word from God informing him that the storm will cease if the sailors throw him into the sea, and the idea of sacrificing a human life in order to appease the wrath of an angry deity seems more in

---

[13] Marvin A. Sweeney, *The Twelve Prophets*, Vol. 1, Berit Olam (Collegeville, MN: Liturgical Press, 2000), 311.

[14] Seven of the other twelve uses of the particle "perhaps" (*'ulay*) in the OT Prophets refer to the possibility of God relenting from sending judgment in response to prayer (Isaiah 37:4; Jeremiah 21:2) or repentance (Jeremiah 26:3; 36:3, 7; Zephaniah 2:3; Amos 5:15).

line with pagan theology than an Israelite understanding of God. For Jonah, death by drowning at sea is preferable to fulfilling God's command to go and preach in Nineveh.

The sailors' concern for Jonah's life, even when he reveals that he is the cause of the storm, contrasts with the prophet's self-absorption. One would expect that the natural reaction would be to kill the man who is responsible for their misfortune. Instead, the sailors only throw Jonah overboard after making every attempt to get the ship to land and praying that the Lord would not hold them accountable for Jonah's death. The sailors also cry out to the Lord in prayer and experience his mercy. The final irony is that Jonah's preaching has inadvertently spared the sailors from death and led to their coming to know the one true God at a time when the prophet is in full flight from fulfilling that responsibility toward the Ninevites. Jonah has failed to understand one of the most important implications of his confession concerning the Lord as Creator of all. The Lord is as concerned about pagan sailors in a storm or wicked sinners in Nineveh as he is about his chosen people Israel or his disobedient prophet fleeing from his presence in the middle of the Mediterranean.

1:17 "THE LORD HAD APPOINTED A HUGE FISH" (THE RESCUE OF THE PROPHET)

The Lord demonstrates his sovereignty in both wrath and mercy. He "hurls" a storm onto the sea in Jonah's direction, but he also "appointed" (*manah*) a "great fish" to swallow Jonah and keep him from drowning. The Lord controls nature to the point that he has this fish in the right place at the right time in order to save the prophet's life. The verb *manah* will appear three more times in chapter four to indicate the Lord's control over nature as he "appoints" a plant (4:6), a worm (4:7), and an east wind (4:8) to continue teaching his prophet about his mercy. The phrase "great fish" does not clearly identify the creature that swallowed Jonah as a whale, as is traditionally understood, and there is no explanation as to how the Lord preserved Jonah's life inside the fish. The significance of the "three days and nights" Jonah spent in the fish is likely that a person was considered truly dead after three days and nights in the grave.[15] Jonah's deliverance is in every way a rescue from the very brink of death.

2:1–10 "Salvation is from the LORD" (Jonah's Thanksgiving Song)

In chapter one, Jonah wanted to die, but he has a change of heart while in the belly of the fish. Jonah prays over his own situation after failing to intercede for the sailors in chapter one. Jonah's prayer follows the form found in several of the psalms of thanksgiving, which express gratitude to God for deliverance from danger and death (see Psalms 30; 40). Hezekiah offers one of these songs when the Lord heals him of a life-threatening illness and promises to extend his life by fifteen years (see Isa 38:9–20). Worshippers offered these songs to God in a celebration at the sanctuary that included fellowship offerings, a meal, and testimony of the Lord's deliverance to family and friends. Remarkably, Jonah offers this thanksgiving psalm while still in the belly of the fish. The Lord's provision of the fish had prevented Jonah from drowning, and Jonah expresses his confidence in his ultimate deliverance from this ordeal.

Jonah's song includes a summary statement of the Lord's deliverance (v. 2), a detailed recounting of the deliverance (vv. 3–7), and a concluding confession of faith in the Lord and promise to fulfill his vows of praise and sacrifice to the Lord (vv. 8–10). In the previous chapter, he had attempted to flee from the Lord's presence; he now expresses his desire to be in God's presence at his temple (vv. 4. 9) and acknowledges that his prayer had come into the Lord's presence at the temple even as he was in the belly of the fish (v. 7).

In the poetic recounting of his deliverance, Jonah employs the imagery of the waters of chaos and the underworld to vividly portray that he was as good as dead when the Lord delivered him. The words for "deep" in verses 3

---

[15] In the Sumerian Descent of Inanna, the goddess tells her servant to lament and petition the gods for her return from the underworld if she has not returned after three days. See Walton, "Jonah," 109. The story of the raising of Lazarus in John 11 mentions that Lazarus had been in the grave for four days (11:39), emphasizing the fact that he was truly dead. In the New Testament, Jonah's three days and three nights in the fish are also typological of the time that Jesus is in the grave prior to his resurrection (Matthew 12:40).

(*metsulah*) and 6 (*tehom*) are elsewhere figurative for life-threatening dangers (Pss 42:7; 69:2, 15; 88:6) and are also used to describe the waters of chaos that the Lord brought under his control at creation (see Gen 1:2; Pss 33:7; 77:16). In Exodus 15:8, the Lord piled up the waters of the deep that were "in the heart of the sea" in order to save the Israelites and destroy the Egyptians, but Jonah had become like God's enemy because of his defiance.

The unleashing of chaos had brought Jonah to the brink of death. Near the beginning of this passage, Jonah prays from the "belly of Sheol," which is ironic in that Jonah remains in the belly of the fish. Sheol is the dwelling place of the dead in the Old Testament, and the Canaanite god of death, Mot, was portrayed as the great swallower who consumed all flesh. Jonah's downward descent begun in chapter one continues in this chapter. The waves overwhelm him in the midst of the sea, and the seaweed that wraps around his head takes him down to the ocean floor. The verb "to go down" (*yarad*) appears once more in verse 6 to suggest Jonah descending to the land of the dead. Jonah's flight from the Lord had taken him much further than Tarshish. The sand bars at the bottom of the sea have become like prison bars, about to entomb him in a watery grave, reminiscent of Sheol's description in Job 16:22 as a place from which there is "no return."

The Lord intervenes by "bringing up" Jonah in response to his prayer and reversing his long descent. Following Jonah's prayer, the fish who obeys the word of the Lord more faithfully than Jonah vomits the prophet onto dry land. Because of God's mercy, the encounter with the fish that initially appears to symbolize death comes to represent new birth and a second opportunity for the prophet to fulfill his prophetic calling.

Jonah's song of thanksgiving appears to be a model prayer, but the remainder of the book will reflect that Jonah's relationship with the Lord is not, in fact, fully restored. There are troubling aspects to Jonah's pious prayer here, just as there were in his orthodox confession of faith in the Lord as Creator in 1:9. A prayer of confession acknowledging his sin would seem to be the proper way to approach God in light of his flagrant disobedience. The prophet even attributes his suffering to God casting him into the sea rather than acknowledging his own sin. Jonah piously contrasts himself to idol worshippers, but chapter one reflects how poorly he compares to the spiritually attuned sailors who came to know the Lord. Jonah celebrates his own deliverance, and rightfully so, but he would not have the same response when the Lord extended his mercy to the Ninevites.

Jonah and Jesus

Jesus taught that the Old Testament as a whole pointed to his suffering and exaltation. While there are no specific messianic prophecies in the book of Jonah, there are patterns and events from the life of Jonah that parallel what will occur in the life and ministry of Jesus. In response to a request from the scribes and Pharisees to give them a sign confirming his identity, Jesus states that the only sign they would receive would be "the sign of Jonah" (Matt 12:38–41; 16:4; Luke 11:29–32). The specific nature of the sign was that the Son of Man would be in the earth three days in the same way that Jonah was in the belly of the fish for three days and nights. The "sign" is simply the analogy between the experiences of Jonah and Jesus. The miraculous rescue of Jonah from certain death anticipated and pointed forward to the greater miracle of the resurrection of Christ. Jesus also states that the men of Nineveh would rise up to condemn the Israelites of his day for their unbelief. If the Ninevites listened to Jonah, then the people of Israel should pay attention to Jesus as the greater prophet and their Messiah.

3:1–10 "The men of Nineveh believed in God" (Jonah Preaches and Nineveh Repents)

At his second commissioning, Jonah obeys and goes to Nineveh in order to announce the city's impending destruction (vv. 1–4). The people and king of Nineveh respond to the message in repentance, and the Lord relents from sending the judgment he had planned for the city (vv. 5–10). The Ninevites' response to Jonah's less-than-stellar sermon (five words in the Hebrew text) is remarkable. R. W. L. Moberly suggests that Jonah's sermon is "subversive of his commission" in that it does not identify the Lord as the source of the warning, explain the reason for the coming calamity, or offer any call for repentance or hope of divine relenting.[16] Nevertheless, his message elicits a response of faith and repentance on the part of both people and king on the first day of his preaching. Like the sailors in chapter one, the Ninevites have no specific way of knowing how to turn away divine wrath, so they try everything in their power to show the depth and sincerity of their

---

[16] R. W. L. Moberly, *Old Testament Theology: Reading the Hebrew Bible as Christian Scripture* (Grand Rapids, MI: Baker Academic, 2013), 186.

repentance. The king's decree reflects that Nineveh's repentance includes both ritual (fasting and the wearing of sackcloth for both people and animals) and ethical (turning from evil and violence) aspects.

The people of Nineveh experience grace and mercy when they "call out" (*qara*) to God, just as the sailors did in chapter one. They "turn" (*shuv*) from their "evil" (*ra'ah*) ways, and the king of Nineveh raises the possibility that the Lord will "turn" (*shuv*) and "relent" (*niham*) from the "calamity" (*ra'ah*) he plans to send against Nineveh. This possibility is precisely what happens, and God "relents" (*niham*) of sending "calamity" (*ra'ah*) when the Ninevites "turn" (*shuv*) from their "evil" (*ra'ah*) ways.[17] The repetitions and wordplays remind us of God's justice when he judges. His judgments of "calamity" (*ra'ah*) are the appropriate responses to the "evil" (*ra'ah*) that people practice, but this episode also reminds us of God's mercy and compassion. Even with Jonah's unqualified message of judgment, "Forty days, and Nineveh shall be overthrown" (NKJV), there was the implied understanding that repentance on the part of those who were targeted for judgment would increase the possibility that God might relent from sending the threatened disaster.[18] The purpose of the prophets announcing judgment ahead of time was not simply to forecast doom but rather to prompt a change of behavior in those who responded to the message. In this sense, the Old Testament prophets had a role something like the Ghost of Christmas Future in Dickens' *A Christmas Carol*. It shows old Scrooge shadows of the future so that he might change his ways and alter the course set for his life before it is too late.

Jeremiah 18:7–10 expresses the principle that the final outcome of prophetic warnings of judgment and promises of salvation depend on how people respond to those announcements and applies this principle to any nation, not just Israel (see also Mic 3:9–12 and Jer 26:17–19). Jonah understood this aspect of prophecy and later reveals that the possibility of the Lord relenting from sending judgment was the reason he did not want to go

---

[17] J. Daniel Hays, *The Message of the Prophets: A Survey of the Prophetic and Apocalyptic Books of the Old Testament* (Grand Rapids, MI: Zondervan, 2010), 305–6.

[18] For further discussion of this feature of biblical prophecy, see Richard L. Pratt Jr., "Historical Contingencies and Biblical Predictions," in *The Way of Wisdom: Essays in Honor of Bruce K. Waltke*, ed. J. I. Packer and Sven K. Soderlund (Grand Rapids, MI: Zondervan, 2000), 183–90.

to Nineveh (see 4:2). The remarkable thing is that both the sailors (1:6) and the king of Nineveh understand this attribute of God as well.

The verb, (*niham*) "relent," can also be translated "to grieve, to be sorry about, to repent, or to change one's mind." The idea of God changing his mind is a difficult one to grasp. At one extreme, some have reduced this concept to a figure of speech so it only appears that God has a change of mind; others have used this image to argue that God has limited foreknowledge of future events. There are obvious anthropomorphic elements in this expression, but the fact that God bases his final decisions on how people respond to him and his directions is one of his distinctive attributes. When people repent and genuinely change their ways, or when they pray for divine mercy in response to the threat of coming judgment (see Exod 32:11–14; Num 14:13–20; Amos 7:1–6), God acts in ways he would not have acted had they not repented or prayed. In his sovereignty, the Lord does not simply impose his will but has allowed human responses to influence the working out of his plans and decrees. The Lord has the freedom to delay or even recall a threatened judgment when people respond appropriately.

There are instances when God will not change his mind because he has made a covenant, sworn an oath, or committed himself to a particular course of action (see Num 23:19; 1 Sam 15:28–29), but his willingness to change on the basis of human response seems to be more the norm.[19] Rather than reflecting a lack of knowledge about the future on God's part, the biblical idea of God changing his mind is more that while he has exhaustive knowledge of all future possibilities (as he does with David and Saul in 1 Sam 23:9–14), he often bases his resolution of a particular situation on the choices and decisions people make in response to his initiatives.

---

[19] God does not relent or turn away from his covenant promises and commitments to restore Israel following exile, to establish a faithful remnant, to send his Messiah, or to establish his everlasting kingdom. How and when those covenant promises become realities, however, are in many ways impacted by human responses to God's initiatives. The statement in Numbers 23:19, "God is not a man who lies, or a son of man who changes His mind" directly relates to how the Lord will not renege on his promises to Israel when Balak hires Balaam to curse them. Jeremiah 31:35–37 and 33:25–26 state that God's covenant promises to Israel are as certain as the fixed order of the sun, moon, and stars. See further, Robert B. Chisholm Jr., "Does God 'Change His Mind'?" *Bibliotheca Sacra* 153 (1995): 387–99.

Though there was genuine repentance on the part of the Ninevites, it does not appear there was a full-fledged conversion on their part to exclusive faith in Yahweh as the one true God. Timmer explains: "The city believed God's word through Jonah, and abandoned their violence and wickedness in the hope that God would spare them. This is a striking moral reform, but there is nothing in Jonah 3 that requires us to say it was more than that."[20] Within only a few decades, Assyria was again involved in "imperial violence" against Israel, leading to Nahum's prophecies in the seventh century BC that Nineveh would be destroyed by an invading army as punishment for its crimes.[21] This prophecy was fulfilled when the Medes and Babylonians destroyed the city in 612 BC.

The emphasis in Jonah 3 is on the mercy and compassion of God. The Lord spares the Ninevites even though their repentance is partial, incomplete, and only appears to last for a short time. The Old Testament reflects elsewhere God's willingness to show mercy to the worst of sinners, even when their repentance is less than ideal. Ahab is the worst of Israel's kings, but the Lord delays the judgment on Ahab's family when the king shows a measure of sorrow for his sinful behavior (1 Kgs 21:27–29). Manasseh was Judah's worst king, but the Lord allowed him to remain on the throne when he repented of his sinful ways as the Assyrians shackled him and prepared to take him away as their prisoner (2 Chr 33:10–17). By refusing to turn from their sinful ways, Israel and Judah forfeited the opportunity to experience this same abundant grace.

4:1–11 "But Jonah was greatly displeased and became furious" (Jonah's Anger Because of the Lord's Mercy to Nineveh)

The final episode returns to dialogue between God and Jonah and delivers the punch line of the book. If the Lord can show mercy to a rebellious prophet, then he can extend the same compassion to the Ninevites. In chapter one, the sailors offer sacrifices and make vows to God when they are saved from death. In chapter two, Jonah expresses thanks and makes vows to God when he is delivered from death. We expect a similar reaction when the Lord

---

[20] Timmer, *A Gracious and Compassionate God*, 103.
[21] Ibid., 104.

spares Nineveh from destruction, but Jonah is instead angry that the Lord has spared Nineveh. Jonah prays to God, just as in chapter two, but now the prophet prays in order to express his anger rather than his thanksgiving.

Continuing the wordplays from chapter three, it was a great evil (*ra`ah*) to Jonah that the Lord had spared Nineveh, and Jonah states that the possibility of God relenting from sending "disaster" (*ra`ah*) because of his gracious and compassionate nature was the reason he had not wanted to go to Nineveh in the first place. In a sense, Jonah's objection to God showing mercy here is understandable. God is forgiving, but can he be depended on to execute justice and carry out his just decisions? The sparing of Nineveh would later have huge implications for Jonah's people, because the Assyrians would be responsible for the destruction and exile of the northern kingdom. Nevertheless, rather than taking Jonah's objection seriously, the narrator parodies Jonah as a pouting prophet who cares only about his own selfish comforts in order to demonstrate how wrong he is in wanting to limit God's compassion. Jonah's heart is no more aligned with God's heart at the end of this story than it was in the beginning when he fled from the Lord instead of going to preach in Nineveh.

We expect a true prophet to rejoice in the repentance of an entire city, but Jonah wants to die because he feels God has betrayed him in not carrying out the judgment on Nineveh. Other servants of God pray for death or wish they had never been born after they experience great adversity. Job lost his family and his health (Job 6:8–10). Moses endured Israel's rebellion (Num 11:15). Samson was enslaved and blinded by the enemy (Judg 16:30). Elijah faced death threats from Jezebel (1 Kgs 19:4), and Jeremiah was the object of various forms of persecution (Jer 20:14–18).[22] Jonah wants to die because he has not gotten his way—the Lord has not destroyed the Ninevites as he desires.

When the Lord asks Jonah if he has the right to be angry over the sparing of Nineveh, the pouting prophet does not even respond to the question. The Lord then uses an object lesson that forces the prophet to wrestle with his improper response to divine mercy. The Lord appoints a vine, a worm, and a scorching east wind to reveal Jonah's extreme selfishness and disregard for the people of Nineveh. Jonah has built a temporary shelter outside of

---

[22] James D. Nogalski, *The Book of the Twelve: Hosea-Jonah*, Smyth & Helwys Bible Commentary (Macon, GA: Smyth and Helwys, 2011), 446.

Nineveh, perhaps waiting out the forty days to see what would actually happen to the city. The leafy vine provided shade that delivered Jonah from the "discomfort" (ra'ah) of the oppressive heat. The next day, a worm eats the vine, and the Lord sends a scorching wind that intensifies Jonah's discomfort. In this object lesson, Jonah experiences exactly what he wishes God would do to Nineveh. Jonah was delivered from "calamity," only to have it return.[23] Rather than thinking God had treated him fairly and repenting, Jonah becomes even angrier and wishes to die.

If Jonah could be concerned for a day-old plant and relief from his physical "discomfort" (ra'ah), then he should share the Lord's concern for the people of Nineveh and the terrible "calamity" (ra'ah) threatened against them. If nothing else, Jonah should at least be concerned with the animals in the city. Jonah had an orthodox belief in Yahweh as the sovereign Creator of all, but in his self-centeredness, he failed to grasp the redemptive concern of the Lord for all that emerges out of this creational theology. The open-ended question, "Should I not care about the great city of Nineveh?" at the end of the book forces readers to wrestle with the selfishness and self-righteousness that keeps us from sharing God's concern for those who need his grace and forgiveness.

Theological Message and Application of Jonah

The book of Jonah affirms the Lord's sovereignty over all. All people are accountable to him for how they live their lives. Jonah may attempt to resist the Lord's command, but the Lord ultimately directs circumstances to conform the prophet to his will. The Lord threatens judgment against the Ninevites for their wicked ways and determines whether their city will survive or be destroyed. Jonah confesses Yahweh as the Creator of all (1:9) and the Lord, as Creator, controls and directs the forces of nature so that they work his will. The Lord "hurls" a storm in the path of Jonah when he attempts to flee his presence. He "appoints" a great fish, a vine, a worm, and a scorching wind to accomplish his purposes in Jonah's life.

The Lord is a God of both justice and mercy. Jonah's confession "Salvation is from the Lord" (2:9) is a central theme in this book and

---

[23] See John H. Walton, "The Object Lesson of Jonah 4:5–7 and the Purpose of the Book of Jonah," *Bulletin for Biblical Research* 2 (1992): 47–57.

highlights three great acts of salvation. The Lord spares the sailors by calming the storm. He delivers Jonah from drowning by providing the great fish, and he relents from destroying the city of Nineveh. The Lord is merciful and gracious, but his grace has conditions. The Lord saves the sailors when they cry out to him in prayer. The Lord spares Nineveh when the people turn from their sinful ways. The proper response to the Lord's salvation is reverence, thanksgiving, and obedience—not the anger that Jonah displays when the Lord saves Nineveh.

The Old Testament reveals a missionary God who has a redemptive plan for all peoples. God calls Abraham so that he might be an instrument of blessing to all peoples (Gen 12:3) and appoints Israel as a "kingdom of priests" so that they might mediate God's presence to the nations (Exod 19:5–6). Gentiles who experience special acts of God's grace include the Egyptians who leave their homeland with the Israelites in the exodus, Rahab the harlot, Ruth the Moabitess, the widow of Zerephath, and Namaan the Syrian general, just to name a few. The Old Testament Prophets are also filled with the missionary promises of Gentile inclusion in the kingdom of God. In the book of Isaiah, the Lord promises that the nations will stream to Zion to worship the Lord (Isa 2:1–4), that Assyria and Egypt will be recognized along with Israel as the people of God (Isa 19:19–25), and that the role of God's Servant-Messiah is to be a light to the nations (Isa 49:5–6). Jonah adds to the rich missionary teaching of the Old Testament by demonstrating that belief in the Lord as a compassionate and merciful God applies as much to his dealings with the nations as it does to his treatment of Israel. God responds to the repentance of foreigners in the same way that he responds to the repentance of his own people (see Jer 12:14–17; 18:5–11).

Among the Book of the Twelve, Jonah is unique in that it provides no word concerning the judgment and salvation of Israel or Judah. The book instead focuses on how the compassionate God who relents from sending judgment against Israel and Judah (Amos 7:1–6; Joel 2:12–14) does the same for the pagan Assyrians. The echo of Exodus 34 in Jonah 4:2 that explains the Lord's mercy toward Nineveh appears elsewhere in the Minor Prophets (Joel 2:13; 3:19–20; Mic 7:18–19) with reference to God's mercy to Israel. The repentance of the Ninevites serves as a rebuke of the refusal of Israel and Judah to turn from their sinful ways.

When Nineveh returned to their sin, Nahum repeated Jonah's message concerning the imminent destruction of the city. Ironically, Nahum echoes the warning of Exodus 34:6 that the Lord "will not leave the guilty unpunished" as the basis for his message that the Lord is about to destroy Nineveh (Nah 1:3). The prophet Zephaniah also prophesies the coming destruction of Nineveh (Zeph 2:13–15). The fulfillment of the prophecies of Nahum and Zephaniah occurred with the destruction of Nineveh by the Medes and Babylonians in 612 BC. The Lord's judgment of the nations that surrounded Israel and Judah is a prominent theme in the Book of the Twelve, especially in the books that immediately precede Jonah (see Amos 1:3–2:3; Joel 3; Obadiah). This judgment would ultimately extend to all peoples, but the sparing of Nineveh prefigures how the Lord would also extend his eschatological salvation to a remnant of the nations along with his people Israel (Zeph 3:9–10; Zech 8:20–23; 14:16–19; Mal 1:11).

At the practical level, the message of Jonah is a reminder that we live under God's sovereignty and must answer to his demands on our lives. Jonah believes his flight from God's presence and his commands will bring freedom and self-autonomy, but ultimately puts him on the path to death and destruction. Jonah's example demonstrates that holding to the right beliefs is inadequate if not accompanied by right attitudes and practices that grow out of those beliefs. Jonah makes three orthodox confessions in the book, but he reflects the wrong response to those beliefs in each instance (see 1:9; 2; 4:2). Jonah's attitude toward the Ninevites should lead believers to assess whether their own lives are driven by selfishness or by God's redemptive concern for the lost who need Christ. The message of Jonah is especially relevant to wealthy and affluent Christians in the West who struggle with the conflict between personal comfort and commitment to God's kingdom agenda. As Thomas Carlisle has expressed in his poem "You Jonah!,"

> And Jonah stalked to his shaded seat
> And waited for God to come around to his way of thinking.
> And God is still waiting for a host of Jonahs in their comfortable
>   houses
> To come around to his way of loving.[24]

---

[24] Thomas John Carlisle, *You Jonah! Poems by Thomas John Carlisle* (Grand Rapids, MI: Eerdmans, 1968).

10

THE BOOK OF MICAH

Introduction

The bedroom of a World War I French military officer named Hubert Rochereau remains exactly as it was at the time when his parents received the news on April 26, 1918, that he had died a day after being wounded in Belgium. Rochereau's parents desired that the photographs on the walls, a jacket on a hanger, a chair tucked under a desk, and other mementos serve as a permanent memorial to their son. It is a sad and poignant reminder of the tragic loss of war.[1] More than 75,000,000 died in the two world wars of the twentieth century. The prophet Micah envisioned a time when the nations would "beat their swords into plows" and "never again train for war." Jerusalem would become the center of Yahweh's earthly

---

[1] http://www.theguardian.com/world/2014/oct/14/french-soldier-room-unchanged -first-world-war. Accessed May 5, 2015.

kingdom, and the nations would stream to Zion to learn the ways of the Lord (Mic 4:1–6).

This idyllic picture did not describe the world of Micah's day. The Assyrians ruled over the Fertile Crescent with an iron fist, and the prophet warned of how the Lord would use the Assyrians to bring judgment against his sinful people in both Israel and Judah. Jerusalem would ultimately be reduced to nothing more than a heap of rubble (Mic 3:12), and the people would be carried away to Babylon as exiles (Mic 4:10). But, judgment would ultimately lead to salvation, and the Lord would restore his people and bring his kingdom of peace to earth. The world today is just as brutal as the one in which Micah lived, but Micah's message continues to offer hope to Christians as they wait for the coming of God's kingdom of peace, earnestly anticipating the city "whose architect and builder is God" (Heb 11:10). Micah's message is also a reminder that lasting peace will not come until all people bow before the sovereignty of the Lord and submit their lives to him.

Micah ministered in the southern kingdom of Judah during the reigns of Jotham, Ahaz, and Hezekiah from approximately 740–690 BC. Micah was a younger contemporary of the prophets Hosea and Amos in Israel and Isaiah in Judah. Micah was from Moresheth (1:1, 14), a village twenty to twenty-five miles southwest of Jerusalem near the fortress town of Lachish. The details of his family situation, personal life, call to ministry, or even the exact span of his preaching career are unknown. His name means, "Who is like Yahweh?" and the closing message in Micah asks the question, "Who is a God like you?" (7:18) as Micah reflects on the Lord's covenant faithfulness to his sinful people.

The resurgence of the Neo-Assyrian Empire under Tiglath-pileser III in the eighth century BC ultimately led to the fall of Israel in 722 BC (see the introductory sections on Hosea and Amos), but the Assyrian expansion westward had devastating effects on Judah as well. In 734–732 BC, the bloody Syro-Ephraimite war occurred when Ahaz refused to join the anti-Assyrian coalition led by Rezin of Syria and Pekah of Israel (see 2 Kgs 16:1–9; 2 Chr 28:5–21; Isaiah 7–8). The Syrian and Israelite armies invaded Judah in an attempt to remove Ahaz from the throne and replace him with a king who would support their alliance. The prophet Isaiah counseled Ahaz to trust in the Lord to protect him (Isa 7:4–11), but Ahaz instead turned to the Assyrians for military assistance (2 Kgs 16:7–9; 2 Chr 28:16–21; Isa 8:5–8).

The armies of Tiglath-pileser III removed the threat, but Ahaz also became an Assyrian vassal. Ahaz was one of Judah's most ungodly kings, and he even introduced an Assyrian altar and worship practices into the temple in Jerusalem in an attempt to appease the Assyrians (2 Kgs 16:10–18). Ahaz also offered one of his own sons as a sacrifice to the gods (2 Kgs 16:2–4; 2 Chr 28:1–4; 22–25).

Ahaz's son, Hezekiah, was determined not to follow in his father's footsteps. He walked in the ways of the Lord and brought about a number of important religious reforms designed to purge Judah of the paganism introduced by his father. At the death of the Assyrian king Sargon II, Hezekiah seized his opportunity to reassert Judah's independence and refused to pay tribute. This led to an Assyrian military invasion under Sennacherib. Sennacherib's armies captured forty-six cities in Judah and even surrounded the city of Jerusalem, demanding Hezekiah's surrender and insisting that the gods of Judah would not protect or deliver him. Renouncing any trust in political or military solutions, Hezekiah turned to the Lord and prayed at the temple for the deliverance of the city (2 Kgs 19:14–19; Isa 37:14–20). The prophet Isaiah assured the king that the Assyrians would not capture the city (2 Kgs 19:20–34; Isa 37:21–35), and the angel of the Lord destroyed the Assyrian army at the gates of Jerusalem. This forced Sennacherib to return to his homeland (2 Kgs 19:35–37; Isa 37:36–38).

Micah experienced opposition as he preached his unwavering message of judgment (2:6–7). One can imagine the abuse heaped upon Micah as he preached in the streets and squares of Jerusalem about how the city and temple would be destroyed. However, a century later, the elders of Judah would remember it was Micah's message of judgment and Hezekiah's response to his message that had led the Lord to relent from destroying Judah when Sennacherib's troops surrounded Jerusalem in 701 BC (see Jer 26:17–19).

The messages of Isaiah and Micah to Judah during the Assyrian crisis mirrored each other in significant ways. Both Isaiah and Micah warned of a future exile to Babylon (Isa 39:6; Mic 4:10). Both promised deliverance from Assyria (Isa 14:25; Mic 4:5–6) and that the Lord would raise up a son from the line of David to rule over his people (Isa 9:6–7; Mic 5:2–3). Both prophets anticipated the exiles would return from Assyria and Babylon (Isa 11:11; Mic 7:12). And both prophets share the eschatological vision of Zion as the highest mountain on the earth, as well as Jerusalem as the center of God's kingdom (Isa 2:2–4; Mic 4:1–5). The oracle in Micah 4:1–5 is perhaps an expanded version of Isaiah's earlier message. The similarities between the two passages may simply reflect the prophets' use of a shared tradition or common source.

Structure

Commenting on the complex structure of Micah, Raymond Dillard and Tremper Longman observe, "It is easy to get lost in the mix of judgment and salvation speeches. The structure is hard to fathom."[2] Despite these difficulties, the simplest and most straightforward understanding of Micah's structure is to divide the book into three major sections (chaps. 1–2; 3–5; 6–7) that are each introduced by the imperative of the verb "to hear" (*shama'*) (1:2; 3:1; 6:1–2).[3] Each of these sections, or panels, exhibits a pattern in which a warning of judgment is followed by a promise of salvation.[4]

Lament is a prominent motif in each of the judgment sections. Micah delivers a mournful eulogy over the doomed towns of Judah in 1:8–16 and announces a woe oracle against Judah's leaders in 2:1–11. The city of Jerusalem writhes in grief like a woman in labor in 4:9–10. Micah mourns

Micah 1–2	Micah 3–5	Micah 6–7
The Judgment of Samaria and Jerusalem and Their Corrupt Leaders (1:1–2:11)	The Failure of Judah's Leaders and the Coming Destruction of Jerusalem (3:1–12)	Judah's Failure to Practice Justice and the Disappearance of the Godly (6:1–7:7)
Salvation: The Promise of the Restoration of the Remnant (2:12–13)	**Salvation:** The Future Kingdom of Peace and Justice Under the Rule of Messiah (4:1–5:15)	**Salvation:** The Vindication of Jerusalem and the Godly and the Removal of Israel's Sin (7:8–20)

---

[2] Tremper Longman III and Raymond B. Dillard, *An Introduction to the Old Testament*, 2nd ed. (Grand Rapids, MI: Zondervan, 2006), 449.

[3] See Leslie C. Allen, *The Books of Joel, Obadiah, Jonah, and Micah*, NICOT (Grand Rapids, MI: Eerdmans, 1976), 257.

[4] Ibid., 257–60.

over the disappearance of the godly from the land in 7:1–6. Announcing national disaster brings great sorrow to Micah as he carries out his mission from God.

The promises of salvation in each section overturn the immediately preceding warnings of judgment. Exile from the land is reversed by a re-gathering of Israel in 2:12–13. The leveling of the temple mount to a heap of ruins is overturned by the elevation of Mount Zion in 4:1–5. The grief of the righteous over Judah's destruction turns to joy in anticipation of the Lord's forgiveness of Judah's sinful ways in 7:18–20. The term "remnant" (*she'erit*) appears in each of these promise/salvation sections as a reminder that the Lord will purify and preserve a faithful minority, ultimately transforming them into a great nation (2:12; 4:7; 5:6–7; 7:18).

The book also reflects an A-B-A structure in that sections with lengthy messages of judgment followed by brief promises of salvation serve as bookends for the middle section of the book.[5] In the middle section, a short message of judgment is followed by a lengthy and detailed message of hope for the future. This particular structure serves to highlight and draw the reader's attention to the promise of the future kingdom of God and the coming Messiah at the center of the book.

The order and arrangement of the oracles in 4:1–5:15 is especially complex, but these messages also reflect a judgment-salvation pattern with an extended message of salvation at the center.[6] Judah will go into exile, but the Lord will rescue his people (4:9–10). The nations have assembled against Zion, but the Lord will turn his people into a mighty army. They will dwell in peace under the rule of the future Messiah (4:11–5:9). The nations that march on Jerusalem will one day come to worship the Lord and learn his ways. The Lord warns that he will destroy Judah's army and demolish her cities, but the purpose of this devastating judgment is to purge the people of their sinful ways (5:10–16). This smaller structure at the middle of the book further accentuates Micah's vision of hope for Israel's future.

---

[5] Ibid., 259–60.
[6] Ibid.

Exposition

Micah 1:1–2:13 (The Coming Judgment of Samaria and Jerusalem)

1:1–7 "The Lord is . . . coming down to trample the heights of the earth" (The Coming of the Lord to Earth as Warrior and Judge)

This opening passage portrays a theophany where God as a warrior comes down from his heavenly temple to mete out judgment on his enemies. As the Lord marches into battle, the mountains and valleys melt before his fiery presence. The target of judgment narrows from the whole earth, to Israel/Samaria, and then to Judah/Jerusalem. Samaria would be judged for its religious apostasy and idolatry, but God's judgment would extend even to the gates of Jerusalem because Judah was guilty of similar sins.

1:8–16 "Disaster has come from the Lord to the gate of Jerusalem" (The Coming Military Invasion of Judah and Destruction of Jerusalem)

The Lord would specifically judge by sending the Assyrian army against the cities of Judah. Micah grieves over the disaster that would befall Judah. This horrible judgment would affect his fellow countrymen, his hometown, and even members of his family. Because the people had become immune to prophetic warnings of judgment, Micah employs a series of vivid puns and wordplays to depict the fate of the various towns that would fall to the Assyrians. As Gary Smith explains, these puns were like a modern preacher saying, "Watertown will be covered with water. Washington will be washed away, and Waterloo will meet its waterloo."[7] The listing of these cities enabled the prophet's audience to imagine the route of the invading army as they marched toward Jerusalem.

"Don't announce it in Gath" in 1:10 recalls the death of King Saul and provides the ominous warning of a similar national disaster in Judah's immediate future (see 2 Sam 1:20). The residents of Beth-leaphrah are told to roll in the "dust" ('aphar) as an expression of mourning. The residents of Shaphir

---

[7] Gary V. Smith, *Hosea, Amos, Micah*, NIVAC (Grand Rapids, MI: Zondervan, 2001), 452.

*Detail of the siege of Lachish recorded on the walls of the palace of Sennacherib at
Nineveh. Assyrian battering rams attack the desperate defenders of the Judean city who
attempt to counteract the assault by hurling flaming torches toward the battering rams.
At the left captives stream out of the doomed city. (Courtesy of the British Museum.)*

("Pleasant Town," from *shaphar*) would be reduced to "nakedness" and
"shame" when taken away as captives. The besieged inhabitants of Zaanan
(*Tsa'anan*) would not be able to "go out" (*yatsa*) because of the enemy troops
surrounding their city. Those living in Beth-ezel ("House Next Door")
would only be able to watch and weep as they observed the collapse of
neighboring towns. Maroth ("Bitter Town" from *mara*) ironically waits for
good news that would not come because "disaster" had reached even to
Jerusalem, the city of *shalom*.

Military preparations would not prevent this disaster. The military gar-
rison of Lachish protected Jerusalem twenty-five miles to the southwest, but
even if the soldiers there were to harness the "horses" (*rakesh*) to the chariots,
it would not halt the enemy's advance. The taking of Lachish opened the
way for the Assyrian army to march on Jerusalem and demand its surrender.
Fortresses and military resources in general had led Judah into the sin of
trusting in its own strength rather than in the Lord as its source of security.
The name of Moresheth-Gath (Micah's hometown) sounded like the word

SENNACHERIB AND THE ASSYRIAN INVASION OF JUDAH

Micah's lament over the cities of Judah in Micah 1:8–16 refers to the Assyrian invasion of Judah carried out by Sennacherib and his troops. The annals of Sennacherib describe his conquest of the cities of Judah:

> *As to Hezekiah, the Jew, he did not submit to my yoke. I laid siege to his strong cities, walled forts, and countless small villages, and conquered them by means of well-stamped earth-ramps and battering-rams brought near the walls with an attack by foot soldiers, using mines, breeches as well as trenches. I drove out 200,150 people, young and old, male and female, horses, mules, donkeys, camels, big and small cattle beyond counting, and considered them slaves. Himself I made a prisoner in Jerusalem, his royal residence, like a bird in a cage. I surrounded him with earthwork in order to molest those who were on his city's gate. Thus I reduced his country, but I still increased the tribute and the presents to me as overlord which I imposed upon him beyond the former tribute, to be delivered annually.*

for "betrothed" (*me'orashah*), and this town would be given away like a bride or her dowry price to the Assyrian captors. The wealth and contribution to national security expected from the ruined city of Achzib would prove to be a "deception" (*'achzab*) for the rulers of Judah. The town of Mareshah (sounds like *yarash*, "to possess") would become the inheritance of the invading "conqueror" (*yoresh*). An allusion to David fleeing from Saul to Adullam (1 Sam 22:1) provides a fitting close to Micah's lament over the impending destruction of Judah, as its leaders would once again have to flee for their lives.

Micah calls for the people of Judah to shave their heads as a sign of mourning for the many who would be killed and exiled in the invasion, in hopes that, by taking this somber message to heart, the people would repent and the Lord would relent from sending this terrible judgment.

2:1–11 "WOE TO THOSE WHO DREAM UP WICKEDNESS" (MICAH'S CONDEMNATION OF THE FALSE PROPHETS)

This judgment speech elaborates on the reasons for the judgment the Lord plans to send against Jerusalem. Micah lays the blame for the corruption of Judah on the privileged and powerful. The wealthy used their resources and influence to exploit the poor and needy. The law of Moses had prescribed generous lending to fellow Israelites (Exod 22:25; Deut 15:7–11) and had stipulated that land was not to be permanently sold or transferred (Lev 25:23–28); thus, each family could have its own inheritance from the Lord. Justice, according to the Mosaic law, involved generosity toward the poor. Those with more than they needed were to share with those who did not have enough. In actuality, wealthy landowners were using the slightest debt of the less fortunate as a pretext for confiscating their property and amassing large estates (see Isa 5:8–10). Because they had devised and carried out their "evil" (ra`ah) (v. 1), the Lord would bring "disaster" (ra`ah) on Judah; those who had oppressed others would lose the lands they had stolen to a foreign invader.

Judah's spiritual leaders had promoted apostasy and actively opposed Micah's ministry as he warned of the coming judgment (2:6–11). The false prophets commanded Micah, "Quit your preaching"—This same verb describes the seductive speech of the adulteress in Proverbs 5:3 and reflects here that Micah's opponents dismiss his message as drivel or hysterical foaming at the mouth.[8] Undaunted by this attack, Micah twice uses the same verb to characterize the preaching of those who oppose him (vv. 6, 11). They are actually the ones babbling because they offer empty promises of hope. Micah's preaching in Judah received the same response as Amos's preaching in Israel (Amos 7:10–17), and both nations were judged for their failure to hear and obey the prophetic word.

Micah's conflict with the false prophets arose over their fundamentally different understandings of Yahweh's covenant relationship with his people.[9] Micah reminded the people that the Lord's blessings were conditioned upon obedience to the covenant commands, while the pseudo-prophets promoted the idea that the Lord would bless and protect his people no matter what. The question, "Is the Spirit of the LORD impatient?" in 2:7 indicates that these prophets and their followers saw Micah as rejecting the proclamation

---

[8] Bruce K. Waltke, *A Commentary on Micah* (Grand Rapids, MI: Eerdmans, 2007), 110–11.

[9] For further discussion of the theme of Micah's conflict with the false prophets, see A. S. van der Woude, "Micah in Dispute with the Pseudo-Prophets," *Vetus Testamentum* 19 (1969): 244–60.

in Exodus 34:6 that the Lord was "slow to anger."[10] Micah reminded them that the covenant between the Lord and Israel did not rule out the possibility of judgment and exile. Unfortunately, the Lord's miraculous deliverance of Jerusalem from the Assyrians in 701 BC only deepened the conviction that he would never allow Judah to fall to its enemies. In the next century, Jeremiah would warn the people of Judah not to listen to prophets who made empty promises of "Peace, peace" (Jer 8:11; 18:8) and who taught he presence at the temple guaranteed their safety, regardless of their behavior (Jer 7:1–15). Micah sarcastically observes that a prophet promising plenty of beer and wine would be just the prophet for a people who only want to hear good news. The prophet employs a wordplay in verse 11 involving "lies" (*sheqer*) that characterizes the message of the false prophets and "beer" (*shekar*) that represents their promises of blessing and abundance.[11]

2:12–13 "I WILL COLLECT THE REMNANT OF ISRAEL" (THE LORD'S PROMISE TO SHEPHERD A FUTURE REMNANT IN ISRAEL)

When the Lord completed his judgment, he would gather and restore the remnant like a shepherd bringing his sheep into the fold. This small "remnant" of survivors would become a large and noisy throng. The image of king as shepherd conveys a ruler who provides security and protection for his people (2 Sam 5:2; Ps 78:70–72), and Israel would find complete security with the Lord as their Shepherd-King (see Psalm 23; Isa 40:10–11; Ezek 34:11–19). The Lord as Israel's shepherd had the power to break through the barriers that would stand in the way of their restoration and return to the land. As Messiah, Jesus would also fulfill the role of Israel's Good Shepherd, delivering them from their enemies (5:4–6; see Ezek 34:23–31) and ultimately even laying down his life for the flock (John 10:1–18).

---

[10] Smith, *Hosea, Amos, and Micah*, 467.
[11] Ibid., 470, n. 29.

3:1–5:15 (The Exaltation of Zion and Israel's Future King)

3:1–12 "ZION WILL BE PLOWED LIKE A FIELD" (THE COMING DESTRUCTION OF JERUSALEM AND THE TEMPLE)

In the second major section of the book, Micah returns to the sins of Judah's leaders. The preaching of the false prophets ultimately emboldened Judah's corrupt civil leaders to continue in their sinful ways—they oppressed the poor because they believed they could sin with impunity. Judah's leaders love and practice "evil" (ra`ah) (vv. 1, 4). Micah compares these oppressors to cannibals who strip off the flesh of the poor and cook them in a pot. Exploitation of the poor was the same as physical violence in God's eyes because it deprived the poor of both their land and their livelihood. The prophet Isaiah compares Judah's rulers to murderers, whose clothes and hands are covered with the bloodstains of their victims (see Isa 1:15, 21–23). Because these leaders had lacked compassion when dealing with the poor, the Lord would not respond to their cries for help in their time of judgment.

Judah's prophets are corrupt and preach for selfish motives. They base whether they preach judgment or salvation on how well they are compensated. Because the people chose to listen to prophets who did not speak for God, the Lord would take away the light of true prophetic revelation. The nation would grope in darkness without direction from the Lord because they had not listened to prophets like Micah who had preached the truth about their sin and given them the opportunity to repent.

Because of the corruption of Judah's leaders, the Lord would destroy Jerusalem and its temple. Jerusalem would share the fate of Samaria, and the temple mount would become a heap of ruins. Micah issued an unqualified prophecy of Jerusalem's destruction, but this prophecy was not carried out in his lifetime. Jeremiah 26 notes that when Judah's leaders later planned to put Jeremiah to death for warning of Jerusalem's impending destruction, Jeremiah reminded them of Hezekiah's response to Micah's preaching and how the Lord had relented from sending judgment because of the king's repentance (Jer 26:15–19). Just as with Jonah and Nineveh (Jonah 3), repentance led to God relenting from sending judgment against Judah when Hezekiah took Micah's warnings to heart.

THE IMPACT OF MICAH'S PREACHING
(Micah 3:9–12 / Jeremiah 26:17–19)

In the century following his ministry, Micah's prophetic warning of the destruction of Jerusalem was remembered as the cause of Hezekiah's repentance that led to the deliverance of Jerusalem from the Assyrian army in 701 BC. The elders recalled Micah's preaching when some were calling for Jeremiah's execution for preaching judgment against Jerusalem and the temple.

Micah's Message	Hezekiah's Response
Micah the Moreshite prophesied in the days of Hezekiah king of Judah and said to all the people of Judah, 'This is what the LORD of Hosts says: "Zion will be plowed like a field, Jerusalem will become ruins, and the temple mount a forested hill." Jeremiah 26:17–18/ Micah 3:9–12	Did Hezekiah king of Judah and all the people of Judah put him to death? Did he not fear the LORD and plead for the LORD's favor, and did not the LORD relent concerning the disaster He had pronounced against them? We are about to bring great harm on ourselves!" Jeremiah 26:19

4:1–5:15 "IS THERE NO KING WITH YOU?" (ZION'S HUMILIATION AND EXALTATION)

This section of the book focuses on the restoration of Israel and the future exaltation of Jerusalem. The placement of this material in the middle of the book highlights its importance. These prophecies include promises of both the return from Assyrian and Babylonian exile in the near future as well as Israel's final restoration in the last days. This section presents some interpretive challenges. The flow and progression of the argument is difficult to follow because the messages jump back and forth from scenes of defeat and humiliation to images of blessing and salvation. The chronology of the events that the prophet portrays is also difficult to determine because the prophet telescopes near and far events together in some confusing ways. The assaults on Zion portrayed in 4:9–13 seem to include both the Assyrian invasion of Micah's day and the Babylonian siege that led to the fall of Jerusalem a century later. Micah 5:1–3 points to the first coming of Jesus in the aftermath of the Assyrian crisis and divine abandonment of Israel, while 5:4–9 looks forward to the Second Coming of Messiah and his reign over all nations. This future reign of Messiah is preceded by the destruction of the Assyrian army without any reference to the long gaps that exist between these events.

The purpose of prophetic visions was not to give a detailed timeline of the future but rather to reflect patterns of how the Lord would act on behalf of his people in the near future until the time of the eschatological kingdom. Bruce K. Waltke explains: "The prophets represent their heralded events as occurring on the same historical horizon, but these occurrences might in fact prove to be separated by ages."[12] The defeat of Assyria and the return from the Babylonian exile are connected to events associated with the first and second comings of Christ because the Lord's actions on Israel's behalf in the near future provide confirmation that he will ultimately fulfill his promises to deliver his people in the distant future. The same pattern of judgment and salvation that characterized God's dealings with Israel in the Assyrian and Babylonian crises would occur on an even grander scale in the last days of Israel's final restoration. The nations would make a final assault on Jerusalem, but the Lord would save his people, and the nations themselves would then stream to Zion to worship him. Reading prophecy in the right way means looking for patterns of how God acts in the working out of salvation history rather than trying to determine detailed timelines or discern exact correspondences between biblical prophecies and contemporary events.

4:1–8 "Come, let us go up to the mountain of the Lord" (The Future Glory of Jerusalem)

The portrayal of Zion's future glory introduced by "In the last days" provides a stark contrast to its present humiliation. The temple mount, reduced to rubble in 3:12, becomes the highest mountain on the face of the earth. The elevation of Zion figuratively signifies that Jerusalem would become the central place on earth. The promise that the Lord would rule with justice and teach the nations his law in the future kingdom envisions a reversal of the unjust practices of the contemporary rulers of Judah and the corrupt teaching of their greedy prophets. Rather than invading and assaulting, the

---

[12] Waltke, *A Commentary on Micah*, 820.

nations would make a pilgrimage to Zion to worship the Lord and learn his ways. Weapons will be turned into farm implements because warfare will be a thing of the past. The image of each man sitting under his vine and fig tree is a picture of Israel enjoying the agricultural blessing of the land without the threat of military attack (see 1 Kgs 4:25; Zech 3:10). The image of a fruitful garden in connection with the eschatological kingdom also suggests that God's design is to restore what was lost at Eden.[13]

Near and Far Fulfillments in the OT Prophets

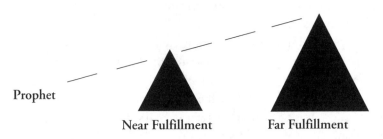

Prophesies often included near and far fulfillments without the prophet necessarily understanding that they were separate events or that these events were separated by long periods of time. In Micah, the judgments of the Assyrian and Babylonian crises anticipate the judgment of the last days, and the deliverance of Jerusalem in 701 BC anticipates the final deliverance of God's people and the coming of Messiah to rule over the earth.

The "On that day" in verse 6 continues the focus on Israel's glorious future. The Lord promises to re-gather his people from exile like a shepherd tending to the crippled and lame in his flock (see 2:12–13; Isa 40:11). The "remnant" of survivors from the exile would become a "strong nation." The dominion of Jerusalem would be restored, and the city would become like a "watchtower" from which the Lord would watch over his people and protect them from their enemies.

---

[13] G. K. Beale, *A New Testament Biblical Theology: The Unfolding of the Old Testament in the New* (Grand Rapids, MI: Baker Academic, 2011), 105.

THE STRUCTURE OF MICAH 4:9–5:6
Like the book as a whole, this section of the book contains alternating messages of judgment and salvation.

4:9–10	4:11–13	5:1–6
'attah Zion in labor pains/ sent away into exile (4:9)	*'attah* Nations besiege Zion and seek to defile her (4:11)	*'attah* Zion under siege and the humiliation of her ruler (5:1)
Zion delivered from exile (4:10)	Zion tramples and crushes her enemies (4:12–13)	The promise of a new David and the defeat of Zion's enemies.(5:2–6)

4:9–10 "YOU WILL GO TO BABYLON; THERE YOU WILL BE RESCUED"
(JUDAH'S COMING EXILE AND FUTURE RESTORATION)

The tone and imagery changes dramatically as the prophet shifts back to the present distress in 4:9–5:1. This section is further divided into three oracles, each introduced by "now" (*'attah*), that contrast Judah's present distress and its future salvation.

In verses 9–10, Daughter Zion is portrayed as a woman in labor, crying out in pain as she is deprived of her king and led away into exile. The image of Zion as a mother in labor is ironic in that many of her residents would be killed or taken away in exile. The prophet's rhetorical, "Is there no king with you?" mocks the people for the misplaced confidence they had put in human kings and military strategies rather than in the Lord. Jerusalem was under assault by the Assyrians in Micah's day, but the prophet looks forward to the future exile in Babylon more than a century later. Babylon was already on the scene in Micah's day and attempted, under its king Merodach-baladan, to lead the resistance against Assyria. When Hezekiah foolishly showed the treasures of his kingdom to the Babylonian envoys, Isaiah warned that the Babylonians would later return to plunder Jerusalem and take captives from the people of Judah (see Isaiah 39). Micah promises that the Lord would ultimately "rescue" (*natsal*) and "redeem" (*ga'al*) Israel from Babylon, using language associated with the exodus from Egypt (see Exod 3:8; 6:6; 15:13).

4:11–13 "MANY NATIONS HAVE NOW ASSEMBLED AGAINST YOU" (JERUSALEM'S PRESENT DISTRESS UNDER ENEMY ATTACK)

Jerusalem is once again under siege in verse 11, and the prophet appears to telescope events relating to the deliverance of Jerusalem from Assyria in 701 BC and the final deliverance of Israel from all its enemies in the last days. The oracle again quickly changes from judgment to salvation. The temple site was originally a threshing floor when David purchased the property (2 Sam 24), and the Lord would use Jerusalem to thresh the enemy nations that had attacked the city. Zion would become like an angry bull with iron horns and bronze hooves and would pulverize its enemies into chaff. In a great reversal, the Lord would once again turn the armies of Israel into a powerful fighting force, and they would defeat the very nations that had subjugated them. The reference to Israel devoting to "destruction" (*haram*) the plunder taken from their enemies recalls how Israel had devoted to destruction the Canaanites and their plunder under Joshua (see Deut 7:2; 13:16; 20:17; Josh 6:17–18).

5:1–6 "ONE WILL COME FROM YOU TO BE RULER OVER ISRAEL" (THE PROMISE OF A NEW DAVID)

The opening of this oracle reverts back to the theme of judgment, as Daughter Zion is once again under siege by her enemies. The timing of the oracle again blends near and far as the siege of Jerusalem leads into the coming of the promised Messiah. Even after the return from exile, Israel would remain under foreign oppression and an even greater bondage to sin and to Satan—Jesus announced that he came to bring the release for prisoners that Isaiah and the prophets had promised (see Isa 61:1–3; Luke 4:18–19). The New Testament further reveals that the complete deliverance and full manifestation of the kingdom of God will not arrive until the Second Coming of Messiah (see Revelation 19–20).

The siege of Jerusalem presents a threat to the promises of the Davidic covenant. The enemy here strikes Israel's ruler (*shophet*—"judge") with a "rod" (*shevet*). Ironically, the word for "rod" here also has the meaning of "scepter," and this symbol of rule is promised to the tribe of Judah and Israel's future king (Gen 49:10; Num 24:17). The Lord promises the Davidic king that he would defeat his enemies with a "rod of iron" in Psalm 2:9, but here it is Zion's enemies that have the upper hand. In the

Assyrian assault on Judah and Jerusalem, Sennacherib boasted that he had trapped Hezekiah "like a bird in a cage." After the fall of Jerusalem to the Babylonians, Nebuchadnezzar slaughtered the sons of Zedekiah and put out Zedekiah's eyes before taking him as a prisoner to Babylon (2 Kgs 25:7; Jer 39:6–7; 52:10–11).[14]

After the present humiliation, the Lord would fulfill his covenant promises by restoring dominion to the house of David. A new ruler would once again come from the obscure village of Bethlehem, just as in the days of David. In contrast to the failed Davidic kings of history, this future rule (Messiah) would fulfill the ideal of what a king should be. Christian readings of Micah 5:2 have often viewed the description of this future ruler's origins "from antiquity" and "from eternity" as a reference to Christ's preexistence, but this verse stresses instead the future Messiah's ancestral connection to David. Gordon Johnston explains that the terms "from antiquity" (*miqqedem*) and "from eternity" (*mime' 'olam*) often refer to earlier periods in Israel's history (see Pss 74:12; 77:5, 11; Deut 32:7; Isa 63:9–11; and especially Mic 7:14).[15] This reference to Messiah's origins in the distant past certainly hints at what is more fully revealed in the New Testament: Jesus is the preexistent Son of God and more than just a human descendant of David (see John 1:1–4; 8:58; Phil 2:5–11; Col 1:15–20).

This new David would only come after the Lord had "abandoned" his people to judgment for a time. The future ideal Davidic ruler would bring peace to Israel by shepherding them (see 4:6–7) and by extending his dominion "to the ends of the earth." He would rule over the enemy nations that had subjugated his people in the past. Should the Assyrians attempt to invade the land, he would repel their assaults. The Assyrians of Micah's day are representative of all of Israel's enemies, including the nations that would assault Israel in the final great Day of the Lord (see Ezek 38–39; Joel 3:1–14; Zeph 3:8; Zechariah 12, 14). The prophet Isaiah even anticipates the time in the future kingdom of God when Israel, Egypt, and Assyria would be unified as the three peoples of God (Isa 19:18–25).

---

[14] Even Jesus as the Messiah would suffer in solidarity with his Davidic predecessors, as his enemies struck him in the head and face (see Matthew 27:30; John 19:3).

[15] Herbert W. Bateman IV, Darrell L. Bock, and Gordon H. Johnston, *Jesus the Messiah: Tracing the Promises, Expectations, and Coming of Israel's King* (Grand Rapids, MI: Kregel, 2012), 125–26.

5:7–15 "Your hand will be lifted up against your adversaries" (Israel's Future Dominion over the Nations)

The restored remnant of Israel would become not only like the refreshing dew and rain, but also like a young lion tearing prey in its military domination over the nations. The purpose of the Lord's judgments on Israel in history and in the last days would be to purge his people of their idolatrous trust in military strength and false gods. The Lord would have to destroy their military equipment, wipe out their cities, and demolish their idols before their hearts would be moved to trust him as their sole source of security. In the last days, this purging judgment would ultimately extend to all nations.

Micah 6:1–7:20 (Israel's Covenantal Failure and the Lord's Covenantal Commitment)

6:1–8 "Listen to the Lord's lawsuit" (The Lord's Covenantal Demands)

The third major section of the book opens with the Lord bringing a formal "lawsuit" (*riv*) against his people with Micah serving as his prosecuting attorney. The proceedings begin with the calling of witnesses. Moses had called on the heavens and earth to serve as witnesses when the Lord entered into covenant with Israel (Deut 32:1), and they had stood as silent observers of Israel's conduct ever since. The Lord begins his case by recalling the good things he did for Israel in making them a people—rescuing them from bondage in Egypt, giving them leaders like Moses, and protecting them in their wilderness wanderings when Balak of Moab enlisted the prophet Balaam to curse them (see Numbers 22–24). The Lord's faithfulness to the people of Israel stands in contrast to their unfaithfulness toward him.

The Lord charges that the people have misunderstood what he expected from them as his covenant partner. The people mistakenly thought they could please the Lord by carrying out religious rituals and offering sacrifices apart from a lifestyle of justice and mercy. John Walton explains that in the ancient Near East at large, "primary obligation to the gods was seen to be in the cultic realm," and "a person's ethical or moral goodness was not as highly valued by the deity as the cultic conscientiousness."[16] Israel's God, however, placed greater emphasis on his moral and ethical demands. To demonstrate the inadequacy of ritual apart from ethics, Micah lists a series of offerings of increasing worth—the standard burnt offering, a valuable young calf, thousands of animals and rivers of oil (something that could only be offered by a king; see 1 Kgs 8:63–64), and finally the sacrifice of a firstborn child.[17] Even the most costly of sacrifices had no value apart from a lifestyle of doing justice, loving faithfulness, and walking humbly before God. "To act justly" required treating others with fairness in accordance with the Mosaic law and carried an obligation to provide for the poor. Loving "faithfulness" (*hesed*) meant a lifestyle of covenantal loyalty and relational commitment toward God and others. One could not love God without also loving one's neighbor. Yahweh's *hesed* with Israel guaranteed the continuation of his covenantal relationship with his people in spite of their unfaithfulness (see 7:18–20), but he also demanded *hesed* from his people as their reciprocal response to his grace (see Deut 7:9, 12; Ps 103:17). Walking "humbly" would guarantee that Israel did not presume upon God's grace. Despite the people's guilt, the Lord's indictment does not conclude with a formal sentence of judgment. Rather, the Lord reminds the people of what he expects from them so they might repent and avoid the coming judgment.

6:9–16 "Can I excuse wicked scales?" (The Lord's Resolve to Judge Injustice and Dishonesty Among His People)

If the lawsuit speech in 6:1–8 lays out the Lord demands from his people, what follows reflects how far Judah had fallen short of these covenant expectations. The Lord would not forget the economic exploitation of the poor through theft, dishonest measures, and deceit. He would strike his people

---

[16] John H. Walton, *Ancient Near Eastern Thought and the Old Testament: Introducing the Conceptual World of the Hebrew Bible* (Grand Rapids, MI: Baker Academic, 2006), 306–307. This reality does not mean that these other religions had no concern for justice, morality, or ethics. See pp. 142–161 in Walton's work for further discussion of this issue.

[17] Child sacrifice is mentioned here only for rhetorical purposes in order to represent the most valued sacrifice imaginable. Sacrifice of the firstborn was a common practice in the ancient Near East, but the Mosaic law allowed for the redemption of the firstborn (Numbers 18:15) and prohibited child sacrifice in general (see Leviticus 18:21; 20:2–5; Deuteronomy 18:10).

with a heavy blow and bring the covenant curses upon them so that the rich and powerful would never enjoy the agricultural produce of the lands they had stolen from others.

7:1–7 "Godly people have vanished from the land" (The Corruption of God's People)

Micah grieved over Judah's spiritual bankruptcy. Righteous individuals were as rare as edible grapes and figs after the harvest. Isaiah also lamented that the righteous were disappearing from the land (Isa 57:1–2). Before the fall of Jerusalem to the Babylonians, the Lord called on the prophet Jeremiah to search the streets of Jerusalem to see if he could find one righteous person (Jer 5:1). Selfishness and greed prevailed to the point that neighbors and even family members could no longer trust one another. The only thing left for righteous individuals to do was to wait for God's ultimate deliverance.

7:8–20 "He will again have compassion on us" (A Final Promise of Restoration)

The Lord would turn Israel's humiliation into vindication and its grief into joy. Judah deserved its judgment, but the righteous could trust that the Lord would act to restore his people. He would turn the tables so the nations that had devastated his people would themselves be humiliated. The cities of Israel would be rebuilt, and the exiles would return from distant lands. Micah prays for the Lord to "shepherd" his people so they might dwell securely in their land, and the Lord promises to perform a second exodus to bring about their deliverance and return. Even the survivors among the enemy nations would worship the Lord.

The Lord's character is the basis of Micah's confidence in the promises to restore Israel. For the third time in the Book of the Twelve, a prophet recalls the central confession found in Exodus 34:6–7 that the Lord is compassionate and forgiving (see Joel 2:13; Jonah 4:2). The Lord will forgive because his anger toward the people that leads to judgment is only temporary. More than simply forgiving, the Lord would declare war on Israel's sin as the greatest enemy of his people (see Isa 59:20–21). He will trample their sins under his feet and cast them into the sea. In spite of Israel's many sins, the Lord would never renege on the covenant promises to Abraham that he swore to fulfill (see Gen 22:15–18).

Theological Message and Application of Micah

Micah's preaching reminded the people that living in covenant with the Lord involved both blessing and obligation. The Lord's judgment would come to both Samaria and Jerusalem because both Israel and Judah had failed to keep his commandments. The lack of justice in the land was the primary indicator of the people's spiritual condition—they could not love the Lord without practicing mercy and kindness toward each other. Jesus also taught the inseparability of the commands to love God and to love one's neighbor (Matt 22:36–39), and James reminds us that "pure religion" is to take care of the poor and needy (Jas 1:27).

Micah confronted prophets who preached the Lord would unconditionally bless his people regardless of their conduct. Micah warned that judgment would reach even to Jerusalem and the temple mount. The Lord's presence at the Jerusalem temple would not protect his disobedient people from the consequences of their sinful behavior. The Lord's blessing and protection of Jerusalem was a vital part of Israel's theological tradition (see Psalms 46; 48; 76), but even the blessing of Jerusalem depended on its leaders and people reflecting the holiness and righteousness that God demanded of them (see Psalms 15; 24). Just like today, the people of Micah's generation flocked to prophets who promoted cheap grace and muted the message of God's wrath and impending judgment. But faithful prophets like Micah told the people what they needed to hear rather than merely what they wanted to hear. The mournful tone of Micah's words of judgment reflects how painful it was to preach of a judgment that would reach even his own hometown, but his willingness to preach this difficult message is what led to repentance and the sparing of Jerusalem from the Assyrian army in the days of Hezekiah. When the people returned to their sinful ways in subsequent generations, the Lord sent his people into exile in Babylon.

Micah also promised that judgment would eventually turn to restoration. The Lord would remain faithful to his covenant promises even though the people had been unfaithful to him. He would forgive the sins of his people and restore a "remnant" to the land that would become a mighty nation. A future Davidic king would rule over his people and deliver them from their enemies. The New Testament portrays another judgment befalling the city of Jerusalem. Jesus warns that Jerusalem would be "trampled by the Gentiles" until the time of its future restoration (Luke 21:24), and when Israel rejects Jesus as her Messiah, the city of Jerusalem is destroyed by Gentiles in AD 70.

Micah's vision of a world without warfare where absolute justice prevails still awaits fulfillment. Nevertheless, the blessings perfectly enjoyed in the future kingdom are at least partially experienced by the church in the present through Christ. Believers have come to the heavenly Zion and enjoy the blessings of God's presence (Heb 12:22–24; Gal 4:21–31); Jesus has replaced the temple as the locus of God's presence (John 1:14). Rather than the nations streaming to Zion, the word of the Lord has gone out to the nations from Jerusalem (Acts 1:8), and the preaching of the gospel is actively bringing about the obedience of the nations (Rom 1:5; 16:26). The church shares God's kingdom agenda in preaching a message of peace among the nations. Jesus and the apostles clearly teach that the blessings of the "last days," promised by the Old Testament prophets, have arrived in their inaugural stages with the first coming of Christ. John and Jesus announce the arrival of the kingdom promised by Isaiah (Isa 52:7–10; Mark 1:15), and Jesus is the eschatological herald who would preach the "good news" to those who needed deliverance (Isa 61:1–11; Luke 4:16–30). Jesus instructed the disciples that his death instituted the "new covenant" promised in Jer 31:31–34 (Luke 22:20; 1 Cor 11:25), and believers live under the benefits and blessings of that covenant (2 Cor 3:6; Heb 8:8–12; 10:16–18). Peter explained that the baptism of the Holy Spirit at Pentecost fulfilled the prophecy of Joel 2:28–32 concerning the pouring out of the Spirit in the last days (Acts 2:17–21).[18] James saw the conversion of Gentiles as fulfilling Amos's prophecy of the rebuilding of David's fallen booth in Amos 9:11–12 (Acts 15:16–17). We should thus understand the fulfillment of Micah's prophecies concerning the eschatological kingdom as both now and not yet.

---

[18] Peter's quotation of Joel 2:28–32 in Acts 2 also suggests a connection to the prophecy in Isaiah 2:1–4//Micah 4:1–4. The exact Greek expression "it will be in the last days" (*estai en tais 'eschatais heterais*) that Peter uses in Acts 2:17 appears in the Septuagint (LXX) only in Isaiah 2:2, thus suggesting that what happens on Pentecost also fulfills in some way what is prophesied in Isaiah 2//Micah 4 as well as Joel 2. See Beale, *A New Testament Biblical Theology*, 104.

11

THE BOOK OF NAHUM

Introduction

Nazi Germany, Imperial Japan—if ever there was a time in history when the forces of evil seemed invincible, the early period of World War II (1939–1942) was that time. Storm the beaches! Man the artillery! Watch your flank! Fire in the hole! (see Nah 2:1). For a prophet to speak of military embattlement in the streets of Berlin or the cities of Japan at the height of Axis power would have seemed a far-fetched hope. Yet in just a few years, Berlin lay in ruins and the cities of Japan were scorched rubble. Imagine a prophet's description of D-Day or the detonation of the atomic bombs over Hiroshima and Nagasaki. Imagine how a prophet in 1940 might have described the death of Hitler and the fall of the Rising Sun. Flying fortresses, pounding shells, steel-hauled tanks, blackened curtains, flashing light, cities aflame—corpses without end! (see Nah 3:3). Would such language bring hope to the victims of Nazi efficiency and Japanese cruelty? Might that prophet have used staccato rhetoric, vivid images, and taunting ridicule? Would he summon the wrath of God on those who brought so much death, destruction, and despair? One might imagine he would.

In like manner, a prophet spoke at the height of the Assyrian Empire. This prophet was Nahum the Elkoshite. His message was one of doom for the mighty Assyrians and their capital city Nineveh, but one of hope for oppressed Judah. The direct opposite of Jonah, Nahum leaves no room for repentance. At this point in history, Nineveh's guilt had reached a tipping point, and God's wrath was sure to be unleashed. From the language of the book, Assyria was still strong in Nahum's day (Nah 1:12), making her fall seem all the more impossible. But she had angered Yahweh, the God before whom the "earth trembles" and "the mountains quake" (Nah 1:5). Just as the fall of Berlin would have seemed impossible to those in the chambers of a concentration camp, so the fall of Nineveh must have seemed impossible for those experiencing Assyrian cruelty (Nah 3:19). Yet from the vantage point of Yahweh, for whom the "clouds are the dust beneath his feet" (Nah 1:3), the fall of Nineveh was certain. Nahum carried God's perspective down to man, even to those bearing the yoke of Assyrian oppression (Nah 1:13).

Understanding when Nahum delivered his oracle is important to the veracity of the message; thankfully, there are clues within the text that provide a chronological bracket. The book must postdate the fall of Thebes, which occurred in 663 BC (Nah 3:8). Furthermore, internal references to the strength of Assyria imply that the book was written before Assyrian dominance waned at the death of Ashurbanipal (626 BC). The power of Nahum's message is neutered if the oracle is dated during or after Assyria's final years, just as an oracle announcing the death of Hitler would have seemed less than prophetic if produced in May of 1945. But as significant as prediction is in Nahum's prophecy, it is the language of Nahum that conveys the power of Yahweh's wrath. Nahum is a master of imagery and literary rhetoric, employing a vast array of metaphors and structural devices to deliver his message. One of the distinguishing features of Nahum is short, staccato repetition, the kind of language that overwhelms the senses. With the words of Nahum one *feels* the prophecy unfold.

Structure

The book of Nahum, like most of the Twelve, is comprised of a mosaic of prophetic sub-genres linked by common themes, language, and style. Yet like all books, there are literary traits that distinguish Nahum among the prophets. First among the literary traits of the book are abrupt, staccato lines of poetry that portray a sense of urgency and chaos in the visions of Nineveh's destruction. A second feature is the taunt. The language of judgment permeates the message of Nahum, but the prophet does more than merely state the case—he actively taunts the enemies of God. Third, Nahum is a master of allusion, utilizing the symbols of Assyria to heighten the effect of poetic justice in the book.[1] Distinctive rhetorical features indicate careful attention given to style and structure in the Nahum book.

The book begins with an opening hymn organized by a partial acrostic (1:2–8). This two-part hymn praises Yahweh as an avenging warrior against the guilty (1:2) but as a stronghold of protection for the innocent (1:7). Transitioning from the hymn, the text follows with a two-fold address condemning the oppressor and comforting the oppressed (1:9–14). The first chapter ends with a call to celebrate the fall of Nineveh (1:15), a fitting conclusion to the announcement of Nineveh's death (1:14).[2]

Chapters two and three form a chiasm with the woe speech of Nahum 3:1–4 acting as the center. Additionally, the call to celebrate in 1:15 corresponds with the final announcement of Nineveh's death in 3:18–19, thus forming an *inclusio* to the chiasm.

Exposition

1:1 (Introduction)

The introduction to Nahum does not provide a list of kings or historical references that aid in the dating of the book, but it does state the oracle is

---

[1] Allusion is based off of Assyrian symbols (2:11–13), geography (1:8; 2:6), culture (2:1, 13), and history (2:8). There are also examples of possible allusion to the language of Assyrian documents and treaties. See Robert B. Chisholm Jr., *Interpreting the Minor Prophets* (Grand Rapids, MI: Zondervan, 1990), 180–81.

[2] The English 1:15 is the Hebrew 2:1, thus functioning in the Hebrew text as an introduction to the visions, taunts, and woe speech that follow.

directed against Nineveh, capital of Assyria. Furthermore, the prophet is introduced as Nahum the Elkoshite. Little is known of Nahum the person, and the location of Elkosh is uncertain.[3] The message of the book, however, does not rely on the background of the prophet or his origins. It is sufficient to simply know that the prophet whose name means "comfort" brought a message of comfort to Judah.

The introduction to Nahum states that it is more than an oracle: it is a book. Nahum is the only prophetic book to refer to itself as just that—a book—thus causing some to reason that Nahum originated as a literary piece rather than a spoken message. However, while Nahum is characterized by substantial literary features and structure, there is little to distinguish it from other prophetic books in this regard. Perhaps the Nahum book is simply stating the obvious—that the prophet's spoken word was later configured into a written word, carrying with it all the prophetic authority of the divine spokesman.

1:2–8 (Parallel Hymns Celebrating Yahweh as Divine Warrior)

A significant feature of the opening hymn is the incomplete acrostic in the Hebrew text. Nahum 1:2–8 incorporates nine of the first eleven letters of the Hebrew alphabet into a loose acrostic, but many features of an acrostic are lacking; successive letters are not always positioned at the beginning of each line or couplet, and some letters are altogether missing.[4] Some speculate that the incomplete acrostic may function to depict elements of judgment or chaos, but this may be reaching. It is perhaps more reasonable to think that Nahum begins his "book" with an adapted version of a preexisting hymn.[5] The original hymn (or psalm) may have reflected a more formalized acrostic, but while being adapted into the book, certain elements of the acrostic were lost. The main point is that Nahum opens his book with

---

[3] This fact suggests Elkosh was a small, insignificant town. There is some irony in a man hailing from a town of little stature proclaiming the demise of the great city Nineveh.

[4] Kenneth L. Barker and Waylon Bailey, *Micah, Nahum, Habakkuk, Zephaniah,* NAC (Nashville, TN: Broadman and Holman, 1998), 164.

[5] J. J. M. Roberts, *Nahum, Habakkuk, and Zephaniah: A Commentary,* OTL (Louisville, KY: Westminster John Knox Press, 1991), 48–49.

a hymn to celebrate God's power as a divine warrior; the complete acrostic was evidently unnecessary to make that case.

1:2–6 "THE LORD IS SLOW TO ANGER BUT GREAT IN POWER" (A THEOPHANIC HYMN, PART 1)

The God described by Jonah as slow to anger, "One who relents (*niham*) from sending disaster" (Jonah 4:2), is in Nahum described as "slow to anger but great in power," a God who will "never leave the guilty unpunished" (Nah 1:3a). Thus, Nahum begins his oracle against Nineveh by highlighting Yahweh's commitment to retribution:[6] no longer will Nineveh know the mercies of a longsuffering God. Nahum 1:2 repeats the Hebrew term *naqam* (vengeance) three times for emphasis . . . no longer will God *niham* from sending judgment (Jonah 4:2), but he will take *naqam* on his enemies (Nah 1:2). In its opening hymn, Nahum's oracle has effectively reversed course from that of the earlier prophet Jonah. The God who in awesome power saved Jonah from the belly of Sheol (Jonah 2:2) would now demonstrate that same awesome power by destroying his enemies.

Using the language of theophany, God is depicted in Nahum 1:3b–6 as a divine warrior, one for whom the "clouds are the dust beneath his feet" (1:3b). Theologians might argue that God is omnipresent—and that is true—but for the ancients, the imagery of Yahweh treading the clouds had far greater impact on the mind than abstract theological convention. With hyperbolic bravado,[7] Yahweh is pictured rebuking the sea, drying up the rivers, and bringing mountains down before him. Not only does this imagery stress his power over creation, it also evokes the memory of his past acts in history (i.e., the parting of the Red Sea).[8] The implication is subtle yet profound—just as the awesome power of God was showcased in the past, it will likewise be showcased in the future.[9]

---

[6] Dan Timmer, "Nahum," in *The Lion has Roared: Theological Themes in the Prophetic Literature of the Old Testament*, ed. H. G. L. Peels and S. D. Snyman (Eugene, OR: Pickwick, 2012), 81.

[7] The language of this opening hymn mirrors the hymns of Amos (4:13; 5:8; 9:5–6).

[8] Chisholm notes that the language of a warrior's battle cry characterizes Nahum's hymn. See Chisholm, *Interpreting the Minor Prophets*, 169–70.

[9] John Goldingay and Pamela J. Scalise *Minor Prophets II* Understanding the Bible Commentary Series (Grand Rapids, MI: Baker, 2009), 23.

1:7–8 "The Lord is good, a stronghold in a day of distress"
(A Theophanic Hymn, Part 2)

Nahum 1:7 mirrors 1:2 in structure and form; however, instead of jealous
and avenging, Yahweh is now described as "good." While this language may
seem contradictory, the propositional statements balance the theology of the
hymn. To the implied audience of Judah, the destruction of Nineveh would
indeed be a demonstration of God's goodness—but for Nineveh, a sign of
his fury. The hymn describes Nineveh's destruction as by "an overwhelming flood" (Nah 1:8). Although "overwhelming flood" could simply be a
metaphor describing Yahweh's wrath, there may also be a kind of prophetic
double entendre at play. As a prophet, Nahum may have been alluding to
the eventual means by which Nineveh was destroyed. Some traditions claim
that the fall of Nineveh (612 BC) occurred in conjunction with the flooding
of the Tigris River. As the river rose, it undercut the city walls, thus allowing enemies entrance into the city. If true, then Nineveh would have indeed
fallen with an "overwhelming flood."[10]

Taking both parts together, the message of the opening hymn of Nahum
is clear. Though Yahweh, the powerful warrior, has been provoked to judgment, he is not a vengeful God whose anger is arbitrary. For those who trust
in him, he is good, a "stronghold in a day of distress." But for his enemies,
"who can withstand His indignation?" (1:6).

1:9–14 (Words from a Prophet)

Although there are literary and thematic links between Nahum 1:2–8 and
1:9–14,[11] the book transitions in verse 9 from hymn to an announcement
of judgment. One of the more significant indicators of this transition is the
shift from third person reflection to second person direct address. Just as the
hymn served double duty by issuing fear to the guilty and comfort to the

---

[10] For a detailed analysis of the destruction of Nineveh by flood, see Walter A.
Maier, *The Book of Nahum* (Grand Rapids, MI: Baker Book House, 1980), 118–26.

[11] For instance, consider the link between verses 8 and 9: with verse 8, Yahweh
will completely destroy Nineveh; in verse 9, Yahweh will bring the "plot" of Nineveh
to complete destruction. The Hebrew phrases are almost identical. On literary and thematic links between 1:2–8 and 1:9–11, see Chisholm, *Interpreting the Minor Prophets*,
172.

oppressed, so the words of the prophet are directed to the afflicted as well as to the condemned.

1:9, 11 "ONE . . . WHO PLOTS EVIL AGAINST YAHWEH" (DIRECT ADDRESS TO NINEVEH)

There is some question concerning the addressee of verse 9. The HCSB and NET understand the second person "you" as Nineveh; what Nineveh plots against the Lord, Yahweh will bring it to destruction. The NKJV and ESV translate 9a as a rhetorical question, leaving readers to doubt the addressee. The NIV translates the "you" into "they," thus inferring that Judah is the addressee; what they (Nineveh) have brought against you (Judah), Yahweh will not allow another time. Given the inherently interpretive nature of rhetorical questions, both approaches are plausible. However, the parallels between 1:9 and 1:11 ("who plots against the Lord/Yahweh") suggest that a similar addressee is in view with each verse. Therefore, it is best to see Nineveh as the addressee. What Nineveh has collectively plotted against the Lord will not occur again. Her people will be consumed like tangling thorns, like the drink of the drunkard, like dry straw enveloped by fire.[12]

Nahum 1:11 introduces an individual who plots evil against Yahweh—a wicked counselor. Structurally, the verse corresponds best with 1:9, with the wicked counselor acting as the head of wicked Nineveh. Drawing again on our comparison to Nazi Germany, one could imagine that the wicked counselor is a kind of Adolf Hitler. If a prophet were to direct God's judgment against Nazi Germany, at some point Hitler himself would be targeted. In the same sense, Nahum's oracle does not neglect to call out the wicked king of Assyria. This is simply the first, albeit cryptic, reference to the king of Assyria in the book of Nahum.[13]

1:10, 12–13 "I WILL AFFLICT YOU NO LONGER" (DIRECT ADDRESS TO JUDAH)

Although the segment from 1:9–14 is characterized by direct address, the interpretive challenge is to consistently determine the addressee. It may help to imagine that the prophet begins verse 9 with a finger pointed at

---

[12] By paralleling three different images of consumption, the text heightens the effect of the metaphor.

[13] See 1:14–15; 3:18–19 for additional references.

personified Nineveh, with personified Judah within earshot. Therefore, after calling out Nineveh in verse 9, the prophet turns to Judah with a word of encouragement—*they* will be consumed—but then quickly turns back to personified Nineveh to continue his announcement of judgment. It is as if there are two parties on the same stage, each receiving their own distinct messages from the prophet, yet able to hear what is directed at the other.

While 1:10 appears to be directed at Judah, verses 12–13 are clearly a message of salvation for Judah. Although in Nahum's day the Assyrians were "strong and numerous,"[14] they would soon be "mowed down," and for Judah, the shackles of Assyrian oppression would soon pass.

1:14 "I WILL PREPARE YOUR GRAVE, FOR YOU ARE CONTEMPTIBLE" (DIRECT ADDRESS TO THE ASSYRIAN KING)

The shift from the feminine pronoun in 1:9, 11 to the masculine in 1:14 implies that no longer is personified Nineveh the addressee, but rather, the wicked counselor of 1:11 is in view. The identity of this contemptible "you" is uncertain; Nahum never mentions the name of any Assyrian monarch in his book. One potential candidate for the wicked counselor—the vile and contemptible one—is the Assyrian king Sennacherib. In his campaign against Palestine (701 BC), he certainly "went out" from Nineveh, plotting evil against Yahweh (Isa 36–37:13).[15] Furthermore, his demise came as the

---

The Boasts of Assyrian Tyrants

"As for the king of Judah, Hezekiah, who had not submitted to my authority, I besieged and captured forty-six of his fortified cities, along with many smaller towns, taken in battle with my batter rams . . . As for Hezekiah, I shut him up like a caged bird in his royal city of Jerusalem. I then constructed a series of fortresses around him, and I did not allow anyone to come out of the city gates." –King Sennacherib (705–681 BC)

"I am powerful, I am omnipotent, I am a hero, I am gigantic, I am colossal!"–King Esarhaddon (680–669 BC)

---

[14] Nahum 1:12 implies that Assyria was strong when Nahum delivered his oracle.

[15] See Maier, *The Book of Nahum*, 196–200, for evidence identifying Sennacherib with the "wicked counselor" of Nahum 1:11. Note, however, that Maier does not argue the same in regard to 1:14.

implied judgment of Yahweh (Isa 37:38). Yet his son did reign on the throne, and the book of Nahum postdates the fall of Thebes (3:8), which occurs decades after Sennacherib's death. A second option exists with Ashurbanipal, the last strong Assyrian monarch. His reign postdates the fall of Thebes, and his wickedness certainly qualifies him as "contemptible." But his demise does not perfectly line up with the language of verse 14.[16] It may be that Nahum's prophecies are, in effect, directed at all the Assyrian kings, with the ultimate demise of the Assyrian monarchy in view. Furthermore, by not naming a specific Assyrian king, Nahum's emphasis lies with the universality of the theological message—tyrants of all ages will not stand. Yahweh will not tolerate the oppression of innocents forever.

1:15 A Call to Celebrate! The King is Doomed!

Speaking with prophetic confidence, Nahum again addresses Judah. Heralding the good news of Assyria's demise, the prophet calls on Judah to proclaim peace, for the wicked one will never march through her again. The wicked king would soon "pass away" (1:12), never again to "pass through" Judah (1:15 ESV).[17] In climactic celebration, Nahum 1:15 functions to concludes the preceding oracles and facilitates an apt introduction to the vision that follows (2:1–10).[18]

2:1–3:17 Sound the Alarm! The Prophetic Watchman on the Walls

Chapters 2 and 3 of the Nahum book are comprised of a chiasm where the "beauty of the poetry combines with the clarity of the brutal imagery to impress as no other form of language could the message of doom for Assyria and hope for Judah."[19] The chiastic structure surrounds a woe oracle at its

---

[16] For a summation of Neo-Assyrian history, including the reign of Ashurbanipal and the fall of the empire, see *Peoples of the Old Testament World*, ed. Alfred J. Hoerth, Gerald L. Mattingly, and Edwin M. Yamauchi (Grand Rapids, MI: Baker, 1994), 87–100.

[17] The repetition of the Hebrew *'avar* heightens the effect. See Chisholm, *Interpreting the Minor Prophets*, 173.

[18] Nahum 1:15 and 3:18–19 act as an *inclusio*, bracketing the chiastic arrangement of visions, taunts, and woe oracle in the book.

[19] Barker and Bailey, *Micah, Nahum, Habakkuk, Zephaniah*, 195.

center (Nah 3:1–3), highlighting the central theme of the book—Nineveh is as good as dead. But Nahum is not content to simply proclaim Nineveh's death; he clothes the central message with the mockery of the taunt and the imagery of the vision so that his audience might participate through the whole spectacle.

Chiastic Structure of Nahum 2–3

A. Call to celebrate (1:15)
    B. The Prophet's Vision (2:1–10)
        C. The Prophet's Taunt (2:11–12)
            D. The Declaration of Yahweh (2:13)
                E. Woe Oracle (3:1–4)
            D'. The Declaration of Yahweh (3:5–7)
        C'. The Prophet's Taunt (3:8–13)
    B'. The Prophet's Vision (3:14–17)
A'. Call to Celebrate (3:18–19)

2:1–2 "One who scatters is coming up against you" (The Prophet's Announcement)

Taking on the role of a watchman on the walls of Nineveh, Nahum announces the coming judgment on Nineveh. Ironically, the enemy is announced as "One who scatters" (2:1). Historically, the "one who scatters" must refer to the coalition of Medes and Babylonians who conquered the city in 612 BC. But theologically, it is Yahweh who is jealous, Yahweh who is good; it is Yahweh who ultimately is the "One who scatters." In describing the defeat of Assyria as a "scattering," Nahum strikes a chord, for the Assyrians were well known for their practice of deporting and importing conquered people into foreign lands. He introduces the conquering army as one who scatters and reinforces that outcome in the conclusion of his book (3:17–18).[20]

---

[20] Adding to other elements of *inclusio*, the motif of "scattering" begins and ends the chiasm running from 2:1–3:17.

Poetic justice is served; Nineveh, the one city who had scattered the nations, would herself be "scattered" in defeat.

Following the introductory announcement, the prophetic watchman calls the troops of Nineveh to her defenses as the enemy encloses her. "Man the fortifications! Watch the road! Brace yourself![21] Summon all your strength!" In the staccato fashion that exemplifies Nahum's rhetoric, the watchman sounds off four battle-themed imperatives. These imperatives offered in quick succession provide a sense of urgency that helps to heighten the intensity of the scene. This battle will be no small skirmish!

Departing for a moment from his vision of Nineveh's destruction, Nahum addresses his Judean audience with one more message of hope. Imagine the prophet sitting personified Judah down to watch a prophetic movie clip of her tormentor's eventual demise. Nahum is rolling the reel, casting his vision on the screen. But as a narrator, he cannot help but add a bit of commentary to the show. Nahum 2 is that commentary.

The primary emphasis in Nahum's prophetic commentary is the restoration of God's people. Capitalizing on the imagery of the vineyard, the "majesty" (or "vine"; the Hebrew words *ge'on/gephen* are very similar, perhaps indicating an intentional wordplay) of Judah is restored, an essential reminder that Nineveh's destruction would bring renewal to Judah. Though the "ravagers have ravaged" the vine branches of Jacob (the Hebrew root *baqaq* is repeated for emphasis), Yahweh would restore those branches, even the vine branches of Israel.[22]

---

[21] Literally, "make strong your loins." In 2:10 the defenders' "loins shake," indicating *inclusio* in the battle vision.

[22] Given the parallel references to Jacob and Israel in 2:2, there is some question regarding the intended audience, (Nahum's historic audience was Judah, the southern kingdom). In Isaiah's oracles of comfort (43:1; 44:1; 46:3), Jacob and Israel are used as parallels within the context of Judah's hope and restoration. Perhaps there is some prophetic inference pointing to the reunification of the divided kingdom as a final aspect of restoration (Ezekiel 37:15–23), especially given the historic role of Assyria in scattering Israel (2 Kings 17:6). When the divided kingdom is restored, Yahweh will gather them "from all around" (Ezekiel 37:21).

2:3–10 "DESOLATION, DECIMATION, DEVASTATION!" (THE PROPHET'S VISION)

In full literary color, Nahum proclaims the destruction of Nineveh. From his prophetic vantage point on the city walls, the action below is described as a medley of battle scenes. With staccato repetition, the language is fast and intense, mimicking the fast pace of battle and the panic of a routed defense. The opening scenes describe an attacking army, the closing scenes a devastated city. There is some ambiguity identifying attacker and defender (2:5),[23] but the general picture is clear. The aggressor presents an overwhelming picture of military might (2:3–4), while the Assyrian defenses flee in terror (2:8). In a streak of poetic justice, the city built on the spoils of conquered nations would herself experience the plunder of a marauding army (2:9), and the city that once exiled so many victims would have her own citizens carried away (2:7).[24]

In the description of the Battle of Nineveh, two points of interest stand out. First is the allusion to flooding waters in verses 6 and 8. Is Nahum simply using the imagery of flooding waters to describe the devastation wrought by an overwhelming army? Is he evoking the imagery of fast-moving waters to describe the pace by which her defenders would flee? Isaiah 8:7–8 uses flood imagery to describe the Assyrian advance into Palestine a century earlier—perhaps the imagery remains intact, but now the tables are turned! Or is this a prophetic glimpse of the historic fall of Nineveh? Coupled with the reference to "an overwhelming flood" in Nahum 1:8, there may be in Nahum 2:6 prophetic corroboration with the ancient testimony of Greek historian Diodorus.[25] The preceding language reads as a visual account, and there is little reason to think that the prophet did not see the river gates open and the palace erode away in his vision. Yet verse 8 appears to be a figurative description of Nineveh's defenses. While formerly as tranquil as a still pool, defenders are now fleeing like waters spilled from a breached dam. Even if

---

[23] Do the attackers stumble in their rush to advance, or are the defenders stumbling in a futile attempt to defend the city walls?

[24] The Hebrew introducing 2:7 is obscure, leading to a variety of attempts in translation. Whatever the identity of that which is "carried away," it is clear that Nineveh is in some sense experiencing the woes of exile. See Marvin A. Sweeney, *The Twelve Prophets*, Vol. 2, Berit Olam (Collegeville, MN: The Liturgical Press, 2000), 439.

[25] Diodorus II 27:1–3.

the primary focus of verse 6 is literal and verse 8 is figurative, one should not rule out a hint of double entendre at work in Nahum's rhetoric.

Second, there is an example of paranomasia wordplay in verse 10. With short staccato strikes, the prophet proclaims the utter destruction of the city: "Desolation, decimation, devastation!" Most English translations, including the HCSB (quoted above), seek to retain the sound-alike qualities of the Hebrew: *buqah, umvuqah, umvullaqah*. Even at a glance, the informal transliteration demonstrates paranomasia. But even more striking than the "sound-alike" feature is the sense of expansion among these three terms. Reading them out loud, one cannot help but speak louder and stronger with each term. The destruction of the city has indeed reached a climax![26]

2:11–12 "Where is the lion's lair . . .?" (The Prophet's Taunt)

Assyrian artifacts often depict its kings and soldiers as lions, imagining them to somehow mimic the king of the beasts. Now Nahum, no stranger to biting rhetoric, capitalizes on Assyrian imagination. Seeing the fall of Nineveh, the prophet sarcastically taunts Assyria—the beast has no lair!

2:13 "Beware, I am against you" (The Declaration of Yahweh)

In the first of two divine declarations, the Lord of Hosts explicitly states to Nineveh, "I am against you" (Nah 2:13; 3:5). The first declaration provides a rhetorical capstone to the vision of Nineveh's fall. It is Yahweh who commands the armies; it is Yahweh who devours the lion. In case anyone might doubt who is behind the demise of Nineveh, the Lord has declared that it was ultimately neither a Babylonian nor a Mede, but rather *he* who brought devastation against Nineveh. In the Lord's judgment of Assyria, even the messengers who once taunted Judah have now been silenced. A few decades prior to Nahum, in the showdown with Hezekiah (2 Kgs 18:19–27), the Assyrian "Rabshakeh" intimidated Judah as Sennacherib's special liaison. He was an ancient propagandist of the first order. There is no lack of irony in the master of the taunt not only being silenced, but now also the subject of a taunt—a fitting judgment indeed.

---

[26] Robertson notes, "Each successive word is slightly longer than the former, so that a rhythmic buildup reinforces the message." See O. Palmer Robertson, *The Books of Nahum, Habakkuk, and Zephaniah*, NICOT (Grand Rapids, MI: Eerdmans, 1990), 94.

3:1–4 "Woe to the city of blood" (Woe Oracle)

Although the staccato style and battlefield imagery of 3:1–3 parallels the material in the preceding chapter, the formulaic introduction "woe" indicates a new literary unit. Woe speeches are common in the Prophets, typically introducing impending judgment. In the case of Nahum 3:1, however, there is no sorrow over fallen Nineveh; as demonstrated in the conclusion of the book, the death of Nineveh will bring rejoicing, not lament. Nineveh is cursed with the devices of her own militaristic barbarism; now the "city of blood" will receive her just reward[27]—dead corpses without end (3:3)!

The woe speech seamlessly transitions into a continued vision of snapshot scenes from the Battle of Nineveh. Again, the staccato style of the report aids the reader in visualizing the imagery. For Nahum's Judean audience, there was great comfort in hearing of Nineveh's impending doom. But Nahum delivers more—his words allow the reader to *feel* the battle raging around them.

It is unclear whether Nahum 3:4 functions as the conclusion to the woe speech or the introduction to Yahweh's declaration of judgment. What is certain is that the impetus behind Nineveh's militaristic barbarism was motivated by her religious commitments. It was not just that Assyria was a bloodthirsty nation, but she was also demonic; her militarism was generated out of an unholy devotion. Of course, Assyria in her idolatry was not unique in the ancient Near Eastern world. Assyria, like other nations, was devoted to multiple gods. And although Assyria's chief deity Ishtar was often worshiped through ritual prostitution, this alone does not seem to be the thrust of Nahum's indictment. The issue was that in her conquests Assyria entrapped other nations to follow her gods. Subjugated peoples became prostitutes to a prostitute—even Judah herself had fallen prey to such advances (2 Kgs 16:10–16).

3:5–7 "I am against you" (The Declaration of Yahweh)

The one who is contemptible (Nah 1:14) will now be treated with contempt (Nah 3:6); this is the declaration of Yahweh! For the second time, Yahweh declares his intentions to utterly shame devastated Nineveh. Yet it is not

---

[27] The Hebrew word for blood (*dam*) is in the plural, an unnecessary construction that functions to emphasize just how bloodthirsty the Assyrian Empire was in character.

the chariots and weaponry of an enemy army, but God himself who brings shame to Nineveh. Through five first person verbal judgments,[28] Yahweh makes it abundantly clear that it is *he* who is against Nineveh. Instead of describing Nineveh's devastation, the text now describes her shame through graphic imagery—with skirts lifted high, the prostitute Nineveh is paraded among the nations, pelted by filth, a spectacle of shame.

3:8–13 "Are you better than Thebes?" (The Prophet's Taunt)

Returning to the rhetoric of the taunt, the prophet asks a rhetorical question: "Are you better than Thebes?" (Nah 3:8). Thebes was the chief city of Egypt conquered by the Assyrians in 663 BC. Ironically, it had many of the same fortifications as Nineveh, with both cities supplied and defended by great rivers. The city of Thebes seemed impenetrable, that is, until Assyria conquered it under Ashurbanipal. Nahum's rationale is obvious: Nineveh should understand that no city is impenetrable. If Thebes could fall, why think that Nineveh could not also experience a similar fate?

Shifting from rhetorical question to a more direct taunt, Nahum mocks defeated Nineveh: she is likened to a drunk (v. 11) whose fortresses are like fig trees (v. 12). Even her once mighty warriors are likened to untrained women on the battlefield (v. 13). A master of metaphorical imagery, Nahum alludes back to the recent defeat of Thebes. Just as the defenders of Thebes were as helpless as drunks, so Nineveh will behave similarly—dazed, confused, and seeking refuge where none exists. Furthering the taunt, Nahum states that defeating Nineveh would be as easy as dropping figs from a "ripe" tree. Merely shaking the tree would drop the fruit; in modern vernacular, defeating Nineveh was "as easy as taking candy from a baby."[29]

As a climax to the taunt, Nahum mocks the ineptitude of Nineveh's defenses. Her gates were wide open, her bars already aflame. There is a sense in which these are literal, but the emphasis is on the figurative. In like manner, while women may have been the last desperate defenders of the city, they were certainly not employed to military service. Rather, Nineveh's once fearsome soldiers are described as being like women—a form of ridicule understood in the ancient world.

---

[28] The HCSB translates three first person verbs, although the Hebrew has five.
[29] Barker and Bailey, *Micah, Nahum, Habakkuk, Zephaniah*, 235.

3:14–17 "Draw water for the siege" (The Prophet's Vision)

The vision of Nineveh's demise in Nahum 3:14–17 begins with an exhortation to prepare the defenses for battle. This is not unlike the introduction to the earlier battle-laden vision of Nineveh's defeat (Nah 2:1, 3–10). One might wonder why a city surrounded by water and towering walls would be called to "draw water for the siege" and build bricks for the defenses. Yet there is a kind of irony in such a call—a sarcastic reference to Nineveh's considerable pride. Nahum calls the people to build defenses even though they thought of themselves as the impenetrable city!

In the vision itself (vv. 15–17), Nahum compares the people of Nineveh to the prey of hungry locusts, and then to the locusts themselves! As prey, Nineveh will be utterly consumed, adding to the metaphors of consumption employed in 1:10. But in a twist of imagery genius, Nahum moves from Nineveh being consumed *by* the locust to Nineveh scattered *like* the locust. The last two lines of verse 15 through verse 17 describe the leaders and emissaries of Nineveh scattered like locusts. Just as Assyria had "scattered" its merchant influence all over the world, so now her merchant traders would scatter like the locusts. In modern vernacular, they would look for "greener pastures,"[30] and seeing Nineveh's fall, they would "take the money and run" (v. 16).

Continuing with locust imagery, Nahum describes the "court officials" and the "scribes" scattering like the locusts. Just as locusts scatter on a warm day, so the inner core of Nineveh's citizenry would abandon the city on that day. The "One who scatters" (2:1) has effectively scattered all who might come to the rescue of the city.

3:18–19 A Call to Celebrate—The King is Dead!

Returning to address the King of Assyria (1:14), Nahum continues to draw on the imagery of people scattered; now, the king's shepherds have slumbered, and as expected, the sheep have scattered. What an irony that a kingdom feared for its practices of scattering conquered people to the ends of the earth would itself be scattered, with "no one to gather them together" (v. 18). What a contrast to the eventual fate of Judah, whose "Good Shepherd"

---

[30] Barker and Bailey, *Micah, Nahum, Habakkuk, Zephaniah*, 240.

(Ezek 34:23–31) would one day gather them from the far corners of the earth (Ezek 37:21–28)!

The final words of the prophet form a fitting closure. Nineveh's wound is fatal; there will be no opportunity to repent. Her end is justified, as the closing rhetorical question implies. The good news proclaimed in 1:15 is the good news heard in 3:19, and all who hear it will applaud the death of the wicked one.

Theological Message and Application of Nahum

The message of Nahum is ancient and timeless. Yes, it is a message about the death of a long-dead empire. But it is also a message about the timeless victory of good over evil, of God over the forces of darkness. There is evil in the world, and it often comes in the form of despotic empires. But all throughout history, as many times as evil has reared its ugly head, it has also been cut off from the earth. Yahweh is the divine warrior who has delivered in the past, who still delivers in the present, and who ultimately will have victory in the future.

Theologically, the God of Nahum is not a distant, detached deity. Rather, he is a God who is provoked and very, very immanent—a divine warrior who not only treads on the clouds, but also tramples the earth. He is a "hands-on" God, one who acts through the course of human history. Many who read Nahum for the first time would consider 1:7 as the high-point of the book. Certainly, he is a "stronghold to those who trust in him." But in times of trouble, the oppressed need to know they have a warrior on their side, One for whom the "clouds are the dust beneath his feet" (1:3). This is the God in whom we trust—the God who "will never leave the guilty unpunished" (1:3). Nahum offers simply one more vivid reminder of this timeless truth.

12

The Book of Habakkuk

Introduction

In times of trouble, it is easy to question God. This is not just the common experience of today's Christians. The saints of old often struggled with what they perceived as an offense or a blind spot in the eyes of divine justice. When righteous people get what the wicked deserve while the wicked go unpunished, wise men are perplexed and the godly are offended (Eccl 8:14; Psalm 73). When God seems distant, his people cry out; but he is often silent, reassurance coming only through the memory of his past activity (Psalm 77).

The prophets, like the sages and psalmists of their day, wrestled with the justice of God in a world gone mad. Habakkuk is the one book that most directly bridges the gap between the psalmist and the prophet, the sage and the seer. He cries out to God with an honest complaint, and God responds with words that, at first, seem unsatisfactory—not quite what the prophet expects out of a holy, omnipotent God. But the dialogue of Habakkuk reveals journey of faith, moving the prophet to a place where he can delight in the mysterious ways of the Lord, even when he does not fully comprehend. The journey of the prophet Habakkuk is set within a distant context, but one that is close to the heart of every believer. In this book, the reader is invited to join the prophet in discovering a God who works in ways difficult to understand, yet wonderful to behold.

The book of Habakkuk is three short chapters, yet it contains a powerful message. Although the reader is given little information by way of introduction, there are a few hints within the book that provide some background to the prophet and his times. While many prophetic books contain the language of the Psalter, no book does so to the extent of Habakkuk. The prayers of Habakkuk mirror the psalms of lament, and even the woe oracles in chapter two are interspersed with temple praises (2:14, 20). Chapter three is itself a psalm, complete with superscription and concluding instructions for the conductor. It is clear that the prophet was familiar with temple liturgy; little else can be concluded about the man, other than the fact he had a close and intimate relationship with God.[1]

Of greater interest for interpretation is the historical background of the book. Habakkuk opens with the prophet crying out to God over injustice in the land. Given that the book presents the Chaldeans as the Lord's instrument of judgment, it is clear that the sins over which Habakkuk laments are those of Judah rather than Israel. Moreover, with judgment yet unfulfilled, one can confidently date the book prior to the successive stages of Babylonian exile (605/597/586 BC). Beyond that, the particulars rest in dating the book either before or after Josiah's reforms in 622 BC (a matter addressed in the exposition of 1:2–4).

Habakkuk is among the most practical books of the Old Testament. While its context of judgment seems distant, the theological issues it raises are near to everyone who has wrestled with the mind of the Lord. Habakkuk questioned God, and God responded. Habakkuk had legitimate concerns over sin and wrongdoing, pining for the day when God would act. Through

---

[1] Additional speculation about the man and his personal background, while interesting, contributes little to the content of the book. See J. J. M. Roberts, *Nahum, Habakkuk, and Zephaniah*, OTL (Louisville, KY: Westminster John Knox, 1991), 85.

a dialogue with the Creator, Habakkuk discovered God would judge his people, in his own timing, in his own way.

Structure

The structure of Habakkuk is rather straightforward, developed around dialogue between the prophet and God. Following a brief introduction, the dialogue begins with the prophet bringing a complaint to God (1:2–4). The Lord then answers the prophet's cry (1:5–11), only to have the prophet respond with a second complaint (1:12–17). Through a mixture of complaints, accusations, rhetorical questions, and affirmations of faith, Habakkuk's prayers incorporate language common to the psalms of lament, prompting God to act.

Chapter two develops God's reply to Habakkuk's second complaint. But prior to the Lord's answer, there is a pause in the dialogue, with the prophet preparing himself in anticipation of the Lord's response (2:1). When the Lord replies, he commands Habakkuk to write the vision on tablets, presumably for future verification (2:2–3). The actual response is twofold: first, there is an accusation of Babylon's guilt (2:4–5) intersected by a brief promise of protection for the faithful (2:4b). Second, the promise of Babylon's judgment follows, but instead of a standard invective pronouncement, Babylon's destruction is proclaimed through the vehicle of a hypothetical taunt song (2:6a). Accentuating the impact of the taunt, it is performed rhetorically by Babylon's victims. Furthermore, the taunt song is comprised of five woe oracles, evoking the image of the dirge, a sure guarantee of death for bloodthirsty Babylon (2:6b–20).

The final chapter is a psalm, introduced with a superscription indicating that Habakkuk is its author (3:1). The psalm itself is comprised of two units, each preceded by a first-person testimonial introduction (3:2, 16). The first unit relates a theophany, a vision of Yahweh's splendor as divine warrior (3:3–15). The second unit is a response in song to Habakkuk's description of the Lord—a hymn of trust that forms a fitting conclusion to the book (3:17–19).

Exposition

1:1 (Introduction)

The introduction to the book is short and devoid of information that would provide a historical context for Habakkuk's complaints and the Lord's responses. But the introduction does describe the book as an "oracle" (*massa*) that the prophet "saw," thus framing the book as the record of a real, historical dialogue.[2]

1:2–4 "Why do You tolerate wrongdoing?" (Habakkuk's First Complaint)

As noted earlier, Habakkuk is characterized by many of the traditions represented in the Psalter. His "oracle" begins not with the prophetic "thus saith the Lord," but rather with the complaint of a psalmist, "How long, Lord . . .?" Thus the prophet does not speak to the people on behalf of the Lord, but he speaks to the Lord on behalf of the righteous. Seeing violence and injustice all around, Habakkuk calls on God to take action and rectify wrongs.

That Habakkuk is concerned about social injustice is clear from the language of 1:2–4, and the balance of the book suggests that his initial complaint is in regards to violence and oppression within Judah. Yet the exact historical context is left unspecified; to what chronological period in Judah's history of social and moral corruption is Habakkuk referring? Prior to Josiah's reforms, which reached their zenith in 622 BC, Judah was reeling from the corruption of its most wicked king, Manasseh. In the early period of Josiah's reign (640–625 BC), corruption was still rampant, and the Neo-Babylonian Empire was yet in its embryonic stages, making the announcement of judgment by Babylon an astounding proposition (1:6). The reforms of Josiah, however, seem an odd interruption to the sequence of impending judgment implied through the dialogue in Habakkuk. Many thus favor a description of corruption following Josiah's reforms but preceding the full ascension of Babylonian power, dating the book early in the

---

[2] For a survey of lexical options and emphases defining "*massa*," see Kenneth L. Barker and Waylon Bailey, *Micah, Nahum, Habakkuk, Zephaniah*, NAC (Nashville, TN: B&H, 1998), 288–90.

reign of Jehoiakim (609 BC). Nonetheless, however one might date the situation of 1:2–4, the general point is intact. Like Habakkuk long ago, the righteous cry out to God because of the world's corruption, violence, oppression, and wrongdoing. Why does God allow wrongdoing to go unanswered? When will God act, and how?

1:5–11 "Look . . . observe—be utterly astounded!" (Yahweh's Response)

While reading the Psalms, one often sees the psalmist bringing his complaints and petitions to God, only to emerge in faith through reflection on the person and past acts of God. In the oracle of Habakkuk, however, the reader actually sees a unique situation in Scripture—God responds directly to the prophet! As one might imagine, when God responds to the cry of the prophet, it is in no small manner. The Hebrew text begins with four imperative verbs, directing the people to vigorously observe what God was doing (1:5–6). The imperatives for "look" (ra'ah) and "observe" (navat) mirror Habakkuk's complaint in verse 3: "Why do You force me to look (ra'ah) at injustice? Why do You tolerate (navat) wrongdoing?" In effect, by using these same words, the Lord is turning the prophet's complaint back on his own head!

What is the Lord's answer to injustice? In Habakkuk's day, he was raising up the Chaldeans, a "bitter, impetuous nation" (1:6). Clearly, this was not the kind of answer the prophet was expecting. It certainly could be that the Chaldeans (Babylonians) had not yet risen to prominence when the Lord unveiled this to Habakkuk. If Habakkuk's complaint originated in the early stages of Josiah's reign, or even earlier during Manasseh's reign, then Babylon was merely a subject within the vast Assyrian Empire. It would be akin to prophesying that God would judge the United States by raising up one of the states—maybe Vermont, perhaps Arizona—an unlikely scenario indeed! But even if Habakkuk's complaint originated during Jehoiakim's reign, when Babylon was a clear threat, it is in part the fact that God *would* use Babylon that is the cause for astonishment. In either case, the theology is clear. God was about to do something in Habakkuk's day that would go beyond his wildest imagination—something that he would not believe even when told directly about it!

Who were the Chaldeans? Historically, they dwelt in the lower Mesopotamian region, eventually expanding to build a dynasty centered in

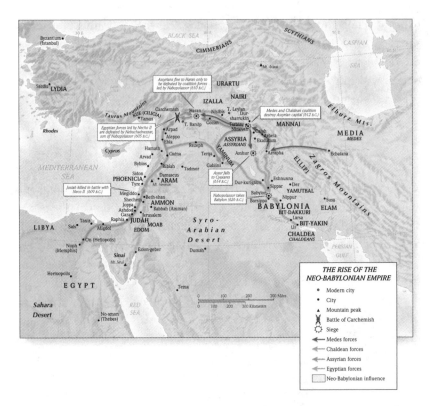

Babylon. Under Nabopolassar and his son Nebuchadnezzar, they expanded their reach through military might, eventually defeating the Assyrians and replacing them as the tyrant of their day. Judah was essentially going to experience a situation like parts of Europe did after World War II, when the tyranny of Hitler was replaced with the tyranny of Stalin. Nebuchadnezzar is never mentioned by name in Habakkuk, but his role is clear. In God's program Babylon would become his instrument of judgment; in Jeremiah, Nebuchadnezzar is even referred to as God's "servant" (Jer 25:9).

The vivid, even hyperbolic description of the Chaldean army in 1:6–11 reminds the reader of Nahum's description of the army that would be used to defeat the Assyrians. Both prophets were describing the Chaldean army, so that should come as no surprise. And both prophets used vivid language to help paint a picture of the near future. This extends beyond metaphors and battlefield imagery. With poetic wordplay, God was setting out to judge violence (vv. 2–3) with violence (v. 9). Similarly, Habakkuk's complaint was of a lack of justice in Judah, that justice "never emerges" and "comes out perverted" (v. 4). Now God would use a nation whose views of justice "stem (lit. 'come out') from themselves" (v. 7).[3] But perhaps more important than wordplay is the allusion to the past warnings of judgment in Deut 28:49–52, where Moses foretold of an enemy swifter than the eagle, besieging cities and laying waste the whole land. Perhaps this announcement should not have been so "utterly astounding" after all. Moses saw it coming almost 800 years earlier.

1:12–17 "So why do You tolerate those who are treacherous?" (Habakkuk's Second Complaint)

Habakkuk's response to the startling revelation of God's plans begins with an affirmation of faith. In the language of the praise psalm, Habakkuk lifts Yahweh up as holy, everlasting, and immortal.[4] Yet, while certain of who God is, the prophet still questions what God is doing. It is clear from God's response (1:5–11) that he would no longer tolerate the wrongdoing in Judah (1:2–4). But then another dilemma emerges . . . would God yet tolerate the wicked Babylonians? Would God remain silent, allowing little Judah to be "swallowed up" by one even more wicked?

To further his point, Habakkuk equates the Babylonians to wicked fishermen and equates helpless Judah to the fish of the sea. Like fishermen with a net, the Babylonians would be indiscriminant in their plunder of Judah. They would not fish with discrimination, "keeping" the wicked and "releasing" the righteous. No, the imperial machine of the Chaldean was his god, and he would worship the net that swallowed whole nations. Would a righteous God really allow such indiscriminate slaughter to go unpunished?

---

[3] Robert B. Chisholm Jr., *Interpreting the Minor Prophets* (Grand Rapids, MI: Zondervan, 1990), 187.

[4] The Masoretic Text reads "we will not die," with many English translations following this reading (KJV, NKJV, NASB, ESV). However, some translations follow an ancient scribal tradition using the second person pronoun, "you will not die" (NRSV, NIV, and HCSB). The NET Bible captures this well with their translation "you are immortal," which fits well in parallel context. However, the MT reading suggests that Habakkuk is affirming some preliminary expectation that "the just shall be delivered by his faithfulness" (Habakkuk 2:4), a theme that coincides well with the book.

2:1 "I will watch to see what He will say to me . . ." (Pause in the Dialogue)

Within the context of the dialogue, Habakkuk now positions himself for the Lord's reply. He stands at the "guard post" and "the lookout tower," imagery suggesting a keen observation and expectation for the Lord's reply. The closing lines of 2:1 are somewhat awkward, reading, "what I should reply about my complaint."[5] The NET Bible provides clarity by its translation of the last line: "and can know how I should answer when he counters my argument." Although the wording is somewhat difficult, the anticipation of continued dialogue is clear.

2:2–5 "But the righteous one will live by his faith" (Yahweh's Second Response)

Yahweh's anticipated response to the prophet arrives. With it, Habakkuk is instructed to write the vision on tablets because its fulfillment will take some time—but to be sure, it will come to pass. Writing the vision on tablets, would create a record of God's revelation for later generations who would see it unfold. While the response to Habakkuk's first complaint would be experienced in his own lifetime (1:5), the fulfillment of this second response would not be realized for a few more generations. The written account let later generations know that a prophet had been among them.

The actual response of Yahweh involves two segments. The first is an accusation against the proud Babylonians (2:4–5) and is presented as the clear statement of God. The second is a collection of woe oracles (2:6–20), presented as a taunt sung by Babylon's victims. While the second section is not portrayed as the word of Yahweh, it functions in the book as the effective decree of Yahweh's judgment—the proud Chaldeans are "as good as dead."[6] The accusation against Babylon centers on their proud imperialism. In conquest, they are first likened to the drunkard consuming his drink, and secondly, to personified Death, whose appetite is never satisfied (v. 5). The actual decree of Yahweh is nothing more than accusation, laying out the

---

[5] This closing thought is the parallel to "what he will say to me," implying that the final line should read "and how I should respond."

[6] "As good as dead" is the language used in the NET Bible's translation of the pronouncements of woe.

guilt of Babylon. The word of her judgment then follows through the taunt song comprised of woe oracles (2:6–20). However, in the midst of Yahweh's proclamation of judgment is a promise of deliverance to the faithful. As a simple contrastive parallel to the pride of the Babylonians (2:4a), one of Scripture's most important theological statements is revealed: "the righteous one will live by his faith" (2:4b).

In the immediate context of Habakkuk's dialogue with God, the statement of 2:4 has the function of reassuring Habakkuk that God would not judge his own people indiscriminately, even as he uses the instrument of Babylonian conquest. Habakkuk 2:4b is therefore saying that righteous individuals will be delivered from death by their faithfulness.[7] Although the wicked in Judah would fall to Babylon, and though the proud Babylonians would, in time, receive their own judgment, God would not turn a blind eye to the righteous. They would be preserved because of their faithfulness.

In the broader context of the book, the statement could be taken as an indirect rebuke to Habakkuk, calling the prophet to believe not only in who God is, but also to trust God in what he does. This certainly coincides with the finale to the book, where Habakkuk affirms his trust in God, no matter what life may bring. Although the Hebrew term 'emunah does not typically communicate the idea of "trust," extended connotations can be expected, especially considering the flexibility applied to the verse in the New Testament. Paul quotes Habakkuk 2:4b twice (Rom 1:17; Gal 3:11), and the writer of Hebrews once (Heb 10:38a), in each case extending its meaning to various facets of God's redemptive program. In Romans 1:17, Paul is saying that God's means to justify the sinner has always been by faith. In Galatians 3:11, Paul is saying that a person is justified by faith, apart from the works of the law. In Hebrews, the emphasis is on faithfulness; those who believe do not "draw back," they demonstrate their faith through their faithfulness (as illustrated by the examples of faithfulness in the Hebrews 11 faith hall of fame). In every context cited, including those in the New Testament, the meaning of Habakkuk 2:4b holds true. People of faith are

---

[7] The term 'emunah is most commonly translated "faith" in English translations, although throughout the Old Testament it typically refers to "constancy," "stability," "reliability," or "faithfulness." Translating 'emunah as "faithfulness," Habakkuk 2:4b is affirming that the righteous will be delivered by their reliance and faithfulness to Yahweh. See Marvin A. Sweeney, *The Twelve Prophets*, Vol. 2, Berit Olam (Collegeville, MN: Liturgical Press, 2000), 472.

faithful, and God will deliver—whether temporally or eternally—the faithful by their faith.

2:6–20 "Woe to him . . ." (A Taunting Song of Woe Oracles)

Habakkuk brings the language of the psalmist and the prophet together more than any other book of the Twelve. In this tradition, Habakkuk envisions the victims of Babylon's cruelty singing a taunt against their oppressor. While displaying language characteristic of a hymn (2:14, 20), this song of "mockery and riddles" ingeniously uses rhetorical questions to bring accusation and the threat of judgment against Babylon. Theologically, the taunt of Habakkuk 2:6–20 mirrors the expectation of the psalmist: although the wicked may prosper, in due time they will be cut off from the earth (see Psalm 1). Stylistically, Habakkuk's song proclaims the death of God's enemies in the manner of the prophetic woe speech; through five woe oracles, Habakkuk proclaims the eventual yet certain death of Babylon. This use of the woe oracle set within a taunt reminds the reader of Nahum's rhetoric, where the central woe oracle (Nah 3:1–3) is bracketed by taunts against Nineveh (Nah 2:11–12; 3:8–13).

The woe oracles essentially proclaim the death of Babylon before her fall;[8] ironically, in the timing of Habakkuk's prophecy, her death is proclaimed not simply at the height of her kingdom, but even prior to her ascension to power (1:6). Through a succession of five escalating oracles, Habakkuk's taunt focuses on the crimes of Babylon. The first three oracles accuse Babylon of greedily building its kingdom through violence and ill-gotten gain; the fourth oracle continues the theme of amassing wealth through violence, but emphasizes the nature of Babylon's judgment. Just as the plunderer will be plundered (2:8), so the one who disgraced nations would be disgraced (2:15–18). In imagery rich language, Babylon's conquests are compared to the intoxicating effects of strong drink—her victims stagger like a drunk, and Babylon is guilty of providing the cup. But poetic justice was about to be served—served as a cup of intoxicating drink delivered straight from the Lord's right hand (2:16)![9] The final oracle does not

---

[8] See the translation of the NET Bible through Habakkuk 2:6–20: "The one who . . . is as good as dead."

[9] Chisholm, *Interpreting the Minor Prophets*, 191.

Five "Woes" within a Taunt	
2:6b–8	"Woe to him who amasses what is not his . . ."
2:9–11	"Woe to him who dishonestly makes wealth . . ."
2:12–13	"Woe to him who builds a city with bloodshed . . ."
2:15–17	"Woe to him who gives his neighbors drink . . ."
2:18–19	"Woe to him who says to wood: 'Wake up!'"

specify the guilt of violence per se, but it centers on the idols that instigate nations to bloodshed (2:18–19). Perhaps some allusion to Habakkuk 1:11 is intended—the marauding armies of Babylon who commit offense, "*Ascribing* this power to his god" (NKJV).

Integral to the taunt are two hymnic interludes set among woe oracles. These praises to Yahweh contrast with the indictments against Babylon. While "countries exhaust themselves for nothing" (2:13), the knowledge of Yahweh's glory fills the earth (2:14). And while the utter disgrace of Babylon will "cover" its "glory" (2:16), the "glory" of the Lord will fill the earth as the waters "cover" the sea (2:14). Likewise, while breathless idols made of "mute stone" "cannot speak" (2:18–19), everyone on the earth is "silent" in the presence of the Lord (2:20).

Although the taunt clearly demonstrates God's wrath against Babylon, by implication God will humiliate all who shed innocent blood in their proud arrogance. Habakkuk first complained of Judah's "violence," and God used violent Babylon to humiliate them. In the end, "everyone on earth" will be humbled in the presence of the Lord (2:20)—no exceptions.

3:1–19 "Yet I will triumph in Yahweh" (A Psalm of Praise)

Chapter three of Habakkuk is clearly a psalm, complete with superscription and musical instruction. Within the psalm there are distinct literary units. Verses 3–15 draw attention to God as a divine warrior, using theophanic imagery similar to Nahum 1:2–8. Verses 17–19 express trust in Yahweh through hymnic celebration, a fitting conclusion to the book. Each of these units is introduced as the prophet hears a report of Yahweh's divine activity (3:2, 16). In a sense, the report Habakkuk heard as a prophet culminates in the praise Habakkuk proclaims as a psalmist. Habakkuk *stood* at the guard post, "watching" to hear what the Lord would say to him, anticipating with wonder his own reply (2:1). In the end, Habakkuk *stood* in awe, hearing the report of an awesome God, seeing him in his radiant power. Through this vision, the prophet replies by proclaiming a hymn of trust, a psalm of praise.[10]

3:2 "I HAVE HEARD . . . I STAND IN AWE OF YOUR DEEDS" (FIRST TESTIMONIAL)

With all the confidence of a prophet who has seen the presence of the Lord, Habakkuk calls upon Yahweh to "revive Your work in these years." The reference to "Your work" employs the same Hebrew term used in Hab 1:5.[11] The God who once responded to an unbelieving prophet, "something (*po`al*) is taking place in your days," is now addressed in faith and expectation: "Revive Your work (*po`al*) in these years." The doubting prophet has become the believing prophet—the prophet who once called for judgment now pleads for mercy, seeing just how awesome the Holy One is!

3:3–15 "YOU MARCH ACROSS THE EARTH WITH INDIGNATION" (A THEOPHANY OF THE DIVINE WARRIOR)

The theophany of 3:3–15 alludes to Israel's history, but the language is clearly that of a prophetic vision; Habakkuk *sees* the God who has acted in the affairs of history.[12] This God is described in awesome terms, through language common to the psalms of Israel. The point is clear—the God who acted in the past is just as awesome as the God who will act in the present and in the future. The Lord's work will be revived in his judgment of Judah (a response to 1:2–4; Habakkuk's first complaint), and alas, will again be revived in his judgment of Babylon (a response to 1:12–17; Habakkuk's second complaint).

The theophany of Yahweh in the psalm incorporates vivid imagery describing a cosmic divine warrior. Although the splendor of his presence causes "age-old mountains" to "break apart" (v. 6), it is not physical creation at which God's wrath is directed. Through the use of rhetorical question

---

[10] Although chapter three is literarily distinct from the rest of the book, the major concerns of the psalm correspond to Habakkuk 1–2. Thematically, the argument for a unified Habakkuk is strong. See Sweeney, *The Twelve Prophets*, 479.

[11] Ibid., 481.

[12] The geographical references in Habakkuk 3:3, 7 allude to the activity of God in the exodus and through the conquest. See Chisholm, *Interpreting the Minor Prophets*, 193–94.

THE BOOK OF HABAKKUK

(v. 8), it is clear that Yahweh's wrath is directed against the nations and that the warrior comes to save his own "anointed" (vv. 12–13). The argument is clear: If this God "tread[s] the sea" in cosmic splendor (v. 15),[13] he is capable of trampling the nations of the earth in his wrath (3:8, 12).[14]

3:16 "I heard, and I trembled within" (Second Testimonial)

In apparent response to the theophany of verses 3–15, Habakkuk trembles in expectation of the divine warrior's judgment, the impending "day of distress." Parallels between 3:2 and 3:16 indicate either an *inclusio* bracketing the theophany or tiered introductions to the separate units of the psalm. Whatever the function of the parallel language, the vision of Yahweh results in trembling awe. Habakkuk's response to the report of Yahweh's splendor moves from petition in 3:2 to patient expectation in 3:16, culminating in the hymn of trust that concludes the psalm and the book (3:17–19).

3:17–19 "Though the fig tree does not bud . . ." (A Hymn of Trust)

In bringing the psalm to a conclusion, Habakkuk expresses his faith and trust in God through one of Scripture's most eloquent hymns. Beginning with the conditional "though," Habakkuk cites (with expectation?)[15] a series of agricultural calamities expressed through escalating parallels. Knowing the judgment that is coming, Habakkuk places his trust in the sovereign providence of God.[16] Whatever the circumstances, and however events unfold, there is no longer doubt in the prophet's mind that his God reigns. The theocentric focus concluding the hymn is accentuated in verse 19 through

---

[13] On the Old Testament imagery related to the sea as a cosmic foe, and the contribution of Habakkuk 3:8–15 to this motif, see Tremper Longman III and Daniel G. Reid, *God is a Warrior*, Studies in Old Testament Biblical Theology (Grand Rapids, MI: Zondervan, 1995), 63–65 and 114–16.

[14] The *inclusio* bracketing Habakkuk 3:8–15 (riding/treading the sea on/with Your horses) enhances the argument prompted by the rhetorical questions (v. 8). The God who treads the sea with horses (v. 15) is really not interested in raging against the sea (v. 8). Instead, his wrath is directed against the nations, and he is surely able to see that through.

[15] See the NET Bible's translation "when" to begin verse 17, implying that these calamities were more than mere possibility.

[16] The use of the personal pronoun is emphatic and indicates a personal experience on the part of the prophet. See Francis I. Andersen, *Habakkuk*, AB (New York, NY: Doubleday, 2001), 347.

the use of the divine personal name preceding by his title: "Yahweh my Lord" (*Yahweh Adonai*).[17] Combined, these names emphasize the immanent, relational, covenant-bound expectation Habakkuk had in a transcendent, sovereign, and all-powerful Lord. It is confidence in *this* God that brings the prophet to the place of triumph!

Theological Message and Application of Habakkuk

The theology of Habakkuk is God centered, yet profound in its impact on humanity. Through his struggle with God, Habakkuk discovers that God is not blind to injustice and will not be silent in judgment. God is a God who hears the cry of the saint, rectifies wrongdoing, and brings justice to the guilty. In the context of Habakkuk, this is demonstrated in the exile of Judah and the fall of Babylon. As a prophet, Habakkuk foretold the judgments described in the book, yet the book functions primarily as a defense of the power and justice of God. Yahweh is revealed in Habakkuk as a divine warrior, radiant in splendor. He is a God who judges wrongdoing and has the power to accomplish the task. The warrior is also wise and will act in his own timing. Though man may not fathom his plan, it is good and just; God will surely bring it to pass.

In the context of Habakkuk, God is demonstrated as sovereign over the nations, directing the events of world history to bring about his own purposes. But God's concern is not merely with the nations. By implication, he is also sovereign over the circumstances of every man, woman, and child. For Habakkuk, God was about to "work a work" in his days that he would not believe, even if it were told to him.[18] Is it too much to ask that God might work a work in our day, which we would not believe even if it was told to us? Indeed, God is a God who can work beyond our wildest imagination! Whatever the circumstances of life, whatever calamities may come, God is in control (3:17–19). The righteous know this—and in that assurance, they too live by faith (2:4b).

---

[17] Barker and Bailey, *Micah, Nahum, Habakkuk, Zephaniah*, 376.
[18] Based on Habakkuk 1:5; using the wording of the NKJV.

13

THE BOOK OF ZEPHANIAH

Introduction

It was once said that the message of the prophets can be summarized by two contrasting themes: things are going to get really, really, really bad, and then things are going to get really, really, really good. At this point in our survey it should be clear that the message of the prophets is a bit more complex than the black-and-white description above, yet the basic thrust of the summary rings true. If ever there was a book that reflects this dichotomy at its core, it is the book of Zephaniah.

Zephaniah does not offer the reader biographical narrative, apocalyptic visions, or prophetic drama. Rather, in three chapters it offers the bread and butter of the writing prophets: announcements of judgment, a call to repentance, and promises of salvation. From the outset, the language of judgment is as horrifying as words can convey. God is pictured as One who pours out the blood of his enemies "like dust" and who discards their flesh "like dung" (1:17). He sweeps away everything "by the fire of His jealousy" and makes "a horrifying end of all the inhabitants of the earth" (1:1, 18). Yet by the conclusion of the book, he is a God who gives fame and praise to the lame, who brings his quietness, peace, and security to his beloved (3:12–20). As striking as this contrast appears, it is the fact that these demonstrate two sides of the same God that leaves a lasting impression on the reader.

Zephaniah preached to the people of Judah in the years following the disastrous reign of Manasseh, Judah's most wicked king. Idols were embedded within the fabric of society, the law was absent, and the people lived under the illusion that God was either impotent or unwilling to act (1:12). But in the face of the people's false sense of confidence, God was about to move—the nation was on the threshold of disaster! In spite of Josiah's nationwide reform (628–622 BC), Judah had become so corrupt that her day of judgment was inevitable. By 586 BC, the day that Zephaniah declared had been realized. Yet in spite of her fall, Judah was not beyond God's care; he would provide a remnant for restoration (3:9–20). Both sides of the divine warrior are presented in Zephaniah: the One who stretches out his hand for disaster (1:4) is the guardian warrior who also delivers his people from disaster (3:17).

Structure

Zephaniah is structured around a progressive application of the Day of the Lord motif. The book opens in chapter one with an oracle of judgment against Judah, replete with references to "that day." The oracle is bracketed by sections describing the decimation of the whole earth, past and future (1:2–3; 17–18). From the greatest breadth of God's wrath, the fury of that day is then directed to the true center of the oracle's intention, Judah (1:4–16). The inner part of the oracle is comprised of three subsets, each with a particular focus. The first addresses the priests and the leadership of Judah (1:4–9), the second the merchants of Jerusalem (1:10–13), and the third the military defenses of the city (1:14–16). To each of these, the Day of the Lord is rapidly approaching, and the fury of God is drawing near (1:14).

Demonstrating that there is still hope the day can be averted, the second chapter begins with a call to repentance (2:1–3). Complementing the call to repentance, Zephaniah shifts to a series of oracles against the nations surrounding Judah (2:4–15). These oracles implicitly offer a warning to wayward Judah, once again brought back into focus in Zephaniah 3:1–5. The whole segment from 2:4–3:7 functions as a series to warn Judah of her impending disaster—although the fall of the nations should have served as a warning, Judah did not take heed (3:7).

With the day of Judah's judgment a foregone conclusion, she is exhorted to wait—only out of judgment will restoration be realized (3:8). And thus Zephaniah 3:8 serves as a transition between the two primary aspects of the Day of the Lord; the day has shifted from a day of judgment to a day of salvation. Zephaniah 3:9–20 concludes the book with a salvation oracle divided into three segments. The first segment foresees the pure worship of a gathered remnant from Judah and beyond (3:9–13). The second segment is a celebration song, exhibiting the traits of a psalm of praise (3:14–17). The final unit repeats the theme of the gathered remnant; this is capped by an affirmation that this is indeed Yahweh's promise (3:18–20).

Within the progressive movement of Zephaniah, the standard array of prophetic literary devices is evident. The distinguishing feature of the book is repetition. Zephaniah uses repetition to heighten and escalate the power of his rhetoric, while also using repeated words and phrases to accentuate contrast. Examples of heightened rhetoric are "I will sweep away" (1:2–3), "face of the earth" (1:2–3), "whole earth . . . consumed by the fire of His jealousy" (1:18; 3:8), "before" (2:2), "seek" (2:3), and the many references to the Day of the Lord and its abbreviated forms (esp. 1:14–16). Meanwhile, the repetition of words such as "*paqad*" (punish, return; 1:8–9; 2:7, 9), "shame" (2:1; 3:5, 11), "fear" (3:7, 15–16), and "gather" (3:8; 18–20) are used in contrastive senses to draw attention to the ultimate twist in fortunes, the double-sided Day of the Lord!

Exposition

1:1 (Introduction)

The reader is introduced to Zephaniah through his lineage and the approximate time of his ministry. Zephaniah is unique among the Twelve in that his revealed genealogy goes back four generations. Assuming that King Hezekiah is in view, Zephaniah's royal ancestry explains the extended genealogy. Of additional interest is the name of his father, Cushi. If Zephaniah's father was

Repetition in Zephaniah	
1:2–3	"I will sweep away" (3x)
1:2–3	"face of the earth" (2x)
1:14–16	"the Day of the Lord" (12x)
1:18; 3:8	"The whole earth will be consumed by the fire of His jealousy" (2x)
1:8–9; 2:7, 9	"punish" or "return" (Hebrew word *paqad*) (3x)
2:1; 3:5, 11	"shame" (3x)
2:2	"before" (3x)
2:3	"seek" (2x)
3:7, 15–16	"fear" (3x)
3:8, 18–20	"gather" (2x)

a Cushite, this may explain the additional references to Cush later in the book (2:12; 3:10).[1]

Zephaniah prophesied during the reign of Josiah. Given the nature of his message, one should assume that he spoke prior to the reforms instituted during Josiah's reign. An approximate date for Zephaniah's prophetic word is therefore set between 640 and 628 B.C. One might imagine that Zephaniah's preaching had a role in prompting the reforms of Josiah (2 Chronicles 34–35).

1:2–18 (An Oracle of Judgment against Judah—The Great Day of the Lord)

The opening oracle of Zephaniah is an announcement of judgment characterized by an emphasis on the Day of the Lord. Reference is made to that "day" fourteen times in chapter one, with the concept introduced in 1:7 and reaching climactic repetition in 1:14–16. The oracle is loosely arranged by a five-part chiastic structure, and repetition features prominently throughout

---

[1] For the historical and theological significance of Cush in Zephaniah, see J. Daniel Hays, *The Message of the Prophets: A Survey of the Prophetic and Apocalyptic Books of the Old Testament* (Grand Rapids, MI: Zondervan, 2010), 334–40.

the oracle. The opening (1:2–3) and closing (1:17–18) segments emphasize the Day of the Lord as judgment upon all mankind, while the central segments emphasize judgment against Judah. The oracle's summary statement is a call to "be silent" in the presence of the Lord (1:7a). This is parallel to Habakkuk 2:20, where Habakkuk (a possible contemporary to Zephaniah) called for everyone on earth to "be silent" in the Lord's presence. The repetition of language links Habakkuk and Zephaniah in the book of the Twelve, but their emphases is slightly different. Habakkuk stood in awestruck wonder as the divine warrior's plan to judge Babylon was unveiled. Zephaniah called for Judah to stand in awestruck fear as the time of God's wrath against his own people was drawing near.

1:2–3 "I will completely sweep away everything" (Judgment against Mankind/ Pictured as a Reversal of Creation)

Opening with hyperbolic fervor, Zephaniah proclaims the Lord's declaration to "sweep away everything" and to "cut off mankind from the face of the earth" (1:2–3). The hyperbolic language functions to evoke the memory of the flood (Gen 6:7; 7:4, 23), where "everything" is swept away (v. 1) and where mankind (*'adam*) is cut off from the earth (*'adamah*). The order of the annihilation of man, animals, birds, and fish also alludes to Genesis 1:20–26, constituting an effective reversal of the creation order.[2] Although the focus of the oracle is on the near judgment of Judah, the argument of 1:2–3 is, in effect, similar to that of Zephaniah's contemporary Jeremiah (see Jeremiah 18). If God once judged the whole world, and intends to one day do it again, why should Judah ever think that God cannot judge her also (see 1:12)?[3]

1:4–9 "Indeed, the Lord has prepared a sacrifice" (Judgment against the Priests and Officials of Judah/ Pictured as a Sacrifice)

Moving from the sign of comprehensive judgment to the scope of particular judgment, Zephaniah calls out Judah for her sins of religious syncretism.

---

[2] Mark F. Rooker, "Zephaniah," in *The World and the Word: An Introduction to the Old Testament* (Nashville, TN: B&H, 2011), 474.

[3] Richard D. Patterson, *Nahum, Habakkuk, Zephaniah*, Wycliffe Exegetical Commentary (Chicago, IL: Moody Press, 1991), 301.

The early years of Josiah's reign were characterized by the syncretistic worship institutionalized by Manasseh some years earlier. Multiple references are made throughout this section to the divided religious loyalties among the priests and nobles of Judah. Ironically, Zephaniah pictures the judgment of these priests and nobles as a sacrifice with consecrated guests of honor (1:7b). The Lord will visit, or "punish" (*paqad*) these guests as they themselves become the object of sacrifice!

1:10–13 "Wail, you residents . . ." (Judgment against the Merchants of Jerusalem/ Pictured by a Lament)

The focus of judgment is now directed against the merchant citizens of Jerusalem, those who amassed wealth and pleasure at the expense of the poor. To demonstrate the force of retribution, the oracle pictures inhabitants from all corners of the city wailing and lamenting the day of God's judgment (1:10–11).[4] Furthering the imagery, God himself is personified as searching Jerusalem with lamps to find the guilty. The language is reminiscent of Amos 3:12–15, where Yahweh intentionally searches out and finds those for whom judgment is due.

Judah was guilty of religious syncretism (1:4–9), but she was also guilty of complacency (1:12–13). The text in verse 12 literally reads, "I will punish (*paqad*) the men who thicken on their dregs." The unusual phrase is likely an ancient idiom, meant to suggest leftover wine congealing and then hardening on its dregs. The hearts of the people had thickened to the point of complacency and hardened to the point of indifference.[5] For this reason, they no longer thought that God would act. Yahweh, however, would remain true to his covenant promises of divine retribution. Those who built houses at the expense of the poor would not dwell in them, and those who processed wine for their pleasure would never partake (Deut 28:30).[6]

---

[4] Note the contrast between the call to silence in 1:7 and wailing in 1:10–11. There is also the contrast between wailing and silence in verse 11.

[5] Patterson, *Nahum, Habakkuk, Zephaniah*, 315–18.

[6] There are two allusions in verse 13. The first is the obvious reference back to Deuteronomy 28:30. Those who believed that the Lord would not act were about to experience the curses for covenant unfaithfulness promised so many years earlier by Moses. Second, and more subtle, Zephaniah balances the idiom regarding wine congealing on the dregs with those who would process wine yet never drink the finish product.

1:14–16 "That day is . . . a day of . . . battle cry" (Judgment against the Fortified Cities/ Pictured by the Bitter Cry)

Expanding out from the core, the movement of the oracle brings God's wrath to the fortified cities of Judah. The priests were judged for their syncretism by sacrifice, and the inhabitants of Judah were judged for their complacency by being chased out from the corners of security within the walled city. Fittingly, the fall of the fortified cities is pictured by the bitter cry of a defeated warrior, rather than the battle cry of the victor (1:14). The irony that runs throughout this oracle is striking.

The stress on the Day of the Lord motif is brought to climax through escalating repetition in this segment of the oracle (1:14–16). By employing six parallel phrases, each beginning with the word "day" (*yom*), Zephaniah creates the sense of intensification throughout the stanza. Additionally, by using pairs of corresponding synonyms,[7] the writer is able to build through language the imagery of Yahweh heaping layer upon layer of wrath upon the condemned.

1:17–18 "The whole earth will be consumed" (Judgment against Mankind/ Pictured as Complete Consumption)

The final segment of the oracle recalls the imagery of sacrifice (blood "poured out") from 1:4–9. It also recalls verses 11–13 in describing the inability of silver and gold "to rescue" in the day of God's wrath. But its primary focus is to recall the judgment on the whole earth that introduced the oracle (1:2–3). This forms an effective *inclusio* that brackets the whole judgment speech. If the whole earth is consumed by God's wrath, how much more will its center—Jerusalem—be consumed to the core?

2:1–3 "Seek the Lord . . . perhaps you will be concealed" (A Call to Repentance)

In the tradition of prophets like Joel, Zephaniah follows his announcement of judgment with a call to repentance—"there's a hope of escape!" Nevertheless, in calling Judah to repentance there is biting irony in the

---

[7] On the specialized relationships between pairings, see Marvin A. Sweeney, *The Twelve Prophets*, Vol. 2, Berit Olam (Collegeville, MN: The Liturgical Press, 2000), 508–9.

invitation. Judah is twice called to "gather together," a term normally used to describe gathering straw for the fire (2:1). Following the reference to the "fire of His jealousy" (1:18), the reader might imagine that Zephaniah is inviting Judah to more judgment. Additionally, Judah is addressed as "undesirable nation," a term usually reserved for the Gentile nations.[8] Judah is described as an undesirable nation, one like the nations described in the speech that follows (2:4–15). But for Judah, even in the midst of judgment there is hope—an opportunity to repent "before" (repeated three times) the "burning" "takes effect" (2:2) and an opportunity to "seek" (repeated three times) the Lord (2:3). In this call to repentance the irony is rich, yet the opportunity profound.

2:4–3:7 (An Oracle of Judgment against the Nations—A Divine Warning for Judah)

Similar to Amos 1–2, Zephaniah incorporates a judgment speech against the nations as a vehicle to warn his people of impending judgment. Addressing nations to the west, east, south, and north, Zephaniah strategically proclaims the destruction of foreign empires and Judah's most antagonistic enemies. Again, similar to Amos 1–2, rhetoric of entrapment is at play. In the mind of the Judean audience, *these* nations were certainly deserving of punishment. But Zephaniah's focus was never the nations. Rather, the oracle of judgment against the nations was a divine warning meant for Judah; it was, in fact, the perfect follow-up to Judah's call to repentance. The oracles of judgment against Gentile nations function not as an end but as a means— a means to warn Judah of what lies ahead if she fails to repent (3:6–7). The point is simply this: If God has demonstrated his power against these nations, should Judah not also fear (3:7)?

---

[8] Some versions understand the verb *kasaph* to denote shame, thus the translation "shameless nation." Either understanding of the verb is plausible in context. The word may also recall the callous complacency of Judah described in 1:10–13. This is reflected by Motyer's translation, "nation devoid of feeling." See J. Alec Motyer, "Zephaniah," in *The Minor Prophets: An Exegetical & Expositional Commentary*, ed. Thomas Edward McComiskey (Grand Rapids, MI: Baker, 1998), 926.

2:4–7 "Woe, inhabitants of the seacoast" (Against the West/Philistia)

The first oracle against the nations is directed to the west, to the Philistine cities along the seacoast of Canaan. Sound-alike wordplay is used to draw attention to the fall of Gaza (`azzah) and Ekron (`eqron). `Azzah will be abandoned (`azuvah), and `Eqron will be uprooted (`aqer). The judgment also reaches to Ashdod and Ashkelon (2:4), and the seacoast will be left uninhabited by the Sea Peoples (2:5–6).

The oracle against the Philistines concludes with an expression of Yahweh's commitment to his covenant promises. Rather than remain uninhabited, the coastlands of Canaan will again be possessed by the remnant of Judah (2:7a) on the day that Yahweh their God returns to them (2:7b). Perhaps most striking is the use of the word *paqad*, translated in the HCSB as "return." The term literally means "to visit," with the context determining whether the visitation is one of blessing or cursing. Earlier, Yahweh was depicted *paqad*-ing in judgment (1:8–9). Now, he is viewed as *paqad*-ing in salvation.

2:8–11 "The Lord will be terrifying to them" (Against the East/Moab and Ammon)

The second oracle is directed against Moab and Ammon, the nations across the Jordan whose fathers were born out of the incestuous relationship between Lot and his daughters (Gen 19:36–38). These nations were continual thorns to the eastern side of Judah, and for this God would solemnly declare their judgment. Ironically, the nations that arose through the escape from Sodom and Gomorrah would themselves become like Sodom and Gomorrah.[9]

2:12 "You Cushites will also be slain" (Against the South/Cush)

Although the oracle is brief, the judgment against Cush (modern-day Sudan) extends the compass of judgment surrounding Judah to the furthest reaches of the known world. Importantly, while the oracle against Cush

---

[9] Robert B. Chisholm Jr., *Interpreting the Minor Prophets* (Grand Rapids, MI: Zondervan, 1990), 208.

does not contain a contrastive expectation of restoration for Judah, there is a connection to this later in the book. When final restoration is promised to Judah following her own judgment, Yahweh's dispersed people will come from "beyond the rivers of Cush" (3:10).

2:13–15 "What a desolation she has become" (Against the North/Assyria)

The fourth oracle is directed against Assyria, effectively rounding out the compass of judgment. In language reminiscent of Nahum, Zephaniah (a near contemporary to Nahum) proclaims God's judgment against the self-assured city of Nineveh (2:15a). If Cush represented the most distant extent of Gentile presence, Assyria represented the most oppressive weight of Gentile power. Yahweh would demonstrate himself able to consume the "whole earth" by the "fire of His jealousy" (1:18; 3:8).

3:1–7 "Woe to the city . . . the oppressive city!" (Against the Center/Jerusalem)

After proclaiming woe on the nations surrounding Judah, Zephaniah refocuses the speech to the true intent of God's anger— punishing Jerusalem! Although the righteous Lord dwelt in the city (3:5), the city did not draw near to God (3:2). Through irony and repetition of structure, Zephaniah brings the accusations home. The very institutions that should have set God's people apart from the Gentiles were guilty of oppressing righteousness. The princes who should have shepherded the people were like lions, and the judges who were to execute justice were like ravenous wolves (3:3). The prophets, rather than reliable preachers of truth, were treacherous; the priests, rather than maintaining the law, profaned the sanctuary (3:4; see Ezek 22:25–28). Unlike in the Gentile nations, all of this was done in the very presence of the Lord by a people who "know no shame" (3:5; see 2:1).

God's wrath against the nations should have been warning enough, but Judah became all the more corrupt (3:6–7). Rather than live in the fear of Yahweh (3:7a), she continued in her rebellion. Therefore, her judgment became all the more inevitable.

3:8 "Therefore, wait for Me . . . until the day . . ." (A Call to Wait)

Following the accusation of Judah's guilt, one might expect further details of the inevitable judgment to follow. But rather than a proclamation of woe, the reader is exhorted to wait. It is not that judgment has been averted; rather, the implied addressee has shifted. Recalling the spirit by which Habakkuk waited for the day of distress (Hab 3:16), the audience must now wait for God's judgment to unfold. Only after it does will the humble see the day of disaster become a day of restoration. Zephaniah now speaks to the righteous people of Habakkuk 2:4, the meek and the humble (Zeph 3:12)—the faithful remnant of Israel (Zeph 3:13).

Beyond making a shift in audience, Zephaniah also moves the Day of the Lord motif from temporal judgment to eschatological salvation. Yet the day of Judah's blessing would be preceded by a gathering of nations, a great assembly where the Lord's verdict would be decided and executed. Chisholm summarizes the transition well: "In short, the humble should wait patiently for the judgment because it would be the first stage in God's program of restoration."[10]

3:9–20 (An Oracle of Salvation)

The concluding oracle of Zephaniah marks a stark contrast to the proclamation of judgment that opened the book. The primary thrust of 3:9–20 is eschatological restoration, where the "on that day" (3:16) and "at that time" (3:19–20) language shifts to a future, blessed expectation. If God's wrath is pictured as a reversal of creation in 1:2–3, then the final oracle envisions a future restoration of creation's ideal.

3:9–13 "For I will then restore pure speech to the peoples" (The Reversal of Babel)

The gathering of nations to judgment in 3:8 becomes a gathering of nations to service in 3:9. To the peoples, a pure speech is restored (lit. "then I will restore to the nations a pure lip"), one of praise to the Lord. Although not specified, the restoration of pure speech may recall the Tower

---

[10] Ibid., 211.

of Babel dispersion in Genesis 11.[11] Although God scattered the nations as they sought to usurp divine authority with a common speech, he will one day restore a speech of common purity to the people under his kingdom domain. Perhaps more significant than the implied connection to the Tower of Babel is the clear correspondence between the nation's "pure lip" in verse 9 and the honest talk of Israel's remnant in verse 13. In Zephaniah's vision of the future, God will bring the nations together with Judah so that all may "serve Him with a single purpose" (3:9). Finally, the remnant of that "shameless nation" (2:1 ESV), who "know no shame" (3:5), will on that day "not be put to shame" (3:11).

3:14–17 "Sing for joy, Daughter Zion" (A Celebration Song)

With a call to celebration, the salvation oracle erupts into a song of praise. The hymn begins and ends with shouts of joy; it coheres around the theme of God-ensured security. For a people who lived in constant fear of foreign oppression and violent affliction, the peace of that day will be worthy of a song!

Instead of impending judgment, the faithful remnant could expect that Yahweh their warrior would bring "quietness with His love" (3:16–17). Although he can be a warrior who consumes the whole earth by the fire of his jealousy (1:18; 3:8), he is also the divine warrior who saves (3:17a). The God of this song rejoices over his people with gladness, delighting in them "with shouts of joy" (3:17). In response, the people shout loudly and sing for joy, rejoicing with all their hearts (3:14). What a contrast to the wailing of Zephaniah 1:10–11!

3:18–20 "At that time I will bring you back" (The Reversal of Exile)

Continuing the theme of eschatological restoration, the oracle concludes with a strong affirmation of God's intentions to restore the meek and faithful remnant of Judah. Verse 18 is rather obscure in the Hebrew, and the difficulty of translation is reflected in the many differences between English versions. But the general sense of the segment is straightforward:

---

[11] Commentators have given varying degrees of credence to this connection. See O. Palmer Robertson, *The Books of Nahum, Habakkuk, and Zephaniah*, NICOT (Grand Rapids, MI: Eerdmans, 1990), 328–29.

Whatever grief the prophet sees among the people of God, he promises relief. Enemy oppression will vanish. Worship opportunities will be purified and renewed. Social injustice will disappear from Israel's agenda. God's elect people will participate in joy and thanksgiving in God's appointed times of worship. People will rejoice, and God will be glorified.[12]

Perhaps most striking is the conclusion to the salvation oracle: "Yahweh has spoken" (3:20). Multiple times through the judgment speeches the authority and guarantee of judgment was reiterated through the statement that what was spoken belonged to Yahweh (1:3, 10; 2:9; 3:8). Now the guarantee of salvation is affirmed through the Lord's own voice—"Yahweh has spoken"—a fitting capstone to the book.

Theological Message and Application of Zephaniah

Undoubtedly the primary theological motif in the book of Zephaniah is the Day of the Lord. The concept permeates the book through frequent repetition, and the full range of its theological flexibility is demonstrated throughout Zephaniah's three chapters. In chapter one, the Day of the Lord is a day of judgment. While its primary focus is Judah, the day is viewed as extending to the whole earth (1:2–3; 17–18). The time of fulfillment in chapter one is also broad. It begins in the distant past with an allusion to the flood event and the reversal of creation (1:2–3). It then moves to the ancient setting of Zephaniah, pointing to impending judgment upon Judah, soon fulfilled by Nebuchadnezzar's army in 586 BC. Finally, the lens redirects to the distant future, with contemporary judgment acting as a precursor to the final eschatological judgment of all humanity (1:17–18).

Chapter two continues the development of the Day of the Lord motif, referring explicitly to the impending judgment of Judah in 2:1–3. However, the text then transitions to the demonstration of Yahweh's wrath against the Gentile nations. These oracles relate to the fall of Judah's contemporaries, functioning as a warning to Judah within her own ancient setting (2:4–15).

[12] Kenneth L. Barker and Waylon Bailey, *Micah, Nahum, Habakkuk, Zephaniah*, NAC (Nashville, TN: B&H, 1999), 498.

In chapter two, the day relates to God's judgment against Judah and the Gentile nations, but all within the ancient setting.

In chapter three, the Day of the Lord carries multiple tiers of reference. Zephaniah 3:8 is an exhortation to wait until the day of plunder, the day of Yahweh's judgment on Judah. For Zephaniah's contemporaries, this day of plunder was fulfilled by the disastrous fall of Jerusalem in 586 BC. The argument of the text, however, is fluid, and the promise of plunder abruptly shifts to include the assembly of all nations. Parallel to 1:17–18, the implied timing of this day is eschatological.

Although remaining eschatological, the subject of that day once again abruptly shifts in 3:9, this time from judgment to restoration. The picture of nations assembled for judgment is transformed into a unified assembly of worship, where the nations join the remnant of Israel to serve God with a single purpose (3:9–13). The day of judgment pictured in chapter one becomes a day of salvation in 3:16—a day in which the scattered of Israel are gathered to receive praise and fame (3:19).

Following the controlling motif of the Day of the Lord, Zephaniah demonstrates the two spheres of judgment and restoration in vivid, even hyperbolic, language. As dreadful as God is in judgment, he is all the more gracious in restoration. The covenant basis behind judgment and restoration is also controlled by the Day of the Lord motif. On this foundation, the stark contrast between the curses of the Mosaic covenant (see esp. 1:13b) and the blessings of the Abrahamic, Davidic, and new covenants are on full display.

Finally, the two sides of the divine warrior are most striking in the book of Zephaniah. In judgment, Yahweh is pictured as a warrior whose indignation is fearsome, who "sweeps away everything" (1:2), who consumes mankind "by the fire of His jealousy" (1:18; 3:8), and who pours out blood "like dust" and "flesh like dung" (1:17). Yet in salvation he is a "warrior who saves," who brings "quietness with His love" (3:17), and who allows none to "be put to shame" (3:11).

The church today might apply the theology of Zephaniah from two alternate contexts. First, consider the church that is worldly, the church that lies complacent in attitude and action. Is this church exempt from discipline and judgment? There is a degree to which many in the church have absorbed a worldly form of religious syncretism. While most in Western Christianity do not follow pagan gods, the length to which the world infiltrates the church is striking. How far off is this from the situation Zephaniah describes in 1:4–9? Additionally, many within the church are complacent, settled down comfortably, and indifferent to the discerning eye of the Lord. Many live as if God will never act, whether by blessing or curse. How different is this from the situation Zephaniah describes in 1:12–13? Perhaps to this church, the message of Zephaniah is primarily one of prophetic warning.

However, for another kind of church, the persecuted church, Zephaniah brings a message of hope and salvation. For the persecuted church, complacency is not an option, and the world offers little temptation to syncretism. With the number of persecuted believers higher in the twentieth and twenty-first centuries than in any other time in history, the message of Zephaniah is more powerful and relevant than ever. To the multitude of believers living under the tyranny of political and religious persecution, the message of Zephaniah is clear: "Therefore wait for Me—Yahweh your God is among you, a warrior who saves" (3:8, 17a).

14

THE BOOK OF HAGGAI

Introduction

Picking up the pieces and rebuilding after a time of disaster is never easy. On August 29, 2005, Hurricane Katrina slammed into the city of New Orleans, forever changing the lives of its residents. Breaches in the city's levees and floodwalls caused flooding to 80 percent of the city. The storm left more than a thousand dead in the city, damaged or destroyed more than 200,000 homes, and caused over $100 billion in damages. Yet, four out of five people making up the city's population before the storm have returned, and New Orleans is once again a vibrant city. One of the local residents who returned to rebuild his home commented, "We had lost everything, but we didn't lose hope."

The story of the Old Testament also concludes with a remarkable story of rebuilding against insurmountable odds. The Lord sent the Babylonian army to destroy Jerusalem as judgment for the sins of his people, but he also graciously provided his exiled people the opportunity to return to their homeland and to rebuild Jerusalem. The prophets Haggai and Zechariah encouraged the postexilic community to rebuild the temple in Jerusalem so that they might again enjoy the Lord's presence and blessing. More importantly, they reminded the people their renewal was not just about returning to the land; their full blessing depended on returning to the Lord.

The book of Haggai consists of a series of four oracles delivered by the prophet over a four-month period in the year 520 BC. Haggai's message was that the Lord had disciplined his people with poor harvests and economic hardships because of their neglect of the temple. When the leaders and people of Judah responded positively to Haggai's challenge, his message turned to one of encouragement and promise. The Lord would be with his people to enable them to finish their work on the temple and would ultimately restore the former glory of the temple and the royal authority of David. Haggai's ministry coincided with that of Zechariah, who also charged the people to finish rebuilding the Lord's house (Ezra 5:1–2; 6:14).

Only the book of Obadiah is shorter than Haggai, and the book contains no biographical information concerning Haggai. His name means "feast/festival" and perhaps reflects that he was born during one of Israel's religious feasts. The book highlights his role as "the prophet" (1:1, 3, 12; 2:1, 10) and "the LORD's messenger" (1:13). The fact that Haggai is not mentioned among those returning to the land in Ezra 2 suggests that he likely came back to the homeland with a later group of returnees.

In 586 BC, the Babylonians sacked Jerusalem, destroyed the temple, and took a large portion of Judah's population into exile. In 539 BC, Cyrus of Persia won a major victory over the Babylonian army at Opis and then captured the city of Babylon. Cyrus issued a decree in 538 BC, allowing the Jews to return to their homeland and to rebuild their temple (see 2 Chr 36:23; Ezra 1:2–4; 6:3–5). Nearly 50,000 Jews returned under the leadership of Sheshbazzar and Zerubbabel, who were appointed as governors of the province of Yehud (Judah), and Jeshua/Joshua, who served as the high priest. The enthusiastic returnees built an altar on the ruins of the temple and celebrated the Festival of Booths in 537 BC (Ezra 3:1–7). In the second

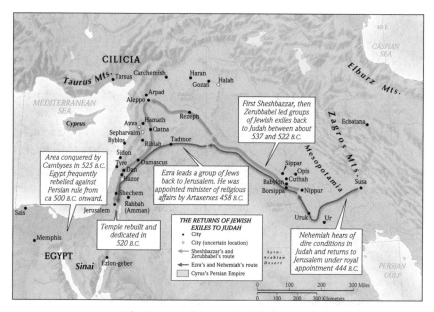

The Returns of the Jewish Exiles to Judah

year, they laid the foundation of the new temple (Ezra 3:8–10; 5:16).[1] External opposition and economic struggles, however, soon caused work on the temple to cease (Ezra 4:1–5; 5:3–5). Resistance to the work from the surrounding peoples and various Persian officials continued throughout the reigns of Cyrus and Cambyses. Darius I (Hystaspes) ascended to the throne in 522 BC, and he immediately faced rebellion and discord throughout the empire. By 520 BC, when Haggai and Zechariah began their ministry, Darius had put down these rebellions and had consolidated his control over the empire.

The people and leaders of Judah faced immediate opposition when resuming their work on the temple. Tattenai, the governor of the province of Trans-Euphrates, wrote a letter to Darius accusing the Jews of

---

[1] An alternate understanding of the chronology involved here is that Zerubbabel and Joshua returned with a second wave of exiles at a later time and that the laying of the foundation in Ezra 3:10 occurs in the second year of Darius (520 BC) at the same time Haggai delivers his second oracle (Haggai 2:1–9). See Mark J. Boda, *Haggai, Zechariah*, NIVAC (Grand Rapids, MI: Zondervan, 2004), 117–19; and Iain Provan, V. Philips Long, and Tremper Longman, *A Biblical History of Israel* (Louisville, KY: Westminster John Knox, 2003), 288.

insurrection, but a search of the royal archives confirmed that Cyrus had earlier authorized the rebuilding of the temple (Ezra 5:6–6:5). Darius issued his own decree with the threat of the death penalty for those who hindered the Jews and even provided funding and resources for the rebuilding project (Ezra 6:6–12). Work on the temple was completed on March 12, 515 BC (Ezra 6:13–15).

The absence of any reference in Haggai to the completion of the temple, along with the intense eschatological expectations attached to Zerubbabel as construction on the temple resumed, reflect that the book of Haggai was put together some time before 515 BC.[2] The specific dating of the oracles in the book provides historical authenticity and would have allowed for later confirmation of Haggai's prophetic promises.[3]

Structure

The four messages in this book are chronologically arranged and joined by a narrative structure that chronicles Haggai's strategic role in challenging the postexilic community to resume the work of rebuilding the temple.

J. Kessler notes the shared elements in these individual messages: (1) a date formula (1:1; 2:1, 10, 20); (2) a conflict or problem (1:2; 2:2–3, 14, 21–22); (3) a call to obedience and faith (1:4–7, 9–11; 2:4–5, 14–17), and (4) a divine promise (1:18; 2:6–9, 18–19, 21–23).[4] These oracles also reflect an A-B-A'-B' pattern, in which the A sections (1:1–11; 2:10–19) contain reproaches and rebuke with the offer of hope, while the B sections (2:1–9, 20–23) contain messages of encouragement and promise.[5] The A sections also parallel one another in the way that they address the issue of agricultural failure and blessing, and the B sections in that they promise that the Lord

---

[2] J. Kessler, "Haggai, Book of," in *Dictionary of the Old Testament Prophets*, ed. Mark J. Boda and J. Gordon McConville (Downers Grove, IL: InterVarsity, 2012), 302.

[3] Richard A. Taylor and E. Ray Clendenen, *Haggai, Zechariah: An Exegetical and Theological Exposition of Holy Scripture*, NAC 21 (Nashville, TN: B&H Reference, 2004), 52–54.

[4] Kessler, "Haggai, Book of," 302.

[5] Ibid.

MESSAGE 1 (August 29, 520 BC)	(1:1–15) Call to Rebuild the Temple and the People's Positive Response
MESSAGE 2 (October 17, 520 BC)	(2:1–9) The Promise of Future Glory for the Temple
MESSAGE 3 (December 18, 520 BC)	(2:10–19) The Promise of Future Blessing to Replace Defilement
MESSAGE 4 (December 18, 520 BC)	(2:20–23) The Promise to Zerubbabel and the Restoration of Davidic Rule

"will shake the heavens and earth" in bringing about Israel's restoration and renewal.[6]

Several recurring expressions serve to unify the four oracles. Yahweh is referred to as "the LORD of Hosts" fourteen times in this short book. Three times, the Lord calls on the people to "think carefully/reflect back" (lit. "set your heart") so they would seriously consider the consequences of their choices and be aware of the blessings that the Lord would provide in response to their obedience (1:5, 7; 2:15). The Lord's promise, "I am with you" (1:13; 2:4) offers hope to the discouraged people. The Lord also promises to "shake the heavens and the earth" and the nations by overturning the present world order in order to accomplish his sovereign purposes on behalf of his people (2:6–7).

The narrative style and arrangement of Haggai reflect the power and importance of the prophetic word. Haggai's preaching moves the people to action, and their positive response to the prophet's message brings blessing in the place of judgment. There is a cause-effect relationship between the people's obedient response to the prophetic word in chapter one and the blessings that are promised in the remaining oracles.

---

[6] C. Hassell Bullock, *An Introduction to the Old Testament Prophetic Books*, updated ed. (Chicago, IL: Moody, 2007), 366.

Exposition

1:1–15 "My house still lies in ruins, while each of you is busy with his own house" (The Call to Rebuild the Temple)

Haggai's first message challenges Zerubbabel, Joshua, and the people to resume the work of rebuilding the Jerusalem temple that had ceased sixteen years earlier. This passage includes both the prophetic oracle (vv. 1–11) and a record of the people's obedient response to the prophet's challenge (vv. 12–15). The prophet rebukes the people for putting their own interests above the Lord's by rebuilding their own houses before first rebuilding the temple. Haggai informed the people that their economic ruin was the direct result of their neglect of the temple. The "ruin" (*harev*) of the temple (vv. 4, 9) had caused the Lord to send the "drought" (*horev*) (v. 11) that devastated Judah's harvests. Eight different references to the Lord speaking in this passage highlight that the prophet's message originates with God.

Haggai's message takes the form of a disputation speech that begins with the assertion of the people he wishes to contest. The people do not believe that the present is the "time" (*'et*) for building the Lord's house. The Lord challenges this thinking by asking why, then, have they invested such effort and expense in constructing their own homes? The repetition of "time" (*'et*), the emphatic "you yourselves," and the contrast between their "houses" and God's "house" all pointedly reflect that they have placed their own comfort and security above the Yahweh's honor.[7]

The term "paneled" (*sephunim*) describing their houses likely refers to expensive wood paneling used in the interior of more wealthy homes and reflects lavish accommodations. This term is used elsewhere with reference to the temple (1 Kgs 6:9) and the royal palace (1 Kgs 7:3, 7; Jer 22:14). The noun form of this word (*sippun*) refers to a "ceiling" in 1 Kings 6:15, and some have seen a reference to "roofed houses" here in verse 4. The KJV reads "ceiled houses." This understanding might seem preferable in light of the overall impoverished condition of the people, but the houses in view here are likely those of the leaders Zerubbabel and Joshua. They control the financial assets of the community at large and have set the wrong agenda in constructing expensive homes for themselves, rather than first seeing to

---

[7] Boda, *Haggai, Zechariah*, 89.

the construction of God's house. These leaders needed to remember the example of David, who lamented that he lived in a "cedar house" while the ark of the Lord was housed in a tent (2 Sam 7:2) and of Solomon, who first built the Lord's house (1 Kings 6) and then his own palace complex (1 Kgs 7:1–14).[8]

Haggai challenged the people to "think carefully" about their ways and to recognize the cause-and-effect connection between the ruined temple and their own impoverished condition (vv. 5–6). They have "planted much" and "harvested little." They are lacking in food, drink, clothing, and wages. Under the Mosaic covenant, the Lord had promised to bless the obedience of his people with agricultural abundance, but he had also warned that he would punish their disobedience with drought, famine, and a lack of good harvests (see Lev 26:19–20; Deut 28:23–24, 38–42). Their disobedience to the Lord had doomed all of their labor to futility. They had become like laborers putting their wages "into a bag with a hole in it." The word for "bag" is used elsewhere to refer to a carrying pouch that was used to hold silver, money, or other valuables (see Gen 42:32; Prov 7:20; Song 1:13).[9]

The second "think carefully" in verses 7–8 offers a more positive motivation. The prophet commands the people to gather the needed timber and to build the Lord's house, with the promise that Yahweh would be "pleased" and "glorified" by their obedience. While the temple was built with cut stones (Ezra 5:8), lumber was also needed to replace the timber burned by the Babylonians as well as to provide scaffolding for the construction project. The verb "to be pleased" (*ratsah*) is often used in the Hebrew Bible to refer to God's acceptance or delight in worshippers and their sacrifices (see 2 Sam 24:23; Ps 119:108; Ezek 20:40).[10] The verb "glorified" also has a close connection to the temple. The "glory" (*kavod*) of the Lord took up residence in the tabernacle (Exod 40:34–38) and the temple (1 Kgs 8:10–11). The rebuilding of the temple would involve a restoring of the Lord's honor. The prophet Ezekiel had declared that the exile brought dishonor to Yahweh's reputation because it appeared he had been unable to protect and deliver his people (Ezek 36:20–23). The continued disrepair of the temple

---

[8] Ibid., 90.

[9] Eugene H. Merrill, *Haggai, Zechariah, Malachi: An Exegetical Commentary* (Chicago: Moody, 1994), 23.

[10] Taylor and Clendenen, *Haggai, Malachi*, 129.

implied that even his own people did not view him as worthy of their honor and devotion.

The prophet concludes his appeal to the people with a final reminder that their economic ruin is the result of their failure to give proper attention to the Lord's house. The message in verses 9–11 echoes verses 5–6, repeating the contrast between the "much" that they had expected and the "little" they actually produced.

Positive responses to the prophetic word are the exception rather than the norm in the Book of the Twelve, but the people began the work of rebuilding the temple three weeks after Haggai's initial message (1:12–15). The leaders and people recognized the words of the prophet as the voice of God and reverenced the Lord enough to take his words seriously. In light of the opposition and challenges facing the people, the promise of Yahweh's presence with them offered the greatest possible encouragement. The Lord "stirring" the hearts of the people to carry through on their commitment to rebuild his house reflects how divine sovereignty and human response cooperate in accomplishing the Lord's purposes. The Lord does not manipulate Israel's response to the prophetic word, but he does reward their choice to obey with enablement to carry out their good intentions.[11]

2:1–9 "The final glory of this house will be greater than the first" (The Lord's Promise to Bless the New Temple)

Haggai gives his second oracle on October 17, 520 BC, almost a month after resumption of the work on the temple. The seventh month of Tishri was the time for the celebration of the Festival of Booths (see Lev 23:33–42; Num 29:12–39; Deut 16:13–15), and the prophet delivered his message on the last day of the feast. Haggai seeks to encourage a disheartened people. The initial enthusiasm for the project has waned, and the people have come to understand the enormity of the work ahead of them. The observance of a major feast in the midst of temple ruins together with a lack of crops at a festival designed to celebrate the harvest (see Exod 23:16) would have especially reminded the people of their desperate plight.[12] Additionally, it was

---

[11] Robert B. Chisholm Jr., *Handbook on the Prophets* (Grand Rapids, MI: Baker, 2002), 452.

[12] Boda, *Haggai, Zechariah*, 118.

already evident to those old enough to remember the splendor of Solomon's temple that the new temple structure would pale in comparison (see Ezra 3:12–13).

Judging by architectural standards, it would have been easy to dismiss the rebuilt temple as "nothing," but Haggai reminds the people that what matters most is not the building itself, but rather Yahweh's abiding presence among his people. The Lord commands the leaders and people to "be strong" in completing what they have started, while also assuring them that his Spirit would be their source of strength. The Lord even promised that the "glory" of this lesser temple would surpass that of the former (vv. 6–9). Using the language of theophany, the Lord of Hosts (Armies) announces that he would soon violently "shake" (ra'ash) the nations (see Judg 5:4; Pss 18:7; 68:8). The reference to shaking "once more" in light of the previous mention of the exodus indicates that the Lord would display his power over his enemies in the same way that he had at the Red Sea (see Pss 68:8; 77:16–18).[13] This cosmic disruption would cause the nations to come to Jerusalem to worship the Lord in recognition of his universal sovereignty.

The expression "treasures of all the nations" in verse 7 literally reads "desire of all the nations," which some Christian interpreters have read as a reference to the Messiah. This phrase instead refers to the tribute that the nations would bring to the temple in honor of the Lord (see Isa 60:5–9; 61:6; 66:20; Zech 14:14). The Lord promises to fill his house with "glory" (kavod), a word that often specifically refers to wealth or splendor (see Gen 31:1; 1 Chr 29:12, 28; Ps 49:17). The statement concerning the Lord's ownership of "silver and gold" in verse 8 also validates this understanding.[14] As Richard Taylor explains, "Haggai envisioned a situation in which God would so move among the non-Israelite nations that they would supply the needed revenues for the project of temple rebuilding."[15] Darius would, in the very near future, provide funding and resources for the work on the temple (see Ezra 6:8–10). In 20 BC, Herod began rebuilding the second temple on a much larger scale, and various renovations continued until the outbreak of the Jewish revolt in AD 66.

---

[13] Merrill, *Haggai, Zechariah, Malachi*, 39.

[14] The NET Bible translates v. 8, "'The silver and gold will be mine,' says the Lord."

[15] Taylor and Clendenen, *Haggai, Zechariah*, 165.

Ultimately, however, this promise anticipates something more than pagan rulers financing the beautification of the temple. The noun "glory" (*kavod*) is used with the verb "to fill" elsewhere to describe the glory of Yahweh filling the tabernacle and the temple (see Exod 40:34–35; 1 Kgs 8:11),[16] and the eschatological hope associated with the temple was the return of Yahweh's glory to dwell among his people (see Ezekiel 40–48; esp. 43:1–7; 44:4). This expectation was fulfilled in part when Jesus, as the incarnated "glory" of God, presented himself at the Jerusalem temple during his earthly ministry (see John 1:14).

2:10–19 "From this day on I will bless you" (Past Defilement and the Promise of Future Blessing)

Haggai delivered his third and fourth oracles on December 18, 520 BC, exactly three months after the people resumed the repair and rebuilding of the temple (see 1:15). This time would prove a pivotal moment for the people of Judah. They experienced judgment for past neglect of the temple, but now they would experience the Lord's blessing. Haggai employs a priestly ruling concerning contact with objects that are ceremonially holy or defiled to teach an important lesson concerning the people's spiritual condition before the Lord.

Meat that was offered as part of a sacrifice was considered holy, or consecrated to the Lord, as was the garment of the worshipper who carried it (Lev 6:27). That purity, however, could not then be transferred from a garment to any other food or drink with which it came in contact. Purity could be conveyed from one object to another but not from the second object to a third one. Ritual defilement or uncleanness, however, could be transferred in this manner. As Mark Boda notes, "Uncleanness is passed on to the third degree; holiness is not. In a word, uncleanness is more contagious than holiness."[17] A person who came in contact with a dead body was defiled and transferred that uncleanness to any object or person that he touched (see Lev 22:1–9; Num 19:22). This message carried a serious warning for the people of Judah. Because of their failure to rebuild the temple, the community was defiled before God, and all of its service to the Lord was

---

[16] Boda, *Haggai, Zechariah*, 125.
[17] Ibid., 144.

tainted. Even with the rebuilding of the temple, repentance was needed for the people to be restored to the Lord and for their worship to be acceptable to him. If they persisted in their disobedience, the people would transfer their defilement to the temple.

Haggai again offered a word of encouragement at a time when it was much needed. Work on the temple had started in earnest, but much labor remained. Their crops were in the ground for the next season, but recent harvests had been poor and unproductive. The commands to "reflect back" in verse 15 and "consider carefully" in verse 18 are the same Hebrew expression (lit. "set your hearts") found in 1:5, 7 where the prophet instructed the people to "consider" their ways. They were to look back and reflect on the want and poverty they had experienced because of the poor harvests the Lord had sent to punish their disobedience. The Lord now counseled the people to pay attention to how he would bless them from that point forward because of their renewed commitment and obedience. As they devoted themselves to rebuilding the temple, the Lord would provide them with an abundant harvest.

2:20–23 "I will . . . make you like My signet ring" (The Blessing of Zerubbabel and the Restoration of Davidic Rule)

Haggai's final oracle is a word of promise directed to Zerubbabel, the governor of Judah and the grandson of King Jehoiachin, who was deported to Babylon in 597 BC. Israel's blessing would include not only the renewal of worship at the temple, but also the restoration of David's throne. Zerubbabel's appointment as the governor of a small province in the Persian Empire was confirmation that the Lord was not finished with the house of David. The Lord had even greater things in store for the future.

God had promised by covenant to establish David's throne forever and had adopted the Davidic kings as his "sons" and vice-regents (2 Sam 7:12–16; Ps 2:6–7). He had promised to crush their enemies and give them dominion over the nations (Pss 2:8–9; 89:20–25; 110). The Lord had instead punished the house of David for its unfaithfulness, and the Babylonian exile appeared to be the end for the Davidic dynasty. As in 2:7, the Lord as the divine warrior once again promises to "shake the heavens" in order to shatter the power of the nations and to elevate Zerubbabel. He would "overturn" (*haphak*) the kingdoms of the earth just as he had "demolished" (*haphak*)

Sodom and Gomorrah (see Gen 19:21, 25, 29; Deut 29:23). The defeat of chariots, horses, and riders recalls how the Lord hurled the Egyptian chariots into the sea at the exodus (Exod 15:1, 4, 9, 21). The kings and armies of the nations would even turn their swords on each other. Ironically, Yahweh announced his intention to overthrow nations when Darius had finally established control over his vast empire.

Jeremiah had announced that Nebuchadnezzar had taken the place of David as Yahweh's "servant" (Jer 25:9; 27:6; see 2 Sam 7:5, 8, 20, 26; Ezek 34:23–24), but now that honored designation is restored to Zerubbabel. Jeremiah had also announced that the Lord had rejected Jehoiachin and would cast him off as his "signet ring" (Jer 22:24–30), indicating that Jehoiachin would lose his royal authority as Yahweh's representative, and that none of his sons would sit on the throne. The signet ring contained the seal of the king used to sign documents and to authenticate royal authority (see 1 Kgs 21:8; Esth 3:10–12). Through Haggai, the Lord reverses the curse placed on Jehoiachin and restores royal authority to Zerubbabel as his "signet ring."

Zerubbabel played an important role in redemptive history as rebuilder of the temple, but the promises of worldwide dominion expressed in this oracle were certainly not fulfilled in his lifetime. The expression "on that day" in verse 23 is commonly used in eschatological contexts in the prophetic literature and points forward to an indefinite time in the future (see Isa 24:21; Hos 2:18, 21; Zeph 1:9–10; Zech 12:3–4). Haggai may have hoped or anticipated that Davidic rule would be restored with Zerubbabel, but the prophecy itself does not give an exact timetable for when these events would occur.[18] Zerubbabel is the contemporary representative of the line through whom the promises of a future Davidic ruler would be fulfilled. As Eugene Merrill explains, Zerubbabel "becomes a code name for the promised Messiah," because he serves "as a link between the Davidic monarchy that had come to an inglorious end in Jehoiachin and that which would be revived in ages to come."[19] Zerubbabel is included in the human genealogies of Jesus found in both Matthew and Luke (see Matt 1:12–13; Luke 3:27), and the New Testament demonstrates how the hopes associated with the royal line of David find their fulfillment in Jesus.

---

[18] Boda, *Haggai, Zechariah*, 163.
[19] Merrill, *Haggai, Zechariah, Malachi*, 58.

The Rejection of Jehoiachin (An End for the House of David)	The Restoration of Zerubbabel (A New Beginning for the House of David)
Jeremiah 22:24–27 "As I live," says the LORD, "though you, Coniah* son of Jehoiakim, the king of Judah, were a **signet ring** on My right hand, I would tear you from it. In fact, I will hand you over to those you dread, who want to take your life, to Nebuchadnezzar king of Babylon and the Chaldeans. I will hurl you and the mother who gave birth to you into another land, where neither of you were born, and there you will both die. They will never return to the land they long to return to." *Jehoiachin	Haggai 2:20–23 The word of the LORD came to Haggai a second time on the twenty-fourth day of the month: "Speak to Zerubbabel, governor of Judah: I am going to shake the heavens and the earth. I will overturn royal thrones and destroy the power of the Gentile kingdoms. I will overturn chariots and their riders. Horses and their riders will fall, each by his brother's sword. On that day"—this is the declaration of the LORD of Hosts—"I will take you, Zerubbabel son of Shealtiel, My servant"—this is the LORD's declaration—"and make you like My **signet ring**, for I have chosen you." This is the declaration of the LORD of Hosts.

Theological Message and Application of Haggai

The message of Haggai is that God's kingdom agenda takes priority over all else in life. By building their own homes before giving attention to the Lord's house, the people put their own personal interests and comforts above Yahweh's honor. Jesus taught his disciples to seek first the kingdom of God and assured them that God as their Father would provide for the necessities of life, such as food and clothing (Matt 6:25–34). In his letter to the Philippians, Paul laments that "all seek their own interests, not those of Jesus Christ" (Phil 2:21), but points to himself and others as counter-models who put serving God and others above self (Phil 2:17–30).

Haggai's preaching also reflects the principle that God rewards obedience and disciplines his people when they disobey, but the specific form of the positive and negative incentives in Haggai was determined by the special relationship between Yahweh and Israel under the Mosaic covenant. The Lord disciplined Israel's unfaithfulness with crop failure and economic ruin and promised to bless their obedience with abundant harvests and prosperity because those were the terms of the covenant he had established with Israel (see Leviticus 26; Deuteronomy 28). The specific terms of this covenant do not directly apply to the church today as the people of God. Droughts in Texas or crop failures in California do not necessarily indicate divine judgment for the United States as they did for ancient Israel as God's chosen people.

Proverbs teaches the general principle that leading a wise life leads to honor and wealth (see Prov 3:13–18), and the Lord promises to provide for those who are generous with their wealth and possessions (see Prov 19:17; 28:27; Luke 6:38; Phil 4:19). Nevertheless, the Lord does not promise economic rewards for the church today in the same way that he did for Israel, and the purpose of financial blessing for the believer is to encourage increased generosity and sacrificial giving (2 Cor 9:6–11). The New Testament places far greater emphasis on how God blesses his people with spiritual and eternal rewards, and we have this greater eternal perspective in light of the resurrection of Jesus.

The priority given to the temple in Haggai connects this book to the larger metanarrative of the Bible. The story of Scripture begins with Adam and Eve enjoying the presence of God in the garden of Eden and concludes with the return of Eden in the New Jerusalem at the end of Revelation.[20] The tabernacle and the temple provided an Eden in a fallen world for the people of Israel. The temple was more than just a place of worship; it was Yahweh's dwelling place where he met with his people and was the locale of his earthly reign as the sovereign King. The destruction of the temple in 586 BC marked a major theological crisis, and it was imperative that the returnees to the land rebuild the temple so they might worship the Lord properly, enjoying the blessings of his presence.

---

[20] For further development of the biblical story from this perspective, see G. K. Beale and Mitchell Kim, *God Dwells Among Us: Expanding Eden to the Ends of the Earth* (Downers Grove, IL: InterVarsity, 2014), and T. Desmond Alexander, *From Eden to the New Jerusalem: An Introduction to Biblical Theology* (Grand Rapids, MI: Kregel, 2009).

Haggai's promises of the Lord filling the temple with his glory (2:7–9) or restoring the dominion of David through Zerubbabel (2:20–23) were obviously not fulfilled historically, and so these promises would find fulfillment in Jesus as the Messiah and in the coming of the eschatological kingdom of God. Jewish intertestamental literature read the Lord's promise to "shake the heavens and earth" in Haggai 2:6–7 as eschatological (2 Bar 32:1–4), as did the New Testament (Heb 12:25–28).[21] The promises of Haggai and other Old Testament prophets concerning the new temple (see Isa 2:2–4; 56:6–7; Ezekiel 40–48; Zech 8:20–23; 14:16–19) are also eschatological in nature and will find their fulfillment in the millennial temple. Understanding these passages (especially the detailed description in Ezekiel 40–48) to refer to a literal temple seems to be the most natural reading of these texts, and the promises associated with this new temple were in no way completely realized in the second temple.[22] This eschatological temple will provide a necessary locale for worship and divine presence in the future earthly kingdom.

Ultimately, however, the canonical development of the temple concept places far greater emphasis on the spiritual blessings of divine presence and fellowship with God than on the architectural structure. Jesus replaces the temple as the locale of God's glory (see Matt 17:1–6; John 1:14; 2:19–22), and his sacrifice for sin on the cross resulted in the rending of the veil in the temple that separated a holy God from sinful humans (Matt 27:51; Mark 15:38; Luke 23:45; Heb 10:19–20). The church has now become a living temple, as the Holy Spirit indwells both the corporate body and individual believers (see 1 Cor 3:16–17; 6:19–20; Eph 2:19–22; 1 Pet 2:4–10). Beyond the temple in the earthly millennial kingdom, Revelation 21–22 anticipates the New Jerusalem where there will be no need for a temple because God

---

[21] George H. Guthrie, "Hebrews," in *Commentary on the New Testament Use of the Old Testament*, ed. G. K. Beale and D. A. Carson (Grand Rapids, MI: Baker Academic, 2007), 998–91. Hebrews 12:25–28 also conveys that believers have a present share in the eschatological blessings promised by Haggai.

[22] For further support of a literal fulfillment of the eschatological temple prophecies in the OT Prophets, see Richard S. Hess, "The Future Written in the Past: The Old Testament and the Millennium," in *A Case for Historic Premillennialism*, ed. Craig L. Blomberg and Sung Wook Chung (Grand Rapids, MI: Baker, 2009), 23–36; and Donald K. Campbell and Jeffrey L. Townsend (ed.), *A Case for Premillennialism: A New Consensus* (Chicago, IL: Moody, 1992), 128–34.

will dwell among his people forever (Rev 21:22). In the New Jerusalem, the fellowship with God that was lost at Eden will be fully restored.

15

THE BOOK OF ZECHARIAH

Introduction

In his book *Christ and Time*, Oscar Cullmann developed the idea of how we as Christians "live between the times" of the first and second comings of Christ, likening the Christian life to the experience of living between D-Day (June 6, 1944) and VE-Day (May 8, 1945) during World War II. The hard-fought battle won on D-Day secured the final victory of the Allied forces on VE-Day at the end of the war.[1] Similarly, we as Christians live between the victory Jesus won over sin and death at his first coming and the ultimate victory of his triumphant return at the Second Coming. Our experience of the blessings we have in Christ is both now and not yet, and

---

[1] Oscar Cullman, *Christ and Time: The Primitive Christian Conception of Time*, Rev ed. (Philadelphia, PA: Westminster John Knox, 1964).

we are called to live faithfully and obediently in anticipation of the second coming of Christ.

Zechariah ministered to the postexilic community in Judah that lived between the times of the return from exile and the ultimate restoration of Israel in the last days. The initial victory of the return from exile called the people to a life of repentance and faithfulness so they might experience the fullness of God's blessing. The community would demonstrate its faithfulness to the Lord by turning from sin and rebuilding the temple. Returning to the land was not enough; more important was their need to return to the Lord.

The message of Zechariah is that Yahweh would bless his people as they rebuilt the temple and would empower Joshua and Zerubbabel as they led this rebuilding project. The return from exile and rebuilding of Jerusalem and the temple anticipated the eschatological restoration and renewal of Israel when all nations would enter Jerusalem to worship the Lord.

Zechariah, whose name means "the Lord remembers," was the son of Berechiah and the grandson of Iddo (Zech 1:1); theirs was a priestly family who was part of the first group of returnees to the land in 537 BC (Neh 12:4). Zechariah likely served as both priest and prophet. Along with the prophet Haggai, Zechariah began his prophetic ministry in 520 BC during the reign of Darius I of Persia. The introductory section of the chapter on Haggai covers the historical background of this period, and the dates given in the books of Haggai and Zechariah provide the following chronology for the ministry of these two prophets.

The temple was completed in 515 BC. The exact duration of Zechariah's ministry is unknown, but the oracles in chapters 9–14, if belonging to the same figure, would suggest the presence of the temple (see 11:13–14) and a ministry that extends beyond the years in the date formula given in the book.

Structure

The book of Zechariah reflects three distinct sections. The first section contains an introductory narrative of the people's positive response to the prophet's call for repentance (1:1–6) and a series of eight night visions that promise the Lord's blessing on the rebuilding of Jerusalem and the temple (1:7–6:15). The night visions in 1:7–6:15 also appear to be arranged in a loosely chiastic structure:

CHRONOLOGY OF THE MESSAGES OF HAGGAI AND ZECHARIAH		
August 520, BC	Haggai 1:1–10	Haggai's first message: *a call to rebuild the temple*
September 21, 520 BC	Haggai 1:12–15	The people's response: *work on the temple resumed*
October 17, 520 BC	Haggai 2:6–8	Haggai's second message: *the future glory of the temple*
October/November, 520 BC	Zechariah 1:1–3	Zechariah's first message: *a call for repentance*
December 18, 520 BC	Haggai 2:18–19, 20	Haggai's third and fourth messages: *the Lord's blessing and the royal authority of Zerubbabel*
February 15, 519 BC	Zechariah 1:7–6:15	Zechariah's eight night visions
December 7, 518 BC	Zechariah 7	Inquiry on the practice of fasting and a call for justice

A   Vision 1: The horsemen and the fate of the nations (1:7–17)

    B   Visions 2 and 3: Obstacles to rebuilding: the Gentile nations (1:18–21; 2:1–12)

        C   Vision 4: The cleansing of Joshua and service at the temple (3:1–10)

        C   Vision 5: Joshua, Zerubbabel and the rebuilding of the temple (4:1–14)

    B   Visions 6 and 7: Obstacles to rebuilding: the sins of the community (5:1–11)

A   Vision 8: Four Chariots and the Fate of the Nations (6:1–8)[2]

---

[2] Tremper Longman III and Raymond B. Dillard, *An Introduction to the Old Testament*, 2nd ed. (Grand Rapids, MI: Zondervan, 2006), 491.

The outer frame of this chiasm reflects the international significance of the rebuilding of Jerusalem, while the middle of this structure highlights the roles of Joshua and Zerubbabel. Both of the visions in the middle also refer to the Lord's "seven eyes" in order to emphasize his presence among his people and his sovereign oversight and protection (3:9; 4:10).[3]

The second major section of the book (7:1–8:23), introduced by the date formula in 7:1, begins with an inquiry concerning the continuation of certain fasts that the Jews had observed during the exilic period and turns into a prophetic exhortation for the community to practice compassion and justice. This section is linked to the book's introduction by its focus on the response of previous generations to "the earlier prophets" (1:4; 7:12) and its calls for repentance. The people's initial repentance in response to the call for rebuilding the temple needed moral and social reforms in accordance with the Mosaic law and the prophet's instructions. The Lord was committed to restoring his people from exile (8:3–8) and bringing all nations to Jerusalem to worship him (8:20–23), but their complete restoration was also conditioned on their obedience (8:14–16).

The third distinct section in the book (chaps. 9–14) is marked off by its use of the heading, "An Oracle: The word of the LORD" (*massa' devar-yhwh*) in 9:1; the use of this same heading in 12:1 further divides this material into two halves. In contrast to the primary focus on contemporary events in chapters 1–8, this apocalyptic-like material has a more eschatological orientation and portrays the final restoration of Israel and the coming of God's kingdom to earth.[4] The return from exile in Babylon was just the beginning of Israel's restoration that would culminate in the last days. Zechariah 9–11 contrasts the blessing of the future kingdom of God with the judgment coming upon the corrupt leaders in the postexilic community. Zechariah

---

[3] Ibid.

[4] Other texts with a similar apocalyptic focus in the Old Testament prophetic books would include Isaiah 24–27; Ezekiel 37–48; Joel 3; and Zephaniah 3. Many passages convey eschatological promises, but these passages would emphasize the otherworldly character of the age to come. These types of prophetic texts are often labelled as proto-apocalyptic or prophetic-apocalyptic in genre. More fully developed use of the apocalyptic genre is found in the books of Daniel and Revelation. For the special features of apocalyptic literature, see Aaron Chalmers, *Interpreting the Prophets: Reading, Understanding, and Preaching From the Worlds of the Prophets* (Downers Grove, IL: IVP Academic, 2015), 120–44.

12–14 portrays the final assault of the nations on Jerusalem and the cleansing and purging of Israel that would lead into the eschatological kingdom of God.

Contemporary scholarship has generally attributed the material in chapters 9–14 to a "Second Zechariah" who comes after the original prophet responsible for chapters 1–8. The reference to "Greece" in 9:13 and some highly speculative reconstructions of how the messages in chapters 9–14 might relate to specific political conflicts in the postexilic community have led to dating this material to the time of Alexander the Great, or even as late as the Maccabean era. Nevertheless, Greece was a significant political power even before the sixth century BC, and the possibility of genuine predictive prophecy should not be dismissed out of hand. Mark Boda concludes that there is nothing in chapters 9–14 that requires a date after 445 BC.[5] The attribution of this book to Zechariah does not preclude the possibility of inspired prophetic activity or later updating of the text that expanded on or provided further clarification of Zechariah's earlier messages.[6] Even scholars not affirming single authorship of the book have recognized the book's essential theological unity.[7]

Exposition

1:1–6 "This is what the LORD of Hosts says: 'Return to Me.'" (Call for Repentance and the People's Positive Response)

The book opens with a narrative account of the Lord directing Zechariah to call the people to repentance. The word "return/repent" (*shuv*) appears in verses 3, 4, and 6. There are also six references in this short section to the Lord speaking. The theme of repentance in the Book of the Twelve as a whole could be summarized by, "Return to Me . . . and I will return to you" (v. 3). In contrast to the Twelve overall, Haggai and Zechariah receive

---

[5] Mark J. Boda, *Haggai, Zechariah*, NIVAC (Grand Rapids, MI: Zondervan, 2004), 29–32.

[6] For some helpful reflection on how prophetic books were put together, see John H. Walton and D. Brent Sandy, *The Lost World of Scripture: Ancient Literary Culture and Biblical Authority* (Downers Grove, IL: InterVarsity, 2013), 224–32.

[7] For a summary of these arguments, see C. Hassell Bullock, *An Introduction to the Old Testament Prophetic Books*, updated ed. (Chicago, IL: Moody, 2007), 378–81.

Zechariah and Haggai began their ministry in the second year of the reign of Darius I, one of Persia's most able administrators who put down a number of rebellions at the beginning of his reign.

positive responses to their preaching—the people have already started their work on the temple when Zechariah begins his ministry. This positive response contrasts with the unwillingness of the generations prior to the exile to listen to the prophets and change their ways. These "earlier prophets" had died, but their message lived on as the words of the Lord, bringing judgment against those who refused to heed them. In verse 6, the people repent and acknowledge the justice of the Lord's punishment of Israel, and Zechariah would call the people to a fuller repentance throughout his ministry (3:7; 6:15; 7:9–13).

Zechariah 1:7–6:15 (Zechariah's Night Visions)

The people's repentance leads to the Lord's promise to bless their work in rebuilding the temple and to restore the city of Jerusalem. These promises are conveyed in a series of eight visions that Zechariah receives on February 15, 519 BC, just a few short months after Zechariah commenced his ministry. In each of these visions, "the Angel of the LORD" provides interpretation and explanation of their significance.

1:7–17 "I AM EXTREMELY JEALOUS FOR JERUSALEM AND ZION" (VISION 1: THE MAN AMONG THE MYRTLE TREES)

In this first vision, Zechariah sees a man who is identified as "the Angel of the LORD" (v. 11) seated on a horse among the myrtle trees. The myrtle tree is an evergreen whose foliage provides concealment for a covert operation. In contrast to Haggai's prophecy that the Lord would soon "shake" the nations (Hag 2:6–7, 20), various angelic riders who have patrolled throughout the earth report that "the whole earth is calm and quiet." By his second year, Darius I had put down several rebellions and had asserted his control over the vast Persian Empire.

This report leads the angel to intercede on behalf of Judah and Jerusalem (v. 12). The reference to the Lord being angry for seventy years recalls Jeremiah's prophecies that the exile would last for this amount of time and suggests that it is time for Judah's judgment to be over (see Jer 25:11–12; 29:10; Dan 9:1–4).[8] The angel appeals to the Lord's "mercy" (*raham*), and the Lord responds that his "mercy" (*raham*) led him to return to Jerusalem

---

[8] The number "70" is likely a round number that signifies a lengthy period of judgment in which those who go into exile will generally not live to see the return. The timing of the 70 years appears to be reckoned in slightly different ways, depending on the context. The time from when the first exiles were taken to Babylon (605 BC) to the decree of Cyrus (538 BC) was 67 years. The time in view here appears to look back 67 years to the fall of Jerusalem and the destruction of the temple in 586 BC.

(v. 16). The Lord also speaks "comforting" (*naham*) words to the angel (v. 13) and promises to "comfort" (*naham*) Zion (v. 17).

The Lord affirms his commitment to his people by declaring, "I am extremely jealous for Jerusalem and Zion" (v. 14), an emphatic construction in Hebrew in which the root word for "jealous" (*qana*) provides both the verb and the object (lit. "I am jealous with a great jealousy"). The word "jealous" is a term of strong emotion that refers both to Yahweh's demand for exclusive devotion from his people (Exod 20:5; Josh 24:19) and his desire to protect and defend them from all harm (Isa 42:13; Exod 35:5–6).[9] In contrast, the identical emphatic construction is used to reflect that the Lord is "fiercely angry" (lit. "angry with a great anger") with the nations for their treatment of Israel. While these nations were Yahweh's instruments of judgment, they had also carried out their own evil intentions against Israel and Judah (see Isa 10:5–7). The great anger of the Lord against these nations contrasts with how he was only "a little angry" with his own people, an ominous warning of the terrible judgment about to befall these peoples.

The Lord promises that the temple would be rebuilt and that Jerusalem would once again be a prosperous city (vv. 16–17). The "measuring line" was used by surveyors to mark boundary and foundation lines for buildings under construction (see Ezek 40:1–3). There is a cause-effect relationship between the people's repentance in 1:1–6 and the Lord's promise here. Because the people had "repented" (*shuv*) (1:6), the Lord promised that he would "return" (*shuv*) to Jerusalem (1:16). The Lord's fierce "anger" (*qatsaph*) against his people would now turn into a fierce "anger" (*qatsaph*) against the nations (1:15).[10]

1:18–21 "These craftsmen have come . . . to cut off the horns of the nations" (Vision 2: The Four Horns and the Four Craftsmen)

In his second vision, Zechariah sees four horns representing the nations that had scattered Israel and Judah into exile. In Scripture, animal horns are frequently used as symbols of strength and military power (see 1 Sam 2:10;

---

[9] Andrew Hill, *Haggai, Zechariah, and Malachi*, TOTC (Grand Rapids, MI: InterVarsity, 2012), 192.

[10] Mark J. Boda, *A Severe Mercy: Sin and Its Remedy in the Old Testament*, Siphrut 1 (Winona Lake, IN: Eisenbrauns, 2009), 336.

Pss 75:10; 89:17, 24; Dan 7:8; 8:8). This vision is connected to the first in that it reflects the judgment of the nations with whom the Lord is angry in 1:15. The number four here likely represents the four points of the compass and thus refers to all the imperial powers of the world that had oppressed the Lord's people.[11]

Zechariah also sees four craftsmen who apparently craft tools or weapons that enable them to break and throw down the horns that have raised themselves up over Israel.[12] The use of craftsmen suggests that these horns are made of iron, which makes them particularly durable (see 1 Kgs 22:11).[13] Persia's defeat of Babylon was a recent example of the fate awaiting all nations that were the enemies of the Lord.

2:1–13 "JERUSALEM WILL BE INHABITED WITHOUT WALLS" (VISION 3: JERUSALEM A GREAT AND PROSPEROUS CITY)

Zechariah next sees a vision of the restored city of Jerusalem. A man with a "measuring line" goes out to survey the layout and boundaries of the city, but a second man runs to inform him that "Jerusalem will be inhabited without walls." Jerusalem would have too many people and animals to fit within the confines of a walled city. Cities without walls in the ancient Near East were vulnerable to enemy attack, and when Babylon later rebelled against Persia, Xerxes ordered its walls taken down.[14] In the place of a physical wall, the Lord's protective presence would be like "a wall of fire," providing absolute security for the city and its inhabitants (v. 5). The image of a city without walls is obviously idealized language, as Nehemiah would repair the protective wall around Jerusalem in 445 BC. The image also anticipates the

---

[11] See the references in 2:6 to how the Jews have been scattered "like the four winds of heaven" and to the four chariots and four spirits in 6:1–8 that patrol the whole earth as agents of Yahweh.

[12] Robert B. Chisholm Jr., *Handbook on the Prophets* (Grand Rapids, MI: Baker, 2002), 458. Contrast the promise in Isaiah 54:6–7 that no weapon forged against Israel would succeed in bringing her down.

[13] Carol L. Myers and Eric M. Myers, *Haggai, Zechariah 1–8*, AB 25B (New York, NY: Doubleday, 1987), 139.

[14] Kenneth G. Hoglund and John H. Walton, "Zechariah," in *Zondervan Illustrated Bible Backgrounds Commentary*, Vol. 5, ed. John H. Walton (Grand Rapids, MI: Zondervan, 2009), 211.

eschatological Zion and the New Jerusalem of Revelation 21–22 where the city gates will never be closed (Rev 21:25).[15]

This vision of a vibrant and thriving Jerusalem certainly contrasts to the city in Zechariah's day, with its small and struggling population. The majority of the exiles had chosen not to return to the land, but the Lord's judgment of Israel's enemies and his return to Jerusalem would cause the Jews to flock home from their various places of exile (vv. 6–10). The call to "escape" from Babylon in verse 7 (and the reference to the shout of "joy" in v. 10) perhaps recalls Isaiah's command for the exiles to "leave" Babylon with "joy" (Isa 48:20), reflecting that the return promised by the earlier prophets has just begun. The Lord would destroy the nations that had afflicted his people, because attacking Israel was like poking a finger in God's eye (v. 9). At the same time, peoples from many nations would accompany the exiles back home and would "join themselves" to the Lord and become his "people" in fulfillment of the Abrahamic covenant (v. 11; 8:20–23; 14:16; see Gen 12:3; 22:18; 26:4).[16]

3:1–10 "I have removed your guilt from you, and I will clothe you with splendid robes" (Vision 4: The Cleansing of Joshua the High Priest)

Zechariah's fourth vision is of a heavenly court scene where Joshua the high priest stands before the angel of the Lord to face an accuser's charge of unfitness for his duties. The word "Satan" in Hebrew here and in Job 1–2 has the definite article (*hassatan*) and thus is used as a title ("the Adversary") rather than a personal name. The term *satan* refers almost exclusively to human adversaries, and in the Psalms, it refers specifically to those who slander the righteous (109:4, 20, 29).[17] Later revelation enables us to see the figure in view here as Satan, "the accuser of the brethren" (Rev 12:9–10).[18] Though Satan may have originally had a legitimate role as prosecutor in the divine

---

[15] J. Daniel Hays, *The Message of the Prophets* (Grand Rapids, MI: Zondervan, 2010), 349.

[16] The Niphal form of this verb for "join themselves" (*lavah*) is also used with reference to the Jews coming from exile to enter into covenant with the Lord in Jeremiah 50:5. See J. Goldingay and P. Scalise, *Minor Prophets II*, NIBC (Peabody, MA: Hendrickson, 2009), 215.

[17] Ibid., 222.

[18] Chisholm, *Handbook on the Prophets*, 460.

council, his hostility toward God and his people both here and in Job (see Job 1:9; 2:4–5) suggests that he no longer exercises this role in a manner that serves the Lord's purposes.

A charge of unfitness against Joshua would seem to have validity because his garments are covered with filth; but the Lord rebukes the accuser, whose words are not even recorded.[19] The way the Lord had rescued Joshua from exile as "a burning stick snatched from the fire" indicated his intention to be merciful to him and to the community at large. Yahweh graciously removed the guilt of his defilement and provided him with clean robes and a turban so Joshua might serve before him (vv. 3–5). The grace Joshua received obligated him to obey the Lord's commands if he wished to lead the people and have access to the Lord's presence (vv. 6–7).

The reinstallation of Joshua as high priest was just the beginning of the Lord's blessings for the leadership of Judah. Joshua and the present leaders of the community were a "sign" confirming that the Lord would fulfill his promise given through the prophet Jeremiah (Jer 23:5–6; 33:15–16) to raise up a "Branch," the future messianic King who would restore the line of David. The image of a "branch" conveyed how new life would emerge from what appeared to be dead (see Ps 132:17). The title "servant" is also elsewhere connected to David and the future Messiah (2 Sam 7:5, 8, 20, 26; Ezek 34:23–24). Zechariah later clarifies that the branch would build the temple, a role that is carried out by Zerubbabel, the governor and Davidic descendant (4:9–10; see Hag 1:8, 12). As in Haggai 2:20–23, it appears that Zerubbabel is the initial fulfillment of promises that are ultimately realized in Christ.

The promise concerning the stone with seven eyes that is set before Joshua in verse 9 has its setting in ancient temple-building and likely refers to the foundation stone of the temple that is inlaid with precious gems.[20] The Lord would bless the rebuilding of the temple, and he would cleanse the people of their sin so that they might worship him. The "seven eyes" seem to signify the Lord's presence at the temple and his omniscient rule over his people (see 4:10). The Lord's blessing of the present generation anticipates the eschatological restoration when Israel will live in peace and prosperity (v. 10; Mic 4:4).

---

[19] Goldingay and Scalise, *Minor Prophets II*, 219.
[20] Hoglund and Walton, "Zechariah," 213.

4:1–14 "Not by strength or by might, but by My Spirit" (Vision 5: The Golden Lampstand and the Two Olive Trees)

Zechariah's fifth vision focuses on Joshua and Zerubbabel as the leaders of the community who would carry out the work of rebuilding the temple. The prophet sees two olive trees representing Joshua and Zerubbabel that supply oil for a lamp. The olive tree appears elsewhere as a positive image for fruitful Israel or prominent leaders (Judg 9:9; Job 15:33; Hos 14:6).[21] The lampstand here is not the traditional menorah, but rather has a bowl at the top with seven lights surrounding it.[22] The lampstand in the tabernacle and temple represented a stylized tree of life, and the seven lights were daily kept burning as a reminder of Yahweh's continual presence at his place of residence among the people (Exod 25:31–40; 37:17–24).[23]

The work of Zerubbabel and Joshua in rebuilding the temple would serve to restore the Lord's presence among his people. The Lord's own Spirit would empower them for this task and would enable them to level the "great mountain" of opposition that stood in their way (vv. 6–9). As in the previous vision (3:9), the "seven eyes" refers to the Lord's sovereign oversight that would accomplish his salvific purposes (v. 10). The expression that the Lord's eyes "scan (*shot*) throughout the whole earth" is the same as the one found in 2 Chronicles 16:9, which states that the Lord examines the earth to bless and strengthen those individuals "whose hearts are completely his."[24] Joshua and Zerubbabel are representative of those who experience Yahweh's blessing because of their devotion to him.

The angelic interpretation of the vision expands on the instrumental roles of Joshua and Zerubbabel (vv. 11–14). Two "gold conduits" from these olive trees provide an abundant source of oil for the lamp. Joshua and Zerubbabel are called "anointed ones" (lit. "sons of oil"), signifying that they are consecrated by the Lord for their leadership roles.[25]

---

[21] Boda, *Haggai, Zechariah*, 274.

[22] See Hoglund and Walton, "Zechariah," 213, for an artist's rendition of this lamp.

[23] Allen P. Ross, *Recalling the Hope of Glory: Biblical Worship from the Garden to the New Covenant* (Grand Rapids, MI: Kregel, 2006), 193–94.

[24] Boda, *Haggai, Zechariah*, 274.

[25] For an alternate interpretation that views Haggai and Zechariah as the two olive trees, see Boda, *Haggai, Zechariah*, 275–76.

5:1–4 "THIS IS THE CURSE THAT IS GOING OUT OVER THE WHOLE LAND" (VISION 6: THE FLYING SCROLL)

Visions 6 and 7 are linked in that both of them focus on the need for moral and social reform in the postexilic community. The initial repentance of the people in the opening section of the book (1:1–6) was a step in the right direction, but their repentance was not yet complete. In vision 6, Zechariah sees a scroll, thirty-feet long and fifteen feet wide, flying through the air. The massive proportions of this scroll, which made it easy to see and read, and the fact that it goes through the entire land reflects its importance and applicability to all the people. This scroll is likely a Torah scroll, in that it announces a curse for violation of two of the Ten Commandments—the eighth commandment prohibiting theft (Exod 20:15) and the third commandment prohibiting "swearing falsely" by the name of Yahweh (Exod 20:7). These two commandments represent the two halves of the law and thus, likely stand for the entire Mosaic law.[26]

5:5–11 "THIS IS THEIR INIQUITY IN ALL THE LAND" (VISION 7: THE WOMAN IN THE BASKET)

In this surreal vision, Zechariah sees a woman, who personifies evil in the land, sealed in a measuring basket with a heavy lid. Two other women with stork wings then lift up the basket and fly away to the "land of Shinar" (Babylon). In Proverbs, both folly and wisdom are personified as women (see Proverbs 8; 9:1–6, 13–18), and the use of a woman to represent evil may be due to the fact that the word "Wickedness" (v. 8) is a feminine noun in Hebrew. More likely, the woman here represents the idol of a female goddess, like the Queen of Heaven (perhaps Asherah or Ishtar), whom a number of the Jews had worshipped during the exilic period (see Jer 44:15–19).[27] The word "Wickedness" (*rish`ah*) is elsewhere associated with the idolatry of pagan nations (Deut 9:4–5; Ezek 5:6–7).[28] An adult woman would not fit inside a basket meant to hold an ephah (approximately five gallons),

---

[26] Eugene H. Merrill, *Haggai, Zechariah, Malachi: An Exegetical Commentary* (Chicago, IL: Moody, 1994), 168.

[27] Boda, *Haggai, Zechariah*, 303–7; Goldingay and Scalise, *Minor Prophets II*, 235–37; and Marvin A. Sweeney, *The Twelve Prophets*, Vol. 2, Berit Olam (Collegeville, MN: Liturgical, 2000), 620–21.

[28] Boda, *Haggai, Zechariah*, 304.

though visionary elements are not always realistic. When the basket is taken away to Babylon, a shrine and pedestal are prepared for it (v. 11). The name "Shinar" for Babylon recalls the Tower of Babel and humanity in rebellion against God (Gen 11:2).

While the Jews prepare a temple for the glory of the Lord, the Babylonians prepare a site for an idol that personifies wickedness. The heavy lead cover placed over the basket and the way in which the woman is pushed down into the basket when the lid is lifted demonstrate the care taken to make sure she does not escape. The people must purge themselves of the idolatrous influences of Babylon and fully devote themselve to the Lord. The removal of the idolatrous image to Babylon may suggest a similar fate for those who worship false gods in the place of Yahweh.

6:1–8 "Go patrol the earth" (Vision 8: The Four Chariots)

This concluding vision of chariots with riders and horses of various colors closely parallels the first vision of the man among the myrtle trees, providing book ends for the night visions that powerfully assert Yahweh's universal sovereignty. These riders are envoys from the heavenly council (see 1 Kgs 22:19–23) who go out from the Lord's presence to patrol the earth. The mountains "of bronze" (v. 1) likely describe the dwelling place of the Lord, and may refer to Mount Zion and the Mount of Olives or possibly even the two massive bronze pillars that had stood at the entrance to Solomon's temple (1 Kgs 7:15–22).

The chariots convey the use of military force not present in the first vision of mounted riders going out on a reconnaissance mission. No army would be able to stand against the Lord's heavenly armies. Two of the four chariots head to the north in the direction of Babylon (see Jer 1:14–15; 6:1; 25:9) to enforce the Lord's rule. The Lord had used Cyrus as his instrument to defeat Babylon (Isa 44:28–45:4), and the recent defeat of Babylon anticipated the Lord's eschatological rule over all nations.[29] There is a progression from the nations of the earth being at rest in the first vision (1:11, 14), and God's Spirit being "pacified" (v. 8) in this final vision.

---

[29] Merrill, *Haggai, Zechariah, Malachi*, 188–90.

6:9–15 "THERE WILL BE PEACEFUL COUNSEL BETWEEN THE TWO OF THEM" (THE CROWNING OF JOSHUA AND THE PROMISE OF THE BRANCH)

This oracle built around a prophetic sign-act (see Jer 13:1–11; 18; Ezekiel 4–5) provides a fitting conclusion to Zechariah's night visions. A group of recent returnees to the land (likely priests) bring an offering from the exiles in Babylon, and a portion of this offering is used to make crowns of gold and silver. Zechariah then places a crown on Joshua the high priest and delivers a special message from the Lord.

The crowning of a high priest, who normally wears a "turban" as part of his vestments (see 3:5), is unusual, and interpreters debate the significance of Zechariah's symbolic act and message. One view is that the prophet invests Joshua with royal authority and promises that Joshua would sit upon the throne as the embodiment of the "Branch" promised to the line of David. In the absence of a Davidic king, Joshua's leadership as high priest typologically represents the coming rule of the future Davidic Messiah.[30]

More likely, Zechariah's sign act and accompanying oracle relate to both Joshua and Zerubbabel.[31] The crowning of Joshua reflects the great honor given to him as high priest, but the message concerning the "Branch" in verses 12–13 applies to Zerubbabel, explaining why there are multiple "crowns" in verse 11. The word for "crown" (`atarah) is one of three words used for royal crowns, but this particular "crown" is not exclusively associated with royalty (see Isa 28:3; Esth 8:15). The application of this oracle to both Joshua and Zerubbabel fits with the dual role given to these two leaders in Zechariah's night visions, and Joshua and the "Branch" are clearly distinguished from one another in 3:8–10. The absence of a Davidic king certainly enhanced the authority of the high priest in the postexilic community, but Zerubbabel would be the one primarily responsible for the rebuilding of the temple. The promise in verse 13 that "there will be peaceful counsel between them" reflects the shared responsibilities of the two. The promises given here concerning Joshua and Zerubbabel reflect the Lord's

---

[30] See, for example, Herbert W. Bateman, Darrell L. Bock, and Gordon H. Johnston, *Jesus the Messiah: Tracing the Promises, Expectations, and Coming of Israel's King* (Grand Rapids, MI: Kregel, 2012), 196–200.

[31] Boda, *Haggai, Zechariah*, 334–43; and Merrill, *Haggai, Zechariah, Malachi*, 193–202.

commitment to fulfill his promises to the houses of David and Levi (see Jer 33:14–28) and point forward to how both royal and priestly expectations would find fulfillment in Jesus.

7:1–8:23 (Questions Concerning Fasting and the Call for Justice)

Zechariah's messages in chapters 7 and 8 come two years after the night visions. At the halfway point in the rebuilding of the temple, the prophet strategically encourages the people to finish the job and to remain faithful to the Lord. Zechariah reminds them of their responsibility to practice justice and compassion (7:8–10; 8:16–17) and also assures them that the Lord would return to Jerusalem and fulfill all of his covenant promises concerning their restoration.

7:1–12 "Show faithful love and compassion to one another" (Fasting Secondary to Compassion)

A delegation from Bethel approaches the priests in Jerusalem for a ruling on whether certain fasting rituals associated with the fall of Jerusalem should continue now that the new temple was nearing completion.[32] The arrival of a delegation from Bethel, the site of one of the apostate sanctuaries of the northern kingdom (1 Kgs 12:28–33), signifies the prospect of Jerusalem once again becoming the place of worship for all Israel.[33] The delegation arrives sixty-eight years after the fall of Jerusalem in 518 BC. In light of Jeremiah's prophecies that the exile would last for seventy years (Jer 25:11–12; 29:10), it seems the larger question raised here regards whether the exile is truly over (see Dan 9:1–4).[34]

Fasting was an appropriate means for expressing repentance and petition for divine mercy (see Joel 2:12–13; Jonah 3:7–10), but Zechariah's response to their inquiry focuses on the motivation behind their fasting.

---

[32] The four fasts commemorated include: (1) the beginning of the siege of Jerusalem in the tenth month (2 Kings 25:1; Jeremiah 39:1); (2) the breaching of the walls of the city in the fourth month (2 Kings 25:3–7; Jeremiah 39:1–10; 52:6–11); (3) the destruction of Jerusalem in the fifth month (2 Kings 25:8–12); and (4) the assassination of Gedaliah in the seventh month (2 Kings 25:25–26; Jeremiah 41:1–3).

[33] Boda, *Haggai, Zechariah*, 355–56.

[34] Ibid., 353.

They were fasting as a ritualistic means of averting divine discipline in the place of genuine repentance. If their repentance had been real, it would have translated into obedience to the Lord and love for one's neighbor. The prophet commands the people to practice "faithful love" (*hesed*) by showing compassion and putting an end to the oppression of the poor.

Zechariah's message here is the same as that of other prophets who had warned that the Lord was displeased with ritual observances apart from a lifestyle of faithful observance of his commands (see Isa 1:10–15; Jer 7:4–8, 21–26; Amos 5:21–24; Mic 6:1–8). The connection here between fasting and social justice particularly parallels Isaiah 58:1–14, where the prophet reminds the people that the Lord desires righting wrongs, freeing the oppressed, and feeding the poor more than the supplicant's denial of food for a day. Persistent sin and mistreatment of the poor still characterized the community (see ch. 5), and Israel would not experience complete restoration and renewal until they had fully returned to the Lord.

8:1–23 "Many peoples and strong nations will come to seek the Lord of Hosts in Jerusalem" (The Promise of Future Blessing)

In chapter 8, the Lord's promise of future blessing provides motivation for the people's faithfulness. Because of his zealous love for Israel, Yahweh would return to Zion and transform it into "the Faithful City." Both young and old would dwell securely within the city. Even though it seemed humanly impossible, the Lord would bring his people back from their various places of exile.

The prophet exhorts the people to "be strong" and promises God will turn their past deprivation into blessing and abundance (vv. 9–13). They will enjoy the blessings of the land in peace as their "inheritance" from the Lord. In light of his promises to bless and restore, the Lord again commands the people to be honest, fair, and just in their dealings with each other (vv. 14–17). The Lord has guaranteed Israel's future restoration by his covenantal promises, but the enjoyment of these blessings for successive generations would be conditioned upon obedience to the Lord's commands.

When the Lord had finished his work of restoration, the fasts of mourning over their past exile would turn into festivals of celebration (vv. 18–19). Disobedience to the Lord had prevented Israel from being an instrument of blessing to the nations, as envisioned in the Abrahamic covenant (see

Jer 4:1–2; Gen 12:3; 26:4), but the return of the exiles and the rebuilding of the temple would cause the nations to travel to Jerusalem to pray and worship. Upon observing the extent of Israel's blessing, foreigners would plead with the Jews to take them to Jerusalem.

In many ways, the return from exile was a disappointment. It did not live up to the expectations associated with the promises of Israel's renewal by the earlier prophets, but Zechariah announces that there will be a final return from exile beyond the return from Babylon. The return from Babylon only partially fulfilled the promises of restoration and renewal of Israel that will be fully realized in the eschatological age. Zechariah more fully develops the details of this eschatological restoration in the next section of the book.

Zechariah 9–14 (Israel's Future Restoration and the Coming Kingdom of God)

The focus moves from the present rebuilding of Jerusalem and the temple to the final restoration of Israel and the eschatological kingdom of God. This section of the book is divided into two halves that are each introduced by the heading, "An Oracle: The word of the LORD" in 9:1 and 12:1. Chapters 9–11 promise that the Lord will save Israel and judge the nations, but also reflect that the corrupt leadership of the present and Israel's rejection of the Lord stand as obstacles to the promised restoration. Chapters 12–14 focus on the judgment of the nations and the cleansing of Israel that lead into the future kingdom of God. The seventeen occurrences of the expression "in that day" in chapters 12–14 reflect the eschatological orientation of this section.

9:1–8 "I WILL SET UP CAMP AT MY HOUSE AGAINST AN ARMY" (THE JUDGMENT OF ISRAEL'S ENEMIES)

Israel's future restoration would involve the judgment of its enemies. The historical judgments of these specific enemies of Israel (some of which had already occurred) anticipate the final judgment of all nations. Yahweh's defeat of Damascus and the other Aramean cities to the north would bring him international renown (vv. 1–2). Tyre to the northwest was known for its impressive fortifications, and the wealth from its extensive maritime trade had made gold and silver as common as dirt on the streets—but the Lord would destroy the city and its treasures (vv. 3–5).

KEY LITERARY GENRES IN ZECHARIAH		
Zechariah 1–6	Zechariah 7–8	Zechariah 9–14
Prophetic Vision Reports: The prophet receives revelation in the form of visions and then provides explanation of visual elements.	*Calls to Repentance:* The prophet calls for the people to practice justice and offers promises of future blessings of Israel as positive motivation for change.	*Prophetic Oracles of Salvation:* Promises of Israel's future salvation and portrayals of what the future kingdom will be like

The Philistines would tremble in fear at their defeat, but the Lord also promises this judgment would purge them of pagan worship practices that included the eating of blood (see Lev 17:10–14; Deut 12:16). Even more remarkable is the promise that a "remnant" from the Philistines would be devoted to the Lord and incorporated into his people. Ekron would be like the Jebusites who were conquered by David but also integrated into Israel (see 2 Sam 5:6–10; 24:16–25). Gentile participation in the worship of the Lord and inclusion in the eschatological blessings of the future kingdom is a prominent theme in Zechariah (2:11; 8:20–23; 14:16).

9:9–17 "Look, your King is coming to you" (The Coming King of Peace and God's Rule over the Nations)

Yahweh would also restore Davidic rule in Jerusalem (vv. 9–10). The future king would come in peace, riding on a donkey, rather than on a horse or in a chariot. Solomon had ridden into Jerusalem at his coronation (1 Kgs 1:33, 38, 44). The Lord's victories as divine warrior would bring an end to warfare, universal dominion for the king (see Ps 72:8), and release of the exiles. In accordance with his covenant with Israel, sealed by blood at Sinai (v. 11; see Exod 24:8), the Lord would rescue his people from the "water-less cistern" just as he had done for Joseph (Gen 37:24). He would restore "double" (*mishneh*) to them as he did for Job (Job 42:10), even though their own sins were the cause of their exile.[35]

---

[35] Merrill, *Haggai, Zechariah, Malachi*, 258, 260.

The Lord's formerly defenseless people would become powerful instruments in his hands as he executed judgment on his enemies, and the image of Judah (south) and Ephraim (north) as his bow and arrow points to the future reunification of Israel (v. 13). The promise of victory for Israel over "Greece" is another example of a specific nation being used as representative of all peoples. This is not a later interpolation into the text, and the reference to Greece is particularly appropriate in that it was the next worldwide empire on the horizon (see Daniel 8, 11). The Lord in battle is like a storm that consumes his enemies (vv. 14–15), and he promises to save and bless his people because they are as valuable to him as the "jewels in a crown" (vv. 16–17).

The initial fulfillment of this prophecy of a coming king and the establishment of Yahweh's rule over the nations occurs as Jesus presents himself as Israel's Messiah at his triumphal entry (Matt 21:1–11; Mark 11:1–11; Luke 19:28–40; John 12:12–15), but the complete and final fulfillment awaits the second coming of Jesus and the eschatological kingdom. As the Sovereign Lord, Jesus will also execute the role of divine warrior in judging and defeating his enemies (Rev 19:11–19).

10:1–11:3 "I WILL RESTORE THEM BECAUSE I HAVE COMPASSION ON THEM" (NEW LEADERSHIP AND A FULL RETURN FROM EXILE)

The theme of Israel's future blessing carries over from the preceding chapter, but this message focuses on two of the obstacles that had impeded Israel's restoration—trust in false gods and corrupt leaders who had led the people astray (vv. 2–3). In light of God's promise to provide abundant harvests (9:17), the prophet exhorts the people to ask the Lord for the rains needed for their crops. The Lord had previously disciplined the people with poor harvests because of their failure to rebuild the temple, but he now promised to bless them (see Hag 1:4, 10–11; 2:15–19). Limited rainfall and few rivers for irrigation in the Promised Land offered a continual test of Israel's faith (Deut 11:11–14), and Israel had often attributed their crops and rains to the Canaanite god Baal (see Hos 2:5–8). If the people would ask, Yahweh would provide the "spring rains" needed to produce a full harvest. These "spring rains" are also symbolic of the Lord's eschatological blessings on Israel (see Hos 6:3; Joel 2:21–25) as they turned to the Lord for guidance. Previously, Israel had also turned to idols and pagan divination that offered nothing more than "falsehood" and "empty comfort."

The people wandered as lost sheep in their spiritual and moral confusion because of their poor leaders. The first half of Zechariah focuses on the positive leadership of Joshua and Zerubbabel, but the second half of this book focuses on how the Lord would judge the corrupt "shepherds" who were leading the people in all the wrong ways. Kings were commonly portrayed as shepherds throughout the ancient Near East (see 2 Sam 5:2; Ps 78:71–72), and "shepherd" was a term for both civil and spiritual leaders in ancient Israel (Jer 3:15; 10:21; 23:1–4; Ezek 34:1–10). As shepherds, these leaders were responsible to protect the people and ultimately to exemplify Yahweh's care for his people (Ps 23:1–11; Isa 40:11), but they often cared only for themselves. A wordplay in verse 3 conveys how the Lord would "punish (*paqad `al*) the leaders" and then "care for (*paqad*) his flock." The verb *paqad* means "visit, attend to" in both positive and negative ways.

With the Lord as their shepherd, the people of Israel would become a powerful nation, like a warhorse in battle (vv. 3–5). A variety of images also portray the strength and stability of the leadership that the Lord would provide for Israel. Their leaders would be like the cornerstone of a building, a peg used to hang heavy items on a wall (see Isa 22:23–25; or possibly a "tent peg"), and a bow in the hand of a warrior. These terms are not exclusively messianic, but the future Messiah would be the perfect embodiment of what they represent. The "cornerstone" image is applied to Jesus in the New Testament (see Matt 21:42; Acts 4:11; Eph 2:20; 1 Pet 2:6–7). With Yahweh as the leader of its armies, Israel would trample its enemies underfoot.

The Lord's promise to "strengthen" his people frames the salvation oracle in verses 6–12. A chiasm at the beginning of this section also stresses the reunification of Israel as one people:

A	I will strengthen	
	B	the house of Judah
	B'	the house of Israel
A'	(I will) deliver[36]	

The ten tribes of the North lost their identity when they assimilated with other peoples in the Assyrian captivity, but God's promise stresses that the restoration would include all of Israel that remained—Israel would again

---

[36] Goldingay and Scalise, *Minor Prophets II*, 284.

be one people. The promise to bring the exiles back from Egypt and Assyria (vv. 10–11) when Assyria was no longer even a power likely reflects the prophet's intent to connect the Lord's promise to save with earlier prophecies of return from exile (see Hos 11:11; Mic 7:12). Yahweh's saving work of restoring his people had just begun, and this deliverance would be like a second exodus (v. 11). The forest fire that consumes the "cedars of Lebanon" and the "oaks of Bashan" offers a powerful visual of the judgment awaiting the enemy nations that had enslaved Israel (11:1–3).

11:4–17 "SO THEY WEIGHED MY WAGES, 30 PIECES OF SILVER" (THE REJECTION OF THE SHEPHERD)

In light of the hopeful messages concerning Israel's future that have preceded, the negative tone of the message that concludes this unit of material in the book is rather surprising. This chapter, however, focuses on the judgment of the worthless shepherds mentioned in 10:2–3 and of the people for following them. Judgment will fall on the community because the people would rather follow leaders who seek to abuse and take advantage of them, than the Lord, who desires to bless them.

This passage possibly recounts a parable or vision given to the prophet, or, more likely, a sign act performed over an extended time before the people for dramatic effect (see 6:9–15). The details of this drama are complex and likely included extended narration by the prophet explaining its significance. Because of the corruption of Judah's leaders, the Lord appoints the prophet to shepherd the people. The prophet's leadership offers a positive alternative to the exploitive shepherds that have come before him, but this sign act would ultimately convey that the Lord would no longer have compassion on his people. He would turn them over to their enemies once again (v. 6).

The message begins hopefully with the prophet displaying two staffs named "Favor" and "Union," reflecting Yahweh's desire to bless the people and reverse the judgments of the past. In a month's time, the prophet even rids the community of three of its worthless leaders. Despite these positive developments, the people "detested" the prophet's leadership and rebelled against him (v. 8). In response, the prophet announced he would no longer shepherd the people. He cut off the staff of "Favor" to show that the people had forfeited the Lord's blessing. Though the people had initially responded favorably to the calls of Haggai and Zechariah to rebuild the temple, they had not been willing to follow other directives from the prophets. As the ultimate expression of their disrespect, the people respond to the prophet's request for payment for his services as their shepherd by giving him thirty pieces of silver, the price of a slave at an earlier time in Israel's history (Exod 21:32). Thus, the fee represented "an insultingly low wage."[37] In response, the prophet throws the silver to the potter at the temple and cuts in two the second staff named "Union." By rejecting the divinely appointed leader, the people have rejected Yahweh.

The sign act concludes as the prophet takes up "the equipment of a foolish shepherd" and then acts the part of the worthless leader the Lord would appoint in the place of the prophet (vv. 15–16). This "equipment" might have included the broken staffs mentioned previously or even implements used in the butchering of sheep.[38] The Lord would punish the people by giving them exactly what they requested—a worthless shepherd who would devour and tear them apart. After punishing the people, the Lord's judgment would then fall on this wicked leader (v. 17).

Zechariah 11:13–14 is one of several passages from Zechariah 9–14 (9:9–10; 12:10; 13:7–9) that are read as messianic texts in the New Testament. Even though 9:9–10 is likely the only one of these passages that is a direct messianic prophecy in its original context, these readings are natural in light of the focus on the eschatological kingdom in Zechariah 9–14. This is typology, where a pattern initiated in the Old Testament is continued and even heightened in some way when applied to Christ in the New Testament. The rejection of the prophet symbolized by paying him thirty pieces of silver anticipates Judas' betrayal of Jesus for the same price (Matt 26:15; 27:3, 9), and the actions of Judas are representative of Israel's national rejection of Jesus as Messiah. This pattern of Israel rejecting the leaders, prophets, and deliverers the Lord raised up for them could be traced through the entire Old Testament.

12:1–9 "I will make Jerusalem a cup that causes staggering" (The Assault on Jerusalem and the Deliverance of the City)

The oracles in chapter 12 promise a reversal of the preceding message of judgment. Rather than giving Israel over to neighboring peoples that would devastate the land (11:6), Yahweh promises the defeat of the nations that

---

[37] Hoglund and Walton, "Zechariah," 223.
[38] Goldingay and Scalise, *Minor Prophets II*, 293.

| THE MESSAGE OF ZECHARIAH 9–14 ||
An Oracle: The Word of the Lord (9–11)	An Oracle: The Word of the Lord (12–14)
THE PROMISE: Coming of Israel's king and judgment of the nations (9:1–11:3) *TWO OBSTACLES TO THE PROMISE:* Israel's corrupt leaders (10:2–3) and Israel's rejection of the Lord (11:4–17)	A "Look" (*hinneh*)—assault on Jerusalem by the nations (12:2–9) B Renewal of Israel: mourning over past sin (12:10–14) B' Cleansing of Israel: cleansing fountain and purging judgment (13:1–9) A' "Look" (*hinneh*)—assault on Jerusalem by the nations (14:1–21)

assault Jerusalem (12:1–9). Rather than Israel continuing to reject the Lord's leadership (11:8), the people will turn to the Lord, mourning over their past rebellion against him (12:10–14). The chapter opens with a confession concerning Yahweh as Creator to remind the people of his power to fulfill his promises and to accomplish his purposes. The Lord would deliver Jerusalem from its enemies, and a series of vivid images portrays the complete and total destruction that will come upon the nations that assault Jerusalem in the last days. Jerusalem would become like a cup of strong wine, causing the nations to stagger like drunkards under God's severe judgment (see Jer 25:15–16; Ezek 23:31–34; Hab 2:16) and a "heavy stone" that brings injury to all who try to move it. The Lord would also transform Judah into a powerful army, and her warriors would destroy their enemies like fire consuming sticks and sheaves. Even the weakest of her warriors would become as mighty as David, and David's house would become like God and the angel of the Lord, who had led Israel through the wilderness to the Promised Land (see Exod 33:2), in its ability to wage war.

12:10–14 "I WILL POUR OUT A SPIRIT OF GRACE AND PRAYER" (THE LORD'S PROMISE TO BRING HIS PEOPLE TO REPENTANCE)

More than deliverance from her enemies, Israel needed a spiritual transformation to break the endless cycle of sin and judgment that had characterized her history. Yahweh would act in grace to enable his people to respond to him as

KEY MESSIANIC TEXTS IN ZECHARIAH 9–14		
OT TEXT	NT TEXT	TYPE OF FULFILLMENT
ZECHARIAH 9:9–10	MATTHEW 21:5 JOHN 12:15	**Direct Prophecy:** 9:9: at first coming of Jesus 9:10: at second coming of Jesus
ZECHARIAH 11:12–13	MATTHEW 27:9–10	**Typology:** Rejection of prophet (paid thirty pieces of silver) Rejection of Jesus (betrayed for thirty pieces of silver)
ZECHARIAH 12:10	JOHN 19:34, 37	**Typology:** Yahweh pierced: Israel rejects the Lord and his prophet Jesus pierced: Israel rejects the Lord and pierces Messiah
ZECHARIAH 13:7	MATTHEW 26:31 MARK 14:27	**Typology:** Worthless shepherd judged/ people scattered in judgment Jesus put to death/ the disciples scattered in fear

they should. Paralleling the promise of Joel 2:28, that he would "pour out" his Spirit on his people, the Lord announces here that he would "pour out a spirit of grace and prayer" (see Ezek 36:25–26). The giving of the Spirit would enable Israel to "mourn" over their past rejection of the Lord. Some form of the verbs "to mourn" (*saphad*) and "to grieve" (*marar*) appear five times in these verses, and this mourning is like the intense grief at the death of an only child or a firstborn son. Another indicator of the intensity of this grief is that it would be "as great as the mourning of Hadad-rimmon in the plain of Megiddo" (v. 11), possibly a reference to the time of national mourning that followed the death of King Josiah when he was killed in battle against the Egyptians at Megiddo

The Lord promises to come down to the Mount of Olives to defend Jerusalem against enemy assault in the last days: "His feet will stand on the Mount of Olives, which faces Jerusalem on the east. The Mount of Olives will be split in half from east to west, forming a huge valley, so that half the mountain will move to the north and half to the south." Zechariah 14:4

in 609 BC (2 Kgs 23:29–30; 2 Chr 35:20–25).[39] This mourning would include all of Israel's families and clans, even the houses of David and Levi (vv. 12–14).

The most difficult interpretive questions in this section centered around the statements "they will look at Me whom they have pierced," and "They will mourn for Him as one mourns for an only child" in verse 10. What does it mean that the people have "pierced" Yahweh, and why do we have a change in pronoun from "Me" to "Him" in these two statements? The verb "to pierce" (*daqar*) appears eleven times in the Hebrew Bible and means "to stab" with a weapon like a sword and often involves a fatal wounding (see Num 25:8; Judg 9:54; 1 Sam 31:4; 1 Chr 10:4; Isa 13:15; Jer 37:10; 51:4). In Zechariah 13:3, it refers to the execution of a false prophet.

Yahweh is clearly speaking in verse 10 and is the One who receives this fatal stabbing that leads to national mourning. The change of pronouns from "Me" to "Him" does not suggest two different figures are being pierced but merely is a dramatic way of emphasizing Yahweh as the One who is

---

[39] Hadad and Rimmon are the names of West Semitic storm gods, like the Canaanite Baal, and some have proposed a reference here to the mourning rituals associated with the dying and rising of these gods. Even if only used as an example of intense mourning, it seems somewhat unlikely for the prophet to highlight a pagan ritual unless ironically highlighting Israel's turning to the Lord.

pierced.[40] The people's piercing of the Lord could refer metaphorically to how deeply the people's rejection has hurt him. Merrill suggests that the prophet is charging the people to "have wounded His holiness and violated His righteousness."[41] Contextually, it seems likely that the "piercing" of the Lord is related to the people's rejection of the prophet as their shepherd in 11:8 and the prophets and priests as a whole throughout their history (1:4; 7:11–12), some of whom were even put to death (see 2 Chr 24:20–21; Jer 26:20–24).[42] In Isaiah 52:13–53:12, the Servant of the Lord who represents "the arm of the LORD" dies for the sins of the nation as a whole, though the idea of vicarious suffering found there is not present in this text.

As in 11:11–13, we do not have here a direct prophecy that refers exclusively to Jesus as Messiah, but we have a typological pattern in which the "piercing" of Jesus becomes the ultimate example of Israel's rejection of Yahweh. John 19:10–34 refers to the piercing of Jesus's side by the Roman solider as a "fulfillment" of Zechariah 12:10, and the irony of this fulfillment is that the crucifixion of Jesus was, in fact, a literal "piercing" of the Lord. The references to the "house of David" in this context would also help to suggest a later messianic reading of this text.

13:1–9 "ON THAT DAY A FOUNTAIN WILL BE OPENED . . ." (THE CLEANSING FOUNTAIN AND THE PURGING JUDGMENT)

Israel's repentance would lead the Lord to provide a cleansing fountain that would wash away its sin and defilement. Washing rituals associated with the removal of ceremonial impurity picture the reality of divine forgiveness (see Num 19:11–12; Ps 51:2, 7; Ezek 36:25). The Lord's actions here are all of grace because he would be the One to prompt their repentance in the first place. This cleansing would be national in scope and would include the house of David for its contribution to Israel's apostasy.

---

[40] Merrill (*Haggai, Zechariah, Malachi*, 320) explains, "From YHWH's viewpoint it is 'Me' that is in focus; from the standpoint of the people it is 'Him.'" These types of pronoun changes are quite common in Biblical Hebrew. In the place of "They will look at **me** whom they have pierced," some Hebrew manuscripts read "they will look at **him** whom they have pierced," or "they will look to the **one** they have pierced," but these scribal changes likely arose as a result of the problematic notion of the piercing of Yahweh.

[41] Ibid., 320–21.

[42] Hill, *Haggai, Zechariah, and Malachi*, 246–47.

The Lord would particularly expunge two sins from his people: idolatry and false prophecy (vv. 2–6). The people would become so zealous against false prophecy that even the parents of a false prophet would have him put to death in accordance with Deuteronomy 13:6–9. Those guilty of false prophecy in the past would give up their deception, refusing to wear the garments of a prophet (2 Kgs 1:8). They would take up other occupations. They would be ashamed of the wounds they had likely inflicted upon themselves as part of pagan cutting rituals associated with seeking the favor of the gods (see 1 Kgs 18:28).

The Lord would graciously cleanse and forgive the repentant, but Israel's purification would also include a severe purging judgment (vv. 7–9). The sword of judgment would fall on the worthless "shepherd" that the Lord appointed when the people rejected the prophet as their shepherd (see 11:8–9, 15–16). This figure is referred to as Yahweh's "shepherd" and his "associate," not because of his exemplary character, but rather because Israel's leaders served as the Yahweh's representatives and received their authority from him. The removal of this leader would cause the people to be scattered as well, and two-thirds of them would be killed. The Lord's judgment would be like a purging fire, and the remnant that remained would be the recipients of the blessings of salvation.

Typology again explains how this passage concerning the judgment of a wicked leader is applied to Jesus in the New Testament (Matt 26:31; Mark 14:27). The striking of the shepherd would again lead to a scattering of the sheep as the disciples abandoned Jesus and fled from him in fear. In contrast to the worthless shepherd, Jesus would fulfill the role of the Good Shepherd, being willing even to lay down his life for the sheep so he might save them from their sins (see John 10:11–18; Heb 13:20–21).

14:1–21 "Yahweh will become king over all the earth" (The Lord's Final Victory and the Worship of the Nations)

This final chapter offers another vision of the nations' eschatological assault on Jerusalem. This "Day of the Lord" would involve divine discipline against Jerusalem, the defeat of the nations, the submission of the nations to Yahweh's sovereignty, and the purification of Jerusalem. Zechariah 12:1–9 has already portrayed a future assault on Jerusalem but without the details found here. These two visions are describing the same event and should be viewed as complementary rather than contradictory. These types of proto-apocalyptic or prophetic-apocalyptic texts that focus on the end of history employ highly figurative and symbolic imagery and often do not line up in exact detail when compared. Zechariah 14 provides the more expanded vision of the eschatological battle and also incorporates the motif of the Lord's purging judgment against his people found in 13:7–9.

The Lord would first use the nations attacking Jerusalem to bring judgment against his own people. Enemy armies would capture and loot the city, rape women, and take half of the city into exile (vv. 1–2). It would be like the Babylonian exile all over again, but then Yahweh would come down to the Mount of Olives with his heavenly hosts to deliver his people (vv. 3–5). The Lord's arrival at this mountain facing Jerusalem "on the east" perhaps suggests a reversal of his abandonment of Jerusalem in the book of Ezekiel at the time of the Babylonian exile (Ezek 11:23; 43:1–5).[43] The Lord now returns in the direction from which he once left in order to defend and deliver the city. As in other theophany texts, Yahweh's arrival is accompanied by an earthquake and the disturbance of nature (see Exod 19:18; Mic 1:3–5; Hab 3:3–10). The severity of the earthquake is compared to the one that occurred during the reign of Uzziah in the eighth century BC (see Amos 1:1–2), and the splitting of the Mount of Olives would provide the remnant of Jerusalem with a valley of escape from enemies.

The Lord's defeat of the enemy nations will usher in the eschatological kingdom and the transformation of the cosmos (vv. 6–11). The prophet employs images that stretch the human imagination to conceive of a world order that is completely different from the realities of the present. The old creation, characterized by the continuous cycle of day and night (Jer 33:25–26), would be replaced by a timeless day. In a land of minimal rainfall where Jerusalem itself was fed by a small spring, the Lord would cause an abundance of fresh water to flow out of Jerusalem eastward to the Mediterranean Sea and westward to the Dead Sea (see Ezek 47:1–12; Joel 3:18). The images of "light" and "living water" also suggest the blessing of God's presence. The Lord himself, rather than the sun and moon, would be the source of light (Isa 60:1–3; Rev 21:25; 22:5). Rivers of water are associated with the presence of God at the temple and in the garden of Eden

---

[43] Boda, *Haggai, Zechariah*, 523.

(Ps 46:4; Gen 2:10–14).[44] Yahweh "will become King over all the earth," and all will acknowledge and submit to his authority.

All of Judah to the north and south of Jerusalem would be made into a level plain, facilitating pilgrimage to the city, and Jerusalem would be elevated to reflect its prominence as the seat of Yahweh's rule over the earth (see Isa 2:1–4; Mic 4:1–4). Those living in Jerusalem would live in the security of the Lord's protection and never again have to face a curse of complete destruction. This phrase translates the Hebrew word *herem*, used for the Lord's command to destroy the Canaanites when Israel entered the land under Joshua (see Deut 7:1–2; 20:16–18; Josh 6:17–18).[45] This type of judgment would never need to occur again because the land would be purged of idolatry and wickedness.

The oracle returns to one final depiction of the Lord's defeat of the enemy nations that would assault Jerusalem in the last days (vv. 12–15). The Lord would send a deadly disease that would consume the troops that attacked Jerusalem and would throw these armies into confusion so they would fight against each other. As at other times in Israel's past, Yahweh supernaturally destroys the enemy while allowing the armies of Israel to fight what amounts to a mop-up operation (see Joshua 6; 10:10–13; Judg 4:15; 5:4–5; 7:15–25; 2 Chr 20:13–30). The promise here of the wealth of the nations coming to Jerusalem confirms Haggai's earlier prophecy that the "glory" of the second temple would surpass that of the first (Hag 2:7–9).

Following this devastating judgment, the survivors of the nations would then come to Jerusalem to worship Yahweh (vv. 16–21; see 2:11; 8:20–23; 9:7). The Feast of Booths (or Tabernacles) was one of Israel's three major pilgrimages but would now be for all peoples. It is likely highlighted here because it was a time of great joy and celebration of the harvest (Deut 16:13–15). The covenant curse of drought the Lord had brought against Israel (Lev 26:18–20; Deut 28:23–24; Amos 4:7–8) would now fall on the nations that refused to come up to worship him. The presence of the Lord and his glory would cover the city to the extent that even common objects like the bells on horses and cooking pots would be as holy as items used at the altar. The promise that Canaanites would no longer be present at the temple should

---

[44] For the association of water with sacred space and the dwelling places of the gods in the ancient Near East, see Hoglund and Walton, "Zechariah," 226, n. 92.

[45] Boda, *Haggai, Zechariah*, 527.

be understood in religious rather than ethnic terms. The temple would no longer be defiled by the worship of false gods like Baal, but Jeremiah had promised that even Canaanites who turned to Yahweh would experience the blessings of salvation (Jer 12:14–17). Israel and the nations would give their allegiance and worship to the Lord alone.

Theological Message and Application of Zechariah

Zechariah highlights repentance as the response the Lord desires from his sinful people. The introduction to the book recounts how the people "repented" in response to Zechariah's preaching (1:1–6), but this initial repentance was just the beginning. Sin and disregard for God's commands still characterized the community (5:1–4), so there was a need for a deeper and fuller repentance. The people must reflect compassion and justice in their dealings with each other (8:14–17) and must turn from idols to give their full devotion to the Lord (10:1–2; 13:3–6). For those who did not repent, the only alternative was purging judgment (5:4–11; 13:7–9).

The motivation for repentance was the Lord's gracious willingness to forgive and restore his people. When the people "repent" (*shuv*), the Lord assures that he has "returned" (*shuv*) to Jerusalem (1:3, 16). The return from exile was proof that Yahweh was no longer angry with his people (1:2, 12, 15; 7:12). The Lord provided clean garments for Joshua and removed his guilt so he might serve as priest (3:4–5); he promised he would "take away the guilt of this land in a single day" as well (3:9). The ultimate expression of mercy was that the Lord would pour out his grace to enable the repentance he desired from his people (12:10–12) and would then provide a fountain of cleansing to remove their guilt and defilement (13:1–2).

Zechariah also affirms the Lord's abiding commitment to his promises to restore Jerusalem. The return from exile had not lived up to the promises of the earlier prophets, but Zechariah clarifies that the present rebuilding of Jerusalem and the temple is merely the prelude to the final restoration and renewal of Israel to occur in the last days. The oracles in Zechariah 9–14 reveal that the pattern of sin-judgment-exile-deliverance would occur again on an even larger scale in the last days. Israel's restoration occurs in stages, beginning with the return from exile, continuing with the first coming of Jesus as inauguration of the kingdom era, and culminating with the second coming of Jesus and the consummation of God's kingdom promises.

The working out of redemptive history in these stages reflects the interplay between divine initiative and human response. The Lord will sovereignly fulfill his purposes to save Israel and to rule over the earth, but when and how these events occur depend in large part on how Israel would respond to his saving initiatives. The Lord delivered the people of Israel from their bondage in Babylon, but the full blessings of salvation and restoration would occur when they fully obeyed the Lord (6:15).

Jesus announced at his first coming that the "kingdom of God" was at hand (Mark 1:15) and that his death would initiate the new covenant promised by Jeremiah (Jer 31:31–34; Luke 22:20). Israel's rejection of Jesus as Messiah, however, necessitated further judgment. Richard Bauckham notes that Jesus's announcement of the impending destruction of Jerusalem (Matt 24:2; Luke 19:42–44; 21:20–24) portrays this event in "scriptural language that strongly suggests that it constitutes a second exile or second stage of the exile of Israel, comparable with the fall of Jerusalem to the Babylonians."[46] The blessings of the eschatological kingdom and new covenant were only for those who believed in Jesus. The death and resurrection of Jesus had given the gift of repentance to Israel (Acts 5:31), but Peter still exhorted the people to "repent and turn back" in order to experience divine forgiveness and the "seasons of refreshing" (Acts 3:19–22). Human unbelief continued to delay the eschatological blessings God had promised to Israel.

The final restoration and renewal of Israel will occur in the last days in connection with the events surrounding the Second Coming. Even then, purging judgment and another experience of exile will precede this final deliverance (Zech 13:7–9; 14:1–2). The Lord would ultimately save his people by acting in sovereign grace to change their hearts—they would mourn over their rejection of him that had culminated in the crucifixion of their Messiah (Zech 12:10). This promise and others of God's covenant faithfulness to Israel enable Paul to confidently assert that the future salvation of the people of Israel would occur in the last days (Rom 11:26–28).

Zechariah had promised the nations would share in the blessings of Israel's salvation and would come to Jerusalem to worship the Lord in the eschatological kingdom (Zech 2:11; 8:20–23; 14:16–19). In Romans 9–11, Paul introduces a twist into the story by stating that it was actually the

---

[46] Richard Bauckham, *The Jewish World Around the New Testament* (Grand Rapids, MI: Baker, 2008), 369.

salvation of the Gentiles and their grafting in to God's people that would bring about the salvation of Israel. Both Jew and Gentile in Christ today enjoy the spiritual blessings of the eschatological era as the people of God.

Leadership is also an important theme in the book of Zechariah, and the Lord uses godly leaders to accomplish his purposes. The preaching of Zechariah led the people to return to the Lord (1:1–6), and the Lord empowers Joshua and Zerubbabel by his Spirit to accomplish the rebuilding of the temple (4:1–14). The contemporary leadership of Joshua and Zerubbabel provided confirmation that the Lord would keep his promise to send the messianic "Branch" (3:8–10; 6:9–15), and the dual roles of priest and king would be fulfilled in the person of Jesus. The Lord would keep his covenant with David by sending a humble leader who would rule over the people in peace (9:9–10), and Israel's future leaders would bring strength and stability to the land (10:4–6). These leaders would be the exact opposite of the corrupt "shepherds" of the present who exploited the people under their care (10:2–3; 11:4–7).

16

THE BOOK OF MALACHI

Introduction

Malachi may speak to the modern reader with greater relevance than any of the other Minor Prophets. Although Malachi reflects an ancient setting, it is easy for the modern reader to identify with the issues of the book. As the prophet mediates between Yahweh and his people, the reader is invited to listen in to a series of hypothetical conversations. One quickly discovers that their conversations with God are not unlike our own; their apathy is like our apathy, their excuses are like our excuses. Yes, there is an emphasis on ancient interests in the book—covenant, the priesthood, and the Mosaic law—yet the principles within Malachi are readily applicable to the modern world.

Relevant content permeates the book. Malachi affirms the love of God for his elect; therefore, the elect are called to love God (1:2–5). He reminds the priests to offer their sacrifices with discernment (1:8–10), knowing that God discerns between the righteous and the wicked (3:18). Later, the prophet calls upon the men of Judah to "watch" their ways (2:16), knowing that God is watching as well (2:14). He exhorts the people to return to God and, with that, God will return to them. After all, in his faithfulness God did not leave them, but rather they left him (3:6–7). The prophet rebukes the people for robbing God of what belongs to him (3:8–9). In turn, God rebukes the curse that plagued their economic prosperity (3:11). Finally, in the later stages of the book, the reader is called to remember the instruction of Moses (4:3), knowing that God remembers the righteous (3:16), and will by no means forget the wicked on the day of judgment (3:5; 4:3). Indeed, the hypothetical conversations mediated by the fifth-century prophet are not unlike those of today.

Malachi is the last book of the Old Testament in canonical order; it is also among the latest books in chronological order. Although the book makes no explicit reference to a Persian setting, the reference to a governor (1:8) suggests a postexilic context. The issues highlighted in the book parallel issues found in Ezra and Nehemiah. These include Judean men divorcing their first wives to marry foreign women (Mal 2:10–16; see Ezra 9–10; Neh 13:23–27), negligence in tithing (Mal 3:8–12; see Neh 13:10–14), and the offering of gifts to the governor (Mal 1:8; see Neh 5:14–18). Finally, reference to the "covenant of the priesthood and the Levites" in Nehemiah 13:29 corresponds to the same covenant in Malachi 2:5–8. Therefore, Malachi can safely be placed in the same context as Ezra and Nehemiah, namely, in the mid to late fifth century BC.

Structure

Malachi follows a structure of disputation speech units, with each unit characterized by hypothetical dialogue between God and the people. There is no set formula among the units, although each includes an assertion by God and an objection by the people. Within these hypothetical dialogues, rhetorical question is frequently used as a strategy to heighten the effect of both assertion and objection. Additionally, the dialogues are often accompanied by oracles that function as an implied response to the people's objections.

There are seven disputation speech units within Malachi,[1] followed by a final prophetic exhortation that concludes the book (4:4–6).[2] Each unit has its own unique structural pattern, and not all contain a corresponding oracle or vision.

Seven Disputation Speeches	
Disputation One	God's Love for His Elect Nation (1:2–5)
Disputation Two	God is Worthy of Honor in Sacrifice (1:6–2:9)
Disputation Three	God Hates Covenant Unfaithfulness (2:10–16)
Disputation Four	God's Justice Vindicated (2:17–3:5)
Disputation Five	God's Faithfulness Affirmed (3:6–7)
Disputation Six	God Blesses the Faithful Giver (3:8–12)
Disputation Seven	God Remembers the Righteous (3:13–4:3)

Exposition

1:1 (Introduction)

The introduction to Malachi provides little by way of historical context, and even the identity of the author is ambiguous. There are no parallel accounts to a prophet named "Malachi," literally translated "my messenger." While it is possible that Malachi is simply a title rather than a proper name, anonymous authorship would be unique among the writing prophets. In keeping with introductions to the other books of the Twelve, it is most likely that the message of the book was mediated through a historical prophet named Malachi.[3]

---

[1] Most commentators see six disputation units within Malachi. The point of departure in this treatment involves the recognition of an independent unit in 3:6–7.

[2] The Masoretic text has three chapters, with Malachi 4:1–6 listed in Hebrew Bibles as 3:19–24.

[3] The introductions to the oracles beginning at Zechariah 9:1 and 12:1 each demonstrate similarity to Malachi 1:1, resulting in speculation that Malachi is an appendage to Zechariah. However, the similarity does not negate the unique existence of Malachi the prophet or the unique position of Malachi the book. Similarity in catchwords may, however, point to editorial ordering in the Book of the Twelve. See Douglas Stuart, "Malachi," in *The Minor Prophets: An Exegetical & Expositional Commentary*, ed. Thomas Edward McComiskey (Grand Rapids, MI: Baker, 1998), 1277–79.

1:2–5 "How have You loved us?" (First Disputation: God's Love for His Elect Nation)

The first disputation speech begins with a hypothetical dialogue followed by a prophetic oracle proclaiming Edom's destruction. The dialogue begins with a bold, propositional assertion by Yahweh: "I have loved you" (1:2a). In response, the people counter with a defiant question: "How have You loved us?" (1:2b). Yahweh then responds with his own question: "Wasn't Esau Jacob's brother?" (1:2c). Yahweh's response continues with a second bold assertion: "Yet I have loved Jacob but Esau I have hated" (ESV, 1:2d–3a). In all, the opening dialogue is highly structured, involving three related chiasms.

The subject of the opening unit provides a glimpse into the situational context of Malachi's day. The people, disappointed in their apparent lack of prosperity, were questioning God's love for them. Having been liberated by the Persians from exile, the people were now living under the thumb of Persian domination, and the meager sense of autonomy experienced in the fifth century BC was certainly not the kingdom promised by earlier prophets. By dwelling on their circumstances, the people questioned the benevolence of God's intentions. God's response was to redirect their attention away from outward circumstances and toward their elect position.

Chiastic Structure in Malachi 1:2–3a

A "I have loved you"
    B Says the Lord
    B' but you ask
A' "How have You loved us?"

A I loved
    B Jacob
    B' Esau
A' I hated

Assertion (1:2a)
    Question (1:2b)
    Question (1:2c)
Assertion (1:2d–3a)

Based in God's choice of Jacob over Esau (Genesis 25:19–26), Israel was bound by a covenant love not experienced by any other nation on earth. If God did not love his elect, he would have destroyed them in judgment, without a remnant or a hope to return to the land. As God's elect people (see Romans 9–11), Israel enjoyed a privileged position; they should never have questioned God's love for them.

The love relationship pictured in Malachi 1:2–3a is not a matter of God loving Jacob more and Esau less. This love was a matter of choice, a matter of election to a privileged covenant position.[4] God's choice of Jacob over Esau demonstrated his love in a manner far more profound than temporal circumstances could ever reveal. The fact that even a portion of the people were back in the land was clear evidence of Yahweh's covenant love for his elect nation!

As a reminder, the prophet paints a picture of Edom's destruction, a foil to the divine election of Israel. While Israel received grace for her sins, Edom received only judgment. And while Israel would receive covenant restoration, Edom's inheritance would be cut off forever (1:3b–4). Clearly, the problem was not that God did not love Israel, but that Israel did not love God.

1:6–2:9 "How have we despised Your name?" (Second Disputation: God is Worthy of Honor in Sacrifice)

The second disputation unit involves the subject of a corrupt priesthood that despised the Lord by offering unclean sacrifices. Essentially, a spirit of apathy and compromise had permeated the ethos of the postexilic community; and the priestly order had come to consider the ceremonial aspects of the Mosaic law a burdensome nuisance (1:13). They profaned the Lord's sanctuary by offering lame and diseased animals in direct violation of the

---

[4] In the context of God's covenantal election, "hate" should be equated with "not chosen." The distinction between Jacob and Esau is not a matter of degrees of affection. Even so, divine choice does lead to relationship and emotive language, both positive and negative. Noting the undertone of imprecation used against Edom by the prophets, one should not be too quick to dismiss the clear statement of indignation in the oracle (1:3b–4). See Andrew E. Hill, *Malachi*, AB (New Haven, CT: Yale University Press, 1998), 165–68.

law (Lev 22:17–25; Deut 15:21). Apathy had led to inattention, and this, in turn, was manifested by ceremonial rebellion.

The second disputation unit is the lengthiest in Malachi, broadly divided into two segments: 1:6–14 and 2:1–9. The first segment involves the disputation proper; the second involves a prophetic warning to the priests.

1:6–14 "I am not pleased with you . . ." (Hypothetical Dialogue between the Priests and Yahweh)

Like the first unit, the second disputation opens with an assertion. In the second unit, however, the assertion is made through self-evident analogy. As one would expect, "a son honors his father and a servant his master" (1:6a). As implied through the twofold rhetorical question, the priests had nonetheless failed to pay respect to their heavenly Father: "But if I am a father, where is My honor? And if I am a master, where is your fear of Me" (1:6b)?

In hypothetical dialogue, the priests respond with defiance: "How have we despised Your name" (1:6d)? Continuing the dialogue, the Lord responds, "By presenting defiled food on My altar" (1:7a). Doubling down, the priests again ask, "How have we defiled You" (1:7b)? The Lord responds in turn, "When you say: 'The LORD's table is contemptible'" (1:7c).

Following the initial dialogue, the evidence against the priests is mounted through a series of arguments characterized by rhetorical question (1:8–9, 13), sarcasm (1:8–10), and continued verbal injection (1:13). The priests were offering the lame and the sick, demonstrating their attitude of contempt not only for their office, but even for Yahweh. In language reminiscent of Amos 5:21–23, Yahweh pronounces his disfavor over corrupt ritualism. Indeed, it would be better to simply shut the temple doors than to continue offering an unacceptable sacrifice before the Lord of Hosts (1:10)!

Of special note in this unit are the two proclamations affirming the greatness of Yahweh (1:11, 14). This motif carries throughout Malachi, and it is represented in the favored divine title of the book, *Yahweh Tseva'ot* (Lord of Hosts). In judgment, Yahweh is magnified "even beyond the borders of Israel" (1:5). Should not the priests, those within the borders of Israel, have feared his name? Apparently, they stood in greater fear of their Persian governor than the Lord of Hosts—a truly absurd proposition (1:8)![5]

---

[5] Chisholm, *Interpreting the Minor Prophets* (Grand Rapids, MI: Zondervan, 1990), 281.

2:1–9 "For the lips of a priest should guard knowledge" (Prophetic Warning to the Priests)

As a complement to the second disputation unit, Malachi 2:1–9 continues the theme of indictment against a corrupt priesthood, but now through a formal prophetic warning.[6] Unless the priests "take it to heart," the blessings of the Lord would be turned to curse, and the economic woes of the day would become increasingly pronounced (2:1–2).[7] The warning was especially shocking to the priests, who were meant to be the shepherds of the people. If they were to continue to offer corrupt sacrifices, Yahweh would take away the privilege of a priestly lineage (2:3a).[8] Furthermore, the priests would be defiled by the very entrails of the defiled food presented on the Lord's altar—it would be spread all over their faces (2:3)! The language is bold and shocking, but standard fare among the prophets (see Nah 3:5–6).

Of special interest within the warning passage are the references to the "covenant with Levi" (2:4, 8). Throughout the book of Malachi it is evident that Yahweh takes his covenant very seriously; the love bestowed in covenant relationship required a reciprocal reverence and awe of his great name (2:4–5; see 1:2–5). The covenant with Levi is somewhat a mystery. It is referenced in Jeremiah 33:21–22 and Nehemiah 13:29, yet its origin is not specifically accounted in the Old Testament. It is not synonymous with the Mosaic covenant, although it certainly complements the broader covenant with Israel. In concert with the Mosaic covenant, it bears the characteristics of a bilateral agreement, offering "life and peace" in exchange for reverence (2:5).[9] The priests had a responsibility to instruct the people in word and deed, demonstrating reverence before Yahweh. But having failed in that

---

[6] The formal introduction in 2:1 suggests that a legal warning is being issued, perhaps with covenant overtones. See Stuart, "Malachi," 1310.

[7] There is some ambiguity over whether the "blessings" are those from Yahweh (see Deuteronomy 28:1–14) or those performed by the priests (see Leviticus 9:22–23; Numbers 6:22–27). Noting that Israel was already experiencing economic distress as a result of covenant unfaithfulness (Malachi 3:8–12), it seems best to recognize this as a warning that covenant blessings from Yahweh were about to become covenant curses (see Deuteronomy 28).

[8] An alternate understanding of "descendants" or "seed" (*zera'*) is agricultural; that is, Yahweh would curse the produce of the land. See Marvin A. Sweeney, *The Twelve Prophets*, Vol. 2 Berit Olam (Collegeville, MN: The Liturgical Press, 2000), 729.

[9] Chisholm, *Interpreting the Minor Prophets*, 283.

obligation, and having despised the name of Yahweh through their irreverence (1:6), he would make them despised before the people (2:9).

2:10–16 "The LORD has been a witness between you and the wife of your youth" (Third Disputation: God Hates Covenant Unfaithfulness)

The third disputation unit is complex and wrought with exegetical challenges, yet the basic thrust of the unit is clear. Among the people there were certain men seeking foreign wives. This, in turn, would lead the whole community into idolatry, the guilt of which had resulted in cataclysmic judgment just a few generations earlier. Worse yet, not only were the men seeking after foreign wives, they were divorcing their Judean wives to do so (2:14–16). Shockingly, they seemed oblivious to Yahweh's disdain over such treacherous behavior (2:14).[10]

The unit opens with a series of parallel rhetorical questions: "Don't all of us have one Father? Didn't one God create us" (2:10a)? These questions set the stage for the dispute to follow, generating a sense of covenant unity among the people.[11] If they were indeed one people under one covenant (2:10b), then why would they profane that relationship by marrying the "daughter of a foreign god" (2:11)? Those guilty of such covenant violation would be cut off from covenant relationship, no longer receiving the benefit of acceptance in ritual offering and worship (2:12–13).

In disputation form, the people respond to Yahweh's rejection with oblivious indifference, astonishingly dismissive of their own guilt (2:14a). Yet in breaking the covenant of their fathers by marrying pagan women (2:10–11), they had preceded this violation with another—breaking the marriage covenant with the wives of their youth (2:14). They had "acted

---

[10] The practice of Judean men divorcing their first wives to marry foreign second wives finds a historical parallel in Ezra 9–10 and Nehemiah 13:23–28.

[11] It is unclear whether the first question relates to "one father" Abraham (implied by the lower case in the NET, NASB, and KJV) or "one Father" Yahweh (implied by capitalization in the HCSB, ESV, NKJV, and NIV). The line of argument in the disputation unit suggests that common lineage is in view ("sons of Abraham, don't marry a foreigner"), while the parallel question in 2:10 suggests common origin ("sons of the living God, do not marry the daughter of a foreign god"). It is impossible to determine the exact designee with certainty.

treacherously" (*bagad*) toward the wives of their youth, divorcing their Judean wives to marry foreign women (2:14–16). In doing so, they had, in effect, acted treacherously against God (2:11).

The Hebrew text of Malachi 2:15–16a is notoriously difficult, as reflected by the many differences among Bible translations. In determining the content of verse 15, it is helpful to note that verse 15 correlates back to verse 10, while also providing commentary on the issue of the sanctity of marriage (as reflected by the end of verse 15). If the intent of verse 10 is to highlight pure lineage based in relationship to Yahweh, then the HCSB translation, "Didn't the one God make us with a remnant of His life-breath? And what does the One seek? A godly offspring . . .," correlates well with "Didn't one God create us?" If, however, the ancestral lineage with Abraham is in view, then one might find the NET Bible translation appealing, understanding "the one" in verse 15 as a reference back to Abraham: "No one who has even a small portion of the Spirit in him does this. What did our ancestor do when seeking a child from God? Be attentive, then, to your own spirit, for one should not be disloyal to the wife he took in his youth."[12] Other translations reflect the sanctity of the marriage covenant, as reflected by the ESV: "Did he not make them one, with a portion of the Spirit in their union? And what was the one God seeking? Godly offspring. So guard yourselves in your spirit, and let none of you be faithless to the wife of your youth."

Compounding the challenges of this unit, the first portion of verse 16 is also difficult. The traditional translation adopted by many English versions has God speaking in the first person with a propositional statement: "I hate divorce" (NASB, NKJV, and NRSV). However, the Hebrew text literally reads, "For he hates divorce," with the Hebrew *san'e* ("hate") in the third person. The classic translation, "I hate divorce" would therefore require that God spoke in the third person, or translators must emend the third person form of the verb to the first person. The HCSB has followed the Hebrew closely: "If he hates and divorces his wife," says the Lord God

---

[12] The NET Bible note explains: "This is an oblique reference to Abraham who sought to obtain God's blessing by circumventing God's own plan for him by taking Hagar as wife (Genesis 16:1–6). The result of this kind of intermarriage was, of course, disastrous (Genesis 16:11–12)."

of Israel, "he covers his garment with injustice."[13] With this translation, the intent is to call out the men for their guilt—those who "act treacherously" (*begad*) against their wives by hating them with divorce are, in fact, covering their own garment with injustice. The meaning of "covering one's garment with injustice" is uncertain, but it may be similar to the modern idiom, "to have blood on one's hands."[14] Those who do such a thing ought to think twice ("watch yourselves carefully"), knowing that God sees such treachery.

2:17–3:5 "Where is the God of justice?" (Fourth Disputation: God's Justice Vindicated)

The fourth disputation unit begins with a brief dialogue followed by an announcement of eschatological judgment (3:1–5). The people were questioning God's justice, claiming that he was blessing the wicked. In the broader situational context, this erroneous theology provided a basis for the people to rationalize their spiritual apathy and sinful ways. But they had forgotten that Yahweh forget the wicked—indeed, there will be a future day of judgment (3:5). On that day no one will ask, "Where is the God of justice" (2:17c)?

2:17 "You have wearied the Lord with your words." (Yahweh's Sense of Justice Questioned)

The fourth disputation involves an assertion by the prophet ("You have wearied the LORD with your words"), a hypothetical (and defiant) question by the people ("How have we wearied Him?"), and a twofold response back to the people ("When you say, 'Everyone who does what is evil is good in the LORD's sight, and He is pleased with them,' or 'Where is the God of justice?'"). The issue behind the dialogue is obvious:—the people were rationalizing their own behavior by citing God's lack of response to the sins of others. They rationalized thus, "If the wicked are blessed, then why bother serving the Lord?" Instead of pondering injustice as the sages

---

[13] Interestingly, the NIV has shifted from the 1984 translation, "I hate divorce" to the 2011 translation, "The man who hates and divorces his wife." The ESV takes a similar approach: "For the man who does not love his wife but divorces her . . . "

[14] There is no biblical or ancient attestation for this idiom. However, the context supports the idea of guilt pictured through the imagery of being "clothed" with injustice. See Stuart, "Malachi," 1343.

of old, or pleading with God as the prophets did, the people used perceived injustice as an excuse: "What good is it to serve God when unrighteousness goes unanswered?"

3:1–5 "BUT WHO CAN ENDURE THE DAY OF HIS COMING?" (YAHWEH'S RESPONSE TO THE QUESTION OF JUSTICE— ESCHATOLOGICAL JUDGMENT)

Yahweh's response to the people's incredulous reasoning takes the form of a prophetic oracle, an announcement of future judgment ensuring that, in God's program, justice will be served. Although the oracle contains interpretive challenges, its prophetic function is clearly tied to the accusations of 2:17. The prophetic announcement is characterized by irony and sarcasm, having the rhetorical effect of reversing the accusations of the people so the pointed finger turns back on them instead of the Lord.

The primary interpretive challenge in the oracle pertains to the identity of three figures in verse one: (1) "My messenger," (2) the "Lord," and (3) the "Messenger of the covenant."[15] In response to the people's accusations that Yahweh does not act, he promises to respond by sending "My messenger" (3:1a). Throughout the Old Testament, a messenger's role is always subordinate to his superior, and in this case, the messenger is clearly distinguished from Yahweh himself. When compared with Malachi 4:5, the parallel language of "sending" identifies this messenger with Elijah, the one who "clears the way" before Yahweh prior to the day of his coming (3:1; see 4:5).

The sarcastic response to the preceding accusations are critical in the interpretation of the two additional figures of 3:1. "The Lord you seek," is a direct response to the second question, "Where is the God of justice (2:17)?" Although the people's question is devoid of sincerity, the Lord they seek is nonetheless coming—the Lord (of justice) will come suddenly to his temple. The "messenger of the covenant in whom you delight" is coming as well (3:1 ESV); this one comes in response to the first accusation that "Everyone who does evil is good in the sight of the LORD, and he

---

[15] The reference to "the Lord" in 3:1 is *ha'adon*, not *Yahweh*. Each reference to "messenger" translates the same Hebrew word *mal'ak*, which with the first person possessive suffix transliterates the name of the prophet, "Malachi."

delights in them" (2:17 ESV).[16] While the parallels are helpful in discerning the relationship between 2:17 and 3:1–5, there is still some question as to whether this second "messenger" is a parallel to "My messenger" or "the Lord."[17] Many view the "messenger of the covenant" as a title for the Lord. This is implied by translations that capitalize the second reference to "messenger," yet keep the first reference in the lower case (see HCSB, NKJV). In this interpretation, the Lord is equated with the "Messenger," taking on the role of a *mal'ak* as he enforces his own covenant.[18] The alternate view is to equate both references to the messenger with Elijah, the one who calls for covenant faithfulness before the "day of His coming" (3:2). This approach distinguishes between "the Lord" and the "messenger of the covenant" in the second half of 3:1.[19]

The oracle continues in response to the people's accusation that God delights in those who do evil. Although the people claim to seek a God of justice, they may be asking for more than they bargained for. In the day of his coming, who will stand? Surely not the priests and the people who were accusing God of wrongdoing—the very same people indicted throughout the book of Malachi (3:2)!

The Day of the Lord is more than just a display of God's wrath. The ministry of the messenger is one of hope in the midst of judgment. To those who fear the Lord, that day will be a day when Yahweh refines and purifies his elect in accordance with his covenant (3:3–4; see 3:1, 16–18; 4:2–3). But to those who do not fear the Lord, it is a dreadful day—a day when the wicked will not stand (3:2, 5).

---

[16] The ESV is quoted at this point because its repetition better reflects the intentional parallelism between the accusation in 2:17 and the response in 3:1.

[17] It is clear that the preparer of the way is distinct from the Lord who comes to *his* temple.

[18] This view is implied by the punctuation of the HCSB: "'Then the Lord you seek will suddenly come to His temple, the Messenger of the covenant you desire—see, He is coming,' says the LORD of Hosts."

[19] This view is implied by the semicolon and the conjunction "and" in the ESV: "'And the Lord whom you seek will suddenly come to his temple; and the messenger of the covenant in whom you delight, behold, he is coming,' says the LORD of Hosts."

3:6–7 "Return to Me, and I will return to you" (Fifth Disputation: God's Faithfulness Affirmed)

Many do not recognize an independent disputation unit at this juncture of the book, either viewing verses six and seven as part of the disputation on tithing (3:8–12), or dividing verses six and seven so that 3:6 concludes the prior unit and 3:7 introduces the following unit on tithing (as per the HCSB subheadings and paragraph breaks). There is an alternative, however. The flow between 3:7 and 3:8 is awkward and wooden, suggesting a unit division between the questions "How can we return?" (3:7) and "Will a man rob God?" (3:8).[20] Adding support for the view that 3:6–7 exists as an independent unit, the allusion to the past in verses six and seven suggest that they function together, while the unit comprising 3:8–12 consistently refers to the present and the future.[21]

The fifth disputation unit moves beyond the justice of God to affirm the faithfulness of God. In spite of the people's propensity to turn away from God, God had not destroyed them (3:6). It was not due to a lack of attention or justice that Israel was spared—it was because of Yahweh's unwavering commitment to his covenant (3:6; see 1:2–5). In the midst of judgment, God continues to call his wayward people to repentance; if they return to him, he will return to them (3:7).

Astonishingly, the people ask, "How can we return?" In a warped sense, they thought God had left them, when in reality, they had left God.[22] The people had demonstrated themselves to be consistently unfaithful to God (3:7a), yet God's faithfulness toward them was always unchanging (3:6). Indeed, once again the problem was not with God, but with the people. God did not need to return to them, but rather, they needed to return to God.

---

[20] It is certainly possible to view the issue of tithing (3:8–12) as the way in which the people might return to God, thus linking verses seven and eight. Nevertheless, there is sufficient cohesion between verses six and seven to see these as comprising an independent unit.

[21] This tie between verses six and seven is implied in the NKJV with the conjunction "yet" ("*Yet* from the days of your fathers . . .").

[22] This is similar to the first disputation unit, where the people thought God did not love them when, in fact, they had not loved God (1:2–5).

3:8–12 "How do we rob You?" (Sixth Disputation: God Blesses the Faithful Giver)

The sixth disputation begins with the Lord's accusation ("You are robbing Me!") preceded by the rhetorical question, "Will a man rob God" (3:8a)? Following the structure of hypothetical dialogue, the people smugly respond by asking, "How do we rob You?" (3:8b), yet the answer was clear: "By not making the payments of the tenth and the contributions" (3:8c). By not giving to God what was already his, the people robbed God (3:8–9). They were already suffering agricultural deprivation, yet they failed to heed the warning. In a manner reminiscent of the situation in Haggai, the people were living under a curse due to their misplaced priorities (Hag 1:10–11). Yet if they would repent of their negligence, God would pour out an abundance of material blessings on them (3:10–11; see Hag 2:19).

What exactly were the people neglecting to give? The payments of the "tenth and contributions" were apparently agricultural; they were gathered into storage to supply "food in My house" (i.e., the temple). They also had a role in providing for the priests and the Levites who administered temple ritual. The tenth (*ma`aser*) was a required tithe, regulated by law and necessary for the welfare of the ceremonial life of ancient Israel (Deut 14:22–29). The contribution (*terumah*) was voluntary, an offering given to supply the needs of those ministering in the name of Yahweh (Num 5:9–10).[23] The people had failed to give the full allotment of required tithes along with voluntary offerings, thereby demonstrating an attitude of indifference to the law, the temple, and ultimately, to God.

3:13–4:3 "They will be Mine" (Seventh Disputation: God Remembers the Righteous)

Similar to the fourth disputation, in this seventh and final unit the people question God's sense of justice. Does Yahweh really discern between the righteous and the wicked? Will there ever be a day of reckoning? In the end, does God really remember the righteous? The unit opens with a hypothetical dialogue typical of Malachi (3:13–15). But rather than respond in dialogue, the prophet responds to the people's complaint through a vision of

---

[23] Eugene H. Merrill, *Haggai, Zechariah, Malachi: An Exegetical Commentary* (Chicago, IL: Moody, 1994), 378.

the heavenly realm, a glimpse into the eschatological future. On a future day, the question of God's justice will be clearly answered—all will know that God has compassion on those who have "high regard for His name" (3:16). Yet beyond the vision of the Lord's remembrance comes a pronouncement of his visitation; not only does Yahweh discern between the righteous and the wicked—he judges as well (4:1–3)!

3:13–15 "It is useless to serve God" (Yahweh's Discernment Questioned)

The final dialogue of Malachi begins with Yahweh's assertion, "Your words against Me are harsh" (3:13a). The people object with yet another defiant question: "What have we spoken against You" (3:13b)? Yahweh's response is to quote and clarify those "harsh words" of the people. Their complaint was that it is "useless to serve God" because of the apparent prosperity of the wicked—"they even test God and escape" (3:15)! Once again the people use perceived injustice as an excuse for their own apathy and sin, justifying their own behavior as they question God's sense of discernment between right and wrong.

3:16–18 "They will be Mine . . ." (The Vision of the Book of Remembrance)

The prophet's response to the people is to provide an answer to their present complaint through a vision of future vindication. In an almost cosmic picture, "those who feared the LORD" are seen speaking to one another, with Yahweh taking notice and listening (3:16a). The text does not describe the content of their conversation. It is clear, however, that this conversation is meant to contrast with the harsh words spoken against Yahweh in 3:13. Perhaps those who feared God were deliberating another conclusion—that Yahweh does discern between the righteous and the wicked![24]

What is clear in the vision is that Yahweh does remember those who have "high regard for His name," and that a "book" records their acts of

---

[24] One option is to understand the sentence "The Lord took notice and listened," as the content of their conversation rather than the Lord's response to their conversation. Thus the verse might be translated, "Then those who feared Yahweh spoke to one another: 'Yahweh has taken notice and listened.'" See Pieter A. Verhoef, *The Books of Haggai and Malachi*, NICOT (Grand Rapids, MI: Eerdmans, 1987), 319–20.

righteousness in perpetuity—they will not be forgotten.[25] Those who fear God are his own special possession;[26] it is to them that the covenant relationship is realized in the most intimate and secure position known (that is, the father/son relationship; see 3:17). Ultimately, the misguided words of the people, "It is useless to serve God," are proven wrong. The cosmic vision is clear: Yahweh does discern, and he will remember (3:18).

4:1–3 "THE SUN OF RIGHTEOUSNESS WILL RISE" (AN ANNOUNCEMENT OF THE COMING DAY OF THE LORD)

Building off of the theme of discernment and future retribution, the prophet reiterates the expectation of the coming Day of the Lord (4:3; see 3:2–5). In that coming day, Yahweh will act on "the difference between the righteous and the wicked" (3:18). For the wicked it will be a day of consuming wrath, but for the righteous it will be a day of healing vindication (4:1–3).

The metaphor "sun of righteousness" requires special attention as it has often been characterized as a messianic title. However, the imagery employed has more to do with the rising sun than with the person of Yahweh—much less with Jesus, the Son of God. Just as the rising of the sun brings a new day, so the Day of the Lord ushers in a new era. And just as that new day dawns, a new reality ensues—the rays of the sun act as wings to dispense "healing" throughout the land. The rising "sun of righteousness" pictures a new day of justice and vindication; it will be a day in which there is no lack of justice, a day where the righteous will be vindicated and the wicked will be trampled underfoot (4:3).[27]

4:4–6 "Remember the instruction . . . Otherwise . . ." (Final Prophetic Warning: Therefore Remember . . .)

The final prophetic warning to the reader functions as an appropriate conclusion to Malachi, tying together the themes of remembrance (3:16–18),

---

[25] The book (or "scroll") may simply function as a metaphorical image depicting the security of Yahweh's omniscient recall. See Merrill, *Haggai, Zechariah, Malachi*, 384.

[26] The phrase "special possession" is the same Hebrew term (*segullah*) used to designate Israel as God's chosen people in Exodus 19:5.

[27] Chisholm correctly notes, "In this context 'righteousness' refers to the vindication that divine judgment brings to the God-fearers and to the restoration of just order in society." See Chisholm, *Interpreting the Minor Prophets*, 289.

the sending of Elijah (3:1), and the warning of a curse (4:6; see 1:4, 14; 2:2; 3:9). It is also a fitting conclusion to the Book of the Twelve and to the whole Old Testament, reminding the reader of covenant obligations and the coming Day of the Lord. The final exhortation additionally provides a bridge to the New Testament, anticipating the messenger Elijah before "the great and awesome Day of the Lord" (4:5; see Matt 11:13–14).

The final warning in Malachi is a curse—ominous indeed, but not a foregone conclusion. Rather than coming to strike the earth with a curse, the messenger comes to turn "the hearts of fathers to their children and the hearts of children to their fathers,"[28] to turn "the disobedient to an understanding of the righteous," and "to make ready for the Lord a prepared people" (Luke 1:17). The final warning of cursing is also a call to repentance and an invitation to salvation.[29]

Theological Message and Application of Malachi

Malachi is at once richly theological and intensely practical. Repeated terminology within the book reveals multiple interests, but the primary theological emphasis in the book involves the motifs of covenant faithfulness and the kingdom of Yahweh. The practical teaching points inherent within each disputation unit then stem from these primary theological motifs.

Within the context of the postexilic community, reassurance of God's covenant faithfulness was a primary concern. Although the people were living under Persian domination, God would stay true to his covenant with Israel. He is the great King, and his name is to be highly revered. Although Israel lived under domination from a foreign power, Yahweh was the God of the heavenly host—so who was really in charge? Yahweh was indeed greater than all the armies of Persia. But service to such a King required covenant faithfulness on the part of his subjects. The theology of Malachi therefore calls God's covenant people to covenant faithfulness in view of the expectation that God will establish his kingdom under his great name.

---

[28] The exact meaning of these words is uncertain. It is perhaps an idiomatic expression whose full meaning is lost, although it may reflect the ministry of turning "the disobedient to an understanding of the righteous," as reflected in Luke 1:17.

[29] See Stuart, "*Malachi*," 1395.

The enduring message of the Twelve is to call sinners to repentance, lest they suffer the wrath of God. Malachi functions to this end, calling the reader to examine one's own faithfulness to Yahweh. In the day of Malachi, the message was clear: live today in light of a future day, "the great and awesome Day of the LORD" (4:5). This message endures.

Teaching Points in Malachi	
Disputation One	As God's elect, we should never question God's love for us. Discipline may be evidence that God does love us!
Disputation Two	Today we offer up our bodies as living sacrifices, meaning our whole lives are dedicated to the Lord. Has this become burdensome? Have we ceased to give God our best?
Disputation Three	Covenant faithfulness begins at home. Those who act treacherously against their spouses have in fact acted treacherously against God.
Disputation Four	Never rationalize sin by thinking that God is unjust—he is just, and the wicked will be judged.
Disputation Five	God is faithful, even when his people are unfaithful. The Lord is always ready to receive struggling believers back.
Disputation Six	Invest your talents and treasures in the things of God. That investment will not return void.
Disputation Seven	We will all one day see that God does indeed remember those who fear his name. Man does not serve God in vain.

CONCLUSION

We began this book with a plea for the church to give greater attention to the Book of the Twelve as a relevant and important part of Scripture. The ministry of the Minor Prophets spans a major portion of Old Testament history, during which God spoke through them to the people of their day. But their messages do not remain in the past. Today, we have an inspired Word from which the Lord continues to guide and direct his people. We would like to conclude this work by suggesting four specific ways in which the message of the Twelve continues to speak to the church as the people of God.

First, the Book of the Twelve enriches the church with its distinctive portrayal of God. In their preaching of judgment and salvation, the prophets reveal both God's justice and grace. When Israel sinned by worshipping the golden calf at the beginning of their history as a nation, the Lord revealed himself as a God who is compassionate, slow to anger, rich in faithful love, and truth (Exod 34:6–7). These attributes led God to keep his covenantal commitments and to forgive the sins of his people. The Book of the Twelve is the story of how Israel experiences these same attributes of Yahweh centuries later. At the beginning of the Twelve, the Lord promises Israel that he cannot give them up and that he would not "vent the full fury" of his wrath even when disciplining them for their sins (Hos 11:8–9).

The Twelve as a whole reflect how the Lord keeps this specific promise to preserve his people. The Lord brings his various "days" of judgment against Israel and Judah, but even at the end, a remnant remains. When the people ask the Lord, "How have You loved us?" (Mal 1:2), the fact that they survived in spite of their repeated rebellion answers the question. When believers today question whether they can be certain that nothing will separate them from the love of God in Christ (Rom 8:37–39), the Book of the Twelve offers powerful testimony to the Lord's enduring faithfulness to his covenant people and promises.

Second, the Book of the Twelve challenges the church with its ethical call for the people of God "to act justly, to love faithfulness, and to walk humbly" with God (Mic 6:8). The covenants between God and his people in the Old and New Testaments involve both blessings and obligations. The prophets challenged Israel's defective understanding of the covenant that led them to believe that being God's chosen people meant that the Lord would bless them no matter what. Enjoyment of the covenant blessings required obedience to the covenant commandments. This obedience was not external conformity to a legal code but was the grateful response from a people transformed by God's grace. The Lord's *hesed* to his people demanded a response of *hesed* from those who had experienced his grace. Today, the responsibility to live transformed lives is increased rather than lessened in the new covenant because the church has received an even greater measure of grace and an even greater demonstration of God's love in the person and work of Jesus Christ.

The primary obligation to which the Twelve calls Israel is exclusive love and loyalty toward Yahweh as the one true God. Paul House reminds us that reverence for the Lord is what anchors our lives and is what leads "to affection for conversion, character, community, friendship, stewardship, service, good work in good places, and concern for others, particularly those in future generations."[1] Ethics flow from a right understanding of God and commitment to him, and Israel had abandoned the principles of love and justice because they had turned away from the Lord. Individuals and societies ultimately become like what they worship. Worship of the violent gods of the ancient Near East produced one kind of society, while devotion to

---

[1] Paul House, "Investing in the Ruins: Jeremiah and Theological Vocation," *JETS* 56 (2013), 6.

Yahweh as a God who rescued slaves from Egypt and who cared for widows and orphans was meant to produce a people with very different values and priorities.

The return to the Lord envisioned by the Twelve would involve return to the ethical standards of Yahweh's commands. Christopher J. H. Wright reminds us, "The prophets uncompromisingly adopt an advocacy stance in favour of the poor, the weak, the oppressed, the dispossessed and the victimized, claiming to speak for the God of justice as they do so."[2] The calls for justice and concern for the needy in the Book of the Twelve should especially serve as a wake-up call for affluent Christians in the West. The Minor Prophets continue to call God's people to guard their hearts against the idolatry of greed and to recognize their responsibility to serve the disadvantaged in their own communities and around the world. The Mosaic law reminded the people of Israel of their obligation to "open their hands" to their needy brothers and sisters so that there would be "no poor" among them (Deut 15:4–11). And the early church took seriously its calling to live out that ideal and to become that kind of community (see Acts 4:32–36). Greater attention to the Old Testament Prophets will help in the restoration of this others-centered ethic in the church and will help to remind followers of Jesus that the priority of preaching the gospel to the nations does not diminish the church's responsibility to minister to the whole person and to implement peace and justice in a fallen world. Expecting that the soon return of Jesus Christ will bring the consummation of the kingdom of blessing and peace promised by the prophets should not lead followers of Jesus to abandon the present world to its sin and decay.

Third, the Book of the Twelve informs the church of the ways in which God deals with his people and the nations. Because of the constancy of God's character, how he dealt with Israel as his people in the past provides a model for how he deals with the church as his people in the present. In our study of the Twelve, we have carefully focused on explaining how the messages of the individual prophets' related to their specific times and circumstances because we believe that a correct understanding of how the prophets' messages applied to their contemporaries is foundational to proper application of how they are relevant to our times. Paul reminds

---

[2] Christopher J. H. Wright, *Old Testament Ethics for the People of God* (Downers Grove, IL: IVP, 2004), 268.

us in 1 Corinthians 10:6 that the things that happened to Israel "became examples for us." Echoing Leviticus 11:44, Peter instructs the church to "be holy, for I [God] am holy" (NIV). Similarly, the Book of the Twelve reveals how the Lord blesses his obedient people and disciplines them when they are unfaithful. The message of the Twelve highlights how the response of his people to his word shapes their destiny. The Lord is willing to relent from judgment when his people seek him and turn from their sinful ways.

The prophets were above all preachers of repentance as they called the people to "turn" from their sin and to "return" to Yahweh so that they might enjoy all of the blessings that he had in store for them. Repentance is a continual and life-long process for God's people. Even when the postexilic community repented by turning to the work of rebuilding the temple, there was still the need to address social issues and where the people stood in their relationship with God. In Revelation 2–3, Jesus issues the same call for repentance to churches that had abandoned their "first love," who were blind to their own spiritual poverty, or who had compromised with the pagan culture around them. In the Book of the Twelve, genuine repentance is rare, but the promise is that the Lord is the One who would ultimately transform the hearts of the people as they turned to him. A lifestyle of repentance does not arise from a slavish fear, but rather from the constant desire to grow in discernment of God's will and to more fully please the Lord (see Phil 1:9–11; Col 1:9–10). God's promise is that he will turn to his people when they turn to him (Zech 1:3; Mal 3:7; James 4:8). Without the focus on grace and the promise of divine enablement, the preaching and teaching based on the Prophets can easily turn into a message of moralism and condemnation.

Lastly, the Book of the Twelve comforts the church with its message of restoration and its anticipation of the eschatological kingdom of God. The book of Lamentations is testimony to the suffering and devastation that the exile brought on the people of Israel, but the prophets announced a message of hope that transcended what appeared to be the end for Israel as the people of God. Israel's failures had brought the judgment of exile, but exile was not God's final word. Beyond the exile, there was the promise of Israel's return to the land, the restoration of the house of David, and the spiritual transformation of God's people so that they would perpetually enjoy the blessings of peace and prosperity in the land. The blessing of Israel would ultimately extend to the nations, and the nations would travel to Jerusalem to worship the Lord and learn his ways. The key promise of the prophets was that the Lord would become "King over all the earth" (Zech 14:9). The prophets convey the promise that the Lord will ultimately triumph over all evil and opposition to his rule, and God's people will share in his victory. They may not provide all the details to satisfy our curiosity of what tomorrow may bring, but they do speak powerfully of the future by painting vivid images of how that kingdom will be completely different from the sin-cursed world of our present experience.

We see in the working out of salvation history that the restoration promised by the prophets arrives in stages. The first stage of restoration came with Israel's historical return to the land following the Babylonian exile. The Lord kept his promise to redeem his people out of exile and to restore them to their homeland, but this return did not exhaust or completely fulfill the prophetic promises of restoration and renewal. With the New Testament, the arrival of the eschatological kingdom of God becomes a reality through the death, resurrection, and ascension of Jesus. Yet the full realization of kingdom promises still awaits a future, Second Coming. Rather than giving a detailed roadmap of how the kingdom will come, the eschatological message of the Twelve allows us to trace the hand of God through various acts of restoration and new creation that will eventually consummate with the future kingdom. Faithful preaching and teaching of the Prophets is all about holding forth this hope of restoration and kingdom apart from the endless speculation about date setting, current events, and eschatological systems that too often distracts from the real focus of the prophetic message.

BIBLIOGRAPHY OF WORKS CITED

Achtemeier, Elizabeth M. *Minor Prophets I*. Understanding the Bible Commentary Series. Grand Rapids, MI: Baker Academic, 1995.

Alexander, T. Desmond. *From Eden to the New Jerusalem: An Introduction to Biblical Theology*. Grand Rapids, MI: Kregel, 2009.

Allen, Leslie C. *The Books of Joel, Obadiah, Jonah, and Micah*. NICOT. Grand Rapids, MI: Eerdmans, 1976.

Andersen, Francis I. *Habakkuk*. The Anchor Yale Bible Commentaries. New Haven, CT: Yale University Press, 2001.

Arnold, Bill T., and Richard S. Hess (ed.). *Ancient Israel's History: An Introduction to Issues and Sources*. Grand Rapids, MI: Baker, 2014.

Baker, David W. *Joel, Obadiah, Malachi*. NIVAC. Grand Rapids, MI: Zondervan, 2006.

Barker, Joel. *From the Depths of Despair to the Promise of Presence: A Rhetorical Reading of the Book of Joel*. Siphrut 11. Winona Lake, IN: Eisenbrauns, 2014.

Barker, Kenneth L. and Waylon Bailey. *Micah, Nahum, Habakkuk, Zephaniah*. NAC. Nashville, TN: B&H, 1998.

Bateman, Herbert W., Darrell L. Bock, and Gordon H. Johnston. *Jesus the Messiah: Tracing the Promises, Expectations, and Coming of Israel's King*. Grand Rapids, MI: Kregel, 2012.

Bauckham, Richard. *The Jewish World around the New Testament*. Grand Rapids, MI: Baker, 2008.

Beale, G. K. *A New Testament Biblical Theology: The Unfolding of the Old Testament in the New*. Grand Rapids, MI: Baker, 2011.

Beale, G. K., and D. A. Carson. *Commentary on the New Testament Use of the Old Testament*. Grand Rapids, MI: Baker, 2007.

Beale, G. K., and Mitchell Kim. *God Dwells Among Us: Expanding Eden to the Ends of the Earth*. Downers Grove, IL: InterVarsity, 2014.

Bleibtreu, Erika. "Grisly Assyrian Record of Torture and Death." *Biblical Archaeology Review* 17 (1991): 1–11.

Block, Daniel I. *Obadiah: The Kingship Belongs to YHWH*. Hearing the Message of Scripture 27. Grand Rapids, MI: Zondervan, 2013.

———. *Israel: Ancient Kingdom or Late Invention?* Nashville, TN: B&H Academic, 2008.

Boda, Mark J. *A Severe Mercy: Sin and Its Remedy in the Old Testament*. Siphrut 1. Winona Lake, IN: Eisenbrauns, 2009.

———. *Haggai, Zechariah*. NIVAC. Grand Rapids, MI: Zondervan, 2004.

Boda, Mark J., and Gordon J. McConville (ed.). *Dictionary of the Old Testament Prophets*. Downers Grove, IL: InterVarsity, 2012.

Bowman, Craig. "Reading the Twelve as One: Hosea 1–3 as an Introduction to the Book of the Twelve (Minor Prophets)." *Stone-Campbell Journal* 9 (2006): 41–59.

Bruckner, James. *Jonah, Nahum, Habakkuk, Zephaniah*. NIVAC. Grand Rapids, MI: Zondervan, 2004.

Bullock, C. Hassell. *An Introduction to the Old Testament Prophetic Books*. Updated edition. Chicago, IL: Moody, 2007.

Carlisle, Thomas John. *You Jonah! Poems by Thomas John Carlisle*. Grand Rapids, MI: Eerdmans, 1968.

Chalmers, Aaron. *Interpreting the Prophets: Reading, Understanding and Preaching from the Worlds of the Prophets*. Downers Grove, IL: InterVarsity, 2015.

Chisholm, Robert B., Jr. *Handbook on the Prophets*. Grand Rapids, MI: Baker Academic, 2002.

———. "'For Three Sins . . . Even for Four': The Numerical Sayings in Amos." Pages 187–95 in *Vital Old Testament Issues: Examining Textual and Topical Questions*. Edited by Roy Zuck. Grand Rapids, MI: Kregel, 1996.

————. "Does God 'Change His Mind'?" *Bibliotheca Sacra* 152 (1995): 387–99.

————. *Interpreting the Minor Prophets*. Grand Rapids, MI: Zondervan, 1990.

Cotterell, Peter, and Max Turner. *Linguistics and Biblical Interpretation*. Downers Grove, IL: InterVarsity, 1989.

Creach, Jerome F. D. *Violence in Scripture*. Louisville, KY: Westminster John Knox, 2013.

Crenshaw, James L. *Joel: A New Translation with Introduction and Commentary*. AB 24. New York, NY: Doubleday, 1995.

Cullmann, Oscar. *Christ and Time: The Primitive Christian Conception of Time*. Rev ed. Philadelphia, PA: Westminster John Knox, 1964.

Dorsey, David A. *The Literary Structure of the Old Testament: A Commentary on Genesis-Malachi*. Grand Rapids, MI: Baker, 1999.

Fee, Gordon D., and Douglas Stuart. *How to Read the Bible for All It's Worth*. 4th ed. Grand Rapids, MI: Zondervan, 2014.

Firth, David G., and Paul D. Wegner (ed.). *Presence, Power, and Promise: The Role of the Spirit of God in the Old Testament*. Downers Grove, IL: InterVarsity, 2011.

Garrett, Duane A. *Hosea, Joel: An Exegetical and Theological Exposition of Scripture*. NAC. Nashville, TN: B&H, 1997.

Goldingay John, and Pamela J. Scalise. *Minor Prophets*. 2 Vols. NIBC. Peabody, MA: Hendrickson, 2009.

Harrison, R. K. *Introduction to the Old Testament*. Peabody, MA: Hendrickson, 2004.

Hays, J. Daniel. *The Message of the Prophets*. Grand Rapids, MI: Zondervan, 2010.

Hess, Richard S. *Israelite Religions: An Archaeological and Biblical Survey*. Grand Rapids, MI: Baker, 2007.

————. "Hezekiah and Sennacherib in 2 Kings 18–20." Pages 23–41 in *Zion City of Our God*. Edited by Richard S. Hess and Gordon J. Wenham. Grand Rapids, MI: Eerdmans, 2004.

Hill, Andrew. *Haggai, Zechariah, and Malachi*. TOTC. Downers Grove, IL: InterVarsity, 2012.

————. *Malachi*. AB. New Haven, CT: Yale University Press, 1998.

Hoerth, Alfred J., Gerald L. Mattingly, and Edwin M. Yamauchi (ed.). *Peoples of the Old Testament World*. Grand Rapids, MI: Baker, 1994.

House, Paul R. *The Unity of the Twelve*. BLS 27; JSOTSup 97. Sheffield, UK: Almond, 1990.

Hubbard, David Allen. *Hosea*. TOTC, 24. Downers Grove, IL: InterVarsity, 2009.

Kaiser, Walter C., Jr. *A History of Israel from the Bronze Age through the Jewish Wars*. Nashville, TN: B&H, 1998.

Köstenberger, Andreas J., and Richard D. Paterson, *Invitation to Biblical Interpretation: Exploring the Hermeneutical Triad of History, Literature, and Theology*. Grand Rapids, MI: Kregel, 2011.

LeCureux, Jason T. *The Thematic Unity of the Book of the Twelve*. HBM, 41. Sheffield, UK: Sheffield Phoenix, 2012.

Lessing, R. Reed. "Amos's Earthquake in the Book of the Twelve." *CTQ* 74 (2010): 243–59.

Linburg, James. *Hosea-Micah*. Interpretation. Louisville, KY: Westminster John Knox, 2011.

Longman, Tremper, III, and Daniel G. Reid. *God is a Warrior, Studies in Old Testament Biblical Theology*. Grand Rapids, MI: Zondervan, 1995.

Longman, Tremper, III, and Raymond B. Dillard. *An Introduction to the Old Testament*. Second ed. Grand Rapids, MI: Zondervan, 2006.

Maier, Walter A. *The Book of Nahum*. Grand Rapids, MI: Baker, 1980.

McComiskey, Thomas E. (ed.). *The Minor Prophets: An Exegetical & Expositional Commentary*. 3 Vols. Grand Rapids, MI: Baker, 1992.

Merrill, Eugene H. *Kingdom of Priests: A History of Old Testament Israel*. Grand Rapids, MI: Baker, 1987.

———. *Haggai, Zechariah, Malachi: An Exegetical Commentary*. Chicago, IL: Moody, 1994.

Merrill, Eugene H., Mark F. Rooker, and Michael A. Grisanti. *The World and the Word: An Introduction to the Old Testament*. Nashville, TN: B&H, 2011.

Moberly, R. W. L. *Old Testament Theology: Reading the Hebrew Bible as Christian Scripture*. Grand Rapids, MI: Baker Academic, 2013.

Myers, Carol L., and Eric M. Myers. *Haggai, Zechariah 1–8*. AB 25B. New York, NY: Doubleday, 1987.

Niehaus, Jeffrey J. *Biblical Theology, Vol. 1: The Common Grace Covenants*. Wooster, OH: Weaver Book, 2014.

————. *God at Sinai: Covenant and Theophany in the Bible and Ancient Near East*. Studies in OT Biblical Theology. Grand Rapids, MI: Zondervan, 1995.

Nogalski, James D., *The Book of the Twelve*. 2 Vols. Smyth & Helwys Bible Commentary. Macon, GA: Smyth & Helwys, 2011.

————. *Literary Precursors to the Book of the Twelve*. BZAW 217. New York, NY: Walter deGruyter, 1993.

Nogalski, James D. and Marvin A. Sweeney (ed.). *Reading and Hearing the Book of the Twelve*. SBLSymS 15. Atlanta, GA: Society of Biblical Literature, 2000.

Osborne, Grant R. *The Hermeneutical Spiral: A Comprehensive Introduction to Biblical Interpretation*. Downers Grove, IL: InterVarsity, 1991.

Pate, C. Marvin, J. Scott Duvall, J. Daniel Hays, E. Randolph Richards, Preben Vang, and W. Dennis Tucker Jr. *The Story of Israel: A Biblical Theology*. Grand Rapids, MI: InterVarsity, 2004.

Patterson, Richard D. *Nahum, Habakkuk, Zephaniah*. Wycliffe Exegetical Commentary. Chicago, IL: Moody Press, 1991.

Paul, Shalom. *Amos*. Hermeneia. Minneapolis, MN: Fortress Press, 1991.

Pratt, Richard L., Jr. "Historical Contingencies and Biblical Predictions." Pages 183–90 in *The Way of Wisdom: Essays in Honor of Bruce K. Waltke*. Edited by J. I. Packer and Sven K. Soderlund. Grand Rapids, MI: Zondervan, 2000.

Provan, Iain, V. Philips Long, and Tremper Longman. *A Biblical History of Israel*. Louisville, KY: Westminster John Knox, 2003.

Roberts, J. J. M. *Nahum, Habakkuk, and Zephaniah*. OTL. Minneapolis, MN: Westminster John Knox, 1991.

Robertson, O. Palmer. *The Books of Nahum, Habakkuk, and Zephaniah*. NICOT. Grand Rapids, MI: Eerdmans, 1990.

Ross, Allen P. *Recalling the Hope of Glory: Biblical Worship from the Garden to the New Covenant*. Grand Rapids, MI: Kregel, 2006.

Routledge, Robin. *Old Testament Theology: A Thematic Approach*. Downers Grove, IL: InterVarsity, 2008.

Ryken, Leland. *A Complete Handbook of Literary Forms in the Bible*. Wheaton, IL: Crossway, 2014.

————. *Words of Delight: A Literary Introduction to the Bible*. Grand Rapids, MI: Baker, 1987.

Ryken, Leland, James C. Wilhoit, and Tremper Longman III (ed.). *Dictionary of Biblical Imagery*. Downers Grove, IL: InterVarsity, 1998.

Sandy, D. Brent. *Plowshares and Pruning Hooks: Rethinking the Language of Biblical Prophecy and Apocalyptic*. Grand Rapids, MI: InterVarsity, 2002.

Sandy, D. Brent, and Ronald L. Giese Jr. (ed.). *Cracking Old Testament Codes: A Guide to Interpreting the Literary Genres of the Old Testament*. Nashville, TN: B&H, 1995.

Seevers, Boyd. *Warfare in the Old Testament: The Organization, Weapons, and Tactics of Ancient Near Eastern Armies*. Grand Rapids, MI: Kregel Academic, 2013.

Seitz, Christopher. *Prophecy and Hermeneutics: Toward a New Introduction to the Prophets*. Grand Rapids, MI: Baker, 2007.

Smith, Billy K., and Frank S. Page. *Amos, Obadiah, Jonah*. NAC 19B. Nashville, TN: B&H Academic, 1995.

Smith, Gary V. *Hosea, Amos, Micah*. NIVAC. Grand Rapids, MI: Zondervan, 2001.

Strazicich, John. *Joel's Use of Scripture and Scripture's Use of Joel: Appropriation and Resignification in Second Temple Judaism and Early Christianity*. Biblical Interpretation Series, 82. Leiden, Netherlands: Brill, 2007.

Stuart, Douglas. *Hosea-Jonah*. WBC 31. Waco, TX: Word, 1987.

Sweeney, Marvin A. *The Twelve Prophets*. 2 Vols. Berit Olam. Collegeville, MN: Liturgical, 2000.

Taylor, Richard A., and E. Ray Clendenen, *Haggai, Zechariah: An Exegetical and Theological Exposition of Holy Scripture*. NAC 21. Nashville, TN: B&H, 2004.

Thiele, Edwin R. *The Mysterious Numbers of the Hebrew Kings*. New Revised ed. Grand Rapids, MI: Kregel, 1994.

Timmer, Daniel C. "Nahum." Pages 79–86 in *The Lion has Roared: Theological Themes in the Prophetic Literature of the Old Testament*. Edited by H. G. L. Peels and S. D. Snyman. Eugene, OR: Pickwick, 2012.

———. *A Gracious and Compassionate God: Mission, Salvation, and Spirituality in the Book of Jonah*. NSBT. Downers Grove, IL: InterVarsity, 2011.

Troxel, Ronald L. "The Problem of Time in Joel." *JBL* 132 (2013): 77–95.

Van Leeuwen, Raymond C. "Scribal Wisdom and Theodicy in the Book of the Twelve." Pages 31–49 in *Search of Wisdom: Essays in Memory of John*

G. Gammie. Edited by Leo G. Perdue, Brandon B. Scott, and William Johnston Wiseman. Louisville, KY: Westminster John Knox, 1993.

van der Woude, A. S. "Micah in Dispute with the Pseudo-Prophets." *Vetus Testamentum* 19 (1969): 244–60.

Verhoef, Pieter A. *The Books of Haggai and Malachi*. NICOT. Grand Rapids, MI: Eerdmans, 1987.

Waltke, Bruce K. *A Commentary on Micah*. Grand Rapids, MI: Eerdmans, 2007.

Waltke, Bruce K., and Michael O'Connor. *An Introduction to Biblical Hebrew Syntax*. Winona Lake, IN: Eisenbrauns, 1990.

Walton, John H. (ed.). *Zondervan Illustrated Bible Backgrounds Commentary*. Vol. 5. Grand Rapids, MI: Zondervan, 2009.

———. *Ancient Near Eastern Thought and the Old Testament: Introducing the Conceptual World of the Hebrew Bible*. Grand Rapids, MI: Baker, 2006.

———. "The Object Lesson of Jonah 4:5–7 and the Purpose of the Book of Jonah." *BBR* 2 (1992): 47–57.

Walton, John H., and D. Brent Sandy. *The Lost World of Scripture: Ancient Literary Culture and Biblical Authority*. Downers Grove, IL: InterVarsity, 2013.

Watts, James W., and Paul R. House (ed.). *Forming Prophetic Literature: Essays on Isaiah and the Twelve in Honor of John D. W. Watts*. JSOTSup 235. Sheffield, UK: Sheffield Academic Press, 1996.

Watts, John D. W. "A Frame for the Book of the Twelve: Hosea 1–3 and Malachi." Pages 209–17 in *Reading and Hearing the Book of the Twelve*. SBLSymS, 15. Edited by James D. Nogalski and Marvin A. Sweeney. Atlanta, GA: Society of Biblical Literature, 2000.

Wiseman, Donald J. "Jonah's Nineveh," *TB* 30 (1979): 44–51.

Wolff, Hans Walter. *Joel and Amos: A Commentary on the Books of the Prophets Joel and Amos*. Hermeneia. Minneapolis, MN: Fortress, 1977.

———. *Hosea*. Hermeneia. Philadelphia, PA: Fortress Press, 1974.

Wood, Leon J. *The Holy Spirit in the Old Testament*. Eugene, OR: Wipf and Stock, 1998.

Yadin, Yigael. *Hazor II: An Account of the Second Season of Excavations, 1956*. Jerusalem, Israel: Magnes Press, 1960.

Zuck, Roy B. *Basic Bible Interpretation*. Colorado Springs, CO: Chariot Victor, 1991.

Name Index

Subject Index

SCRIPTURE INDEX

Malachi